THE PICKERING MASTERS

THE WORKS OF
IRVING FISHER

Volume 3. *The Rate of Interest*

THE WORKS OF
IRVING FISHER

EDITED BY
WILLIAM J. BARBER

ASSISTED BY ROBERT W. DIMAND AND KEVIN FOSTER

CONSULTING EDITOR: JAMES TOBIN

VOLUME
3

THE RATE
OF INTEREST

Routledge
Taylor & Francis Group

LONDON AND NEW YORK

First published 1996 by Pickering & Chatto (Publishers) Limited

Published 2016 by Routledge
2 Park Square, Milton Park, Abingdon, Oxon OX14 4RN
711 Third Avenue, New York, NY 10017, USA

Routledge is an imprint of the Taylor & Francis Group, an informa business

Copyright ©Taylor & Francis 1996
Introduction © William J. Barber, 1997

BRITISH LIBRARY CATALOGUING IN PUBLICATION DATA
The works of Irving Fisher. – (The Pickering masters)
  1. Fisher, Irving, 1867–1947 – Criticism and interpretation
  2. Economics
  I. Barber, William J. (William Joseph), 1925–   II. Tobin, James, 1918–
330.1′57′092

ISBN 13: 978-1-13876-420-0 (hbk) (vol-03)

LIBRARY OF CONGRESS CATALOGING-IN-PUBLICATION DATA
Fisher, Irving, 1867–1947.
    The rate of interest.
      p.   cm. –– (The works of Irving Fisher ; v. 3)
    Includes index.
    ISBN 1–85196–228–X
      1. Interest rates. I. Title. II. Series: Fisher, Irving,
1867–1947.   Selections.   1996 ; v. 3.
HB119.F5A25   1996 vol. 3
[HB539]
330 s––dc20
[332.8′2]   96–12203
                                                                      CIP

CONTENTS

★ Denotes extract

ACKNOWLEDGEMENTS

We would like to thank the following for granting their kind permission to reproduce texts in this volume:

MIT Press: "A Reply to Critics", *Quarterly Journal of Economics* XXIII: 3 May 1909, 536–41*

Academy of Political Science: "Capital and Interest", *Political Science Quarterly* XXIV:3, September 1909, 504–16*

American Academy for the Advancement of Science: "Why has the Doctrine of Laissez-Faire Been Abandoned?", *Science*, January 4 1907, 18–27

* Denotes extract

Editorial Introduction
with Selected Document

The Rate of Interest, published in 1907, was a logical sequel to *The Nature of Capital and Income* (which had appeared in 1906). Indeed Fisher regarded them as companion volumes and had sought – unsuccessfully – to persuade his publisher to make an advance announcement of the projected second volume at the time the first was being promoted. The first of the two books had demonstrated the crucial role of the interest rate in determining capital values through the discounting of the prospective income stream. What remained to be shown was how the interest rate itself was determined. Fisher assigned himself that task in the 1907 work.

There could be no denying the centrality of this topic in controversies between members of rival doctrinal schools at the turn of the century. This issue was at the core of the ideological divide separating Marxists – who interpreted interest-taking as an illegitimate form of "exploitation" – and economists engaged in shaping the architecture of neo-classicism. For the latter, an interest rate was not only a valid return for a productive contribution; it also promised to provide an analytic bridge between a theory of production and a theory of income distribution. Even so, there was still plenty of room for intra-familial disputation among neo-classical theorists about the specifications of the "correct" theory of interest.

Useful insight into the form in which Fisher structured his presentation in *The Rate of Interest* can be gleaned from an inspection of his treatment of two fellow contributors to discourse on the subject. At first glance, one of them – John Rae (1796–1872), to whose memory the book was dedicated – would seem to be an unlikely candidate for the homage Fisher paid him. After all, Rae – an eccentric Scotsman who had emigrated to Canada in 1822 – had produced but one work in political economy and it had left virtually no mark. By contrast, the other, Eugen von Böhm-Bawerk (1851–1914) was a figure of recognized stature. With the publication of *A History and Critique of Capital and Interest Theories* (first edition, 1884; second edition, 1900) and *The Positive Theory of Capital* (first edition, 1889; second edition, 1900), he had established himself as a towering presence in the field. These studies were agenda-

1

setting documents; it was altogether to be expected that Fisher should feel obliged to define himself in relation to Böhm-Bawerk. Fisher had asked Böhm-Bawerk (whom he had met when visiting Vienna in 1894) to assist in that exercise by inviting him to review material while still in draft.

In 1897, Fisher first learned of Rae's sole work in political economy – entitled *Statement of Some New Principles on the Subject of Political Economy, Exposing the Fallacies of the System of Free Trade, and of Some Other Doctrines Maintained in the 'Wealth of Nations,'* published in Boston in 1834.[a] A graduate student at Harvard, C.W. Mixter, had rescued it from oblivion.[b] Fisher was quick to grasp the significance of Rae's contribution of 1834 when Mixter's "discovery" was professionally noticed. He then described it as **"truly a masterpiece, a book of a generation or a century ... written before the world was ready for such painstaking analysis."**[c]

Subsequently, Fisher encouraged Mixter to prepare a new edition of Rae's book (which appeared in 1905 in a revised format and with an amended title – *The Sociological Theory of Capital*). Fisher hailed its publication with unrestrained enthusiasm. **"Had the conditions been different,"** he wrote, **"Rae to-day might have ranked in the history of economic science as the peer of Adam Smith or John Stuart Mill."** Fisher held it to be unfortunate that economists of Rae's generation were **"too much committed to the classical economy, which to them possessed finality, and were not to be roused from their 'dogmatic slumbers' by an obscure provincial schoolmaster like Rae."**[d]

It is ironic that Rae's work received far more notice a quarter-century after his death than it had during his lifetime. As a schoolmaster in Canada, he had operated largely in intellectual isolation. Moreover, his contemporaries might have been disposed to dismiss him on grounds that he possessed no credentials likely to qualify him to produce fundamental insights. As far as political economy was concerned, he was largely self-taught (though he had taken a degree at the University of Aberdeen and had studied medicine for several years at the University of Edinburgh). Neglected as it was, his *Statement of Some New Principles* was not completely ignored. Nassau Senior, Professor of Political Economy

---

[a] This work has been reissued as the second of two volumes prepared by R. Warren James, *John Rae, Political Economist: an Account of His Life and a Compilation of His Main Writings*, University of Toronto Press, 1965.

[b] See C.W. Mixter, "A Forerunner of Böhm-Bawerk," *Quarterly Journal of Economics*, XI (January 1897), 161–90.

[c] "A Neglected Economist," *Yale Review*, February 1897, 457. This note, though unsigned, was written by Fisher.

[d] I.F., Review of *The Sociological Theory of Capital*, *Yale Review*, November 1905, 333.

in the University of Oxford, knew the book and drew it to the attention of John Stuart Mill. Mill, in turn, had spoken appreciatively of Rae's description of contrasting attitudes toward saving observable in different societies. As for Rae's analytic argument, Mill took no notice.

What, then, did Fisher find so appealing in Rae's *Statement of Some New Principles*? An answer to this question must begin by disposing of a potential source of confusion. Despite the language of the sub-title, the book was not a militant protectionist tract. To the contrary, the qualifications to Adam Smith's case for free trade were argued primarily on "infant industry" grounds. From Rae's perspective, the "legislator" had a positive role to play in shaping policies to promote capital accumulation and to provide a climate favorable to technical progress. These conclusions emerged in the context of an inquiry into the "laws" regulating the increase or diminution of "wealth" in various nations of the world. Rae's statement of this program was congruent with the spirit of classical economics in the tradition of Smith. What made Rae's argument distinctive was the way he explained the process of capital accumulation.

In Rae's view, economic progress turned fundamentally on a society's capacity to create "instruments" to enlarge production – an activity involving "the sacrifice of some smaller present good for the production of some greater future good."[a] Given the state of the arts at any moment, a considerable array of instruments could conceivably be created. Rae proposed that they be "ordered" according to the length of time required for the instrument to generate additional outputs valued at twice the cost of the instrument's creation. (Rae worked with a labor theory of value in which both the instrument and its outputs were measured in terms of standardized labor units embodied in them.) Self-evidently, instruments with the most rapid pay-back period deserved priority. What, then, would govern the extent to which instruments in the inferior "orders" would be created? Rae maintained that the outcome depended upon the interactions between an "accumulative principle" and an "inventive principle."

Rae's innovative ingenuity was on display in his discussion of these two principles. He clearly broke new ground when analyzing the conditions influencing the "effective desire of accumulation." An analogous conception in mainstream classical doctrine held accumulation to be primarily a function of saving arising from the profits of a capitalist class. Rae instead argued that the strength (or weakness) of the accumulative principle involved questions of inter-temporal choice in which decisions about sacrificing present goods for future ones were heavily conditioned

---

[a] John Rae, *Statement of Some New Principles on the Subject of Political Economy*, University of Toronto Press edition, 1965, 118.

by cultural and social conditions. Thus, a community's willingness to make provision for the future would be influenced by considerations such as the following: the prevalence of "social and benevolent affections" that inclined its members to care about the well-being of others and, particularly, of posterity; the "extent of the intellectual powers" (which Rae associated with foresight and prudence); the stability of a society – as promoted in a regime of law and order – which reduced life's uncertainties and increased life expectancy.

The moral of this part of the tale was that a society in which the accumulative principle was strong would create more instruments of the lower orders – and more instruments altogether – than one in which the accumulative principle was weak. To drive that point home, Rae presented copious illustrations of divergent cultural patterns, distinguishing accumulating societies (e.g., Holland, Britain, and Western Europe more generally) from those not noted for accumulation (e.g., North American Indian tribes, Asians and Africans in general). But he also took note of individual behavioral differences within societies: even in the accumulating ones, those in hazardous occupations (such as soldiers and sailors) were notorious prodigals. He also pointed out that social envy could erode the accumulative principle. Lower income groups, he observed, had a tendency to practice wasteful dissipation when attempting to imitate the consumption standards of higher income groups. In his judgment, it was pernicious when "consumption is conspicuous."[a]

There was genuine novelty as well in the way Rae presented his conception of an "inventive principle." Invention that fed technical advance was a vital cog in economic progress because it enabled society "from the same outlay to produce greater returns, or from less outlay to produce the same returns." The effect of such improvement, in Rae's terms, was "to carry instruments into orders of quicker return" and thus more instruments would be created.[b] It was clearly in the interest of the community to promote this healthy outcome. Accordingly, the "legislator" should encourage "discovery" – through, for example, support to education, research, and the free interchange of ideas. When foreigners enjoyed a technological advantage, the "legislator" had a clear duty to import the invention and to domesticate it. In most instances, Rae believed that the "accumulative" and "inventive" principles worked in tandem. But he identified an important exception when they were at odds: war tended to energize the inventive faculty, while its uncertainties dampened the "effective desire to accumulate."

---

[a] Thorstein Veblen, the author of *The Theory of the Leisure Class* (1898) in which the expression "conspicuous consumption" was popularized, knew Rae's work, but did not cite it.
[b] Rae, *op. cit.*, 258–59, 261.

In what respects did Fisher build on the "foundations" Rae had laid (as he stated he was doing in the dedication)? In *The Rate of Interest*, a number of building blocks were in evidence. There was an overlap in their discussions of investment options, though Fisher – who was not encumbered by a labor theory of value – could approach that issue with greater sophistication. Rae's influence was more marked in Fisher's treatment of "time preference" (an expression Rae had not used). Fisher's elaboration of the concept contained more than trace elements of Rae's thinking about the impact of social and cultural factors on attitudes toward provision for the future. Fisher appropriated many of Rae's illustrations and supplemented them with his own. To Fisher's latter-day readers, a number of his examples have a decidedly unattractive ring, notwithstanding the fact that he was following in Rae's footsteps. His comments on the "present- mindedness" exhibited in the "happy-go-lucky" attitude of negroes in the American South are a case in point. Fisher's text made numerous references to racial characteristics that would be denied acceptability in scholarly standards of a later day.[a] It should be pointed out, however, that Fisher also noted that "there is now accumulating much testimony to show that there is more error than truth in the common opinion as to the relatively great importance of heredity as compared with environment" (*The Rate of Interest*, p. 298). Behavioral attributes should thus not be regarded as immutable, but amenable to conditioning through education and training.

Fisher held Rae's analysis of invention in particularly high regard. Much of Rae was woven into the fabric of Fisher's account of the role of technical progress in creating new investment opportunities. Fisher's discussion of the conditions most favorable to the stimulation of invention, nonetheless, bore the stamp of his personal style. He did not follow Rae by suggesting that war could excite the "inventive faculty." Fisher proclaimed instead the importance of "hygiene" – by which he meant health maintenance through a regime of proper diet and exercise – to the enhancement of creativity.[b]

As Fisher explained in *The Rate of Interest*, he and Böhm-Bawerk also occupied some common ground. Nevertheless, formidable differences remained. Some of their features were revealed in their respective appraisals of John Rae. In the first edition of his historical survey of capital and interest theories, Böhm-Bawerk had made no mention of Rae.

---

[a] Aspects of this matter have been noted by Mark Aldrich, "Capital Theory and Racism: From Laissez-Faire to the Eugenics Movement in the Career of Irving Fisher," *Review of Radical Political Economy*, 7 (Fall 1975), 33–42. Details on Fisher's role in the eugenics movement will be taken up in Volume 13.

[b] For documentation on Fisher's crusades for "hygiene," see Volume 13.

Thanks to Mixter's "rediscovery," Rae's contribution received extended treatment in the second edition in 1900. While recognizing Rae's *Statement of Some New Principles* as a remarkably prescient study for its time, Böhm-Bawerk – unlike Fisher – concentrated on what he took to be its shortcomings. Fisher responded when reviewing the English translation of the supplementary material prepared for the second German edition of *Capital and Interest*. His observations in that context in 1905 foreshadowed a point of view he was to develop in *The Rate of Interest*:

"In our opinion, Böhm-Bawerk's criticisms of Rae are only partially deserved, and some of the faults which he finds will prove on examination to be virtues. He takes issue with Rae for making two determinants of the rate of interest, the first, a psychological one, 'the effective desire of accumulation,' and the second, a technical one, 'the order of instruments,' i.e., the rate of their return on their cost of production. According to Böhm-Bawerk, Rae has failed to show how these two regulators of the rate of interest cooperate. He admits that the first is valid and that it is practically identical with his own 'preference for present over future goods.' He therefore concedes to Rae full credit for having anticipated him in the statement of this part of the agio theory. But he maintains that, so far as the influence of the technical factor is concerned, not only is Rae's treatment at variance with his own, but that Rae's is wrong and his own right. In our own opinion, Rae's treatment, though not entirely free from the defects mentioned by Böhm-Bawerk, is actually nearer the truth than Böhm-Bawerk's. The latter's theory of the so-called 'technical superiority of present over future means of production' will prove, on close examination, to be entirely illusory. We shall ourselves attempt later in a book on capital to justify this view."[a]

In *The Rate of Interest*, Fisher devoted a chapter and appendix to his critique of Böhm-Bawerk's views. Presumably his criticisms would have come through with a still sharper bite had he not reacted to Böhm-Bawerk's comments on manuscript while still in draft. The correspondence that passed between the two men seems not to have survived. Böhm-Bawerk was later to refer to it, observing that Fisher had deleted some passages intended for "polemical color." But the two men could not concur on what Böhm-Bawerk took to be the main point: namely, his "thesis on the higher productivity of longer roundabout methods" of production.[b]

---

[a] I.F., Review of *Recent Literature on Interest, 1884–1899, A Supplement to 'Capital and Interest*,' by Eugen von Böhm-Bawerk (English translation by William A. Scott and Siegmund Feilbogen, 1903) *Yale Review*, August 1905, 221–23.
 [b] Eugene von Böhm-Bawerk, *Capital and Interest, Vol. III: Further Essays on Capital and Interest*, translated by Hans F. Sennholz, Libertarian Press: South Holland, Illinois, 1959, 220.

By 1930 – when Fisher published a revised statement of his doctrine as the *Theory of Interest* – he stressed points of convergence with Böhm-Bawerk's teaching. The Fisher of 1907 preferred to emphasize product differentiation. And he took specific aim at Böhm-Bawerk's claim concerning the productive superiority of the lengthier periods of production. Arguments Fisher deployed for that purpose contained some arresting features. Rae's analysis of invention, for example, proved to be a convenient argumentative tool: with its aid, it could be shown that – in an environment of technical progress – productivity improvements could be generated when the period of production was shortened.

Fisher was also at pains to demonstrate imprecisions and ambiguities in the very concept of a "period of production." Modern readers may find his treatment of this point in Appendix IV, section 2 to be particularly intriguing. Using a numerical example, he there considered the respective merits of alternative income streams, concluding that "it is not true that one of the alternatives will be chosen if the rate of interest is high, and the other if the rate of interest is low" (as Böhm-Bawerk's analysis would hold). To the contrary, one of the alternatives would "be most the economical if the rate of interest were either very high or very low, whereas the other alternative would be chosen in case the interest were at a more moderate level" (p. 352). In his challenge to Böhm-Bawerk, Fisher thus anticipated the "re-switching problem" that was to figure so prominently in controversies between economists at Cambridge (U.K.) and at Cambridge (U.S.) in the 1960s and 1970s.[a]

Yet another differentiating feature in the conceptual apparatus deserves mention. In the Böhm-Bawerkian scheme of things, capital was viewed as the "produced" or "artificial" factor of production – in contradistinction to land, which was regarded as the productive factor "given by nature." There was a lingering residual here of the social class categories of income distribution around which much of the European classical tradition had been organized. Böhm-Bawerk spoke from that perspective when attacking Fisher's conceptual framework from which social class distinctions were purged. The discipline needed to be protected, Böhm-Bawerk insisted, from "capricious terminological distinctions" which were "patently in conflict with deep-rooted usage in scientific as well as popular language." He maintained that "usage in all languages . . . regularly attributes definitely conflicting interests to the owners of capital

---

[a] The principals in these "re-switching" debates appear to have been unaware of Fisher's contribution. Fisher's priority, however, has been noticed by others: e.g., K. Velupillai, "Irving Fisher on 'Switches of Techniques': a Historical Note," *Quarterly Journal of Economics*, November 1975, 679–80; Mark Blaug, *Economic Theory in Retrospect*, Third edition, Cambridge University Press, 1978, 557.

on the one hand and on the other hand to the landowners and still more unmistakably to the workers."[a] Had Böhm-Bawerk elected to do so, he could have extended this indictment to other American economists – and not just to Fisher. Indeed social class "blindness" had become a marked characteristic of the distribution theories produced in the United States.[b]

With respect to its place in the flow of formal economic argument, Fisher's performance in *The Rate of Interest* is noteworthy for yet another reason. The diagram presented on p. 409 of the text was a pioneering formulation and one which has left a formidable legacy. For Fisher's purposes, this construction was designed as a demonstration of optimal inter-temporal allocation of consumption between two time periods. Latter-day international trade theorists have adapted this apparatus to illustrate the gains from trade and have used it extensively. But Fisher, though he used a different terminology, was the first to incorporate indifference curves, production possibility curves, and a market price line into a common diagram to represent gains from exchange. Fisher's priority in this matter has been pointed out by Thomas M. Humphrey.[c]

---

[a] Böhm-Bawerk, *Capital and Interest, Vol II: Positive Theory of Capital*, English translation by George D. Huncke, Libertarian Press: South Holland, Illinois, 1959, 40.

[b] In the 1920s, for example, Frank A. Fetter remarked on this phenomenon, observing that such departures from European orthodoxy "arose naturally in America where were lacking the artificial feudal limitations upon the sale of land, and where land-holders were not marked off socially from capitalist merchants as a separate class. Here land was readily bought and sold and was from the earliest settlement the chief object of investment with a view to speculative profit." ("Clark's Reformulation of the Capital Concept," as reprinted in Frank A. Fetter, *Capital, Interest, and Rent: Essays in the Theory of Distribution*, Murray A. Rothbard, ed., Sheed Andrews and McMeel: Kansas City, 1977, 122.)

[c] See Thomas M. Humphrey, "The Trade Theorists's Sacred Diagram: Its Origin and Early Development," *Federal Reserve Bank of Richmond Economic Review*, 74:1, January/February 1988, 3–15.

THE RATE OF INTEREST

THE RATE OF INTEREST

ITS NATURE, DETERMINATION AND RELATION TO ECONOMIC PHENOMENA

BY

IRVING FISHER, Ph.D.

PROFESSOR OF POLITICAL ECONOMY, YALE UNIVERSITY

New York

THE MACMILLAN COMPANY

1907

TO

𝔗𝔥𝔢 𝔐𝔢𝔪𝔬𝔯𝔶

OF

J O H N R A E

WHO LAID THE FOUNDATIONS

UPON WHICH

I HAVE ENDEAVORED

TO BUILD

PREFACE

THE problem of interest has engaged the attention of writers for two thousand years, and of economists since economics began. And yet, with the exception of what has been accomplished by Rae, Böhm-Bawerk, Landry, and some others, very little progress has been made toward a satisfactory solution. Even these writers can scarcely claim to have established a definitive theory of interest. While the value of their work is great, it is chiefly negative. They have cleared the way to a true theory by removing the confusions and fallacies which have beset the subject, and have pointed out that the rate of interest is not a phenomenon restricted to money markets, but is omnipresent in economic relations.

The theory of interest here presented is largely based upon the theories of the three writers above mentioned, and may therefore be called, in deference to Böhm-Bawerk, an "agio theory." But it differs from former versions of that theory by the introduction explicitly of an *income concept*. This concept, which I have developed at length in *The Nature of Capital and Income*, is found to play a central rôle in the theory of interest. The difficult problem is not whether the rate of interest *is* an agio, or premium, for of this there can be no question, but upon what does that agio depend and in what manner? Does it depend, for instance, on the volume of money, the amount of capital, the productivity of capital, the "superior productivity of roundabout processes," the labor of the capitalist, the helplessness of the laborer, or upon some other condition?

vii

The solution here offered is that the rate of interest depends on the character of the income-stream, — its size, composition, probability, and above all, its distribution in time. It might be called a theory of *prospective provision of income*.

As in *The Nature of Capital and Income*, mathematics have here been relegated to appendices. These appendices are not, however, mere translations into mathematical language of the theory verbally expressed in the text. Mathematics can properly claim no place in economic discussions except as they add something not expressible, or at any rate only imperfectly expressible, in ordinary language.

Parts of Chapters V and XIV with their appendices have appeared in somewhat different forms in *Appreciation and Interest*. My thanks are due to the American Economic Association for permission to use portions of this monograph unaltered. Since it appeared a decade ago, the view expressed in it, to the effect that appreciation of money should, and to some extent does, lower the rate of interest expressed in money, has gained considerable currency, though it is still unfamiliar to most persons. It has been thought wise to present again the statistical evidence in its favor, and to bring the statistics down to date.

In the preparation of this book I have received important aid from many persons. For general criticism I am indebted to my wife, to my colleagues, Professors H. C. Emery and J. P. Norton, and to my friend Richard M. Hurd, President of the Mortgage-Bond Company of New York City. My thanks are also due to Finance Minister Böhm-Bawerk for his kindness in reading and criticising the chapter devoted to his theory of interest; to Professor Clive Day for facts and references on the history of interest rates; to Dr. Lester W. Zartman for a large part of the statistical computation and for many helpful criticisms; to two of my students, Mr. Harry G. Brown and Mr. J. H. Parmelee, for valuable aid in proof-reading, including many keen and fruitful suggestions; and to my brother, Herbert W. Fisher, for a most searching and valuable criticism of the mode of expression and exposition.

IRVING FISHER.

NEW HAVEN, July, 1907.

CONTENTS

FIRST SUMMARY

SECOND SUMMARY

ANALYTICAL TABLE OF CONTENTS

CHAPTER I

CRUDE THEORIES

CHAPTER II

PRODUCTIVITY THEORIES

CHAPTER III

COST THEORIES

xiii

21

CHAPTER IV

Böhm-Bawerk's Theory

CHAPTER V

Appreciation and Interest

CHAPTER VI

TIME-PREFERENCE

CHAPTER VII

FIRST APPROXIMATION TO THE THEORY OF INTEREST
(ASSUMING INCOME RIGID)

CHAPTER VIII

SECOND APPROXIMATION TO THE THEORY OF INTEREST
(ASSUMING INCOME FLEXIBLE)

CHAPTER IX

CLASSES OF OPTIONS

CHAPTER X

INVENTION

CHAPTER XI

THIRD APPROXIMATION TO THE THEORY OF INTEREST
(ASSUMING INCOME UNCERTAIN)

CHAPTER XII

RÔLE OF INTEREST IN ECONOMIC THEORY

CHAPTER XIII

APPLICATION TO ACTUAL CONDITIONS

26

CHAPTER XVI

INDUCTIVE REFUTATION OF "MONEY-THEORY"

CHAPTER XVII

SUMMARY

GLOSSARY

APPENDICES

PART I. CRITICISM

THE RATE OF INTEREST

CHAPTER I

CRUDE THEORIES

§ 1

IF the theory to be presented in this book is correct, the rate of interest in any community is an index of the preference, in that community, for a dollar of present over a dollar of future income. The task of justifying this theory will be facilitated by a brief preliminary review of rival theories. A complete history of theories of interest has been made unnecessary by Böhm-Bawerk's admirable *Capital and Interest*.[1] For the same reason, it is not necessary to combat many of the special theories advanced by individual writers. The theories which are here selected for criticism are for the most part those which have the greatest currency, either in economic literature or in the unexpressed but none the less firmly rooted ideas of business or professional men. Experience shows that nearly every student of economic science has almost unconsciously acquired a number of crude and usually false ideas on this important subject. Such, for instance, is the idea that interest is the price paid for the "use of money"; or that it represents the "productivity" of capital or the "fecundity" of plants and animals; or that it represents some

---

[1] English translation by Smart, (Macmillan) 1890. See also *Recent Literature on Interest*, English translation by Scott & Feilbogen, (Macmillan) 1903.

3

"cost" to the producer, such as the cost of the capitalist's personal exertion in controlling capital, or the "cost of waiting"; or that it constitutes a species of legalized plunder perpetrated by the employer on the employed. Before the correct theory of interest can be securely implanted in any mind, these ideas must first be eradicated. To accomplish this is the object of the present and of the next three chapters.[1]

§ 2

An objection, formerly common, to the practice of taking interest was that interest is "unnatural." The word employed among the Greeks to signify interest or usury was τόκος, "offspring"; and Aristotle declaimed against the taking of interest, on the ground that money could not have "offspring," — a curious instance of the influence of terminology on thought.

Interest-taking between Jews was forbidden by the Mosaic laws, and similarly, in Rome, interest-taking between Romans was prohibited. Many biblical texts show the hostile attitude of the writers, both in the Old and New Testaments, toward the practice, and the Church Fathers through the Middle Ages for over a thousand years waged a ceaseless but fruitless war against interest-taking. St. Thomas Aquinas stated that interest was an attempt to extort a price for the use of things which had already been used up, as for instance, grain and wine.[2] He also declared that interest constituted a payment for *time*, and that time was a free gift of the Creator to which all have a natural right.[3]

[1] These chapters for the most part may be said to be a brief epitome, under a changed classification, of Böhm-Bawerk's exhaustive *Capital and Interest*.

[2] This criticism against the legitimacy of interest is very nearly revived by Böhm-Bawerk in his criticism of the modern "use" theory of interest. *Op. cit.*, Chap. VIII.

[3] This theory is not unlike one of the objections made to land-rent by the single-tax advocates; namely, that *space* is a free gift of nature.

The unpopularity of interest-taking increased until the thirteenth century; but the practice persisted, and as business operations increased in importance, certain exemptions and exceptions from its general prohibition were secured. Pawnshops, banks, and money-lenders were specially licensed, and permission was granted for buying annuities, and taking land on mortgage for money loaned. One of the subterfuges by which the allowance of interest was excused suggests the true idea of interest as an index of the relative preference for present over future goods. It was conceded that, whereas a loan should be nominally without interest, yet when the debtor delayed payment, he should be fined for his delay (*mora*), and the creditor should receive compensation in the form of "*interesse.*" Through this loophole it became common to make an understanding in advance, by which the payment of a loan should be "delayed" year after year, and with every such postponement a "fine" should become payable.

Some of the Protestant reformers, while not denying that interest-taking was wrong, admitted that it was impossible to suppress it, and that it should therefore be tolerated. This toleration was in the same spirit as that in which many reformers to-day defend the licensing of vicious institutions, such as saloons, racetracks, lotteries, and houses of prostitution.

In the sixteenth century interest-taking began to find some definite champions. Calvin attempted to discriminate between interest-taking which was right and interest-taking which was wrong. Among the wrong kinds he classed the taking of interest from the poor and from those in urgent need, and the taking of interest in excess of a legal maximum.

In order to defend interest, its champions began to construct theories to account for the phenomenon. Most of these early theories were little more than a shifting of the problem. It was seen that capital earned income whether it was lent or not. The income which a lender obtains through a loan contract may be called *explicit interest;* but it was clear that the borrower was enabled to pay this interest because the capital which he borrowed earned it for him. The income which capital thus earns may be called *implicit interest.* The earliest attempt to construct a theory of interest merely explained explicit interest in terms of implicit interest. Salmasius and Locke, both in the seventeenth century, attempted thus to explain interest. They tried to justify the taking of interest in a loan on the ground that an equivalent to that interest was obtained by the borrower from the capital he borrowed, and might have been obtained by the lender of the capital had he retained it. If, they said, a man lends $1000, he is entitled to interest upon it because, had he used it in business himself, he could have made profits by means of it. But beyond the bare statement that unlent capital yields income, these theories did not go. The real problem—"why capital yields income to the user"—was left untouched.

§ 3

The theories just described are for the most part obsolete to-day; yet we have a number of other theories almost equally crude. If a modern business man is asked what determines the rate of interest, he may usually be expected to answer, "the supply and demand of loanable money." But "supply and demand" is a phrase which has been too often forced into service to cover up difficult problems. Even economists have been prone to employ it to describe economic causation which they could not unravel. It was once wittily remarked of the early writers on economic problems, "Catch a parrot and teach him to say 'supply and demand,' and you have an excellent economist." Prices, wages, rent, interest, and profits were thought to be fully "explained" by this glib phrase. It is true that every ratio of exchange is due to the resultant of causes operating on the buyer and seller, and we may classify these as "demand" and "supply." But this fact does not relieve us of the necessity of examining specifically the two sets of causes, including utility in its effect on demand, and cost in its effect on supply. Consequently, when we say that the rate of interest is due to the supply and demand of "capital" or of "money" or of "loans," we are very far from having an adequate explanation. It is true that when merchants seek to discount bills at a bank in large numbers and for large amounts, the rate of interest will tend to be high, and that when merchants do not apply in large numbers and for large amounts, the rate of interest will tend to be low. But we must inquire for what purposes and from what causes merchants thus apply to a bank for the discount of loans, and why it is that some apply to the bank for loans and others supply the bank with the funds to be loaned. The real problem is: What causes make the demand for loans, and what causes make the supply? This question is not answered by the summary "supply and demand" theory. The explanation is not simply that those who have much capital supply the loans and those who have little capital demand them. In fact, the contrary is quite often the case. The depositors in savings banks are the lenders, and they are usually poor, whereas those to whom the savings bank in turn lends the funds are relatively rich.

§ 4

There is another phrase often employed by business men to explain the rate of interest or, at all events, its existence. It is often said that interest is the price paid for the "use of money." As an explanation this is almost as superficial as "supply and demand"; for it is clear that the "use" of money is to facilitate exchange, and that, except in rare instances (as when a bank borrows a chest of gold to reinforce its cash reserve), the money borrowed does not remain long in the hands of the borrower. If interest is a payment for use, it is payment for the use, not of the borrowed money, but of that for which the borrowed money is expended. For this reason the final explanation of the rate of interest is not to be sought in any monetary cause.

A special version of the theory that interest depends on the "use of money" is found in the very persistent belief that the quantity of money in circulation governs the rate of interest, — that the rate is high when money is scarce, and low when money is plentiful. The shallowness of this theory has been exposed repeatedly by economists from the time of Hume to the present. It requires only a little reflection to see that, although an increase of the quantity of money in circulation will increase the supply of loans, it will also equally increase the demand. For instance, a piano dealer who borrows $10,000 in order that he may add to his stock in trade 50 pianos costing $200 apiece would, if the supply of money were doubled, require a loan of double the amount; for such an inflation of the currency would double the cost of his stock, and in order to obtain 50 pianos — costing now $400 apiece instead of $200 — he would have to borrow $20,000 instead of $10,000.

In spite of such reasoning, showing that an inflation of the currency must act on the demand for loans as surely as upon the supply, the theory that an abundance of money lowers the rate of interest is nevertheless widely accepted even among intelligent business men. Yet facts do not, any more than *a priori* reasoning, lend support to this belief.[1]

The probable reason for the persistence, among business men, of the opinion that an abundance of money reduces the rate of interest is the observed fact that the rate of interest is high when the reserves in banks are low, and *vice versa*, and that the rate in a loan center can be materially reduced by bringing to that center a supply of actual

[1] A statistical discussion is contained in Chap. XVI, *infra*.

money to relieve the "stringency." This is true, and it is not denied that money plays a part in determining the rate of interest. But the part which it plays is chiefly as a puppet of other and mightier factors. The fundamental causes at work in a "money" market are not monetary at all, but economic. The economic causes operate through money and seldom show themselves save under a money disguise; but, generally speaking, money is only their instrument, not an independent factor. If money is plentiful for loan purposes, it is because its owners decide to apply it for these rather than for other purposes, and not because money in general is plentiful. The owners of money determine the purpose to which it shall be applied. To understand the real causes at work in the loan market, we must go back of the money itself and learn the reasons for bringing it into that market instead of spending it in other markets, — the meat, fish, fruit, or grocery markets, for instance. The abundance or scarcity of money for loan purposes is merely a sign or symptom of those more fundamental causes operating upon the rate of interest.

A full consideration of the manner in which money in loan centers is related to the rate of interest must, however, be deferred to Chapters V, XIV, and XVI. In the present chapter we are content merely to point out that the theories of which it treats are crude and superficial. They contain a modicum of truth, but they do not reach the root causes of interest. It is true that explicit interest is dependent upon implicit interest; but this being so, the question still remains, What determines implicit interest? Again, it is true that the rate of interest, like every other ratio of exchange, depends on "supply and demand"; but the question is, What constitutes the supply and demand? And again, it is true that interest varies with loanable funds; but what causes the variation of those funds? To answer these ulterior questions, more careful and elaborate theories have been constructed. These will be considered in the three following chapters.

CHAPTER II

PRODUCTIVITY THEORIES

§ 1

In the previous chapter it was shown that the problem of interest is not confined to contract or *explicit* interest, but includes the much broader field of natural or *implicit* interest. The existence of implicit as distinct from explicit interest needs emphasis, for the reason that, to most persons, the "rate of interest" means simply the explicit rate of interest in a loan contract. When a personal note, mortgage, or corporation bond is issued, the "rate of interest" is explicitly named in it and agreed upon by the contracting parties. But after its issue and before maturity, this note or bond may change hands; and as the price of sale is seldom exactly par, the investor evidently "realizes" a "rate of interest" on his investment different from the rate named in the written instrument. This rate is not explicit, but implicit. It is *implied* by the price of the note or bond, and can be ascertained from bond tables.[1] This implicit rate of interest is such that when it is used for calculating the present values of the future payments of the bond (the "principal" and "interest"), the sum of those present values will be the price of the bond.

It is evident that not bonds and notes alone, but all securities, *imply* in their price and their expected returns a rate of interest. There is thus an implicit rate of interest in stocks as well as in bonds. In the case of stocks the element of chance enters also; but while this adds somewhat to the intricacy of the calculation, it still requires the

[1] See *The Nature of Capital and Income*, New York (Macmillan), 1906, Chap. XIII.

employment of a rate of interest.[1] In the same way all instruments of wealth, such as land, *imply* a rate of interest. This is recognized when land is sold on the basis of a number of "years' purchase." In like manner, machinery, dwellings, furniture, and, in fact, all articles of wealth, as was shown in *The Nature of Capital and Income*, are valued by discounting expected income; and all discounting of income can be calculated only by means of a "rate of interest." There is thus an "implicit rate of interest" in the value of every capital-good. It is, to be sure, often difficult to work out this rate definitely, on account of the elusive element of chance; but it has an existence in all capital. From this it is clear that the extent and importance of the interest problem cannot be grasped until implicit interest is recognized; and, as a matter of history, it was only after implicit interest was in some degree thus recognized that any theory of interest worthy of the name was evolved.

§ 2

The first writer who attempted to explain natural or implicit interest, as distinct from contractual or explicit interest, appears to have been Turgot. His explanation consisted simply in shifting the onus of the problem on to land. He explained that interest must be obtainable from the use of capital in general, because it is obtainable from the use of land in particular. He reasoned that, were it not likewise obtainable from other capital, every one would invest in land. A man with $1000 worth of other goods would, if he received no increase, prefer to sell these goods and buy $1000 worth of land, from which he could obtain say $50 a year. Land, he explained, evidently yields interest because it yields a perpetual series of crops, the land being bought for so many "years' purchase" of those crops. This number of years' purchase, he said, was de-

[1] See *The Nature of Capital and Income*, Chap. XVI.

termined by "supply and demand"; but back of this convenient phrase he did not penetrate.

Turgot's shifting the problem to land might naturally have revealed the true theory of interest as lying in the preference for present over future goods; for when one asks why land does not have an infinite value, equal to the entire value of its infinite future crops, the answer becomes at once obvious, namely, that no one would prize crops to accrue a million years hence on an equal footing with crops of to-day. Yet this explanation was never made.

Turgot's theory may be regarded as a particular species of the numerous productivity theories, differing from the others chiefly in that he took his starting-point from the productivity of a particular form of capital, instead of from the productivity of capital in general. At the basis of all the thought of Turgot, as of other physiocrats, is the idea that land is the source of all human revenue.

§ 3

This idea few share to-day; yet there are many who, consciously or unconsciously, ascribe the phenomena of interest to the productivity of capital in general. When the rate of interest is 5 per cent., nothing at first sight seems more obvious than that this is so because capital will yield 5 per cent. Since capital is productive, it seems self-evident that an investment of $100 in productive land, machinery, or any other form of capital will receive a rate of interest proportionate to its productivity. Yet a very slight examination will suffice to show the inadequacy of this explanation.

The productivity theory in its simplest or "naïve" form, as Böhm-Bawerk calls it, confuses what we have distinguished [1] as physical-productivity and value-return. It takes no account of the great gap between the physical-

[1] See *The Nature of Capital and Income*, Chap. XI.

productivity of a factory — the ratio of its output to the size of the plant — and its value-return — the ratio of the value of the output to the value of the factory.[1]

It is evident that if an orchard of ten acres yields 100 barrels of apples a year, the physical-productivity, ten barrels per acre, does not of itself give any clew to what rate of return on its *value* the orchard yields. To obtain the value-return, we must reduce both income and capital to a common standard of value. If the net annual crop of apples is worth $1000 and the orchard is worth $20,000, the ratio of the former to the latter, or 5 per cent., is a rate of value-return; and if this rate is maintained without depreciation of the value of the orchard, this rate of value-return is also the rate of interest.

It seems at first sight very easy to pass from quantities to values, — to translate the ten acres of orchard and the 100 barrels of apples into dollars. But this apparently simple step begs the whole question. The important fact, and the one lost sight of in the productivity theory, is that the value of the orchard depends upon the value of its crops; and in this dependence lurks implicitly the rate of interest itself. The statement that "capital produces income" is true only in the physical sense; it is not true in the value sense. That is to say, *capital-value does not produce income-value*. On the contrary, income-value produces capital-value. It is not because the orchard is worth $20,000 that the annual crop will be worth $1000, but it is because the annual crop is worth $1000 that the orchard will be worth $20,000. The $20,000 is the discounted value of the expected income of $1000 per annum; and in the process of discounting, a rate of interest of 5 per cent. is implied. In general, it is not because a man has $100 worth of property that he will get $5 a year, but it is because

[1] Certain theories, which Böhm-Bawerk calls "indirect productivity theories," have taken account in some degree of the distinction between the relation of quantity and value of income to quantity and value of capital, and have attempted to bridge the chasms between them, but, as Böhm-Bawerk has shown, without success.

he will get that $5 a year that his property is worth $100. In short, when capital and income are measured in *value*, their causal connection is the reverse of that which holds true when they are measured in *quantity*. The orchard produces the apples; but the value of the apples produces the value of the orchard.

§ 4

We see, then, that present capital-*wealth* produces future income-*services;* but future income-*value* produces present capital-*value*. The order to be observed in the study of capital and income is consequently as follows: (1) quantity of capital, or capital-wealth, (2) quantity of income, or income-services, (3) value of income, (4) value of capital. This order is shown in the following scheme: —

	Present Capital	Future Income
Quantities	Capital-wealth ⟶	Income-services
		↓
Values	Capital-value ⟵	Income-value

This scheme signifies that (1) any capital-wealth, such, for instance, as land, railways, factories, dwellings, or food, is the means for obtaining income-services, whether these be preparatory services like production of crops, transportation, and manufacturing transformations, or final services like shelter and nourishment. This first step in the sequence pertains to the study of the "technique" of production and involves no rate of interest. (2) The income-services are next reduced to a single denomination, such as dollars of gold. This step pertains to the study of prices, and, when applied to the *final* services, such as shelter and nourishment, does not directly involve any rate of interest. (3) From the income-value thus obtained is computed the value of the original capital by the process of discounting. This final process introduces the element of interest. It is clearly with this last process that we are concerned in the study of interest.

The paradox that, when we come to the *value* of capital, it is income which produces capital, and not the reverse, is, then, the stumbling-block of the productivity theorists. It is clear, of course, in any ordinary investment, that the selling value of a stock or bond is dependent on its expected income. And yet business men, although they are constantly employing this discount process in every specific case, usually cherish the illusion that they do so because their money could be "productively invested" elsewhere. They fail to observe that the principle of discounting the future is universal, and applies to any investment whatsoever, and that in such a discount-process there is necessarily involved a rate of interest. Consequently, any attempt to deduce the rate of interest from the ratio of the income from capital to the value of that capital is a *petitio principii*.

§ 5

The futility of the ordinary productivity theory may be further illustrated by observing the effect of a change of productivity. If an orchard could in some way be made to yield double its original crop, the productivity of that capital in the physical sense would be doubled, but its yield in the sense of the rate of interest would not necessarily be affected at all, certainly not doubled. For the orchard whose yield of apples should increase from $1000 worth to $2000 worth would itself correspondingly increase in value from, say, $20,000 to something like $40,000, and the ratio of the income to the capital-value would remain about as before, namely, 5 per cent. To raise the rate of interest by raising the productivity of capital is, therefore, like trying to raise one's self by one's boot-straps.

One cannot escape this conclusion (as has sometimes been attempted) by supposing the increasing productivity to be universal. It has been asserted, in substance, that though an increase in the productivity of one orchard would not appreciably affect the total productivity of capital, and hence would not appreciably affect the rate of interest, yet if the productivity of all the capital of the world could be doubled, the rate of interest would be doubled. It is true that doubling the productivity of the world's capital would not be entirely without effect upon the rate of interest; but this effect would not be in the simple direct ratio supposed. Indeed, an increase of the productivity of capital would probably result in a decrease, instead of an increase, of the rate of interest. To double the productivity of capital might more than double the value of the capital. That it would fail to do so has not been shown by the productivity theorists, much less that capital would remain unchanged in value.

§ 6

The same objections which have been indicated in relation to the productivity theory apply to what Böhm-Bawerk calls the "use theories." These, in fact, are a special and improved form of the productivity theory. The ordinary productivity theory regards capital as producing an unspecified something called its "product," whereas the use theory regards that something specifically as a use or service. This accords to some extent with a correct theory of services, but nevertheless it is still subject to the objections which have just been made to the other productivity theories. If a machine renders a service or use of which the annual value is reckoned at $100, and the life of the machine is ten years, this $1000 of services distributed over a decade gives, of itself, no intimation as to the rate of interest. Here, again, we must first know the rate of interest itself in order to know the value of the machine. Suppose that the rate of interest, on the basis of which the machine is valued, is 5 per cent. Then the value of the machine, when new, would be $772, this being the discounted value, at 5 per cent., of the income above specified. This capital-value is, of course, derived from the expected income, and not *vice versa*. If, for any reason, the services of the machine are doubled in quantity, and the price of these services remains unchanged, their value will rise and become $200 a year for each of the ten years. But the effect will not be to double the rate of interest; it will rather be to double the capital-value of the machine, and instead of being worth $772, which is the discounted value, at 5 per cent., of $100 a year for ten years, it will now be worth $1544, which is the discounted value, at 5 per cent., of $200 a year for ten years.

Actually, of course, the doubling of the income-services performed by the machine will lower the price of those services and affect the manufacture of the machine which performs them. When the effects are complete, the resultant income-value of the services of the machine may rise above, fall short of, or remain stationary at $200 a year, according to the extent of the fall in the price of the services. As a consequence of such a changed income-value, the capital-value of the machine may also change in either direction, or remain stationary. The capital-value follows the rate of interest, not the reverse. Whatever the effect on the rate of interest involved in these events, it is not the simple one, imagined by the use theorists, of a rise or fall proportionate to a rise or fall in income-services, or even to a rise or fall of income-value.

The objections which have been urged to the productivity and use theories apply with still greater force in cases where the depreciation of capital is offset so as to "standardize"[1] the income. It is sometimes said that interest is the income which capital yields beyond what is neces-

---

[1] See *The Nature of Capital and Income*, Chap. XIV.

sary to replace the capital. But in the cost of replacement which maintains the capital there lurks again the very rate of interest to be explained.

Let us examine the case of a factory plant of ten machines, each like the one just described. Suppose that these ten machines are evenly distributed through the years, as to wear — that, for instance, the life of each machine is ten years and that, accordingly, the cost of renewal is the cost of one machine annually. Let us imagine a man buying these ten machines for $4556. Knowing that the cost of each machine is $772 and its annual use is $100, he will calculate that he is "making 5 per cent. on his capital," because he will receive 10 × $100 or $1000 a year in service from his machines, and will spend each year for replacement $772. This leaves a net income of $228, which, divided by the capital invested, $4556, makes just 5 per cent. If asked why the rate of interest is 5 per cent., this owner is likely to answer, because outfits like his yield 5 per cent. on their cost, over and above the cost of replacement. A little reflection, however, will show that the rate of interest is implicitly assumed in his calculation. Not only the $4556 of capital, *but even the $228 of income,* are calculated on the assumption of a rate of interest of 5 per cent.

That this is true of the capital, $4556, is evident by repeating, with reference to the entire ten machines, the calculations already explained for one. Each machine is valued by discounting its future annual services of $100 for its lifetime. One of the machines is new and has a life of ten years; consequently, it is worth, as already seen, $772, this being the discounted value of ten annual instalments of $100 each, on the assumption of a 5 per cent. interest rate as the basis for the calculation. The life of the next machine is only nine years, making, by a similar reckoning, a present value of $711; the life of the third machine, eight years, making its value $646, and so on. Thus the total for the ten machines is $772 + $711 + $646 + $578

+ \$508 + \$433 + \$355 + \$272 + \$186 + \$95, or \$4556.   It is clear that this item and each of the ten sums of which it is composed are calculated only by the aid of a rate of interest.

So much for the capital; now let us turn to the net income of \$228. The gross income is \$100 per machine for ten machines, or \$1000, and from this is deducted the cost of replenishing one machine. This cost is \$772, leaving \$228 as net income. But this cost of replacement, \$772, is the capital-value of a machine, and is obtained by means of a rate of interest, namely, 5 per cent. The reason, then, that the \$4556 yields \$228, or 5 per cent., is not because of the productivity of the machines, but because 5 per cent. is *assumed* in the calculation both of the \$4556 and of the \$228. The 5 per cent. emerges at the end only because it was put in at the beginning.[1]

Were the productivity the source of the rate of interest, we should expect a double productivity to double the rate of interest. But the reasoning used in the case of the orchard shows that not only will the value of the use of the machinery be doubled, but the cost of each new machine may be doubled, so as to leave the rate of interest at 5 per cent.

As stated above, the doubling in productivity would naturally result in lowering the price of the services produced, so that the *value* of the doubled quantity of services might be less than double the value of the original quantity of services. Consequently, the value of the new machines and the cost of replacing an old machine by a new one might not be double what they were before. But they certainly would not be unaffected.

The process of adjusting supply and price reconciles what has been said with the old cost-of-production theory of value. The reader may have felt that we have treated the value of the machines and the cost of replacement as though they had no relation whatever to the cost of producing the machines. One cannot deny that the classical

[1] For a mathematical formulation, see Appendix to Chap. II, § 1.

economists were partly right in ascribing value to cost of production. But cost of production affects the value of a capital good only *indirectly* by affecting the scarcity of its products or uses. The value of its products or uses depends on its marginal utility. The marginal utility is dependent on the scarcity, and this scarcity depends, in turn, partly on cost of production, so far as this cost of production has any independent existence.[1]

§ 7

Extreme cases are always instructive, even when they are impossible of realization. As an extreme case, let us imagine a community in which the rate of interest is zero. In this case we can scarcely fail to observe the wide difference between physical-productivity and value-return; for we shall find that the disappearance of interest does not carry with it the disappearance of physical-productivity, though it does bring about the cessation of value-return. Consider a plant of ten machines, of which the annual use is worth, as before, $100. The value of a new machine to last ten years will now be, not $772 as before, but $1000, this being the capital-value of ten annual instalments of $100 each, reckoned at full value, or, if we prefer to say so, each discounted at zero per cent. Similarly, the value of a machine one year old, having nine more years of life, would be, not $711 as before, but $900; of one two years old, $800, and so on, making a total value, not of $4556, but $1000 + $900 + $800 + $700 + $600 + $500 + $400 + $300 + $200 + $100, or $5500. This is the capital-value of the plant. We next seek the *net* annual income from the ten machines. Strange as it may seem, this net income, if the plant is exactly kept up, would be zero; for the *gross* annual income from the ten machines is 10 × $100, or $1000, and the deduction for the cost of a new

---

[1] See *The Nature of Capital and Income*, p. 173.

machine is, as we have seen, also $1000. Consequently the net income is zero, and the value-return, being $\dfrac{\text{zero}}{5500}$, is also zero. Yet the case supposed does not imply any reduction in physical-productivity; the machines produce the same amount of work as when the rate of interest was supposed to be 5 per cent.

It may be asked how it is possible that the plant, if it yields no income, could have any value. We have found it worth $5500 and yet it yields no net income. The answer is that the annihilation of net income which we have witnessed takes place only so long as the up-keep of the plant is maintained. At any time that the owner of the plant sees fit to do so, he may draw income from the plant to any amount up to $5500, but no more. If, for instance, he decides at the end of ten years to withdraw from manufacturing, he may discontinue his annual renewals and obtain in the first year thereafter his $100 income from each of the ten machines, or $1000 in all, without any deduction for up-keep. During the next year, as one machine will have been worn out and unreplaced, he will obtain the income from only nine machines, or $900, and likewise, in the years succeeding this, he will obtain $700, $600, etc., until the last machine is worn out and no capital remains. The total of this income is evidently $5500.

In other words the owner of the machines, as long as he keeps up his capital, obtains no net income, but he has the possibility at any time of obtaining a total net income of $5500 simply by letting his plant run down. The possibility of obtaining this return keeps the value of the capital at $5500 as long as it is kept up. His capital is like a fixed treasure and remains $5500.[1] The process of keeping up the capital is virtually to keep the $5500 in cold storage, so to speak.

[1] For a mathematical treatment of this peculiar case, see Appendix to Chap. II, § 2.

If it be asked what motive could ever prompt any one to keep up his capital when, as long as he does so, all income is foregone, the answer is that, under our assumption of zero interest, there would be no preference for the immediate over the remote income of $5500. The owner of the plant would just as willingly wait a hundred years for his $5500 as to receive it now. In actual fact, men are not thus willing to wait, and therein lies the unreality of our assumption that interest is zero. In our supposititious case the element of time-preference was abstracted with the element of interest. But this imaginary case shows that absence of interest is quite compatible with the presence of physical-productivity, and that, therefore, whatever element is responsible for the existence of interest in the actual world, that element cannot be physical-productivity.

§ 8

It was with a view to meeting some of the difficulties which have just been pointed out in the productivity theories, that Alexander Del Mar and Henry George suggested their theory of interest,[1] basing it on the productivity of those particular kinds of capital which reproduce themselves. They state that, were all capital inanimate, the phenomena of interest would not exist, because inanimate capital is incapable of increasing; but that the organic forms of capital are capable, without labor, of reproducing and increasing with time. Money, as Aristotle said, is barren, and coal and iron cannot breed. Were all capital of this non-increasing kind, it would, said Henry George, not yield interest. But a flock of sheep, herd of cattle, or group of Belgian hares will, from its own natural powers of breeding, increase and multiply; it will, as it were, ac-

[1] Del Mar, *Science of Money*, (Macmillan) 1896, p. 144. Henry George, *Progress and Poverty*. For a general criticism of this theory, see Dwight M. Lowry, "The Basis of Interest," *American Academy of Political and Social Science*, March, 1892, pp. 53–76.

cumulate at compound interest. In like manner a forest will grow, and crops will spring up. These seem to show a rate of interest in Nature herself. Mr. George contends that a man who puts $1000 into a savings bank can demand that it receive interest, for the reason that he might invest it in a flock of sheep and let it accumulate naturally. According to this theory, interest exists because plants and animals grow, because the seed becomes the crop, the sapling becomes a tree, the egg a chick, and the chick a hen. The conclusion is drawn that, in the last analysis, the rate of interest consists in the "average rate of growth of animals and plants."

We may remark at the outset that this theory, like the land-yielding theory of Turgot, is one-sided and partial, inasmuch as it makes the rate of interest from all capital depend on the rate of interest from one particular form of capital; and it does not seem likely, *a priori*, that any theory of interest can be true which does not apply alike to all forms of capital which yield interest. But, aside from this preliminary objection, a specific examination of his theory will show that Henry George has not escaped the fatal error of assuming a rate of interest in order to prove it. We propose to make a thorough reëxamination of this theory, not because it has attracted any special attention or been accepted by others than its author or authors, but because it puts the productivity theory on its strongest grounds — stronger grounds than its opponents have usually acknowledged or understood — and more especially because, in a dormant state, it seems to exist in the minds of a great many persons.

§ 9

Let us imagine a forest growing at a certain rate, such, for instance, that an acre of spruce containing 100 cords of wood suitable for making wood pulp will, if let alone, in five years amount to 200 cords. Here is an increase of 100 per cent. in five years, which is at the rate of about 15 per cent. per annum. Does this 15 per cent. represent a natural rate of interest? Would 100 cords of this year's timber exchange for 115 cords of next year's timber? If so, we certainly have a simple physical basis for the rate of interest quite independent of the psychological element.

But a little consideration will show that there is an error in the reasoning. If the supply of wood pulp is decreasing as years go on, while the demand is steadily increasing (and these conditions correspond to the facts as they are to-day), it may well be that 100 cords of this year's timber would exchange for a relatively small amount of next year's timber, say 105 cords, in spite of the fact that it grows at 15 per cent. per annum instead of 5 per cent. That this rate of exchange of present wood for future wood is quite compatible with a much greater rate of growth will become apparent as soon as we consider that *growing timber* is not the same thing as *cut wood*. It is clear that to cut young timber which is growing very fast is like killing the goose that lays the golden egg, and to reckon the value of the growing timber as only equivalent to the wood contained in it is like reckoning a live goose equivalent to a dead one. The value, in cut wood, of 100 cords of rapidly growing timber will be considerably greater than 100 cords of cut wood. If, for instance, the possessor of the growing timber has the option, besides that of cutting it, of allowing it to stand for five years and then obtaining a stumpage of 200 cords, he will allow it to stand, for these 200 cords due five years hence are worth, in present estimation, discounted at 5 per cent., 157 cords. Thus his present 100 cords of standing timber is equivalent to 157 cords of present cut wood. The value of a tree at any time is therefore not necessarily the physical amount of wood then in it; it may be the discounted value of the future wood which the tree will produce if left to grow. It will actually be whichever of the two happens to be the greater. For, of various optional employments of his capital, the investor selects the one which offers the maximum present value.[1] Were it true that the value of a tree in wood were always simply the physical amount of wood it contains, it would be a matter of indifference whether a tree were cut at the sapling stage or any other, whereas we know that part of the art of lumbering consists in selecting the right age for cutting.

The case may be illustrated by Figure 1. Let AB repre-

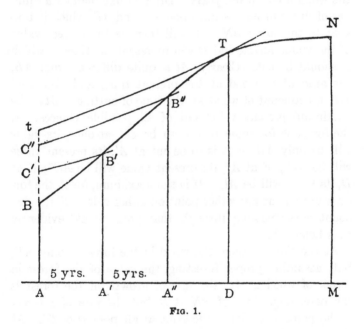

FIG. 1.

sent the number of cords of wood on an acre of growing trees, $A'B'$ the amount of wood which may be expected at the end of five years, $A''B''$ what may be expected in ten years, and so on for successive years until the forest reaches its maximum growth, MN, at the end of AM

[1] See *The Nature of Capital and Income*, pp. 221–222.

years. The percentage-slope [1] of the curve BN at any point, therefore, represents the rate of growth of the forest. The value at present of the forest in terms of cords of wood will be represented, not by the height AB, but in a different manner, as follows: If from B' the discount curve [2] $B'C'$ be drawn, the ordinates of which will represent the discounted values of $A'B'$ at any times, AC' will represent the present value of $A'B'$, the wood if cut in five years. Similarly, AC'' will represent the present value of $A''B''$, the wood if cut in ten years. Draw in like manner a number of discount curves until one is found, tT, which is tangent to the curve BN. At will then be the correct value of the young forest, and D will represent the time at which it should be cut. Clearly, At is quite different from AB, the amount of wood at the present time, and also from DT, the amount of wood at the time of cutting. At is the maximum present value out of all possible choices. If the forest is for some reason to be cut at once, its value will be only AB; if it is to be cut at A', its present value will be AC'; if at A'', its present value will be AC''; if at D, its value will be At. At is the maximum, for if the forest were cut at any other point on either side of T the discount curve passing through that point would evidently pass below tT.

At the time A, then, the wood in the forest is only AB, but, assuming proper foresting, the value of the forest in terms of wood is At; the rate of growth of the forest is the percentage-slope of BN at B, but the rate of interest is the percentage-slope (the same at all points) of tT. At the point of tangency alone, namely, T, are the rate of growth and rate of interest identical, and to that extent there is truth in the thesis that the rate of interest is the rate of growth. This element of truth in the organic

---

[1] By percentage-slope is meant the ratio of the slope to the ordinate. See *The Nature of Capital and Income*, Appendix to Chap. XII, § 2.

[2] See *The Nature of Capital and Income*, Chap. XIII.

productivity theory will be more fully discussed when
we come to develop our own theory of the rate of interest. But that this element of truth is insufficient to
afford a determination of the rate of interest is evident
when we consider that the point at which the forest is to
be cut itself depends, among other causes, upon the rate of
interest. If the interest rate rises, the discount curves employed become steeper and the point of tangency T moves
toward the left; that is, the forest will be cut earlier. This
is undoubtedly one reason for the fact that forests in the
United States have hitherto been cut early ; the owners
have not felt that they could afford to "lose the interest"
in waiting. In Europe, on the other hand, where interest
rates have been low, forestry culture, though often involving fifty years' waiting, has been profitable. It would
not be correct, of course, to ascribe the difference in forest
policy wholly to a difference in the rate of interest, for
the European policy has also been more enlightened than
the American.

Not only does the most favorable time for cutting depend
upon the rate of interest, but the rate of interest itself
depends upon the future distribution of the times of cutting of many forests. If all the forests of a country are
young, there will be a relative scarcity of present wood and
a consequent enhancement of the rate of interest (in terms
of wood) which will make for early cutting. In the United
States at the present time the reverse is the case. There
is a present abundant supply of spruce for wood pulp.
But a single edition of a large metropolitan Sunday newspaper will use up two acres of spruce. We have, therefore,
to contemplate a growing scarcity of wood, and probably
at the same time an increasing demand for it. The effect
is to enhance the value relatively of future wood, that is,
to lower the rate of interest in wood. This shifts the point
of tangency T toward the right and introduces a tendency to postpone cutting, as is manifested by speculation
in spruce forests.

§ 10

From what has been said it is clear that although interest enters into the processes of nature, it is not because of their physical expansion, but because they require time. It is not because the seed grows into crops or the egg into a chick that there is interest, but because the crops or the chick are unavailable until a future time. The type of interest is a "time-lock" like those used on the doors of some banks. Nature holds many treasures in her storehouse, but she will not unlock them all at once.

The conclusion, therefore, from our study of the various forms of the productivity theory is that physical-productivity, of itself, has no such direct relation to the rate of interest as is usually ascribed to it; and in the theories which we have examined, the rate of interest is always surreptitiously introduced. It is, however, quite true that the productivity of capital does *affect* the rate of interest; for it affects the relative valuation of present and future goods by affecting the relative endowment of the present and the future. It is quite true, in particular, that the rapidity of growth of the organic world will affect the rate of interest by redistributing income between different points of time and by opening up a series of choices to the owner as to the time of cutting his forests or of reaping the rewards of other sorts of organic growth. It follows that the rate of growth will coincide at certain points with the rate of interest. These small grains of truth in the productivity theories will be fully incorporated in our study at a later stage.

CHAPTER III

§ 1

WE turn now from those theories of interest based mainly
on the idea of *productivity* to those based mainly on that of
cost.

The first of the cost theories to be examined resembles
closely the productivity theories, the only difference being
that the "cost of production of capital" takes the place of
the value of capital. In the productivity theories, the rate
of interest was sought in the ratio between the income
from capital and the *value of that capital*. In the cost
theory now considered, on the other hand, the rate of interest is sought in the ratio between the income from capital and the *cost of that capital*. This theory is subject to
many of the objections which apply to the productivity
theories. In the first place, it is necessary, before the
ratio of income to cost can be regarded as even commen-
surable with a rate of interest, that income and cost shall
have been reduced to a common denomination of value,
as, for instance, dollars. A loom renders its return, or service, by the operation called weaving. The cost of the
loom, on the other hand, consists of raw materials, the use
of tools, dies, lathes, and other machine-shop appliances,
together with human labor. Only when these miscellaneous items are reduced to some common standard of value
does the ratio of income to cost become a mere percentage
like the rate of interest. But when this reduction to a
common standard is effected, the suspicion immediately
arises that, after all, the question of interest may have

29

been begged in the process,—that the labor, materials, and use of tools all derive their value as costs, in part, at least, from discounting the prospective product to which they contribute. In other words, since the cost of capital must be obtained by a process of valuation, this valuation may involve the very rate of interest to be determined.

Nevertheless, the theory which seeks the rate of interest in the ratio of return to cost of capital has certain advantages over that which seeks it in the ratio of return to value of capital; for there are some costs which are not merely the discounted value of expected services. There are two kinds of costs, (1) "interactions"[1] and (2) labor-and-trouble. The value of the former is always determined by discounting some future service; the value of the latter is determined (to the laborer) by the irksomeness or "undesirability" of labor compared with the desirability of money. We are not called upon, however, to strengthen the cost theories by recourse to this distinction between costs which involve discounting and costs which do not; for the cost theories as actually held and advocated take no account of such a distinction, and the costs usually cited are mainly costs which do involve discounting,—in other words, interactions. Such costs certainly cannot be taken as a sufficient foundation for explaining the rate of interest. The tailor reckons among his costs the value of the cloth which he buys; the manufacturer of the cloth reckons among his costs the value of the yarn; the producer of the yarn reckons in his cost the value of the wool. But the value of the wool is found in part by discounting the value of the yarn to which it contributes; that of the yarn, by discounting the value of the cloth; that of the cloth, by discounting the value of the clothes.

It is seldom possible in practice to find a case so pure as not to be obscured by a number of different elements; but let us, for the sake of illustration, consider

[1] See *The Nature of Capital and Income*, Chaps. VII–X.

a dealer in trees, who buys saplings and sells them after
they are full grown.   In this case there are few other
costs besides the cost of *buying* the saplings.   We can here
see clearly the fallacy involved in regarding the rate of interest as determined by the ratio of the value of the full-
grown tree to the cost of the sapling; for the cost of buying
the sapling is evidently itself obtained by discounting the
value of the tree.   In fact, in this case the cost theory
becomes identical with the productivity theory; for the
cost of buying the sapling is nothing more nor less than the
value of the sapling.   The only distinction between them
is a formal one: the cost of buying the sapling is regarded
as pertaining to the income and outgo account; the value
of the sapling, to the capital account.   Since, then, the
cost of buying the sapling is the discounted value of the
tree, this cost can be computed only by discounting, and
discounting presupposes a rate of interest.   In many
cases, therefore, "cost" is merely the discounted value of
"return."   The cost, in these cases at least, depends on
the rate of interest, not the rate of interest on the cost.

§ 2

It is true that an article sometimes costs less (or more)
than the discounted value of the returns.   The ratio of
future return to present cost may then temporarily differ
from the rate of interest on loans.   Thus, a manufacturer
calculates that a newly invented machine will earn him
$10 a year for twenty years.   If we suppose he is willing
to invest on a 5 per cent. basis, namely, that subjectively
he values this year's goods at a premium of 5 per cent.
compared with next year's goods, then the price he is
willing to pay for the machine is $125, this being the
present worth, at 5 per cent., of $10 a year for twenty years.
But it may be that the cost of obtaining the machine is
not $125 but, say, $100, which corresponds to an 8 per

cent. basis.   Here seems to be a natural rate of interest of
8 per cent., in defiance of an interest rate of 5 per cent. employed by the manufacturer in discounting his returns.
The manufacturer, by investing $100, makes 8 per cent. —
not, apparently, because he or any one else discounts the
future at that rate, but simply because of the productivity
of the machine in relation to its cost.

But such a disharmony between the 8 per cent. realized
and the 5 per cent. employed in discounting will be only temporary.   It will work out its own correction, for the manufacturer who finds he can invest at 8 per cent. when he
is willing to invest at 5 per cent. will increase his investment until the returns fall to 5 per cent.   He will buy
more machines; but the more he buys, the less will he
make from each successive machine.   The tenth machine
will not increase his income rate by $10 over and above
what it would be with only nine machines, but by, let us
say, only $6.25.   This reduction may be due to outrun-
ning his market and reducing the price he can get, or by
increasing the cost of running, or in other ways.   He will
buy machines up to the point where the last increment
earns 5 per cent., and by the "law of indifference" he will
impute this same rate to all the machines.   In other words,
however much the ratio of return to cost may temporarily
deviate from the rate of preference for present over future
goods, such deviation is done away with at the margin of
final choice.   Excessive rates of return could never serve
as a permanent basis for market values, for the rush to
secure these excessive returns would reduce them.   If, on
the other hand, the cost of the machine is $150, represent-
ing a basis of about 3 per cent., while the manufacturer
continues willing to invest only on a 5 per cent. basis,
there may seem to be a natural rate of 3 per cent.   Here,
too, the apparent disharmony will work out its own correction.   The manufacturer will cease buying machines to
replace the old ones which have worn out, until through
such limitation the returns have increased to 5 per cent.

In either case, when equilibrium is established the value of
the machine is the discounted value of its future uses.
For the individual purchaser, the cost of the machine
appears as a fixed quantity, and he so adjusts the number
of machines that the return of the marginal machine is
5 per cent. on this cost.   For the market as a whole, however, the situation is reversed; the price of the machines is
determined by their prospective return.

§ 3

So far as the cost theories of interest relate to *labor*
cost, they are free from the objection of begging the question, which has just been offered to the more general cost-
theory; and yet, the ratio of return on labor to the labor
invested cannot, by itself, afford a sufficient basis for the
rate of interest, for the reason that neither the return nor
the labor are fixed quantities.   With an increase in the
amount of capital, the return will decrease, and the labor
of obtaining it will increase.   This, in fact, is the well-
known "law of diminishing returns."

To render our reasoning clear, we shall take a classical
illustration of Roscher's.   Let the labor sacrificed in producing a fishing net be reckoned at 100 fish.   This valuation of
labor by the laborer is not quite like the valuation of the
machine.   Instead of being the value of future income discounted, it is the value of present outgo in the form of
effort.   We cannot, therefore, maintain that in valuing the
net the rate of interest is surreptitiously introduced.   Our
objections are now confined to the fact that both the labor
of making the net and its return are not fixed elements to
which the rate of interest is adjusted, but are themselves
adjustable to that rate.   With the net, the fisherman is
enabled to catch 30 fish a day, whereas without it he could
catch but 3.   We may suppose that the net will last 90
days, getting in all 2700 fish.   This is the return on the

labor invested, which has been reckoned at 100 fish. If the net requires care and attention, and this be reckoned at 3 fish a day, there is still an excess of 30 − 3, or 27 fish a day to be credited to the net itself. For the 90 days this amounts to 2430 fish. Even if, for other reasons, we make further reductions, the return may still be a very large one compared with the 100 fish invested, — let us say 2000 fish.

The question now is, does the excess of this return over the labor invested explain interest? Certainly not. Granted that such an extraordinary return on one's labor invested were initially realized, it is evident that nets paying so handsomely would be made in large numbers, and that, as their numbers were increased, the labor and sacrifice of making each additional net would increase, or else the product obtained from each additional net would decrease, or both. In this way the excess of return over cost would be doubly reduced. Why should not this excess be reduced to zero? Evidently nothing in the physical nature of the net itself, or the condition of the fisheries, or the amount of labor involved in producing a net, will suffice to explain the point at which the process will cease and nets no longer be produced. On the contrary, it is evident that physically it would be possible to greatly overproduce the nets. It is also clear that the fisheries could not continue to yield fish indefinitely. The result might be that, as the nets were increased in number, the labor of obtaining materials and making nets would increase until, let us say, a net would cost labor reckoned equivalent to 1000 fish; at the same time the yield of each net might fall to, say, 10 fish a day for the 90 days, or 900 fish in all. Here would be an investment of 1000 for a return of only 900. The reason that this result would not, intentionally at least, be reached, is evidently not to be sought in any physical facts as to the net, the fish, and the labor of producing them, but in the fact that the net makers would of their own volition cease producing nets before such a superabundance was put upon the market. In fact, they would even refuse to invest 1000 for an equal return of 1000. In other words, the production of nets would proceed only up to the point where the excess of return over cost corresponded to the relative preference for present over future fish. The reason, then, that the product keeps above the cost is simply that those who make nets decide to stop making them at a point earlier than that of equality between cost and return, and their decisions so to do are based not on a physical but on a psychical fact — their relative valuations of present sacrifice and future return.

Leaving our special illustration, let us put the matter in general terms. It is often stated by economists that any capital will be constructed only so long as its marginal utility is equal to or greater than the marginal disutility or marginal cost of its construction. The greater the desire for its services and the less the cost of production, the more of it will be produced before its marginal utility falls to the level of its marginal cost. But the proper statement would be, not that the marginal utility of the services of a capital instrument tends to *equal* the marginal cost of the instrument, but that it tends to reach a level slightly *above* that cost, such that the *present* or *discounted* estimate of the marginal utility of future services will equal marginal cost.

§ 4

Sometimes the argument of the cost theorists takes a slightly different form. It is said that the net, for instance, receives interest because it "saves labor." If by "saving labor" is meant that the net costs less than it produces, — that the labor of constructing and tending the net, measured in fish, is less than the number of fish caught by the net, — the argument is merely a repetition, in different words, of the argument which has just been stated and criticised, that the net receives interest because it produces something over and above its cost. If, on the other hand, by "saving labor" is meant simply that the net catches more fish than its owner could catch without it (30 fish a day instead of 3), the argument is superficial; it leaves entirely out of account the cost of constructing the net, which is evidently an essential factor in reckoning the rate of return. For aught which this statement of "labor-saving" contains, the net might have cost or be worth 10,000 fish. Such a net, though "saving labor" for 90 days, would never earn its original cost, and there could be no interest, in spite of this "saving of labor."

The adherents of the labor-saving theory of interest may put their case in a third and stronger form. They may say (1) that the net first costs labor to produce, (2) that it afterward saves labor in operating, and (3) that the labor subsequently saved exceeds the labor originally expended. The excess of the labor saved over the labor expended, both being measured, say, in fish, is, according to their theory, the source of interest. There is an element of truth in the theory as thus stated, and this element will be incorporated into the constructive argument in Chapter VIII. But the element of truth is inadequate to form a complete theory of interest for the reason that the excess of labor saved over labor spent is not a fixed excess, but depends on the voluntary choice of the fishermen as to the number of nets they propose to make. Their choice depends on how much present labor they are willing to spend in order to save themselves a given amount of future labor; it depends, in other words, on their relative valuation of present and future labor.

§ 5

In the example of the net, labor-sacrifice and return were both measured in a common objective standard, — fish.

66

A still more elementary case is that in which both cost and return are measured in a common subjective standard, — utility. The desirability of the fish and the labor-cost of obtaining them are comparable magnitudes, the one being utility (or desirability) and the other disutility (or undesirability).

To change our illustration, let Robinson Crusoe be suddenly placed on a fertile island suitable for banana growing. He will be able at first, owing to the great fertility, to get a high degree of satisfaction in consuming bananas by the expenditure of a low degree of labor in planting and cultivating the trees. But the same objections apply as before; for the excess of subjective satisfaction over subjective effort is no more fixed than any other excess of return over cost, and Crusoe may, if inclined, be so industrious in his raising of bananas as to vastly increase the labor of raising them, or, by satiating himself with them, decrease the satisfaction which they yield, or both. This process will proceed far enough to reduce the excess of satisfaction over effort to such dimensions as Crusoe's relative valuation of present effort and future satisfaction will allow. The stopping point is determined by him, not by any natural yield of the soil. The mere fact that the island is naturally fertile, so that labor is especially productive, cannot determine the degree of intensive culture which Crusoe may apply to it.

The same principles apply to every unusually lucrative employment. Man is continually hunting, as it were, for bargains with Nature; but he deals at Nature's bargain counter only up to a definite point, — a point decided upon by him and not by Nature. We cannot obtain a true and complete explanation of interest without recourse to the psychological element of human choice.

Those who have made the most successful use of the cost theory of interest are John Rae [1] and Adolphe Landry,[2]

[1] *The Sociological Theory of Capital*, edited by Professor C. W. Mixter, (Macmillan) 1905.

[2] *L'Intérêt du Capital*, Paris (Giard & Brière), 1904.

and both of these expressly admit that the ratio of return to cost can influence the rate of interest only as the marginal excess of return over cost harmonizes with the degree of preference for present over future goods. No objection is here offered to the general reasoning of Rae and Landry. Their results and those shown in the present book are for the most part in agreement. The chief difference, in so far as the present topic is concerned, grows out of the fact that neither Rae nor Landry made use of any definite theory of income, the relation of cost to income, and the distinction between labor-costs and "interactions."

§ 6

Some economists, whom Professor Böhm-Bawerk classifies as the "labor theorists of the English school," have attempted to explain the rate of interest as a sort of wage for the labor of producing capital. This theory is very crude and does not need extended discussion; for it is evident that the labor which produces the capital very seldom receives the interest. Suppose that a tree twenty-five years old is worth $3, and was planted at a cost of $1 worth of labor. The laborer was paid $1 when the tree was planted; evidently not he, but the capitalist who pays him, receives the $3 twenty-five years later and thereby enjoys an increase of value of $2. If this $2, which is interest, is produced by the laborer who planted the tree, why does he not get it? It is quite true that the laborer produces this "surplus value," and yet he is forced to let another receive it.

This paradox has been made use of by the socialists, who maintain that interest *ought* to go to the laborers who produce the capital, but that they are robbed of it by the capitalist. This "exploitation theory of interest" consists virtually of two propositions: first, that the value of any product usually exceeds its cost of production; and, secondly, that the value of any product *ought* to be exactly equal to its cost of production. The first of these propositions is true, but the second is false. Economists have usually pursued a wrong method in answering the socialists, for they have attacked the first proposition instead of the second. The socialist is quite right in his contention that the value of the product exceeds the cost. In fact, this proposition is fundamental in the whole theory of capital and interest. Ricardo here, as in many other places in economics, has been partly right and partly wrong. He was one of the first to fall into the fallacy that the value of the product was normally equal to its cost, but he also noted certain apparent "exceptions," as for instance, that wine increased in value with years. As a matter of fact, as Böhm-Bawerk has fully shown, this increase of value, instead of being exceptional, is universal in the whole realm of production. It is just because the value of a product does exceed its cost that there exists the possibility of any perpetual net income.[1] Not only, therefore, is there no necessity that cost should equal return, but on the contrary, it never can normally do so. By making cost of production a corner-stone of the theory of value, the classical economists weakened their system greatly.[2]

In attempting to prove that the laborer should receive the whole product, the socialist thus stands on stronger ground than has sometimes been admitted. He cannot be an-

[1] See Chap. II and its Appendix, where it is shown that if each machine costs exactly what it returns, and if the up-keep of a group of machines is maintained, the net annual income from the group is zero.

[2] Besides the error that the cost of production theory omits the interest element, there was the error that most costs of production — all "interactions," in fact — are themselves not the cause but the result of value, being future values discounted. See *The Nature of Capital and Income*, Chaps. X, XIV, XVII. This objection to the cost theory of value does not apply to labor-cost; but even labor-cost is not a necessary or universal accompaniment of value. A mineral spring may produce a valuable water without labor-cost. Land also is largely costless except for the cost of transferring it, which is an "interaction." Other classical examples of articles which have no cost of production are autographs of Milton and similar memorabilia.

69

swered offhand by saying that capital aids labor, and that
the owner of a plow deserves an interest payment for its
use quite as truly as the laborer who operates the plow
deserves wages for his labor. The socialist contends that
the payment for the use of the plow should belong, not to
the man who holds it, but to the man who made it. He is
quite correct in believing that the value of the uses of the
plow is entirely due to the laborers who made it, but
that, nevertheless, the capitalist, not the laborer, enjoys the
value of these uses. The capitalist is, as a matter of fact,
always living on the product of past labor. A millionaire
who gets his income from railroads, ships, and houses, all
products of labor, is reaping what labor sowed. The capitalists of to-day are receiving compound interest on the
labor of yesterday.

§ 7

But it does not follow that in this any injustice has been
done to the laborer. Let us revert to the case of the tree
which was planted with $1 worth of labor, and 25 years
later was worth $3. The socialist virtually asks, Why
should not the laborer receive $3 instead of $1 for his work?
The answer is that he may receive it, provided he will wait
25 years for the $3! As Böhm-Bawerk says: [1] —

"The perfectly just proposition that the laborer should receive
the entire value of his product may be understood to mean either
that the laborer should *now* receive the entire *present* value of his
product, or should receive the entire future value of his product
in the future. But Rodbertus and the socialists expound it as if
it meant that the laborer should *now* receive the entire *future*
value of his product."

To take another example: if a number of laborers work
upon a railroad which requires 5 years before it can be
completed, and which, when completed, is worth $7,000,000,
there is no reason, if the laborers are willing to wait until
the road is completed, that they should not own and

---

[1] *Capital and Interest*, p. 342.

operate it. They would then be receiving, in the future, the future value of their product. If, however, they are paid at the time their work is being done, they may be paid in one of two ways. One is by having assigned to them such parts of the road as they have created so that they may retain the same until it is a finished product to return income to them in future years. The other method, and the one which they much prefer, is to be paid in cash, convertible immediately into food, clothes, and other enjoyable income. Under these circumstances the road, which is to be worth $7,000,000, will be paid for in wages, not by $7,000,000, but by, say, $5,000,000, distributed at the rate of $1,000,000 a year for the 5 years required to build the road.

Socialists would cease to think that this is extortion if they would try the experiment of sending a colony of laborers into the unreclaimed lands of the West, letting them develop and irrigate those lands and build railways on them, unaided by borrowed capital. The colonists would find that interest had not disappeared by any means, but that by waiting they had themselves reaped the benefit of it. They would need to wait, let us say, 5 years before their railway was completed. At the end of that time they would own every cent of its earnings, and no "capitalist" could be accused of robbing them of it. But they would find that, in spite of themselves, they had now become capitalists, and they had become so by stinting for those 5 years, instead of receiving in advance, in the shape of food, clothing, and other real income, the discounted value of the railroad. This example was almost literally realized in the case of the Mormon settlement in Utah. Those who went there originally possessed little capital, and did not pay interest for the use of other persons' capital. They created their capital, and passed from the category of "laborers" to that of "capitalists." It will be seen that capitalists are not robbers of labor, but labor-brokers who buy work at one time and sell its products at another. Their profit on the transaction (or rather, that part of it which is interest) is due to the time elapsing between the labor and its return to the capitalist.

§ 8

Among those who have attempted to justify interest-taking on a labor basis is a peculiar group of theorists who maintain that interest does actually go to the laborer — not the laborer who produces the capital, but the laborer who *manages* it. In other words, the "entrepreneur," "under-taker," or "enterpriser" is the one who creates interest and therefore deserves it. This is another of the many at-tempts to maintain that every economic product must be a mere equivalent for some corresponding labor-outgo. The only evidence the adherents of this school can offer for the truth of their theory is, however, that capital can produce nothing without proper management. If, they say, no one lifts a finger to make capital productive, it will not be productive, and the man who plans, organizes, and controls the use of capital is the one who creates interest and ought to receive it. This theory, however, is evidently fallacious, if not self-destructive. For the person who receives interest, *par excellence*, is not the active "entrepreneur," but his "sleeping partner." If the active capitalist produces the interest on the capital he borrows from his sleeping partner, who "does not lift a finger," why does he surrender any of it to that partner? Is the sleeping part-ner "exploiting" his active associate? Of course it is true that the mere investor could get no interest were it not for some intelligent, active management of capital. But this management is paid for in the shape of entre-preneur's profits. The mere fact that the entrepreneur's work is usually indispensable to the production of income would not justify his receiving all of that income. In fact, we may conversely state that the capital intrusted to the

entrepreneur is quite as indispensable to him as is his work
to the inactive capitalist.

§ 9

So determined have been the attempts to justify interest
on the ground of some cost of production that, in the absence of any other item which can be called cost, a special
constructive cost called "abstinence" or "waiting" has
been invoked to meet the emergency. Certain French
economists have even gone so far as to call this the "labor
of saving." The abstinence theory in its various forms
holds that the capitalist, by abstaining from the consumption of his capital, obtains a reward in the shape of interest.

The abstinence theory bears a close resemblance to the
"agio" theory of interest, which is believed by the writer
to be essentially correct. In fact, it has been claimed by
some writers that the abstinence theory differs from the
agio theory merely in words. This claim is perhaps true
of certain versions of the theory, and against these no criticism need here be offered, unless it be a verbal one. If by
saying that interest is the reward of waiting or abstinence
it is only meant that men prefer not to wait for the future,
but to enjoy the present, the only objection which need be
offered is that the mode of statement is somewhat unhappy;
it implies, apparently, that future rewards are caused by
making present sacrifices, rather than that present sacrifices are caused by the prospect of future rewards.

But in the sense in which the abstinence theory is usually
held, it differs from the agio theory not only in words but
in essence. As Böhm-Bawerk has shown, it assumes that
"abstinence" is an independent item in cost of production,
to be added to the other costs and to be treated in all ways
like them. With this proposition issue is here joined. If
"abstinence" or "waiting" or "labor of saving" is in any
sense a cost, it is certainly a cost in a very different sense
from all other items which have previously been con-

sidered as costs. An illustration will make clear the difference between true costs and the purely constructive cost of waiting. According to the theory that waiting is a cost, if planting a sapling costs $1 worth of labor, and in 25 years, without further expenditure of labor, this sapling becomes worth $3, this $3 is a mere equivalent for the entire cost of producing the tree. The items in this cost are, it is claimed, $1 worth of labor and $2 worth of "waiting."

According to the theory of the present book, however, the cost of producing the tree is the $1 worth of labor, and nothing more. The value of the tree, $3, exceeds that cost by a surplus of $2, the existence of which as interest it is our business to explain. At first it would seem a mere matter of words whether we call the $2 a surplus above cost, or an item constituting another cost, known as "waiting." But examination will show that the two so-called "costs" are radically different.

If waiting is a cost like other costs, it should be subject to the law of discount, according to which the capital-value of any article of wealth is equal to the discounted value of its expected income less the discounted value of its expected outgo. The value of the tree which has just been mentioned, taken, say, at the end of 14 years, will actually be about $2, and this is the discounted value of the $3 of income which the tree will yield at the end of eleven more years. According to our own theory, this $3 is the only future item of income or outgo. But according to the theory here criticised, besides this positive item of income, $3 due in eleven years, we have to deal with a series of eleven negative items called "waiting," distributed through these eleven years, and amounting to the interest, — about 10 cents for the first year and gradually increasing to 15 cents for the last year. Now if these costs really exist, they ought to be discounted and their discounted value deducted from the discounted value of the $3 of expected income. But we should then have to assign a value to the tree not of $2, as it actually is, but of about $1, which is erroneous. If the waiting-items were *bona fide* annual costs, — like, for instance, actual labor-costs of pruning the trees, — the process of discount would properly be applied to them. The fact that it cannot be applied to the so-called "cost of waiting" without leading to an erroneous result is a proof that the "cost of waiting" differs radically from true costs.

Thus, the theory that waiting is a cost or outgo is a fallacy exactly the inverse of the fallacy that saving is income explained in *The Nature of Capital and Income.*[1] Both have to deal with the increase of capital-value; the one theory regards this increase as income, the other as outgo. As a matter of fact, it is neither income nor outgo, but increase of capital only.

§ 10

As an answer to the objection just urged against treating waiting as a cost, namely, that it cannot be discounted, it might be pointed out by the abstinence theorists that while waiting-cost is certainly not a discountable cost, its inclusion in the list of costs obviates the necessity of discounting the other items of cost or of income. If all income and all cost items, including waiting, are counted at full value, capital may be valued simply by taking their net sum, without subjecting any item to the discounting process. To count "waiting" as a cost, then, appears as an alternative method of keeping accounts. Accepting this answer for the sake of argument, we observe that while it obviates the objection to the abstinence theory of cost so far as its application to *capital* value is concerned, it leaves objections equally great to its application to *income*. If waiting is a cost like other items, it must be included on the outgo side of the income account. To show how this

[1] Chap. XIV. Cf. as to the fallacy here considered, Böhm-Bawerk, *Recent Literature on Interest* (Macmillan), 1903, p. 35 n.

would apply to the cost of the tree, the following table is presented : —

INCOME		OUTGO	NET INCOME	CAPITAL VALUE AT END OF YEAR
1st year	00.00	Labor 1.00		
		"Waiting" .05		1.05
2d year	00.00	"Waiting" .05		1.10
3d year	00.00	"Waiting" .05		1.15
* * * * * * *	* *	* * * * *		* *
14th year	00.00	"Waiting" .10		2.00
* * * * * * *	* *	* * * * *		* *
25th year, from sale of tree	3.00	"Waiting" .15		3.00
Total	3.00	3.00	00.00	

According to this method of accounting, we see that during the year in which the sapling is planted its cost consists of labor to the extent of $1, expended, let us say, at the beginning of the year, and 5 cents' worth of waiting suffered during the course of the year. During the second year a waiting cost of about the same amount is incurred, and so on for each succeeding year, the cost of waiting gradually increasing as the tables of compound interest would indicate, until in the fourteenth year it amounts to 10 cents, and in the twenty-fifth year to 15 cents. The total cost for the 25 years will then be $3, and the return to the planter at the end, from the sale of the tree, will also be $3. Consequently, if we take the whole period from the first application of labor to the final sale of the tree, the net income will be zero. This result is, to say the least, somewhat surprising, but not so much so as some other results of the same bookkeeping, as the following additional examples will show.

Suppose a person owns an annuity amounting to $100 a year for 10 years. According to any ordinary method

of keeping accounts, his income consists of this $100 a year
each year.   But if we count the waiting as a cost, we shall
find that the income for each year is less than $100.   The
owner of such an annuity will, during the first year, have
to suffer "waiting" to the extent of $39, supposing interest
is at 5 per cent.; for this is the increase in value of his annuity during that year, due to his waiting for the future
instalments of income of which his annuity consists.[1]   His
net income during that year, therefore, according to such
accounting, is not $100, but $100 − $39, or $61.   During
the second year his income is somewhat greater, for the
cost of "waiting" is only $35.   His net income is, therefore,
$100 − $35, or $65.   Similar computations carried out for
succeeding years result in the following table: —

	INCOME	OUTGO	NET INCOME	CAPITAL VALUE AT BEGINNING OF YEAR
1st year	money, $ 100	"Waiting" $ 39	$ 61	$ 772
2d year	money, 100	"Waiting" 35	65	711
3d year	money, 100	"Waiting" 32	68	646
4th year	money, 100	"Waiting" 29	71	578
5th year	money, 100	"Waiting" 25	75	507
6th year	money, 100	"Waiting" 22	78	432
7th year	money, 100	"Waiting" 18	82	354
8th year	money, 100	"Waiting" 14	86	272
9th year	money 100	"Waiting" 9	91	186
10th year	money, 100	"Waiting" 5	95	95
	$ 1000	$ 228	$ 772	

Is it good bookkeeping to introduce a new and strange
element of cost which results in making the net income
of the annuitant not the $100 which he actually receives,

[1] This is evident, since the value of his annuity, capitalized at 5 per
cent., reckoned at the beginning, is $772, whereas, reckoned at the end
of the first year, before his $100 is paid, it is $811.

but the sums given in the table; namely, $61, $65, $68, and so forth?

To push this criticism to the limit, let us finally consider a perpetual annuity of $100 a year. In this case we shall find that the "cost of waiting" each year is $100; for the value of such an annuity, reckoned at 5 per cent., is $2000 reckoned at the beginning of each year, and $2100 reckoned at the end. If this cost of waiting is to be regarded as a deduction from income, like other costs, we are forced to conclude that the owner of such a perpetual annuity receives each year no income whatever! For, if we deduct from the $100 of money-income the $100 of waiting, the remainder each year is zero!

It may be said that we have not always a mere *annuity* to deal with but a definite capital such as a *house* or a *factory* which has involved cost in its construction and the "sacrifice" of waiting for an income, whereas the capital might have been consumed at once. In all such cases, however, we are dealing with the very same principle. The possession of the house or factory, like the title to the annuity, is valuable *only because* of the service or the income which it is expected to yield. If there is for the house or factory an initial labor-cost or expense, this is also true of the annuity. On the other hand, the one as well as the other may come by inheritance and so involves no cost to its owner. What it is desired to emphasize is that in any case the present value is the discounted value of the expected future services or income and that it is *not* any sacrifice or cost of waiting which produces this value but that, on the contrary, it is the existence of this future value which prompts the waiting.

§ 11

It is obvious that the theory which calls "waiting" a cost has worked out its own absurdity. The most that can be said in its favor is that it makes the capital-value of any article equal to its cost of production. The idea that the value of an article should equal its cost seems to possess a certain fascination for many, if not most, students of economics. That it is false has been sufficiently shown by Böhm-Bawerk through reasoning somewhat similar to the foregoing. That it is absurd when carried to its logical conclusion is evident when we consider what happens if the same method of bookkeeping is carried out with respect to the future as well as the past. It is a poor rule which will not work both ways. This rule, applied to future expected income and outgo, yields the strange result that the capital value of any article is normally not less than, but equal to, the expected income. Thus, to revert to the case of the tree, let us take its value at the end of 14 years. It is then worth $2, which, in the parlance of the abstinence theorists, is equal to its previous cost of production, consisting of $1 worth of labor plus $1 worth of waiting during the 14 years. It is also, in like manner, equal to the future income to be derived from it, which consists of $3 worth of actual receipts from the sale of the tree, due at the end of eleven more years, less the cost of waiting for those $3, which amounts to $1.

In the same way, the ten-year annuitant just considered has, at the beginning, property worth $772. This, according to any proper bookkeeping, is the discounted value of the future income of $100 a year for 10 years, the total amount of which is $1000. But, according to the abstinence theorists, the income which he receives for the whole period is, as has been shown, not this $1000, but $772, which is just equal to the value of the property. Pursuing the method of limits, we find that for the owner of a perpetual annuity the same proposition would hold good. According to the true and ordinary method of reckoning, the total income from such an annuity is infinity, although its present capital value is only $2000. But

according to the abstinence theorists the income itself is
not infinite, but only $2000.[1]

Those who are enamored of the simplicity and neatness
of the formula of the abstinence theorists, by which the
capital value is not greater than *past* cost of production,
but exactly equal to it, can scarcely be attracted by the
exaggerated simplicity of the inverse theorem which is
also involved; namely, that the capital value of any *future*
expected income is not less than that income, but exactly
equal to it also.

§ 12

The fallacy of the abstinence theorists lies in the simple
fact that waiting has no independent existence as a "cost."
We can never locate it in time, nor estimate its amount,
without first knowing some *other* more tangible costs.
Waiting means nothing unless there is something waited
for, and the cost of waiting can only be estimated in proportion to the magnitude of what is waited for.

It will doubtless take a long time for many to accept the
doctrine that the value of capital is not only less than its
future expected income, but normally greater than its past
cost. Even to those who do not formally accept any cost
theory of interest, the interest itself will seem in some
sense to be a cost; and in most books on economics, interest, however explained, is regarded as one of the costs
of production. It is true that for a debtor who pays interest, the interest is, to him, a real cost, and is debited on

---

[1] Lest the non-mathematical reader should be puzzled by this
result, which seems to contradict the fact already brought out, that
under the pseudo-reckoning of the abstinence theorists the net income is zero every year, it must be remembered that this zero income
is repeated an infinite number of times, and that when we deal with
infinity we can get reliable results only by the method of limits.
The mathematical reader will find no difficulty in showing, by the
method of limits, that there is a "remainder term" which will, in
the supposed accounting, make the total income distributed through
all eternity simply equal to the capital value, $2000.

his books. But we need only to be reminded of the debit and credit bookkeeping which was considered at length in *The Nature of Capital and Income* to see that this item is counterbalanced on the books of the creditor, to whom this interest is by no means a cost, but an item of income. For society as a whole, therefore, even in the case of interest which is explicitly paid, it cannot be said that it constitutes a cost of production. In the case of a person who works with his own capital, the truth of this statement is even more evident. Economists who state that the independent capitalist must charge off interest as one of his costs of production seem to forget that such self-paid interest must be charged back again as income also. The fallacy of assuming that interest is a cost is doubtless due to the habit of regarding production from the point of view of the "enterpriser." Since he usually *pays* interest, he comes to think of it purely as a cost.

We have devoted considerable space to the refutation of the abstinence theory, because its errors are so subtle and insidious as to beguile many of the best and most wary of economists.

§ 13

The results of the present chapter may be summed up by grouping the cost theories under two heads: those which regard interest as in some sense a cost; and those which regard interest as a surplus above cost. As we have seen, the contention of the first group is erroneous, whether the concept of cost employed is the "cost of producing capital," the "cost of managing," organizing, or investing it, or the purely constructive cost of "waiting," "abstinence," or "labor of saving." The contention of the second group, which considers interest as a surplus above cost, is correct; but the explanations which are given of this surplus are incorrect, or at any rate, incomplete, whether those explanations take the fanciful form of the socialists that interest is extortion, or the mere statement of fact of the cost productivity theories, that nature yields a surplus above cost. In this last statement, however, lies the only grain of truth which can be ascribed to the cost theories. Although nature does not of herself yield a fixed surplus above cost, which may be called interest, she offers a series of such opportunities of getting a surplus, of which opportunities man takes advantage, and with respect to which he adjusts his efforts to his returns until the surplus yielded corresponds to his subjective preference for present over future goods. In other words, just as in the case of the theories based on productivity, we find that the theories based on cost have an element of truth only as far as the opportunities presented by nature are reviewed in the mind of man and decided upon according to his time preference.

CHAPTER IV

§ 1

In the preceding three chapters the most common of the existing theories of interest have been stated and criticised. There remains one, however, which has received a large degree of currency among economists. Hitherto, in order to condense our review, we have employed the impersonal method and have rarely discussed the special interpretations which individual writers have made of the several theories. In the present chapter, however, we shall depart from this practice. The reason for criticising Böhm-Bawerk's specific theory is that, unlike the theory of any other individual writer, it has become widely accepted. *Capital and Interest* and *The Positive Theory of Capital* have become economic classics. There can be no question that they deserve the high esteem in which they are held, for they contain the material, both in their destructive criticism and in their constructive argument, for a correct theory of interest. For the most part, Böhm-Bawerk's work will doubtless always stand. At only one vital point do we regard it as defective.

Böhm-Bawerk's theory is called by him the "agio theory" of interest, since it finds the essence of the rate of interest in the agio or premium on present goods when exchanged for future goods. This theory is in the main accepted by the present writer as the natural and proper starting-point for any rational discussion of the subject. Böhm-Bawerk has presented the agio theory clearly and forcibly, and has disentangled it from the crude and incorrect

53

notions with which it had previously been associated. It is only when he attempts to add to it his special feature of a "technical superiority of present over future goods" that he has impaired rather than improved it.

The agio theory may be said to have been foreshadowed by mediæval writers, some of whom stated that interest could be justified by *mora* or "delay"; and the theory appears in a crude form in the abstinence theories of Senior and others, which were discussed in the preceding chapter. In a more definite form it was advanced by John Rae in 1834, in a work which has hitherto received far less attention than it deserved;[1] and in a less complete form, and quite independently of Rae, by Jevons,[2] Sax,[3] and Launhardt.[4] But excepting Rae, none of these writers can compare with Böhm-Bawerk for the thoroughness with which the theory is worked out.

Böhm-Bawerk distinguishes two problems: (1) Why does interest exist? and (2) What determines any particular rate of interest? In answer to the first problem, he states virtually that this world is so constituted that most of us prefer present goods to future goods of like kind and number. This preference is due, according to Böhm-Bawerk, to three circumstances: (1) the "perspective

---

[1] Böhm-Bawerk reintroduced independently the main argument of Rae. Several years later Rae's book was unearthed and brought into prominence by Professor C. W. Mixter. The original being out of print, Professor Mixter has edited a reprint, rearranged for modern readers, under the new title, *The Sociological Theory of Capital* (Macmillan), 1905. Rae's work labored under the disadvantage, compared with Böhm-Bawerk's, of being written before the modern theory of value had been expounded. Its shortcomings are chiefly due to this fact. On the other hand, it surpasses Böhm-Bawerk's treatise in some respects, notably in its treatment of invention. See Böhm-Bawerk's comments on Rae in *Recent Literature on Interest* (Macmillan), 1903, and the reply by Mixter, "Böhm-Bawerk on Rae," *Quarterly Journal of Economics*, May, 1902, pp. 385–412.

[2] *Theory of Political Economy*, London, 3rd ed. (Macmillan), 1888.

[3] *Grundlegung der theoretischen Staatswirthschaft*, Vienna, 1887.

[4] *Mathematische Begründung der Volkswirtschaftslehre*, Leipsic, 1885.

underestimate" of the future, by which is meant the fact that future goods are less clearly perceived and therefore less resolutely striven for than those more immediately at hand; (2) the relative inadequacy of the "provision" for present wants as compared with the provision for future wants, or in other words, the relative scarcity of present goods compared with future goods; (3) the "technical superiority" of present over future goods, or the fact, as Böhm-Bawerk conceives it, that the "roundabout" or "capitalistic" processes of production are more remunerative than those which yield immediate returns.

The first two of these three circumstances are undoubtedly pertinent, and will be incorporated, under a somewhat different form, in the theory of the present book. It is the third circumstance — the so-called technical superiority of present over future goods — which we believe to contain essential errors.

§ 2

According to Böhm-Bawerk, labor invested in long processes of production will yield larger returns than labor invested in short processes, and will therefore confer a "technical advantage" upon those who have the command of that labor. In the reasoning by which Böhm-Bawerk attempts to prove this "technical superiority," there are three principal steps. The first consists of postulating an "average production period" representing the length of the productive processes of the community; the second consists of the proposition that the longer this average production period, the greater will be the product; and the third consists in the conclusion that in consequence of this greater productiveness of lengthy processes, present goods possess a "technical superiority" over future goods.

We shall endeavor to show that the third of these steps contains a fatal error. The first step also is not wholly satisfactory.

85

A serious defect in Böhm-Bawerk's concept of an average production period is that it lacks sufficient definiteness to form a basis for the reasoning that he attempts to base upon it. He begins by stating that every article is the result of the coöperation of land and labor, and (abstracting the element of land) he proceeds to consider the period of production for the element of labor. If, he says, an article costs 100 days' labor, of which 20 days must be spent 10 years before the completion of the article, 20 days 9 years before completion, and thereafter 5 days in each succeeding year until completion, whereupon 20 days' labor are spent in finishing touches, the production period for this article is the *average age* of these several brief terms of labor; namely,

$$\frac{20 \times 10 + 20 \times 9 + 5 \times 8 + 5 \times 7 + 5 \times 6 + 5 \times 5 + 5 \times 4 + 5 \times 3 + 5 \times 2 + 5 \times 1 + 20 \times 0}{100} = \frac{560}{100}$$

or 5.6 years.[1] In other words, all the labor expended in the production of the article is regarded as concentrated at one point of time 5.6 years prior to its completion. This point is what mathematicians call the "center of gravity" of the various portions of labor expended. First, in regard to the location of this point, we may ask why the particular method of averaging which Böhm-Bawerk employs is assumed by him to be the correct one. His average is a "weighted arithmetical mean." There are many other possible methods of averaging any series of numbers. The particular kind of average chosen in any special problem is a matter of prime importance in cases, like the present, in which the numbers are widely divergent. In cases in which the numbers do not vary widely, there is little practical need of distinguishing between the different methods of averaging. Experience with index numbers shows, for instance, that the arithmetical, geometrical, and harmonical "means" and an

[1] *The Positive Theory of Capital*, English translation, London (Macmillan), 1891, p. 89.

infinite number of other "means," [1] will agree very closely. But where, as in the present case, some of the elements averaged are very small and others very large, their means will differ widely according to the different methods of averaging. Thus, in the example used by Böhm-Bawerk, if we apply, instead of the weighted arithmetical, the weighted geometrical mean, we shall obtain 0 years, [2] instead of 5.6 years as the average. The weighted harmonical mean will also be 0.

But suppose the question of the correct formulation of the average production period for an individual article to have been satisfactorily settled, in what manner is it proposed to combine the production periods of different articles? Here are involved, considerably magnified, all the well-known difficulties of constructing a suitable index-number. Supposing the average production period of cloth is 2 years and iron 5 years, how are we to obtain the average production period for cloth and iron? No one would maintain that in such averaging between different commodities, they should all be assumed as equally important. They must be *weighted*. To obtain the average of 2 and 5 for the cloth and iron, are we to weight these two commodities according to the value of the amounts annually consumed? If so, will not the rate of interest be involved in the value of the cloth and the iron?

Again, Böhm-Bawerk's theory of the production period requires us to combine a number of seemingly disconnected time-elements. Thus, the "period of production"

---

[1] For a mathematical statement of this topic, see Appendix to Chap. IV, § 1.

[2] To be exact, not quite 0 years; for it is physically impossible to have the last instalment of labor, namely, 20 days, all put in at an instant. Böhm-Bawerk speaks of this 20 days of labor as immedilately preceding the finishing of the productive process. It, like the other elements of labor, is located in the past, though its remoteness from the present is very small, let us say one day, or $\frac{1}{365}$ years. Then the geometrical mean would be, not zero, but
$$\sqrt[100]{10^{25} \times 9^{20} \times 8^5 \times 7^5 \times 6^5 \times 5^5 \times 4^5 \times 3^5 \times 2^5 \times 1^5 \times \left(\tfrac{1}{365}\right)^{25}}$$ or 1.3 years.

of obtaining water from a well is not, by Böhm-Bawerk's method of estimation, the time consumed in merely sending down and drawing up the bucket. His theory requires us to add to this interval of time some fraction of the time of digging the well, and to this, some fraction of the time of making the spade by which the well was dug, and then, some fraction of the time of making the machinery by which the spade was manufactured, and again, some fraction of the time of constructing the tools by which the machinery was made, and so on, thus carrying our calculations indefinitely into the past. Waiving other objections, what is to insure that the items representing the distant past will be, as Böhm-Bawerk alleges,[1] negligible quantities? Such an assertion as to the convergence of the mathematical series in question should receive substantiation.

Professor Fetter[2] and others[3] have criticised Böhm-Bawerk's concept of a production period so fully that we need not mention additional perplexities.[4]

§ 3

Passing over the second step,[5] to which no objection is offered, we come to the third and crucial step in Böhm-Bawerk's theory of the technical superiority of present goods; namely, that the productiveness of long processes confers a special "technical advantage" to the possessor of present goods or labor. This advantage produces, so Böhm-Bawerk believes, a preference for present over future goods which is entirely apart from and in addition to the preference due to the perspective underestimate of the future or

---

[1] *The Positive Theory of Capital*, p. 88.

[2] See "The Roundabout Process in the Interest Theory," by F. A. Fetter, *Quarterly Journal of Economics*, Vol. XVII (November, 1902), p. 13 *passim*. *Cf.* Taussig, *Wages and Capital*, p. 12.

[3] See Lexis, *Jahrbuch für Gesetzgebung, Verwaltung und Volkswirtschaft*, 1895, pp. 332–337; Bortkiewicz, *ibid.*, 1906, p. 69.

[4] See, however, Appendix to Chap. IV, § 2.

[5] See Appendix to Chap. IV, § 3.

that due to the underendowment of the present. Granting for the moment the validity of the concept of a production period, and that the longer the period, the greater
its product, it may still be shown that no such "technical
superiority" follows. Since Böhm-Bawerk regards this
part of his theory as the most essential of all, and repeatedly states that the theory must stand or fall by the truth
or falsity of that part, it becomes necessary to examine his
claim in considerable detail.

Böhm-Bawerk supports his assertion of the existence of
a "technical superiority" [1] by elaborate illustrative tables,
reproduced below: —

A MONTH'S LABOR AVAILABLE IN 1888 YIELDS

For the Economic Period	Units of Product	True Marginal Utility of Unit	Marginal Utility Reduced in Perspective	Amount of Value of Entire Product
1888	100	5	5	500
1889	200	4	3.8	760
1890	280	3.3	3	840
1891	350	2.5	2.2	770
1892	400	2.2	2	800
1893	440	2.1	1.8	792
1894	470	2	1.5	705
1895	500	1.5	1	500

A MONTH'S LABOR AVAILABLE IN 1889 YIELDS

For Economic Period	Units	True Marginal Utility	Reduced Marginal Utility	Value
1888	—	5	5	—
1889	100	4	3.8	380
1890	200	3.3	3	600
1891	280	2.5	2.2	616
1892	350	2.2	2	700
1893	400	2.1	1.8	720
1894	440	2	1.5	660
1895	470	1.5	1	470

[1] *The Positive Theory of Capital*, p. 266.

89

A MONTH'S LABOR AVAILABLE IN 1890 YIELDS

For Economic Period	Units	True Marginal Utility	Reduced Marginal Utility	Value
1888	—	5	5	—
1889	—	4	3.8	—
1890	100	3.3	3	300
1891	200	2.5	2.2	440
1892	280	2.2	2	560
1893	350	2.1	1.8	630
1894	400	2	1.5	$\overline{600}$
1895	440	1.5	1	440

A MONTH'S LABOR AVAILABLE IN 1891 YIELDS

For Economic Period	Units	True Marginal Utility	Reduced Marginal Utility	Value
1888	—	5	5	—
1889	—	4	3.8	—
1890	—	3.3	3	—
1891	100	2.5	2.2	220
1892	200	2.2	2	400
1893	280	2.1	1.8	504
1894	350	2	1.5	525
1895	400	1.5	1	$\overline{400}$

Beginning with the first table we see that it represents, in the second column, the units of product obtainable in various years through the investment of a month's labor in 1888. Thus, a month's labor in 1888 may be invested so as to produce 280 units in the year 1890, or 470 units in the year 1894.

The third column gives the marginal utility of the product to the investor in the various years. This column is formed on the assumption that the individual is in "gradually improving circumstances," so that in 1895 a unit of product will be estimated in his mind at 1.5 units of utility, whereas in 1888 the same unit would have been estimated at 5.

The fourth column shows the *present* valuation of the aforesaid marginal utilities. Thus, the unit of product in 1895, while worth 1.5 units of utility at that date, is, when foreseen in perspective, worth only 1.

The fifth column shows the (subjective) value of the product. This is obtained by multiplying the number of units of product by the reduced marginal utility; that is, multiplying the items in the second column by the corresponding items in the fourth column.

Beginning with the first table, Böhm-Bawerk selects the maximum figure (underscored) in the last column. This maximum signifies that a month's labor available in 1888 would best be invested so as to mature in 1890, because the present value of the product attainable in 1890, but reckoned in 1888, is the maximum, 840, of all the present values. In the same way it is seen from the second table that a month's labor available in 1889 will be so invested as to mature in 1893; for, when thus invested, it has its maximum present value (reckoned in 1888). But this maximum present value is only 720, which is less than the previous maximum present value of the product (840) if the labor were invested in 1888. There is, therefore, says Böhm-Bawerk, a "technical advantage" in having the labor available in 1888 over having it available only in 1889. In the same way, it is still less advantageous to have a month's labor available in 1890, as the product is in that case worth only 630 in the present (1888). Likewise, a month's labor available in 1891 is still less valuable, having a value (in 1888) of only 525. Thus we see that the longer the labor is deferred the less the value of its best product, as reckoned in the present (1888).

§ 4

The result is correct; but Böhm-Bawerk is mistaken in ascribing any part of the result to the fact that the longer

processes are the more productive. In his tables he
assumes the existence of one or both of the *other* two
factors, — the relative overprovision for the future as
compared with the present, and the perspective undervaluation of the future, due to lack of intellectual imagination and of self-control. Examination will show that
it is these elements, and these alone, which produce the
advantage of present over future goods which the tables
display.

Böhm-Bawerk has curiously deluded himself, as well as
many of his followers, on this point. He says:[1] —

> "I repeat emphatically that this result is not an accidental one,
> such as might have made its appearance in consequence of the par-
> ticular figures used in our hypothesis. On the single assumption
> that longer methods of production lead generally to a greater out-
> put, it is a necessary result; a result which must have occurred,
> in an exactly similar way, whatever might have been the figures
> of quantity of product and value of unit in the different years."

As a matter of fact, however, the result does not at all
follow from "the single assumption that longer methods
of production lead generally to a greater output." It
has nothing whatever to do with that assumption. In
other words, it has nothing to do with the fact that the
series of numbers in the *second* column of the tables increases, but with the fact that the series of numbers in the
fourth column decreases.

If we should make the opposite assumption from that
of Böhm-Bawerk, namely, that the longer the productive
process the smaller will be the return, the very same result
would follow. The labor would still be invested at the
earliest possible moment. Let the figures in the second
column decrease instead of increase; the only difference
would be that the month's labor available in 1888 would
now be so invested as to bring immediate returns instead

---

[1] *The Positive Theory of Capital*, p. 268.

of being invested in a two years' process as before. The present value, in 1888, of the investment of the month's labor of that year in an immediately returning process would be, as before, the product of 100 by the marginal utility, 5, or 500, whereas if the labor were invested for a year the present value would be less; for its amount is found, as before, by multiplying the number of units of product (now assumed less than 100) by the marginal utility (which is less than 5). Likewise, the month's labor available in 1889 would also be invested so as to yield an immediate return and would possess a value of 100×3.8, or 380. If similar calculations are performed for each year and the results are compared, it will appear that the investment in 1888 yields the highest return, just as it did on the previous hypothesis.

Again, the same result would follow if the productivity increased and then decreased in all the tables, as follows: 100, 200, 230, 200, 100, etc. For examination will show that the labor available in 1888 would have a maximum value of 200×3.8, or 760; that available in 1889, a value of 200×3, or 600; that in 1890, a value of 230×2, or 460; that of 1891, 230×1.8, or 414, etc. These results, 760, 600, 460, 414, etc., constitute a descending series, and show again the greater desirability of labor which is available early as compared with labor which is available late. It is just as easy to show that if the productivity first decreases and then increases, the same advantage of present over future labor will result.

Such illustrative figures could be reproduced indefinitely. The reader can readily convince himself by trial that as long as the column of "reduced marginal utility" decreases, the column of "units of product" may be of *any description whatever*, without in the least affecting the essential result that the earlier the month's labor is available, the higher is its value.[1]

---

[1] For a mathematical proof, see Appendix to Chap. IV, § 4.

§ 5

On the other hand, if the conditions are reversed and the fourth column of "reduced marginal utility" does *not* decrease, the earlier available labor will *not* have a higher value, whatever may be the character of the second column of "units of product."

Böhm-Bawerk, however, specifically denies this:[1] —

"The superiority in value of present means of production, which is based on their technical superiority, is not one borrowed from these circumstances [*i.e.*, the perspective underestimate of the future and the relative underendowment of the present]; it would emerge of its own strength even if these were not active at all. I have introduced the two circumstances into the hypothesis only to make it a little more true to life, or, rather, to keep it from being quite absurd. Take, for instance, the influence of the reduction due to perspective entirely out of the illustration, and we get the following figures:—

A MONTH'S LABOR OF THE YEAR

		1888	1889	1890	1891	
YIELDS FOR THE ECONOMIC PERIOD	1888	500	—	—	—	UNITS OF VALUE
	1889	800	400	—	—	
	1890	924	660	330	—	
	1891	875	700	500	250	
	1892	880	770	616	440	
	1893	924	840	735	588	
	1894	940	880	800	700	
	1895	750	705	660	600	

It is, as Böhm-Bawerk remarks, still true that the month's labor available in 1888 is more highly valued than the same month's labor available at a later date. But he has carefully retained in his illustration *one* of the "two circumstances" which he stated could be discarded; namely, the

---

[1] *The Positive Theory of Capital*, p. 268.

relative overprovision for the future.   To leave one of these two circumstances effective instead of both is merely to change slightly the series in the fourth column of the previous tables; namely, to change it from the descending series, 5, 3.8, 3, 2.2, 2, 1.8, 1.5, 1, to another descending series, 5, 4, 3.3, 2.5, 2.2, 2.1, 2, 1.5.   The change in the particular numbers is quite immaterial as long as the series is still descending.   It does not matter whether the descent is due to perspective, or to the relative overprovision for the future, or to both.   The essential fact is that the numbers in the fourth column still constitute a descending series. The only fair test of the independence of Böhm-Bawerk's third factor — the alleged technical superiority of present over future goods — would be to strike out *both* the other elements (underestimate and overprovision of the future) so that there should be no progressive decrease in marginal utilities; in other words, to make the numbers in the fourth column all equal.   Böhm-Bawerk, for some reason, hesitates to do this.   He says:[1] —

"But if we were also to abstract the difference in the circumstances of provision in different periods of time, the situation would receive the stamp of extreme improbability, even of self-contradiction."

This is very true indeed; for to abstract both the underestimate of the future and underprovision for the present is to abstract the *whole* basis for interest and not a part merely.   Yet this is no reason for refusing to push the inquiry to its limit.   The consideration of this extreme case will in fact show clearly the error of Böhm-Bawerk; for although we shall have abstracted all true foundation for interest, there will be left what Böhm-Bawerk wrongly imagines to be a basis of interest.   Let us, therefore, make all the factors in the "reduced utility" column alike, say 5.   The tables for 1888 and 1889, condensed, would then read as follows: —

[1] *Ibid.*, p. 269.

A MONTH'S LABOR AVAILABLE

For Economic Period	IN 1888 YIELDS			IN 1889 YIELDS		
	Units of Product	Reduced Utility	Value	Units of Product	Reduced Utility	Value
1888	100	5	500	—	5	—
1889	200	5	1000	100	5	500
1890	280	5	1400	200	5	1000
1891	350	5	1750	280	5	1400
1892	400	5	2000	350	5	1750
1893	440	5	2200	400	5	2000
1894	470	5	2350	440	5	2200
1895	500	5	2500	470	5	2350
						2500

The figures in the value columns for 1888 and 1889 are here absolutely alike; hence the maximum of the former, if there be a maximum, must be identical with the maximum of the latter.

Though Böhm-Bawerk did not consider this case in his tables, he speaks of it briefly in his text, but seems to be somewhat puzzled by it. He says:[1] —

"If the value of the unit of product were to be the same in all periods of time, however remote, the most abundant product would, naturally, at the same time be the most valuable. But since the most abundant product is obtained by the most lengthy and round-about methods of production, — perhaps extending over decades of years, — the economic center of gravity, for all present means of production, would, on this assumption, be found at extremely remote periods of time — which is entirely contrary to all experience."

Böhm-Bawerk's confusion here is probably to be ascribed to his insistence on the *indefinite* increase of product with

[1] *Ibid.*, p. 269.

a lengthening of the production period. Had he admitted into his possibilities the particular possibility that the product would ultimately decrease with a lengthening of that period, the error which he had committed would have made itself too evident to escape his notice. As it was, he found himself dealing with an infinite series; and as the history of mathematics shows, it is not easy in such inquiries to keep clear of pitfalls. Yet even in the hypothesis of a law of *indefinite* increase in returns with increased length of productive period, the error, though concealed, exists and may be shown.

In order not to tamper prematurely with any of Böhm-Bawerk's hypotheses, let us then still assume this law of indefinite increase of value proportionately with the length of the productive process. The result of such a fact would be simply that productive processes indefinitely long would be chosen by investors. The possessor of a month's labor, whether available in 1888 or 1889, would invest it in an *infinite* production process, — a result extremely fantastic, but involved in the hypothesis. We need not assume that the product of an infinite production period is itself infinite. The increasing product may approach a definite limit. This ought, in fact, to be assumed; for we could not imagine that a finite earth would have an infinite product. To fix our ideas, let us suppose that with each year after 1895, with which Böhm-Bawerk breaks off his table, the product leaps up halfway toward 1000 units. Thus, in 1896 the product rises to 750, a rise of half the interval between 500 units (the product of 1895) and 1000 units. In 1897 it becomes, in like manner, 875, in 1898, 937.5, etc. The limit of such a series is 1000 units. A month's labor, whether available in 1888 or 1889, will now have the same maximum value, exactly 1000, and there will be no " technical superiority" in present over future goods whatever.

It is noteworthy that in treating this case Böhm-Bawerk shifts his ground. For the case of undiminished marginal utilities, the only comparison which he makes between the two series (that for 1888 and that for 1889) is not a comparison between their maxima, such as he made in his previous cases, but a comparison between individual terms. He states in a footnote:[1] —

" . . . The month's labour of 1888 remains superior to that of 1889. For, as regards any one remote period, say, the year 1988, the former, as employed in a process longer by one year, could produce a somewhat greater product than the latter."

Such an individual comparison is, of course, beside the point; but granted that it should be made at all, why is it made between two items relating to the *same calendar year?* Why not make it between two items relating to the *same production period?* Why conclude that a month's labor of 1888 is superior to that of 1889 because, say in 1892, the first yields 400, whereas the second yields only 350, rather than conclude that they are equal, since, in a four years' process, the labor of 1888 yields 400, and that of 1889 yields also 400? That the fruition is deferred one year in the latter case is no disadvantage under the present hypothesis, for we have expressly eliminated from consideration any overprovision or underestimation of the future; it becomes a matter of entire indifference whether the 400 is obtained in 1892 or 1893.[2]

§ 6

Thus far we have not altered any of Böhm-Bawerk's hypotheses; but if we allow ourselves to assume, as prac-

[1] *Ibid.*, p. 269.
[2] Cf. Bortkiewicz, "Der Kardinalfehler der Böhm-Bawerkschen Zinstheorie," *Jahrbuch für Gesetzgebung, Verwaltung und Volkswirtschaft,* 1906, pp. 71–73.

tically we ought to assume, that *sometime* the product decreases, no matter for how long a production period, we shall have a more practical illustration of the fact that the labor available in 1888 and that available in 1889 stand on a perfect equality.

Let us assume that Böhm-Bawerk's table of products holds true as far as he carries it, 1895, but that thereafter the numbers decrease, as in the next table. In this table are also given the products of a month's labor available in 1889 and other years: —

PRODUCT OF A MONTH'S LABOR AVAILABLE IN

For the Economic Period	1888	1889	1890	1891	1892	
1888	100	—	—	—	—	
1889	200	100	—	—	—	
1890	280	200	100	—	—	
1891	350	280	200	100	—	
1892	400	350	280	200	100	
1893	440	400	350	280	200	Units of Product
1894	470	440	400	350	280	
1895	500	470	440	400	350	
1896	490	500	470	440	400	
1897	480	490	500	470	440	
1898	460	480	490	500	470	
1899	430	460	480	490	500	
1900	410	430	460	480	490	

If, as before, we suspend the operation of the two "circumstances " (overprovision and underestimation of future) and employ for the "reduced utility" the constant number, 5, we have the following table for the "*value*" columns: —

A MONTH'S LABOR AVAILABLE IN

Yields in Value for the Economic Period	1888	1889	1890	1891	1892	
1888	500	——	——	——	——	
1889	1000	500	——	——	——	
1890	1400	1000	500	——	——	
1891	1750	1400	1000	500	——	
1892	2000	1750	1400	1000	500	
1893	2200	2000	1750	1400	1000	
1894	2350	2200	2000	1750	1400	Value
1895	2500	2350	2200	2000	1750	
1896	2450	2500	2350	2200	2000	
1897	2400	2450	2500	2350	2200	
1898	2300	2400	2450	2500	2350	
1899	2150	2300	2400	2450	2500	
1900	2050	2150	2300	2400	2450	

This table of values is simply the previous table of products magnified fivefold, and is only given separately lest there be any possible room for doubt that the reasoning applies to "value" as well as to "product." We see clearly that the labor of 1888 will be invested in a seven-year productive process maturing in 1895, and having a present value, reckoned in 1888, of 2500 units of value; that the labor of 1889 will likewise be put into a seven-year productive process, maturing in 1896, and having a present value in 1888 of 2500. Similarly, the labor of each succeeding year matures seven years later, but is worth to-day (1888) its full value of 2500.

Our conclusion is that if we eliminate the "other two circumstances" (relative underestimate of, and over-provision for, the future), we eliminate entirely the superiority of present over future goods, and the supposed third circumstance of "technical superiority" therefore turns out to be non-existent.

The fact is that the only reason any one can prefer

the product of a month's labor invested to-day to the product of a month's labor invested next year is that to-day's investment will mature earlier than next year's investment. If a fruit tree is planted to-day which will bear fruit in four years, the labor available to-day for planting it is preferred rather than the same amount of labor available next year; because, if the planting is deferred until next year, the fruit will likewise be deferred a year, maturing in five instead of four years from the present. It does not alter this essential fact to speak of the possibility of a number of different investments. A month's labor to-day may, it is true, be spent in planting slow-growing or fast-growing trees; but so may a month's labor invested next year. It is from the preference for the early over the late fruition of *any* productive process that the so-called "technical superiority of present over future goods" derives all its force.   The imagined "third circumstance" producing a superiority in present goods is only the first two circumstances in disguise.

§ 7

But our distinguished author attempts to prove that his "third circumstance" — the alleged technical superiority of present goods — is really independent of the first two, by the following reasoning: [1] —

". . . If every employment of goods for future periods is, not only technically, but economically, more remunerative than the employment of them for the present or near future, of course men would withdraw their stocks of goods, to a great extent, from the service of the present, and direct them to the more remunerative service of the future.   But this would immediately cause an ebb - tide in the provision for the present, and a flood in the provision for the future, for the future would then have the double advantage of having a greater amount of productive instruments directed to

[1] *Ibid.*, pp. 269, 270.

its service, and those instruments employed in more fruitful methods of production. Thus the difference in the circumstances of provision, which might have disappeared for the moment, would recur of its own accord.

"But it is just at this point that we get the best proof that the superiority in question is independent of differences in the circumstances of provision : so far from being obliged to borrow its strength and activity from any such difference, it is, on the contrary, able, if need be, to call forth this very difference . . . We have to deal with a third cause of the surplus value, and one which is independent of any of the two already mentioned."

The argument here is that if "the other two circumstances" which produce interest, namely, underestimate of the future and underendowment of the present, are temporarily absent, they will be forced back into existence by the choice of roundabout processes. In other words, the "technical superiority of present goods" produces interest by restoring the "other two circumstances." But this is tantamount to the admission that "technical superiority" actually depends for its force on these "other two circumstances" and is not "independent." The essential fact is that its presence does not produce interest when the other two are absent. In short, the "technical superiority" of present goods is a delusion,[1] and the only way in which the existence of long processes of production acts on interest is by overendowing the future and underendowing the present, thus creating a "scarcity value" of present goods.

Since the foregoing criticism on Böhm-Bawerk's theory of the technical superiority of present over future goods was first written, very similar criticism has been made by Adolphe Landry[2] and by Ladislas von Bortkiewicz.[3] So far as the writer knows, Landry is the first to have set forth clearly and definitely the fallacy contained in Böhm-

---

[1] Cf. Bortkiewicz, "Der Kardinalfehler der Böhm-Bawerkschen Zinstheorie," *Jahrbuch für Gesetzgebung, Verwaltung und Volkswirtschaft*, 1906, pp. 61–90.

[2] *L'Intérêt du Capital.*

[3] *Loc. cit.*, pp. 61–90.

Bawerk's theory of "technical superiority." Every reader of Böhm-Bawerk, however, must have felt dissatisfied with his explanations; and sundry expressions of Böhm-Bawerk's suggest that he was dissatisfied himself. His theory of technical superiority stands out as incongruous with the rest of his work, and is more in keeping with the productivity theories which he has done so much to demolish. It would seem as though, like a successful warrior, he had been haunted by the ghosts of his slain enemies. As Professor Fetter has said:[1] —

"It has been a surprise to many students of Böhm-Bawerk to find that he has presented a theory, the most prominent feature of which is the technical productiveness of roundabout processes. His criticism of the productivity theories of interest has been of such a nature as to lead to the belief that he utterly rejected them. But evidently such is not the case. Critics have pretty generally agreed that the theory of the roundabout process is a productivity theory of interest."

It is, therefore, somewhat strange to find Böhm-Bawerk strenuously insisting on the importance of his "technical" theory. He writes:[2] —

"The statement of how the productivity of capital works into and together with the other two grounds of the higher valuation of present goods, I consider one of the most difficult points in the theory of interest, and, at the same time, the one which must decide the fate of that theory. It is just at this point that we discover the chief weakness in Jevons's otherwise suggestive work. None of the groups of phenomena concerned escaped his keen observation; what did escape him was the way in which they work into one another."

And, referring to Launhardt, he says:[3] —

"But, on the other hand, it is a sensible omission that the difference between the values of present and future goods is traced

[1] "The 'Roundabout Process' in the Interest Theory," by Frank A. Fetter, *Quarterly Journal of Economics*, Vol. XVII, November, 1902.
[2] *The Positive Theory of Capital*, p. 277, footnote.
[3] *Ibid.*, p. 278.

exclusively to this factor, and that the much more important factor that coöperates with it, that of the greater productiveness, does not get even the scanty consideration it gets from Jevons."

Before leaving the subject, justice requires that we should dissent from Böhm-Bawerk's opinion that he has made no substantial contribution to the theory of interest aside from his particular "technical" feature. His work in historical criticism is a model both for the historian and for the critical analyst, and his enunciation of the agio theory, while partially anticipated by Jevons, Sax, and Launhardt, was so much more clearly and perfectly worked out that it gains an almost independent form in his hands. The only writer who has equaled Böhm-Bawerk was one with whom the latter was not acquainted, namely, John Rae. His valuable contribution to the subject was, through a curious chain of circumstances, lost to two generations of readers, and has only recently been revived and made accessible through Professor Mixter.

If we cast out from the agio theory Böhm-Bawerk's special feature, his alleged "technical superiority of present goods," the theory which remains is believed to be correct. It is, however, still incomplete, for there remains the gap which Böhm-Bawerk sought to fill, — the formulation of the exact manner in which the "technique" or actual conditions of production enter into the determination of interest. In Part III we shall attempt to supply this deficiency.

PART II. First Approximation

CHAPTER V

§ 1

In the four preceding chapters we have criticised those theories of interest which enjoy the greatest currency in present economic and business circles. Inasmuch as we have found radical defects in all of them, our best course now is to formulate *de novo* what seems to us to be the correct theory. At the outset we need to note an oversight common to all the theories reviewed. In none of them is any account taken of the fact that the number expressing the rate of interest depends upon the monetary standard of value in terms of which that rate of interest is expressed. To say that the rate of interest is 4 per cent. means [1] that the quantity of this year's goods which is worth $100 is equivalent to the quantity of next year's goods which is worth $104. In this statement we observe that the "goods" which are considered are expressed not in their own special units, — pounds, bushels, yards, etc., — but in terms of a standard of value. The standard of value chosen is usually money. This money, the $100 and $104, is nominally exchanged; but actually it merely measures the "goods" which are exchanged. When a man lends $100 this year in order to obtain $104 next year, he is really sacrificing not one hundred dollars in money, but one hundred dollars' worth of goods such as food, clothing, books, or pleasure trips, in order to obtain next year not one hundred and four dollars in money, but one hundred and four dollars' worth of other goods which he desires.

---

[1] See Glossary at end of this volume ; also the writer's *The Nature of Capital and Income* (Chap. XI), the nomenclature of which book is followed in the present work.

77

Yet the fact that both sets of goods are *measured* in money introduces a monetary factor into the problem of interest. Interest, being a premium in the exchange between the *money* values of this year's and next year's goods, is therefore not wholly an affair of goods, but is partly one of money. The relation of the rate of interest to goods will form the subject of subsequent chapters. The present chapter is devoted to a study of the relation which subsists between the rate of interest and the monetary standard in terms of which it is expressed.

The monetary standard affects the rate of interest in so far as there is a *change* in the value of that standard in reference to other standards. Could it always be assumed that the monetary standard was invariable in value with reference to all goods, the rate of interest reckoned in money would be the same as though it were reckoned in terms of the goods themselves. But if money and goods are to change with reference to each other — in other words, if the money standard "appreciates" or "depreciates" — the number expressing the rate of interest will be affected.

§ 2

The influence of monetary appreciation or depreciation on the rate of interest will be different according to whether or not that appreciation or depreciation is foreseen. If it is not foreseen, the appreciation of money necessarily injures the debtor, because, the purchasing power of money being increased, the principal of his debt, when due, represents a larger quantum of goods than was anticipated when the debt was contracted. But if the appreciation is foreseen, any increased burden in the "principal" may be offset by a reduction in the rate of interest. This fact, strangely enough, has seldom been recognized. The assumption has been tacitly made that contracting parties are powerless to forestall gains or losses due to an upward or downward movement of the monetary standard. Yet no reason has been given to show that it is any more difficult to make allowance for a change in the unit of value than for a change in any other unit. If the unit of length were changed, and its change were foreknown, it is clear that contracts would be modified accordingly. Suppose, for instance, that a yard were defined (as possibly it once was) as the length of the king's girdle, and suppose the king to be a child. Everybody would then know that the "yard" would probably increase with the king's age, and a merchant who should agree to deliver one thousand "yards" ten years hence would make his terms correspond to his expectations. It would be strange if, in some similar way, an escape could not be found from the effects of changes in the monetary yardstick, provided these changes were known in advance. To offset a foreseen appreciation, it would only be necessary that the rate of interest be correspondingly lower, and to offset a foreseen depreciation, that it be correspondingly higher.[1]

If a debt is contracted optionally in either of two standards and one of them is *expected* to change with reference to the other, the rate of interest will by no means be the same in both. A few years ago, during the uncertainty as to the adoption or rejection of "free silver," a syndicate offered the United States government the alternative of some $65,000,000 of bonds on a 3 per cent. basis in gold, or on a $3\frac{3}{4}$ per cent. basis in "coin." Every one knew that the additional $\frac{3}{4}$ per cent. in the latter alternative was due to the mere *possibility* that "coin" might not continue at full gold value, but sink to the level of silver. If the alternative had been between repayment in gold and a — not merely possible but actual — repayment in silver, the additional interest would obviously have exceeded $\frac{3}{4}$ per cent.

[1] For the history of the theory of appreciation and interest, see Appendix to Chap. V, § 1.

§ 3

The relation between the rate of interest and the rate of a foreseen appreciation or depreciation of money may be readily illustrated. In order to illustrate the theory, we may imagine two specified standards of value diverging from each other, in either of which loan contracts may be expressed. Let the two standards be gold and wheat, and let a bushel of wheat be first worth \$1. If the two standards did not diverge, that is, if the price of wheat in terms of gold held good till next year, it is clear that the rate of interest in a gold contract and a wheat contract would be the same; if it were 4 per cent. in gold, it would be 4 per cent. in wheat also. This may be expressed as follows : —

If to-day   100 dollars is the equivalent of 100 bu. @ \$1 per bu., then next year 104 dollars is the equivalent of 104 bu. @ \$1 per bu.

But let us suppose that the price of wheat rises from \$1 to \$1.01. We then readily see that : —

Whereas to-day   100 dollars is the equivalent of 100 bu. @ \$1 per bu., next year 104 × 1.01 dollars is the equivalent of 104 bu. @ \$1.01 per bu.

If we calculate out the 104 × \$1.01, we shall obtain \$105.04 as the sum which next year should be repaid in gold to be equivalent to 104 bu. payable in wheat. In other words, if 4 per cent. is the interest in the wheat standard, its equivalent is $5\frac{4}{100}$ per cent. in the gold standard; or, again, if the rate of interest in wheat is 4 per cent., an appreciation of wheat of 1 per cent. is exactly offset by a rise of $1\frac{4}{100}$ per cent. in the rate of interest in gold. It is thus a matter of indifference whether, under our supposed circumstances, a man who borrows \$1000 expresses his contract in gold and agrees to pay $5\frac{4}{100}$ per cent. interest or translates the same contract into terms of wheat, borrowing the value of

1000 bushels and agreeing to pay 4 per cent. interest. By the first form of contract he pays back $1000 of gold principal and $50.40 of gold interest; by the second, he pays back the value of 1000 bu. as principal and of 40 bu. as interest. At the end of a year his debt by the one reckoning is $1050.40, by the other, 1040 bu., and these are equivalent.

It is to be noted that we have been regarding gold or wheat as standards of value and not as media of exchange. In either contract the actual liquidation need not be made either in actual gold or wheat. The speculator who sells wheat "short" comes very close to using wheat as a standard, but not as a medium.

The relative change in the two standards may be spoken of either as an appreciation of wheat relatively to gold, or as a depreciation of gold relatively to wheat. We are not compelled to inquire which is the "absolute" change. If we use the first of these two modes of expression, we may say that since one bushel changes in value from $1 to $1.01, wheat has appreciated 1 per cent.; if we use the second mode of expression, we may say a gold dollar has fallen in its wheat value from one bushel to $\frac{100}{101}$ of a bushel, and has therefore depreciated by $\frac{1}{101}$ or $.99\frac{1}{101}$ per cent.[1]

$$\S\ 4$$

In our numerical example, the appreciation (1 per cent.) of one standard relatively to the other, and likewise the depreciation ($.99\frac{1}{101}$ per cent.) of the latter standard relatively to the former, are not quite so great as the difference ($1\frac{4}{100}$ per cent.) in the rate of interest. This slight disparity must always exist so long as the rate of interest is reckoned annually or discontinuously. But the shorter the period of "compounding," the less the disparity; that is, the more

[1] For the general formula connecting the rates of interest in any two diverging standards, see Appendix to Chap. V, § 2.

nearly equal are the two magnitudes: (1) the rate of
divergence between the two standards, whether measured
as appreciation or depreciation, and (2) the difference
between the rates of interest in the two standards. When
the rates are "reckoned continuously," the disparity disappears altogether.[1]

§ 5

Having established the truth and generality[2] of the
principle connecting the rates of interest in two standards
and the appreciation of one of them relatively to the other,
we next inquire what limits, if any, are imposed on the
three magnitudes; namely, the two rates of interest in
the respective standards and the rate of relative appreciation between the standards. From what has been said
it might seem that, when the appreciation is sufficiently
rapid, the rate of interest in the upward-moving standard,
in order to equalize the burden, would have to be zero or
even negative. For instance, if the rate of interest in gold
is 4 per cent., and if wheat appreciates relatively to gold
at 4 per cent. also, the rate of interest in wheat, if perfectly
adjusted, would have to sink to zero! But we know that
zero or negative interest is practically impossible. Wheat
would be hoarded, and this action would effectually prevent the rate of interest in terms of wheat from passing
below the zero mark. But this very limitation on the
possible rate of interest carries with it a limitation on the

---

[1] For the mathematical demonstration of this proposition, see
Appendix to Chap. V, § 3. For the significance of "continuous"
reckoning, see *The Nature of Capital and Income*, Chap. XII; also
Chap. XIII and Appendix. We have here an example of the fact
there observed that, considered mathematically, the analytical relations connected with the rate of interest are simplest when that rate
is reckoned continuously. Since, however, the rate of interest reckoned continuously is so rarely used in practice, we shall adhere, in
the remainder of our discussion, to the system of annual reckoning.

[2] For mathematical proofs, numerical illustrations, and formulæ
see Appendix to Chap. V, §§ 4 to 9 inclusive.

possible rate of appreciation. If interest on money, for instance, were 4 per cent., it would be impossible for wheat to have a foreknown appreciation of 10 per cent. per annum relatively to money; for it would immediately be bought and held for the rise. It would therefore rise *at once* to the discounted value of its future expected value, and its succeeding rise could not exceed the rate of interest.[1]   In other words, if interest is 4 per cent., it is impossible that wheat should be worth $1 to-day and $1.10 next year foreknown to-day. For, under these circumstances, holding for a rise would give a sure return of 10 per cent. The lowest price of present wheat possible would be the $1.10 discounted at 4 per cent., or about $1.06. At this figure the rate of interest in gold is 4 per cent., but *in wheat* it is zero per cent. We should have: —

To-day $106 equivalent to 100 bu. @ $1.06 per bushel.
Next year $110 equivalent to 100 bu. @ $1.10 per bushel.

and the two alternative forms of contract would be: for $106 this year $110 are returned next year, or (about) 4 per cent., and for 100 bu. this year 100 bu. are returned next year, or zero per cent. Every case of holding wheat or land or other wealth for a rise may be, in fact, regarded as a case of zero interest in terms of these articles as standards of value.

The same principle which prevents the rate of interest in wheat or land from being negative also prevents a negative interest in money. A lender, rather than exchange $101 to-day for $100 next year, would hoard his $101. It is important to emphasize the fact that the limits imposed on the rates of interest and appreciation come from the possibility of hoarding money without loss. If money were a perishable commodity, like fruit, the limit would be pushed into the region of negative quantities.

[1] See *The Nature of Capital and Income,* on the rate of rise of " discount curves," Chap. XIII.

One can imagine a loan based on strawberries or peaches, contracted in summer and payable in winter, with *negative* interest.[1] Or, again, we may define a "dollar" as consisting of a constantly increasing number of grains of gold, the weight of which is to double yearly. *Such "dollars" cannot be hoarded without necessarily becoming fewer with time,* and if interest in the old fixed-weight dollars is 5 per cent., it will be *minus* 47½ per cent. in the new dollars of increasing weight; for he who borrows $100 (2580 grains) to-day will need to pay back only $52.50 (2709 grains) one year hence.

§ 6

The relation existing between interest and appreciation implies, then, that the "rate of interest" is always relative to the standard in which it is expressed. The fact that interest *in money* is high, say 15 per cent., may merely indicate that general prices are expected to rise at the rate of 10 per cent., and that the rate of interest in terms of *goods* is not high, but only 4½ per cent.

We thus need to distinguish between interest in terms of money and interest in terms of goods. The first thought suggested by this fact is that the rate of interest in money is "nominal," and that in goods "real." But this distinction is not sufficient, for no two forms of goods maintain, or are expected to maintain, a constant price ratio toward each other. *There are therefore just as many rates of interest in goods as there are forms of goods diverging in value.*

Is there, then, no absolute standard of value, as utility, in terms of which "real" interest should be expressed? To this we reply that any absolute standard is absolute only for a particular individual.[2] The fact that a dollar

[1] Cf. Böhm-Bawerk, *The Positive Theory of Capital*, pp. 252, 297; Landry, *L'Intérêt du Capital*, p. 49.

[2] Marshall, *Principles of Economics*, Vol. I, 3d ed. New York (Macmillan), 1895, p. 198, and *Royal Commission on Depression of*

is a smaller unit to a millionaire than to a poor laborer
has as its consequence that, as the millionaire grows poorer
his dollar grows larger, while as the laborer grows richer
his dollar grows smaller.   On account of such changes in
personal fortunes, the dollar will be constantly appreciating and depreciating in different degrees among different
men and classes.   But if the dollar appreciates in terms
of absolute utility in the eyes of one man, and depreciates
in a corresponding standard of utility in the eyes of another,
the rates of interest in the men's "absolute" standards
must be different in the two cases; for the rates of interest to both persons in terms of objective units, such as
money, *must by the operations of the market be the same.*
If, in the gold standard, $100 to-day is equivalent to $104
due one year hence, both for him who is growing richer
and for him who is growing poorer, the rates in terms of absolute utility will be different for the two men.   Thus, suppose that the dollar to-day is worth to each man one unit of
utility, but that one year hence, to the man who is growing
richer, the dollar will be worth slightly less — let us say,
$\frac{99}{100}$ of one unit of utility.   Consequently, when he considers
$100 to-day as equivalent to $104 due next year, he is
virtually contrasting in his mind 100 units of utility to-day
with $104 \times .99$, or about 103 units of utility next year.   His
rate of interest, therefore, in terms of absolute utility, is
3 per cent.   Similar calculations for the man whose fortunes were declining, and to whom the marginal utility of
the dollar was increasing 1 per cent. per annum, would
show that whereas $100 to-day is equivalent in his esti-
mation to $104 next year, 100 units of present utility are
equivalent to about 105 units of next year's utility.   To
him, therefore, the rate of interest in the absolute standard
would be 5 per cent.

Trade, 1886, p. 423; the writer's "Mathematical Investigations in
the Theory of Value and Prices," *Transactions of the Connecticut
Academy*, New Haven, 1892, pp. 11–23, 86–89; A. C. Pigou, "Some
Remarks on Utility," *Economic Journal*, March, 1903, p. 60.

From this explanation it is very evident that if we seek to postulate an absolute standard of value in which the rates of interest are to be reckoned, we cannot fix one which will be uniform for all the individuals in the market. Supply and demand operate only to make *objective* rates equal.   Hereafter we shall confine ourselves to a study of objective interest; and since the objective standard usually employed is money, the rate of interest, unless otherwise specified, will be taken in this book to mean the rate of interest in terms of the money standard.

As was observed at the beginning of this chapter, it makes a great difference whether the relative divergence of the different standards is or is not known in advance. In actual fact it usually happens that future appreciation or depreciation is neither entirely foreseen nor entirely unforeseen.   An intermediate condition is usually maintained.   When prices are rising, the rate of interest is usually high, but not as high as it should be to compensate for the rise; and when prices are falling, the rate of interest is usually low, but not as low as it should be to compensate for the fall.   The facts as they are actually found in the market will be given in Chapter XIV.

CHAPTER VI

§ 1

IN the last chapter we saw that the number expressing the rate of interest depends on the standard of value in which present and future goods are expressed. We saw how the rate of interest in one standard is to be derived from the rate of interest in any other standard.

It is clear that this translation of the rate of interest from one standard to another does not constitute *a complete determination of the rate of interest in any standard whatever;* for it assumes that the rate in *some one* standard is already known, and merely enables us on the basis of this known rate to calculate the rates in other standards. The case is similar to the conversion of temperature from the Fahrenheit system into the Centigrade or the Réaumur, which clearly does not determine temperature itself; or, to the conversion of the price of cotton in dollars into its price in shillings or francs, which does not determine the price of cotton itself. The relation which has been shown between appreciation (or depreciation) and interest therefore solves merely the problem of *translating* the rate of interest from one standard into another; but the problem of *determining* the rate of interest is still left untouched. This problem — the problem of determining the rate of interest — now demands attention.

In our theory we shall find a place for each of the partial truths which we have found in the foregoing review of the productivity, cost, and agio theories. Our presentation may, in fact, be classified as a form of the agio theory, differing from Böhm-Bawerk's version chiefly by the omission of

87

the "technical advantage of present over future goods," and from agio theories in general by the explicit introduction of the income-concept. The income-concept plays the central rôle.

The theory of interest bears a close resemblance to the theory of prices, of which, in fact, it might be regarded as a part; for, as was shown in *The Nature of Capital and Income*, Chap. XII, the rate of interest expresses a price in the exchange between present and future goods. Just as in the ordinary theory of prices the ratio of exchange of any two articles is based on a psychological or subjective element, — their comparative marginal utility, — so in the theory of interest the rate of interest, or the premium in the exchange between present and future goods, is based on a subjective prototype; namely, the preference for present over future goods.

This "time-preference" is the central fact in the theory of interest.[1] It is what Rae calls the "effective desire for accumulation," and very nearly what Böhm-Bawerk calls the "perspective undervaluation of the future."[2] It is the (percentage) excess of the present desirability[3] of present goods over the present desirability of an equal amount of future goods.

[1] Cf. Bullock, *Introduction to the Study of Economics* (Silver, Burdett & Company), 1900, p. 390; Fetter, *Economics*, New York (Century Co.), 1904, p. 135.

[2] At least, as applied to objective goods. Böhm-Bawerk applies it to subjective pleasures, which he translates into objective goods at a ratio depending on the "relative provision for present and future needs." As we have seen in § 6 of the preceding chapter, it is possible to translate the rate of interest (and, it might have been added, the rate of preference) from an objective to a subjective standard, or *vice versa*, provided we know the rate at which the two standards are diverging. We prefer to base our reasoning in this book on rates of preference and rates of interest expressed in terms of an objective, monetary standard. As we have seen, the rate of preference expressed in terms of subjective standards will be different for different individuals.

[3] Or "ophelimity," or "utility." See *The Nature of Capital and Income*, Chap. III.

§ 2

But what are these "goods" which are thus contrasted?
At first sight it might seem that the "goods" compared
may be indiscriminately *wealth, property*, or *services*.[1]   It is
true that present machines are preferred to future machines;
present houses to future houses; land possessed to-day
to land available next year; present food or clothing to
future food or clothing; present stocks or bonds to future
stocks or bonds; present music to future music, and so on.
But a slight examination will show that some of these
cases of preference are reducible to others.   When present
capital (whether capital-wealth or capital-property) is preferred to future capital, this preference is really a preference for the income of the first capital as compared with
the income of the second.   The reason we would choose a
present fruit tree rather than a similar tree available in
ten years is that the fruit production of the first will occur
earlier than that of the second.   The reason one prefers
immediate tenancy of a house to the right to occupy it in
six months is that the uses of the house begin six months
earlier in one case than in the other.   In short, capital-
wealth available early is preferred to capital-wealth of
like kind available at a more remote time, because the
income of the former is available earlier than the *income*
of the latter.   For the same reason, early capital-property
is preferred to late capital-property of the same description.
For property is merely a claim to future income; and the
earlier the property is acquired, the earlier will the income accrue, of the right to which the property consists.

Thus, all time-preference resolves itself into the preference for early income over late income.   Moreover, the
preference for present income over future income resolves
itself into the preference for present *final* income over future
final income.   The income from an article of capital which

---

[1] For definitions of these terms, see Glossary.

consists merely of an "interaction"[1] or "preparatory service"[2] is desired for the sake of the final income to which that interaction paves the way. We prefer present bread baking to future bread baking because the enjoyment of the resulting bread is available earlier in the one case than in the other. Present weaving is preferred to future weaving, because the earlier the weaving takes place the sooner will the cloth be manufactured, and the sooner will the clothing made from it be worn by the consumer.

When, as is usually the case, exchange intervenes between the weaving and the use of the clothes, the goal in the process is somewhat obscured by the fact that the manufacturer feels his preference for present weaving over future weaving, not because the clothes will be more early available, but because he will be enabled to sell the cloth earlier. To him, early sales are more advantageous than deferred sales, because the earlier the money is received the earlier can he spend it for his own personal uses, — the shelter and the comforts of various kinds constituting *his* real income. It is not he, but his customers, those who buy the cloth he manufactures, that base their preference for present cloth over future cloth on the earlier availability of the clothes which can be made from it. But in both cases the mind's eye is fixed on some ultimate enjoyable income to which the interaction in question is a mere preparatory step. We thus see that all preference for present over future goods resolves itself, in the last analysis, into a *preference for early enjoyable income over late enjoyable income*. This simple proposition would have received attention before had there been at hand a clear-cut concept of income.

§ 3

In *The Nature of Capital and Income*[3] it was shown that income ultimately consists of the stream of conscious-

---

[1] See Glossary.
[2] See *The Nature of Capital and Income*, Chap. IX.
[3] Chap. X.

ness. Or, if we prefer to stop just short of this subjective income, we may say that income consists of the objective services which impinge upon our persons and are on the point of producing the subjective effects on consciousness. In short, the income-stream consists of nourishment, clothing, shelter, amusements, the gratification of vanity, and other miscellaneous items. It is this income-stream upon which attention now centers. Henceforth, instead of speaking vaguely and loosely of the preference for present "goods" over future "goods," we shall speak of the preference for *present enjoyable income* over *future enjoyable income*. "Present" and "future" are, of course, used in a comparative sense only; in a more accurate statement we should substitute "early" and "deferred."

It should be noted that the preference for present over future goods, when thus reduced to its lowest terms, rids the values of the contrasted present and future goods of the interest element. When any other goods than enjoyable income are considered, their values already imply a rate of interest. When we say that interest is the premium on the value of a present house over that of a future house, we are apt to forget that the value of each house is itself based on a rate of interest. We have seen [1] that the price of a house is the discounted value of its future income. In the process of discounting there lurks a rate of interest. The value of houses will rise or fall as the rate of interest falls or rises. Hence, when we compare the values of present and future houses, both terms of the comparison involve the rate of interest. If, therefore, we undertake to make the rate of interest depend on the relative preference for present over future houses, we are making it depend on two elements, in each of which it already enters. The same is true of all capital, and also of those items of income which we have called interactions; for the value of an interaction is the discounted value of the ultimate income

[1] See *supra*, Chap. II, and *The Nature of Capital and Income*, Chap. XIII.

to which that interaction leads. We could not rest satisfied
in the statement that interest is the premium on the
value of present tree-planting over that of future tree-
planting; for the value of each tree-planting itself depends
on the rate at which the future income from the tree is
discounted. But when present *ultimate* income is compared with future *ultimate* income, the case is different,
for the value of ultimate income involves no interest whatever. We see, therefore, that the reduction of the problem
of interest to a comparative value of present and future
enjoyable income avoids the difficulty of making interest
depend on magnitudes which themselves depend directly
on interest.

§ 4

Having seen that time-preference is really a preference
for early enjoyable income compared with remote enjoyable income, we next note that this preference depends
on the entire future income-stream, that is, the amount of
income and the manner in which it is distributed in time.
It depends on the relative abundance of the early and
remote incomes — or what we may call the time-shape of
the income-stream. If future income is particularly abundant, its possessor would evidently be willing to sacrifice
a large amount of it for the sake of a relatively small
amount of present income.[1] Thus, in winter, the possessor
of a strawberry patch might be willing to sell two boxes of
strawberries, due in six months, for one available to-day,
while in strawberry season he might, on the contrary, be

---

[1] It is noteworthy that, though lacking any definite theory of
income, those writers who have made the most successful analysis
of the rate of interest have, in substance, made it depend, to some
extent, at least, on income. Thus Böhm-Bawerk, as has been observed,
gives as one of the "three circumstances" affecting the "preference
for present goods" the "relative provision for present and future";
and Landry virtually states the same relation, on p. 55 of *L'Intérêt
du Capital*.

willing to give up two boxes of his then abundant crop for the right to one box in the succeeding winter.

It is, therefore, not necessary here to distinguish, as Böhm-Bawerk does, between the principles which lead to the *existence* of interest and those which regulate the *rate* of interest; for to determine the rate of interest will include the determination of whether the rate must necessarily always be greater than zero. As a matter of fact, the rate may theoretically be negative, as in the case just mentioned of strawberries in strawberry season, or in the case cited by Böhm-Bawerk himself, of ice in winter. The reason such negative interest is not actually encountered in the market is that perishable articles such as ice and strawberries are never used as standards of value. We express our rates of interest in money, even if our contracts relate to strawberries or ice. But money possesses durability, and may be hoarded without loss. This explains why the rate of interest in terms of money can never be negative.[1]

The proposition that the preference of any individual for present over future income depends upon his prospective enjoyable income corresponds to the proposition in the theory of prices, that the marginal utility of any article depends upon the quantity of that article; both propositions are fundamental in their respective spheres.

When it is said that the time-preference of an individual depends on his enjoyable income, it is meant that the rate of preference for, say, $100 worth of this year's enjoyable income over $100 worth of next year's enjoyable income depends upon the entire character of the individual's income-stream.

An income-stream is made up of a large number of different elements, some of which contribute to nourishment, others to shelter, others to amusement, etc. In a complete enumeration of these elements, we should need to distinguish the use of each different kind of food, the

_____
[1] See *Supra*, Chap. V, § 5.

gratification of every variety of human want. Each of these constitutes a particular filament of the income-stream, extending from the present out into the indefinite future and varying at different points of time in respect to size and probability of attainment. A man's rate of time-preference, therefore, depends on the size and probability at various moments of the entire collection of income-elements. For the graphic representation, however, of size and distribution in time, it is simpler to lump together these innumerable elements of income, expressed in terms of money. We may say, therefore, that an individual's time-preference depends on the following four elements : —

1. On the *size* of the income-stream.
2. On its *distribution in time,*—according as it accrues evenly or unevenly, and if unevenly, according to the periods at which it is expected to be relatively abundant and the periods at which relatively scarce.
3. On the *composition* of the income-stream,—what part consists of nourishment, what part clothing, what part shelter, etc.
4. On the *probability* of the income-stream and its constituent elements.

We shall consider these in order.

§ 5

Our first step, then, is to show how a person's time-preference depends on the *size* of his income. In general, it may be said that the smaller the income the higher is the preference for present over future income. It is true that a small income implies a keen appreciation of future wants as well as of immediate wants. Poverty bears down heavily on all parts of a man's life, both that which is immediate and that which is remote. But it enhances the utility of immediate income *even more* than of future income. This result is partly rational, because of the importance, by supplying present needs, of keeping up the continuity of life and the ability to cope with the future; and partly irrational, because the pressure of present needs blinds one to the needs of the future. As to the rational side, it is clear that present income is absolutely indispensable, not only for the present, but even as a precondition to the attainment of future income. "A man must live." Any one who values his life would prefer to rob the future for the benefit of the present, so far, at least, as to keep life going. If one has only one loaf of bread he would not preserve it for next year; for if he did he would starve in the meantime. A single break in the thread of life suffices to cut off all the future. And not only is a certain minimum of present income necessary to prevent starvation, but the nearer this minimum is approached the more precious does present income appear, relatively to future income.

As to the irrational side, the effect of poverty is often to relax foresight and self-control and tempt one to "trust to luck" for the future, if only the all-absorbing clamor of present necessities is satisfied.

We see, then, that a low income tends to produce a high time-preference, partly from lack of foresight and self-control, and partly from the thought that provision for the present is necessary both for itself and for the future as well.

§ 6

We come next to the influence upon time-preference of the distribution of income in time — the *time-shape* of the income-stream. The concept of the time-shape of one's income-stream is fundamental in the following chapters. Four different types of time-shape may be distinguished:

uniform income, as represented in Figure 2;[1] increasing
income (Fig. 3); decreasing income (Fig. 4); and fluctuating

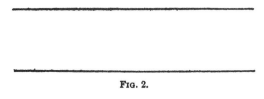

FIG. 2.

income (Fig. 5).   The effect of possessing an increasing income is to make the preference for present over future

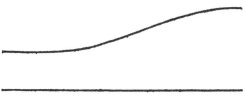

FIG. 3.

income higher than otherwise, for it means that present
income is relatively scarce and future income abundant.

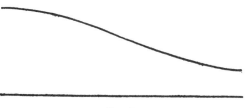

FIG. 4.

A man who is now enjoying an income of only $1000 a
year, but expects in ten years to be enjoying one of
$10,000 a year, will prize a dollar to-day far more than a
dollar due ten years hence.   He may, in fact, borrow

[1] In these curves, time is represented horizontally and rate of
flow of income vertically, as in *The Nature of Capital and Income*,
Chap. XIII.

money to eke out this year's income, and make repayment
by sacrificing from the more abundant income ten years
later.   Reversely, a gradually decreasing income, making,
as it does, present income relatively abundant and future
income scarce, tends to reduce the preference for present
as compared with future income.   A man who has a salary
of $10,000 at present, but expects to retire in a few years
on half pay, will not have a very high preference
for present income over future.   He will want to save
from his present abundance to provide for coming
needs.

The extent of these effects will of course vary greatly with
different individuals.   Corresponding to a given ascend-

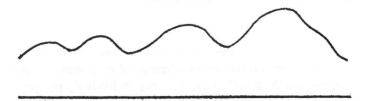

FIG. 5.

ing income, one individual may have a preference of 10 per
cent., and another only 4 per cent.   What we need here
to emphasize is merely that, given a descending instead
of an ascending income, both of these individuals would
experience a reduction of time-preference, — the first, say,
to 5 per cent. and the second, say, to 2 per cent.

If we consider the combined effect on time-preference of
both the *size* and *time-shape* of income, we shall observe
that those with small incomes are much more sensitive to
time-shape in their feeling of time-preference than are
those with large incomes.   For a poor man, a *very slight*
stinting of the present suffices to enhance enormously his
preference for present over future income;   and reversely,
a *very slight* increase in his present income will suffice to

enormously lessen that preference.   A rich man, on the other hand, requires a relatively large variation in the comparative amounts of this year's and next year's income to suffer any material change of time-preference.

It is clear that the dependence of time-preference on time-shape of income is practically identical with what Böhm-Bawerk calls the "first circumstance" making for the superiority of present over future goods:[1]

"The first great cause of difference in value between present and future goods consists in the different circumstances of want and provision in present and future. . . . If a person is badly in want of certain goods, or of goods in general, while he has reason to hope that, at a future period, he will be better off, he will always value a given quantity of immediately available goods at a higher figure than the same quantity of future goods."

§ 7

We come next to the influence of the *composition* of the income-stream on the time-preference of its possessor.   An income worth $5000 may, for one individual, comprise one set of enjoyable services, and for another, an entirely different set.   The inhabitants of one country may have relatively more house-shelter and less food-element in their incomes than those of another.   These differences will have an influence in one direction or the other upon the time-preference.   Diminution of any one constituent of income would have an effect upon the time-preference similar to the effect of diminution of income in general.   A decrease of the food element would be felt especially, both because this element usually forms a considerable part of income and because it is a prime necessity.

Were we to pursue the subject in detail, we should need to resolve a person's income into the elements of which it is composed, — nourishment, shelter, clothing, and other gratifications.   As we have seen, the income-stream is a complex magnitude consisting of a large number of sepa-

[1] *The Positive Theory of Capital*, p. 249.

rate filaments, one for each separate constituent. Any individual's rate of preference depends on this complex magnitude in its entirety. Theoretically a change in any of these individual partial income-streams will influence the rate of preference. A bread famine, a large wheat crop, the outlook for the fuel supply, electric light service, shoes, or diamonds, all should be taken into account in a statement designed fully to cover the influence of the income-stream upon time-preference.

It is not necessary to formulate the concept of "composition" of an income-stream in such a way as to divorce it from the concepts of size and time-shape; for the composition of an income-stream is included in a statement of the size and time-shape of each filament of which that income-stream consists. We content ourselves by considering all these elements of income lumped together in a single sum of money value. We need not here concern ourselves with the principles which govern the valuation of the sum. These principles constitute the theory of prices, not of interest; and these prices, as we have already observed, being prices of *final* or enjoyable elements of income, do not, like the prices of capital or of interactions, embarrass us by direct dependence on the rate of interest which we are seeking to solve. Assuming, then, the elements of which incomes are composed to be adjusted according to the principles which regulate prices, we shall hereafter usually treat an income-stream as a homogeneous quantum expressible in terms of gold or some other monetary standard. Our task is therefore reduced to answering the question: Enjoyable incomes being expressed in terms of money, what determines the rate of interest in terms of this same money?

§ 8

We come finally to the element of *risk*. Income, being future, is always subject to some uncertainty, and this un-

certainty must naturally have an influence on the rate of
time-preference of the possessor. We have seen that time-
preference is the preference for $1 *certain* added to im-
mediate income over $1, also *certain*, added to income
one year hence. The influence of risk on time-preference
therefore means the influence of uncertainties in the
anticipated income of an individual upon his relative
valuation of present and future small increments of income, both increments being *certain*. The manner in
which risk operates upon time-preference will differ according to the particular periods in the future to which the risk
applies. If the possessor of income regards the income
of the immediate future as fairly well assured, but fears the
loss of income in more remote periods, he may be aroused
to a high appreciation of the needs of that remote future and
save from his present *certain* abundance in order to provide
for the later *possible* scarcity. Income in which this sort
of risk exists tends, therefore, to produce a low rate of
time-preference for income which is immediate and certain as compared with income which is remote and uncertain. In actual fact, such a type is not uncommon. The
remote future is usually less known than the immediate
future. This means that the risk connected with distant
income is greater than that connected with income near
at hand. The chance of disease, accident, disability, or
death is always to be reckoned with, but under ordinary
circumstances is greater in the remote future than in the
immediate future. Consequently there is usually a tendency toward a low time-preference. This tendency is
expressed in the phrase to "lay up for a rainy day."

But the influence of risk is not always in the direction of
lowering time-preference. Sometimes the relative uncertainty is reversed, and immediate income is subject
to higher risk than remote income. Such is the case
in war or other temporary threat of misfortune. Such is
also the case when an individual is assured a permanent
position with a salary after a certain time, but in the mean-

time must obtain a precarious subsistence. In these cases the effect of the risk element is to enhance the estimation in which immediate income is held. Again the risk may, instead of applying especially to remote periods or especially to immediate periods, apply to all alike. Such a condition largely explains why salaries and wages are lower than the average earnings of those who work for themselves. Those who choose salaries rather than profits are willing to accept a low income in order to get rid of a precarious one. Since a risky income, if the risk applies evenly to all parts of the income-stream, is nearly equivalent to a low income, and since a low income, as we have seen, tends to create a high time-preference, risk, if uniformly distributed in time, must tend to raise time-preference.

We see, then, that risk tends in some cases to increase and in others to decrease the rate of time-preference. But there is a common principle in all these cases. Whether the result is a high or a low time-preference, the primary fact is that the risk of losing the income in a particular period of time operates as a virtual impoverishment of the income in that period, and hence increases the estimation in which it is held. If that period is a remote one, the risk to which it is subject makes for a high appreciation of remote income; if the period is the immediate future, the risk makes for a high appreciation of immediate income; if the risk is in all periods of time, it acts as a virtual decrease of income all along the line.

There are, however, anomalous individuals in whom caution is absent or perverted. Upon these, risk will have quite the opposite effects. Some persons, who see great speculative chances in the remote future, may treat that future as though it were especially well-endowed, and therefore be willing to sacrifice a large amount of their "great expectations" in the future for the sake of a relatively small addition to their present income. In other words, they will have a high time-preference. The same individuals, if receiving an income which is risky for all periods of time alike, might have, as a result, a low instead of a high time-preference.

The income to which risk applies may be either the income from articles of capital external to man, or the income from man himself. In the latter case the risk of losing the income is the risk of death or invalidism. This risk — the uncertainty as to human life and health — differs somewhat from the uncertainty of income dependent on objective capital; for the cessation of life not only produces a cessation of income from the human machine, but a cessation of the enjoyment of all income whatsoever. For persons who have children whose future welfare they have at heart, this consideration loses much of its force. A man with wife and children is willing to pay a high insurance premium in order that they may continue to enjoy an income after his death, while an unmarried man, or a man who cares only for self-indulgence and wishes to "make the day and the journey alike," will not try to continue the income after his death. Uncertainty of life in the latter case is especially calculated to produce a high degree of time-preference. Sailors offer a good example. They are natural spendthrifts, and when they have money use it lavishly. The risk of shipwreck is constantly before them, and their motto is, "A short life and a merry one."

The effect of risk, therefore, is manifold, according to the degree and range of application of risk to various periods of time; according to the cautious or incautious character of the individual; according to whether or not the risk in question applies to human life, and if so, according to whether or not the individual's interest in the future extends beyond his own lifetime. The manner in which these tendencies operate upon the rate of interest will be discussed in Chapter XI.

§ 9

The proposition that the preference for present over future income depends upon the income, its size, time-shape, composition, and probability, does not deny that it may depend on other factors also, just as, in the theory of prices, the proposition that the marginal utility of an article depends upon the quantity of that article does not deny that it may depend on other elements as well. But the dependence of time-preference on income is of most importance, for time-preference is a preference *for* income. It is in the same way that the dependence of the marginal utility of bread on the quantity of bread is more important than its dependence on the quantity of some other commodity, such as butter. As to the dependence of this time-preference for income on other factors than that income, these other factors may conveniently be regarded as affecting the " form of the function" which expresses its dependence on income. In this light may be considered the influence of "the personal equation." It is clear that the rate of time-preference which corresponds to a specific income-stream will not be the same for everybody. One man may have a time-preference of 5 per cent. and another 10 per cent., although both have the same income. The difference will be due to the personal characteristics of the individuals. These characteristics are chiefly five in number : [1] (1) foresight, (2) self-control, (3) habit, (4) expectation of life, (5) interest in the lives of other persons. We shall take these up in order.

(1) First, as to foresight. Generally speaking, the greater the foresight, the less the rate of time-preference, and *vice versa*.[2] In the case of primitive races and uninstructed

---

[1] Cf. Rae's *Sociological Theory of Capital*, p. 54. Also Böhm-Bawerk, *The Positive Theory of Capital*, Book V, Chap. III.

[2] To be exact, we should observe that lack of foresight may either increase or decrease time-preference. Although most persons who lack foresight err by failing to give due weight to the importance of future needs, or, what amounts to the same thing, by overestimating the provision existing for such future needs, cases are not lacking in which the opposite error is committed; that is, the individual exaggerates the needs of the future or underestimates the provision likely to be made for them. In order not to complicate the text, only the former

classes of society, the future is seldom considered in its true proportions. The story is told of such a person that he would not mend his leaky roof when it was raining, for fear of getting more wet, nor when it was not raining, because he did not then need shelter. Among such persons, the preference for present gratification is powerful because their comprehension of the future is weak. In regard to foresight, Rae states:[1]—

"The actual presence of the immediate object of desire in the mind, by exciting the attention, seems to rouse all the faculties, as it were, to fix their view on it, and leads them to a very lively conception of the enjoyments which it offers to their instant possession. The prospects of future good, which future years may hold out to us, seem at such a moment dull and dubious, and are apt to be slighted, for objects on which the daylight is falling strongly, and showing us in all their freshness just within our grasp. There is no man, perhaps, to whom a good to be enjoyed to-day, would not seem of very different importance, from one exactly similar to be enjoyed twelve years hence, even though the arrival of both were equally certain."

The sagacious business man represents the other extreme; he is constantly forecasting. These differences in degrees of foresight produce corresponding differences in the dependence of time-preference on the character of income. Thus, for a given income, say $1000 a year, the reckless might have a time-preference of 10 per cent., when the forehanded would experience a preference of only 5 per cent. In both cases the preference will depend on the size of the income, being higher the lower the income; but the particular rates corresponding to a particular income in the two cases will be entirely different. Therefore the rate of preference, in general, will be higher in a community consisting of reckless individuals than in one consisting of the opposite type.

and more common error will be hereafter referred to when "lack of foresight" is mentioned. But the reader may in each such case readily add the possibility of the contrary error.

[1] *Sociological Theory of Capital*, p. 54.

(2) We come next to self-control. This trait, though distinct from foresight, is usually associated with it and has very similar effects. Foresight has to do with *thinking*, self-control with *willing*. A weak will usually goes with a weak intellect, though not necessarily, and not always. The effect of a weak will is similar to the effect of inferior foresight. Like those workingmen who cannot carry their pay home Saturday night, but spend it on the way in the grogshop, many persons cannot deny themselves any present indulgence, even when they know definitely what the consequences will be in the future. Others, on the contrary, have no difficulty in stinting themselves in the face of all temptations.

(3) The third characteristic of human nature which needs to be considered is habit. That to which one is accustomed exerts necessarily a powerful influence upon his valuations and therefore upon his time-preference. This influence may be in either direction. Rich men's sons, accustomed to the enjoyment of a large income, are apt to put a higher valuation on present compared with future income than would persons of the same income who were brought up under different conditions. If they suffer a reverse of fortune, they find it harder to live moderately than those of equal means who have risen instead of fallen in the economic scale; and this will be true even if foresight and self-control are the same in the two cases.

(4) The fourth circumstance which may influence the form of the function by which time-preference depends on the character of income has to do with the uncertainty of life of the recipient of that income. We have already seen in a different connection that the time-preference of an individual will be affected by the prospect of a long or short life, both because the termination of life brings the termination of the income from labor, and because it also terminates the enjoyment of all income. It is the latter fact in which we are here interested; the expectation of life affects the dependence of time-preference on income. There

will be differences among different classes, different individuals, and different ages of the same individual. So far as age is concerned, the usual course of events is as follows: The time-preference in the early periods of life is high because foresight and self-control are weak. Children are notorious spendthrifts. A little later, when the individual has acquired some self-control and foresight, he will still have a high rate of preference, but for another reason, — the prospect of an ascending income-stream. His present income is small, but he looks forward to having an ample income in five or ten years. As the time of marriage and middle life approaches, the opposite tendency may assert itself. Foreseeing the needs of middle life and anticipating no increase in the provision for those needs, he will cease to borrow and begin to save. After he has passed middle age, when his children have become self-supporting, and he looks forward to declining years, matters are reversed again. He will want to enjoy his income while he may, the income beyond his death being of no significance to him except as it can be bequeathed to his descendants. The prospect of death plays an important rôle in the thoughts of the old. One evidence of this is the prominence given to it in all philosophical and religious systems.[1] The philosophy of Horace, for instance, was summed up in the maxim "*carpe diem*," which is practically the same as the still older maxim, "eat, drink, and be merry, for to-morrow we die." The chance of death may be said to be the most important *rational* factor tending to make the rate of time-preference high, and anything that would tend to prolong human life would tend at the same time to reduce the rate of time-preference. As Rae says:[2] —

"Were life to endure forever, were the capacity to enjoy in perfection all its goods, both mental and corporeal, to be prolonged

[1] See Metchnikoff, *Nature of Man*, English translation, New York (Putnams), 1903, Part II.

[2] *The Sociological Theory of Capital*, pp. 53–54.

with it, and were we guided solely by the dictates of reason, there could be no limit to the formation of means for future gratification, till our utmost wishes were supplied. A pleasure to be enjoyed, or a pain to be endured, fifty or a hundred years hence, would be considered deserving the same attention as if it were to befall us fifty or a hundred minutes hence, and the sacrifice of a smaller present good, for a greater future good, would be readily made, to whatever period that futurity might extend. But life, and the power to enjoy it, are the most uncertain of all things, and we are not guided altogether by reason. We know not the period when death may come upon us, but we know that it may come in a few days, and must come in a few years. Why then be providing goods that cannot be enjoyed until times, which, though not very remote, may never come to us, or until times still more remote, and which we are convinced we shall never see? If life, too, is of uncertain duration and the time that death comes between us and all our possessions unknown, the approaches of old age are at least certain, and are dulling, day by day, the relish of every pleasure."

The shortness of life thus tends powerfully to raise the rate of time-preference. This is especially evident when the income-streams compared are long. A lover of music will prefer a piano at once to a piano available next year, because, since either will outlast his own life, he will get one more year's use out of the piano available at once.

From what has been said it is clear that there are three periods in his life when a man's time-preference is especially high: (1) in early life it is high because of youthful recklessness; (2) in the preparatory stage, because future income seems relatively abundant; and (3) late in life, because future income seems relatively superfluous.

(5) But whereas the shortness or uncertainty of life tends to raise the rate of time-preference, its effect is greatly mitigated by the fifth circumstance, the care for the welfare of posterity. Probably the most powerful cause tending to reduce the rate of interest is the love of one's children and the desire to provide for their good. When these sentiments decay, as they did at the time of the decline and fall of the Roman Empire, and the fashion is to exhaust wealth in

self-indulgence and leave little or nothing to offspring, the rate of time-preference and rate of interest will be high. At such times the motto, "After us the deluge," indicates the feverish desire to squander in the present, at whatever cost to the future.[1]

In a community like the United States, where parents regard their lives as continuing after death in the lives of their children, there exists a high appreciation of the needs of the future which tends, therefore, to produce a low rate of time-preference. It is this sentiment which is responsible for the enormous extension of life insurance. At present in the United States the insurance on lives amounts to $20,000,000,000. This represents, for the most part, an investment of the present generation for the next. The investment of this sum springs out of a low time-preference, and tends to produce a low rate of interest.

Not only does the regard for posterity lower interest, but the increase of posterity has in part the same effect. So far as an increase in the size of a family reduces the income *per capita* of that family, it operates, like impoverishment, to increase time-preference. So far as it adds to future needs rather than to immediate needs, it operates, like a descending income-stream, to diminish time-preference. Parents with large families feel the importance of providing for future years far more than parents otherwise similar but with small families. They try harder to save and to take out life insurance. In other words, their rate of preference for present over future income is lowered. An increase of population, therefore, will, other things being equal, reduce the rate of interest. This proposition must not be thought to conflict with the reciprocal proposition that the same prudent regard for the future which is created by the responsibilities of parenthood itself tends to diminish the number of offspring. An increase of population tends toward a low time-preference, but reciprocally a low

[1] See Rae, *The Sociological Theory of Capital*, p. 97.

time-preference tends to check such increase.   Hence it is that the thrifty Frenchman and Scotchman have small families.

§ 10

Time-preference, therefore, depends for each individual on his income; that is, its size, time-shape, composition, and probability; but the *form* of this dependence differs according to the various circumstances of the individual. The circumstances which will tend to make his time-preference high are (1) shortsightedness, (2) a weak will, (3) the habit of spending freely, (4) the shortness and uncertainty of his life, (5) selfishness, or the absence of any desire to provide for posterity.   The reverse conditions will tend to make his rate of preference low; namely, (1) a high degree of foresight, which enables him to give to the future such attention as it deserves; (2) a high degree of self-control, which enables him to abstain from present income in order to increase future income; (3) the habit of thrift; (4) the probability of long life; (5) the possession of a family and a high regard for their welfare after his death.

The resultant of these various tendencies in any one individual will determine the degree of his time-preference *in relation to any particular income.*   This result will differ as between individuals, and as between different times for the same individual.   The essential fact, however, is that *for any given individual at any given time, his time-preference depends in a definite manner upon the size, shape, composition, and probability of his income-stream.*

§ 11

This view, that the rate of time-preference and consequently the rate of interest depend upon income, needs to be contrasted with the common view, which makes the

rate of interest depend merely on the scarcity or abundance
of capital. It is commonly believed that where capital is
scarce, interest is high, and where capital is plentiful, interest is low. In a general way there is undoubtedly some
truth in this proposition; and yet it contains a misinterpre-
tation of borrowing and lending. It is true that when and
where men are anxious to lend, interest is low, and when
and where men are anxious to borrow, interest is high.
But it is not true that the more capital a man has the more
anxious he is to lend, and the less capital he has the more
anxious he is to borrow. The willingness to lend or borrow depends primarily, not upon the amount of one's
capital, but upon the character of the income which he
gets from it, — whether this income is large or small, immediate or deferred, of what elements it consists, whether
it is certain or uncertain.

The proposition that abundance of capital tends to
lower interest is thus very superficial; for abundant
capital merely means abundant income. Capital-value is
discounted income. Behind, or rather beyond, a capital
of $100,000 is the income which that capital represents.
To fix attention on the $100,000 capital instead of on
the income is to use the capital as a cloak to cover up
the real factor in the case. Moreover, capital-value is
itself dependent on the rate of interest. The capital-value
of a farm will be doubled if the rate of interest is halved.
In such a case there would be found more capital in
farms; for the farms in a community would rise, say, from
$10,000,000 to $20,000,000. But it is not the rise in capital which produces the fall in interest. On the contrary,
it is the fall in the interest rate which produces the rise in
the valuation of capital. If we attempt to make the rate of
interest depend on capital-value, then, since capital-value
depends on two factors, — the prospective income *and the
rate of interest*, — we thereby make the interest rate depend
partly on income and partly on itself. The dependence
on itself is of course nugatory, and we are brought back to

its dependence on income as the only fact of real significance.

But even as thus amended and explained, the proposition that the rate of interest depends on the amount of capital is not satisfactory. The mere amount of capital does not tell us much about the income for which that capital stands. To know that one man has a capital worth $100,000, and another $200,000, shows, to be sure, that the latter man may have an income of double the value of the former; but it tells us absolutely nothing as to the "time-shapes" of the two incomes; and the time-shape of income has, as we have seen, a most profound influence on the time-preference of its possessor.

Let us suppose two communities similar in population, distribution of wealth, and all other particulars except in the amount of their capital and the character of the income which that capital represents. One of these two communities we shall suppose has a capital of $100,000 invested, as in Nevada, in mines and quarries nearly exhausted, while in the other community there is $200,000 of capital invested in young orchards and forests, as in Florida. According to the theory that abundance of capital makes interest low, we should expect the Nevada community to have a high rate of interest compared with the Florida community. But it is evident that, unless other circumstances should interfere, the opposite would be the case; for Nevada has to contemplate a decreasing future income, and in order to offset the depreciation of capital which follows from this condition,[1] she would be seeking to lend or invest part of the income of the present or immediate future, in the hope of offsetting the decreased product of the mines in the more remote future. The Florida planters, on the contrary, would be inclined to borrow against their future crops. If the two communities are supposed to be commercially connected, it would be Nevada which would lend to Florida, notwithstanding the fact that the lending community was the

[1] See *The Nature of Capital and Income*, Chap. XIV.

poorer in capital of the two. From the illustration it is
clear that the mere amount of capital-value is not only
a misleading but a very inadequate criterion of the rate of
interest.[1]

Apologists for the common statement that abundance
or scarcity of capital lowers or raises interest might be inclined to argue that it is not the total capital, but only the
"loanable capital" which should be included, and that the
Nevada community had more "loanable capital" than the
Florida community. But the phrase "loanable capital"
is merely another cloak to cover the fact that it is not
the amount of capital, but the decision to lend or
borrow it, which is important. To give this proposition
meaning, "loanable capital" must be taken, not in the
literal sense of capital which *can* be lent, — for all capital
is loanable in this sense; but in the sense of capital which
persons are *willing* to lend. Hence, to state that in any
community there is abundance of loanable capital is merely
to state that there is in that community a willingness to
lend a great deal of capital. Consequently, the proposition
that the rate of interest, or preference for present over
future goods, is low when loanable capital is abundant
becomes reduced to the platitude that the rate of preference
for present over future goods is low when men wish to lend.

But it may be said, surely in a money market there exists
at one time a large visible supply of loanable money and at
another time a small visible supply, and this supply affects
the rate of interest. This, again, is a true but a superficial
statement. A little examination will show that the abundance or shortage of loanable bank funds is merely a
measure of the decision of merchants to discount or deposit, —
in other words, to borrow or lend, — and does not give us any
clew as to the reason why they do so. The money or credit

---

[1] One of the few defects in Rae's analysis of interest is his emphasis on the accumulation of capital. Since this accumulation is
merely in anticipation of future income, the emphasis belongs on the
latter.

is, of course, the mere vehicle by which the bank acts as an intermediary or broker between borrowers and lenders, and does not represent any independent factor in the case.

We end, therefore, by emphasizing anew the importance of fixing our eyes on income and not on capital. It is only as we look through capital-value, beyond to the income which it represents, that we reach the efficient causes which operate upon the rate of interest. The absence hitherto of a definite theory and conception of income has prevented economists from doing this. Borrowing and lending are in form a transfer of capital, but they are in fact a transfer of income of which that capital is merely the present value. In our theory of interest, therefore, we have to consider not primarily the *amount* of capital of a community, but the income for which that capital stands.

§ 12

Unfortunately for purposes of exposition, the relation between time-preference and income cannot be expressed in a simple schedule or curve, as can the relation between demand and price, or supply and price, or utility and quantity consumed, for the reason that income means not a single magnitude merely, but a conglomeration of a number of magnitudes. As mathematicians would express it, to state that time-preference depends on the character of income, its size, shape, composition, and probability, is to state that time-preference is a function of all the different magnitudes which need to be specified in a complete description of that income. A geometrical representation, therefore, of the dependence of time-preference on the various magnitudes which characterize income, would be impossible. For a curve can only represent the dependence of a magnitude on one independent variable; even a surface can only represent dependence on two; but for our requirements we should need a space of n dimensions. We may represent the relation between time-preference and income by a "schedule" like the ordinary "demand schedule" and "supply schedule," if we make a list of all possible incomes, specifying for each individual income all its characteristics, — its size, time-shape (that is, its relative magnitude for each successive time-interval considered), its composition (or the amount, at each period, of each individual constituent, as nourishment, shelter, etc.), and the certainty or uncertainty attached to all these elements. Having thus compiled a list of all possible incomes, it would only be necessary for us to assign to each of them the rate of time-preference pertaining to it. Such a schedule would be too complicated and cumbersome to carry out in detail; but the following will roughly indicate some of the main groups of which it would consist. In this schedule we have represented by the three vertical lines three different classes of income, — two extreme types and one mean type, — so that the corresponding rates of time-preference range themselves in a descending series of numbers. We have also represented by the three vertical columns three different classes of individuals, two being of extreme types of individuals, and the third of a mixed or medium type. Thus the numbers in the table descend as we proceed either down or toward the right, the lowest number of all being in the lower right-hand corner.

DESCRIPTION OF INCOME				CORRESPONDING TIME–PREFERENCE to an individual who is		
SIZE	TIME-SHAPE	COMPOSITION	PROBABILITY	shortsighted, weak-willed, accustomed to spend, without heirs	of a mixed or medium type	farsighted, self-controlled, accustomed to save, desirous to provide for heirs
small	increasing	food scanty	precarious	20%	10%	5%
of a mixed or medium type				10%	5%	2%
large	decreasing	food abundant	assured	5%	2%	1%

Out of the large number of possible incomes represented in such a schedule, of course only one can be the actual income of the individual. The one which exists in any case is to a large extent a matter of choice, as we shall see in the next chapter. Since time-preference may be varied by voluntarily varying the character of the income-stream on which it depends, it follows that the shortsighted, weak-willed spendthrift individual may not have, as a matter of fact, any higher rate of time-preference than his farsighted, self-controlled, abstemious brother. In fact, where a loan market is in full operation, the tendency is for the two individuals to select such income-streams as will bring their time-preference into unison. How this is accomplished will form the subject of the following chapter.

CHAPTER VII

FIRST APPROXIMATION TO THE THEORY OF INTEREST
(ASSUMING INCOME RIGID)

§ 1

In the last chapter we saw that the rate of preference for present over future goods was, in the last analysis, a preference for present over future income; that this preference depends, for any given individual, upon the character of his income-stream, — its size, time-shape, composition, and probability, — and that the nature of this dependence varies with different individuals. The question at once arises, will not the rates of preference of different individuals be very different, and if so, what relation do these different rates have to the rate of *interest?* John Rae assumed that the rates differed widely, and that the rate of interest was a sort of average of their different magnitudes. But this is incorrect. In a nation of hermits, in which there was no mutual lending and borrowing, the time-preferences of individuals would diverge widely; but in modern society, borrowing and lending tend to bring into equality the rates of preference in different minds. It is only because of the limitations of the loan market that absolute equality is not reached.

The chief limitation to lending is due to the risk involved, and to the difficulty or impossibility of obtaining the security necessary to eliminate or reduce that risk. Those who are most willing to borrow are oftentimes those who are least able to give security. It will then happen that these persons, shut off from the loan market, experience a higher rate of time-preference than the rate of interest ruling

117

in that market. If they can contract loans at all, it will be only through the pawn shop or other high-rate agencies.

But, for the moment, let us assume a perfect market, in which the element of risk is entirely lacking, both with respect to the certainty of the expected income-streams belonging to the different individuals, and with respect to the certainty of repayment for loans. In other words, we assume that each individual is initially possessed of a fore-known income-stream, and that he is free to exchange any part of it to some other person, in consideration of receiving back at some future time an addition to his income for the prospective period. We assume further that to buy and sell various parts of his income-stream (by loans, etc.), is his only method of altering that income-stream. Prior to such exchange, his income-stream is *rigid*, *i.e.* fixed in size, time-shape, and composition. The capital-instruments which he possesses are each capable of only a single definite series of services contributing to his income-stream. These assumptions that each man's income-stream is initially *certain* and *fixed*, will be used in our *first approximation* to the theory of interest.

§ 2

Under these hypothetical conditions, the rates of time-preference for different individuals would be perfectly equalized. Borrowing and lending evidently affect the time-shape of the incomes of borrower and lender; and since the time-shape of their incomes affects their time-preference, such a modification of time-shape will react upon and modify their time-preference, and bring the market into equilibrium.

If, for any particular individual, the rate of preference differs from the market rate, he will, if he can, adjust the time-shape of his income-stream so as to harmonize his preference rate with the interest rate. Those who, for a given income-stream, have a rate of preference above the market rate, will sell some of their surplus future income to obtain an addition to their present meager income. This will have the effect of enhancing the value of the future income and decreasing that of the present. The process will continue until the rate of preference of this individual is equal to the rate of interest. In other words, a person whose preference rate exceeds the current rate of interest will borrow up to the point which will make the two rates equal. Reversely, those who, with a given income-stream, have a preference rate below the market rate, will sell some of their abundant present income to eke out the future, the effect being to increase their preference rate until it also harmonizes with the rate of interest.

To put the matter in figures, let us suppose the rate of interest is 5 per cent., whereas the rate of preference of a particular individual is 10 per cent. Then, by hypothesis, the individual is *willing* to sacrifice $1.10 of next year's income in exchange for $1 of this year's. But in the market he is *able* to obtain $1 for this year by spending only $1.05 of next year. This ratio is, to him, a cheap price. He therefore borrows, say, $100 for a year, agreeing to return $105; that is, he contracts a loan at 5 per cent. when he is willing to pay 10 per cent. This operation, by increasing his present income and decreasing his future, tends to reduce his time-preference from 10 per cent. to, say, 8 per cent. Under these circumstances he will borrow another $100, being willing to pay 8 per cent., but having to pay only 5 per cent. This operation will still further reduce his time-preference, until it has been finally brought down to 5 per cent. Then, for the last or "marginal" $100, his rate of time-preference will agree with the market rate of interest. As in the general theory of prices, this marginal rate, 5 per cent., being once established, applies indifferently to all his valuations of present and future income. Every comparative estimate of present and future which he actually makes must be "on the margin" of his income-stream as actually determined. The above-men-

tioned 10 per cent. and 8 per cent. rates are not actually
experienced by him ; they merely mean the rates of prefer-
erence which he *would* have experienced had his income
not been transformed to the time-shape correspondent to
5 per cent.

In like manner, if another individual, entering the loan
market from the other side, has a rate of preference of
2 per cent., he will become a lender instead of a borrower.
He will be *willing* to accept $102 of next year's income for
$100 of this.   But in the market he is *able*, instead of the
$102, to get $105.   As he can lend at 5 per cent. when he
would gladly do so at 2 per cent., he jumps at the chance
and invests, not one $100 only, but another and another.
But his present income, being reduced by the process, is
now more highly esteemed than before, and his future
income, being increased, is less highly esteemed. The result
will be a higher relative valuation of the present, which,
under the influence of successive additions to the sums lent,
will rise gradually to the level of the market rate of interest.

In such an ideal loan market, therefore, where every individual could freely borrow or lend, the rates of preference
for present over future income for all the different individuals would become equal to each other and to the rate
of interest.

§ 3

To illustrate this reasoning by a diagram, let us suppose
the income-stream to be represented as in Figure 6, and that
the possessor wishes to obtain a small item X' of immediately ensuing income, for a somewhat larger item X''
later on. He therefore modifies his income-stream from
$ABCD$ to EBD. But this change will evidently produce
a change in his time-preference. If the rate of time-preference corresponding to the income-stream represented by
the unbroken line is 10 per cent., the rate of preference corresponding to the broken line will be somewhat less, say

8 per cent. If the market rate of interest is 5 per cent., it is evident that the person will proceed to still further borrowing. By repeating the operation several times he

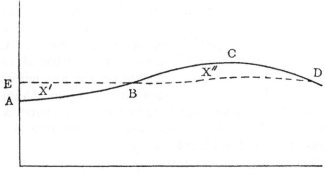

Fig. 6.

can evidently produce almost any required conformation in his income-stream. If, instead of borrowing, he wishes to lend (Fig. 7), he surrenders from his present income-

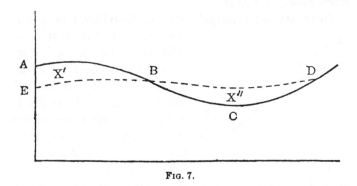

Fig. 7.

stream the amount X' for the sake of the larger amount X'' at a later time. He will engage in the former series of operations if, at the start, his subjective preference for present goods exceeds the market rate of interest, and in the latter, if it falls short of that rate. After the operations are completed and the final conformations of the income-streams are determined, the rates of time-preference are all brought into conformity with the market rate of interest.

The loan is effected under the guise of money. We do

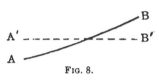

FIG. 8.

not confessedly borrow and lend incomes, but money. Yet money — that universal medium in practice and universal stumbling-block in theory — merely represents capitalized income. A hundred dollars mean the power to secure income, — any income the present value of which is $100. When, therefore, a person "borrows" $100 to-day and

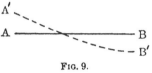

FIG. 9.

returns $105 next year, in actual fact he secures the title to $100 worth of future income — immediately future, perhaps — and parts with the title to $105 worth of income more remotely future.

There are six principal types of individuals in a loan

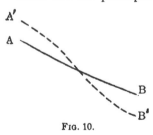

FIG. 10.

market. In the first type (Fig. 8) the individual is supposed to be possessed of an increasing income-stream AB which in his mind results in a rate of preference above the market rate. This leads him to borrow, and relatively to level up his ascending income-stream to such a position as $A'B'$. The second type of individual already possesses a uniform income-stream AB (Fig. 9), but, nevertheless, being of a spending type, experiences a rate of preference also above the market rate, and will therefore modify his income-stream to the curve $A'B'$. The third type is represented in Figure 10. This individual has a rate of preference in excess of the market rate, even with a descending curve *AB*. The consequence is that by borrowing he obtains a curve *A'B'* of still steeper descent.

The preceding three cases are of borrowers. In like manner there are three types of lenders. Figure 11 represents a descending type of income *AB* which, by lending present income in return for future income, is converted into a relatively uniform income *A'B'*; Figure 12 represents a

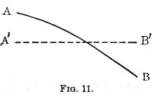

Fig. 11.

uniform income converted, by lending, into an ascending income; and Figure 13 an ascending income converted into a still more steeply ascending income.

In all cases we see that the borrowers change their income curve by tipping it down in the future and up in the present;

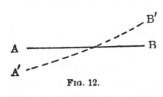

Fig. 12.

whereas the lenders tip their income curves in the opposite direction. Of the three types of borrowers and of lenders, the first in each group of three (see Figs. 8 and 11) is the usual and normal case. In both these cases the effort is to transform the given income into a more uniform one, the rising curve (Fig. 8) being lowered and the falling curve (Fig. 11) being raised toward a common horizontal position. Figure 10 and Figure 13, on the other hand, represent extreme and unusual cases. The former (Fig. 10) typifies the spendthrift who, in spite of lessening income, borrows, and the latter (Fig. 13) typifies the miser who, in spite of rapidly increasing income, saves even more.

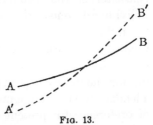

Fig. 13.

But whatever the personal equation, it remains true that, for each individual, the more ascending his income curve the higher his rate of preference, and the more descending the curve, the lower the rate. If the descent is sufficiently rapid, the rate of preference could be made zero or even negative. In these cases, the income is such that its possessor would sacrifice present income to future, even if the market rate of interest were zero.[1]

These are, of course, not the only types which could be considered, but they are some of the most important. To them we may add the type of fluctuating income, as represented in Figure 14, which may result in alternate bor-

Fig. 14.

rowing and lending so as to produce a more nearly uniform income-stream.

It must not be imagined that the classes of borrowers and lenders correspond respectively with the classes of poor and rich. Personal and natural idiosyncracies, early training and acquired habits, accustomed style of living, the usages of the country, and other circumstances discussed in Chapter VI, will, by influencing foresight, self-control, regard for posterity, etc., determine whether a man's rate of preference is high or low, and therefore whether he becomes a spender or a saver. So far as the character of the income-stream itself tends to place an individual in one or the other of these classes, the nature of the influence is in accordance with the principles stated in Chapter VI in respect to the four features, size, time-shape, composition, and probability. As to size, the larger the income the more likely, in general, is its possessor to become a lender, because large incomes, in general, reduce the rate of preference for present over future income; as to time-

[1] This is the case mentioned by Carver (*Theory of Distribution*, pp. 232–236), when he remarks that a man with $100 in his pocket would not think of spending it all on a dinner to-day, but would save at least some of it for to-morrow.

shape, ascending incomes are apt to make the possessors
borrowers, and descending incomes to make them lenders;
as to composition, incomes well endowed with the food
element are less apt to make their possessors borrowers
than incomes of the contrary type; and as to probability,
incomes which are uncertain tend sometimes to make
their possessors borrow, sometimes to lend.

§ 4

But borrowing and lending are not the only ways in which
one's income-stream may be modified. The same result
may be accomplished simply by buying and selling property;
for, since property rights are merely rights to particular income-streams, their exchange substitutes one such stream for
another of equal value but differing in time-shape, composition, or certainty. This method of modifying one's income-
stream, which we shall call the method of sale, really includes
the former method of loan; for a loan contract is at bottom
a sale, as Böhm-Bawerk has so clearly shown. That is,
it is the exchange of the right to present or immediately
ensuing income for the right to more remote or future income. A borrower is a seller of a note of which the lender
is the buyer. A bondholder is regarded indifferently as a
lender and as a buyer of property. The concept of a loan
may therefore now be dispensed with by being merged in that
of sale. By selling some property rights and buying others
it is possible to transform one's income-stream at will,
whether in time-shape, composition, or probability. Thus,
if a man buys an orchard, he is providing himself with future
income in the use of apples; if, instead, he buys apples, he
is providing himself with similar but more immediate
income. If he buys securities, he is providing himself
with future money, convertible when received into true
income. If his security is a share in a mine, his income-
stream is less lasting, though it should be larger, than if
the security is stock in a railway. Purchasing the right to

155

remote enjoyable income is called *investing;* to immediate enjoyable income, *spending.* These, however, are purely relative concepts, for "remote" and "immediate" are relative terms. Buying a winter overcoat or a carpet may be called investing, and on the other hand, buying a factory or a ship may be called spending. And yet the antithesis between "spending" money and "investing" is important; it is the antithesis between immediate and remote income. The adjustment between the two determines the time-shape of one's income-stream. Spending increases immediate income but robs the future, whereas investing provides for the future to the detriment of the present.

Popular usage has devised many other terms and phrases in this field, most of which, like "spending" and "investing," while containing meaning of importance, include also the alloy of misconception. Thus, the phrase "capital seeking investment" means that capitalists have property for which they desire, by exchange, to substitute other property, the income from which is more remote. It does not mean that the inanimate capital has of itself any power to "seek investment"; it does not mean that there is any hard and fast line between invested and uninvested capital. Again, the phrase "saving capital out of income" means "not spending," — reserving money which would otherwise be spent for immediate enjoyable income in order to exchange it for remoter income; it does not mean the creation of new capital, though it may lead to it. Many needless controversies have centered about the phenomenon of "saving," chiefly because neither "saving" nor "income" was clearly defined.[1]

From what has been said it is clear that by buying and selling property an individual may change the conformation

---

[1] Thus, by "saving," some writers understand that capital necessarily increases, and hence the income-stream is made to ascend; others, like Carver (*loc. cit.* p. 232), apply the term broadly enough to include the case where a descending income is simply rendered less descending. The latter view harmonizes with that here presented.

of his income-stream precisely as though he were specifically lending or borrowing. Thus, if a man's original income-stream is $1000 this year and $1500 next year, and if, selling this income-stream, he buys with the proceeds another yielding $1100 this year and $1395 next year, he has not, nominally, borrowed $100 and repaid $105, but he has done what amounts to the same thing, — increased his income-stream of this year by $100 and decreased that of next year by $105, the $100 being the modification produced in his income for the first year by selling his original income-stream and substituting the final one, and $105 being the reverse modification in next year's income produced by the same operations. The very same diagrams which were used before may be taken to represent these operations. A man sells the income-stream $ABCD$ (Fig. 6) and with the proceeds buys the stream EBD. The X' and X'' are, as before, $100 and $105, but now appear explicitly as differences in the value of two income-streams instead of direct loans and returns.

<h2 style="text-align:center">§ 5</h2>

In passing we may note that interest-taking cannot be prevented by prohibiting loan contracts. To forbid the particular form of sale called a loan contract would leave possible other forms of sale, and, as was shown in *The Nature of Capital and Income*, the valuation of every property-right involves interest. If the prohibition left individuals free to deal in bonds, it is clear that they would be still borrowing and lending, but under the name of "sale"; and if "bonds" were tabooed, they could change the name to "preferred stock." It can scarcely be supposed that any prohibition of interest-taking would extend to all buying and selling; but as long as buying and selling of any kind were permitted, the virtual effect of lending and borrowing would be retained. The possessor of a forest of young trees, not being able to mortgage their future

return, and being in need of an income-stream of a less
deferred type than that receivable from the forest itself,
would simply sell his forest and with the proceeds buy, say,
a farm, with a uniform flow of income, or a mine with a
decreasing one.   On the other hand, the possessor of a
capital which is depreciating, that is, which represents an
income-stream great now but steadily declining, and who
is anxious to "save" instead of "spend," would sell his
depreciating wealth and invest the proceeds in such instruments as the forest already mentioned.

It was in such a way, as for instance by "rent purchase,"
that the medieval prohibitions of usury were rendered
nugatory.   Practically, at the worst, the effect of restrictive
laws is simply to hamper and make difficult the finer adjustments of the income-stream, compelling would-be borrowers to sell wealth yielding distant returns instead of
mortgaging it, and would-be lenders to buy the same,
instead of lending to the present owners.   It is conceivable
that "explicit" interest might disappear under such restric-
tions, but "implicit" interest would remain.   The young
forest sold for $10,000 would bear this price, as now, because
it is the discounted value of the estimated future income;
and the price of the farm bought for $10,000 would be de-
termined in like manner.   The rate of discount in the two
cases must be the same, because, by buying and selling,
the various parties in the community adjust their rates
of preference to a common level, — an implicit rate of interest thus lurking in every contract, though never specifically appearing therein.   Interest is too omnipresent a
phenomenon to be eradicated by attacking any particular
form; nor would any one undertake it who perceived the
substance as well as the form.[1]   In substance, the rate of
interest represents the terms on which the earlier and later
elements of income-streams are exchangeable.

[1] Cf. Fetter, *Principles of Economics*, New York (Century), 1904,
pp. 134, 135.

§ 6

The fact that, through the loan market, the marginal rate of time-preference for each individual is made equal to the rate of interest, may be stated in another way, namely, that the total present desirability or utility of the individual income-stream is made a maximum. For, consider again the individual who modifies his original fixed income-stream by borrowing until his rate of preference is brought into unison with the rate of interest. His rate of preference was at first 10 per cent.; that is, in order to secure an addition of $100 to his present income, he was willing to sacrifice $110 of next year's income. But he only needed to sacrifice $105; that is, he was enabled to get his loan for less than he would have been willing to pay. He was therefore a gainer to the extent of the present desirability of $5 of next year's income. The second $100 borrowed was equivalent, in his present estimation, to $108 of next year's income, and the same reasoning shows that, as he pays only $105, he saves $3; that is, he adds the present desirability of $3 due next year to the present "total desirability" or "total utility" of his income-stream. In like manner, each successive increment of loans adds to his present total desirability, so long as he is willing to pay more than $105 of next year's income for $100 of this year's income. But, as he proceeds, his gains and his eagerness diminish until they cease altogether. At, let us say, the fifth instalment of $100, he finds himself barely willing to pay $105; his present total desirability is then a maximum, and any further loan would decrease it. A sixth $100, for instance, is worth in his estimation less than $105, say $104, and as, in the loan market, he would have to sacrifice $105 next year to secure it, the contracting of such a loan would mean a loss of desirability to the extent of $1 due in one year. Thus, by borrowing up to the point where the rate of preference for present over future income is equal to the rate of interest, the individual secures the greatest "total desirability."

Similar reasoning, applied to the individual on the other side of the market, whose rate of preference is initially less than the market rate of interest, will show that he also will maximize his present total desirability by lending up to the point where his rate of preference corresponds to the rate of interest. At the beginning, $100 this year has to him the same present desirability as $102 due one year hence, whereas in the market he may secure $105. It is then clear that by lending $100 he gains the present desirability of $3 due one year hence. By lending each successive $100 he will add something to his total present desirability, until his rate of preference for present over future income is raised to a level equal to that of the rate of interest. Beyond that point he would lose by further lending; but at that point he will stop, and his present total desirability will therefore be a maximum.

§ 7

We are now in a position to give a preliminary answer to the question, What determines the rate of interest? Thus far we have regarded the individual only, and have seen that he conforms his rate of preference to the rate of interest. For him the rate of interest is a relatively fixed fact, since his own time-preference and resulting action can affect it only infinitesimally. His rate of preference is the variable. In short, for him individually the rate of interest is cause, and the rate of preference, effect. For society as a whole, however, the order of cause and effect is reversed. This change is like the corresponding inversion of cause and effect in the theory of prices. Each individual regards the market price, say, of sugar, as fixed, and adjusts his marginal utility to it; whereas, for the entire group forming the market, we know that the price of sugar is due to its marginal utility to the consumer.[1] In the same way, while for the individual the rate of interest determines the rate of preference, for society the rates of preference of the individuals determine the rate of interest. The rate of interest is simply the rate of preference, upon which the whole community may concur in order that the market of loans may be exactly cleared.

To put the matter in figures: if the rate of interest is set very high, say 20 per cent., there will be relatively few borrowers and many would-be lenders, so that the total extent to which would-be lenders are willing to reduce their income-streams for the present year for the sake of a much larger future income will be, say, 100 million dollars; whereas, those who are willing to add to their present income at the high price of 20 per cent. interest will borrow only, say, one million. Under such conditions the demand for loans is far short of the supply and the rate of interest will therefore go down. At an interest rate of 10 per cent. the present year's income offered as loans may be 50 millions, and the amount which would be taken at that rate only 20 millions. There is still an excess of supply over demand, and interest must needs fall further. At 5 per cent. we may suppose the market cleared, borrowers and lenders being willing to take or give respectively 30 millions. In like manner it can be shown that the rate would not fall below this, as in that case it would result in an excess of demand over supply and cause the rate to rise again.

Thus, the rate of interest is the common market rate of preference for present over future income, as determined by the supply and demand of present and future income. Those who, having a high rate of preference, strive to acquire more present income at the cost of future income, tend to raise the rate of interest. These are the borrowers, the

[1] See the author's "Mathematical Investigations in the Theory of Value and Prices," *Transactions of Connecticut Academy*, New Haven, 1892, p. 28.

spenders, the sellers of property yielding remote income, such as bonds and stocks. On the other hand, those who, having a low rate of preference, strive to acquire more future income at the cost of present income, tend to lower the rate of interest. These are the lenders, the savers, the investors.

The mechanism just described will not only result in a rate which will clear the market for loans connecting the present with next year, but, applied to exchanges between the present and the remoter future, it will make similar adjustments. While some individuals may wish to exchange this year's income for next year's, others wish to exchange this year's income for that of the year after next, or for a portion of several years' future incomes. The rates of interest for these various periods are so adjusted as to clear the market for all the periods of time for which contracts are made.

If we retain our original assumption that every man is initially endowed with a fixed and certain income-stream which, by borrowing and lending, can be freely bought and sold and thereby redistributed in time, the foregoing discussion gives us a complete theory of the causes which determine the rate of interest, or rather, the *rates* of interest for various time-periods. These rates of interest would, under these circumstances, be fully determined by the following four conditions, to which all the magnitudes in the problem of interest must conform:—

(1) The rate of time-preference of each individual for present income, as compared with remoter income, depends upon the character of his income-stream, as finally modified and determined by the very act of borrowing or lending, buying or selling.

(2) Through the variations in the income-stream produced by loans or sales, the rates of preference for all individuals in the market are brought into equality with each other and with the market rate of interest.

This condition is equivalent to another; namely, that

each individual exchanges present against future income, or *vice versa*, at the market rate of interest up to the point of *maximum desirability*.

(3) The market rate of interest will be such as will just clear the market; namely, will make the loans and borrowings cancel each other for each period of time.

(4) All loans are repaid with interest; that is, the present value of the payments, reckoned at the time of contract, equals the present value of the repayments. More generally, the modifications or departures from a person's original income-stream effected by buying and selling are such that the algebraic sum of their present values is zero.

These four conditions not only determine the rate of interest, but determine also all the other variable elements which enter into the problem; namely, the individual rates of preference (equal to the rate of interest) and the amounts which are borrowed and lent.

The formulation of these four determining conditions constitutes our first approximation to the theory of interest. The sufficiency of the four conditions and their coördination may be made clear by means of the mathematical statement contained in the Appendix to this chapter.

PART III. Second and Third Approximations

CHAPTER VIII

SECOND APPROXIMATION TO THE THEORY OF INTEREST (ASSUMING INCOME FLEXIBLE)

§ 1

HITHERTO we have assumed that the income-stream flowing from any given article of capital is both fixed and certain. We now abandon the first part of this hypothesis. Still assuming that all income-streams are certain, that is, can be definitely foreseen, we now introduce the hypothesis that they are not fixed, but flexible; that is, that the owner of any capital-wealth or capital-property is not restricted to a single use to which he may put it, but has open to his choice several different uses, each of which constitutes a separate optional income-stream.

For instance, the owner of land may use it in more than one way. He may use it to grow crops, graze animals, plant forests, extract minerals, support buildings, or for other purposes. Again, the owner of a building may use it for office purposes, for apartments, or for stores. Most raw materials can be used for any one of a number of purposes. Iron may be wrought into steel rails or into machinery, implements, tools, armor for ships, or girders for buildings. A derrick may be used for quarrying stone, building a house, or unloading a boat. A ship may be used to carry any sort of cargo, and over any one of numerous different routes. Hammers, saws, nails, and other tools may be used in almost numberless ways.

Perhaps the most adaptable of all instruments of wealth is man himself. He may be simply a passive enjoyer or

137

"transformer"[1] of the services of other wealth, and as such derive his satisfactions in sensual, esthetic, intellectual, or spiritual ways; or, he may also be an active producer, and as such perform physical or mental work. If his work is physical, it may consist in anything from wielding a pick and shovel to the deft manipulation of the instruments employed in the jeweler's art. If his work is mental, he may be a bookkeeper, clerk, superintendent, director, lawyer, physician, editor, teacher, or scientist.

In consequence of such a range of choice, the same set of productive instruments may result in very different income-streams. Their energies may be directed at will to produce cheap frame houses or durable stone ones; to equip a city with horse cars, trolleys, or underground rapid transit; to secure an income-stream which shall consist largely of the pleasures of the table, or of the amusements of the theater, or of the gratification of social vanities, — in short, to select one particular income-stream out of a thousand possible income-streams differing in size, composition, and time-shape, as well as in probability, though in this chapter the element of uncertainty is supposed absent.

Owing to this great range of choice, the owner of capital may modify the income-stream he derives from it, not simply by the devices of borrowing and lending or of selling and buying, but also by changing the use or employment to which his capital is put. It should be noted, however, that this third method of modifying an income-stream really includes the other two. Just as buying and selling virtually include borrowing and lending, so the change from one use of capital to another may be said to include buying and selling, and therefore also to include borrowing and lending. This is evident if we consider that one method of employing capital is to sell it. In fact, a merchant regards himself as "using" his stock in the exclusive sense of selling it.

This method of modifying the income-stream is therefore

[1] See *The Nature of Capital and Income*, Chap. X.

a general one. But, while it includes the other methods, it includes much else so different from the methods of borrowing and lending or buying and selling that we shall need to distinguish the new method from the old. There are two principal reasons for keeping the new method separate. First, the former and narrower methods of modifying income-streams cannot be applied to society as a whole. Society as a whole cannot borrow and lend, nor buy and sell; and yet it can radically change the character of its income-stream by changing the employment of its capital. Secondly, when borrowing and lending or ordinary buying and selling are employed to modify an income-stream, the present values of the original income-stream and of the modified income-stream are the same. But when an income-stream is modified by a change in the use of the capital yielding it, its present value may not remain the same.

§ 2

The choice among the various optional income-streams will fall on the one which has the maximum desirability. As among income-streams of different sizes but alike in composition and time-shape, the most desirable will of course be the largest; as among income-streams of different composition but alike in other respects, the most desirable will be that in which the marginal desirabilities of the different constituents are proportional to their several prices, in accordance with a fundamental principle in the theory of prices; finally, as among income-streams differing in time-shape, the most desirable is found in accordance with the principles which govern the rate of interest. It is therefore with the differences in time-shape that we are here chiefly concerned.

To illustrate these differences, let us suppose an individual possessed of a piece of land almost equally good for lumbering, farming, or mining. He thus has the *option* of using it in any one of three different ways: (1) in farming, which, let us say, will give him a regular and indefinite succession of crops with an income-stream of the type A in Figure 15; (2) for forest purposes, with very slight returns for the first few decades, and larger returns in the future, as indicated by the curve B; (3) for mining purposes, in which case we shall suppose that, as the mining plant is already set up and the richest ore lies close to the surface, the income is greatest for the early years and thereafter gradually decreases until the mine is exhausted. This is shown by curve C. What are the principles upon which the owner of the land chooses among these three income-streams?

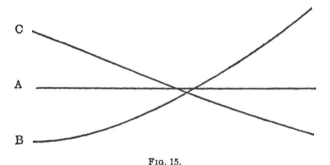

FIG. 15.

We shall suppose, as heretofore, that there is a uniform rate of interest, and that any individual is free either to borrow or lend at that rate to any required amount. Under this hypothesis the choice among the options will simply depend on the one which gives the maximum present value, reckoned at the market rate of interest. Thus, if the use of the land for forestry purposes yields the following sums: zero for the first two years, $300 for the third, $400 for the fourth, $500 for the fifth, and $500 thereafter forever,—then the value of the land, if the rate of interest is 5 per cent., will be $8820. If the land is used for mining purposes, it will yield an income-stream of quite a different character, let us say, as follows: $2000

the first year, $1800 the second, $1600 the third, and so
on diminishing annually by $200 to the point of exhaustion.
The present value of these sums is $9110. If, finally, the
land is used for farming purposes and yields a net income
of $450 a year perpetually, the present value will be $9000.
Under these conditions the choice will evidently fall on the
mining use, because, for mining purposes, the land is worth
$9110, which is greater than $8820, its value for forestry
purposes, and than $9000, its value for farming purposes.

The particular income-stream selected will leave its im-
press on the time-shape of the total income-stream of the
individual who owns it. For, as was seen in *The Nature
of Capital and Income*,[1] the total final income-stream of
any individual is simply the sum of the incomes flowing
from all the articles of property belonging to him. Hence,
if one selects the mining use for his land, whereby the
income-stream gradually decreases, its tendency will be
to produce a similar decrease in the total income-stream
possessed by the individual. This tendency may, of course,
be counteracted by some opposing tendency, but will have
full sway if the income from all other capital than the
land remains the same in value and time-shape.

It is true that the income from the mine is not final
enjoyable income, but consists of "interactions." But
these interactions are readily transformed, through a chain
of credits and debits, into final enjoyable income. The
ore of the mine is exchanged for money, and the money
spent for enjoyable services or for commodities which soon
yield enjoyable services, so that the "enjoyable" income
follows closely behind the "intermediate" income from the
mine, and almost exactly copies it in time-shape.[2]

§ 3

Yet the possessor of the mine is not compelled to copy in
his final enjoyable income the mine's fluctuations of natural

[1] Chaps. VII–X, XVII.
[2] See *The Nature of Capital and Income*, Chaps. VIII, IX, XVII.

income. He may, for instance, prefer as his model an even
flow of income such as he could get from the farm-use of
his land. He will not, however, on that account choose
this farm-use in preference to the mining-use; for the mining-use has the larger present value, and the undesirable
time-shape of its income-stream can be remedied by the
methods explained in the previous chapter, — by *lending*
at interest the proceeds of its earlier output and postponing
enjoyable income to later years; or, more generally, by
buying with the early proceeds such property as will
yield returns at such future times as are most desired, —
in short, by "investing" instead of "spending." [1] The
difference is merely that if he "spends" the yield from his
mine, he is exchanging it for property from which enjoyable income comes promptly, whereas if he "invests," he
is exchanging it for property from which enjoyable income
comes more tardily. If he "spends" the mine's income
as fast as he receives it, for food, clothing, shelter, travel,
amusements, his "enjoyable" income simply shadows the
"intermediate" income from the mine; but if he "invests"
the mine's income in more durable forms, such as furniture,
or still better, dwellings, or stocks and bonds, his enjoyable income lags further behind the income from the mine
on which it depends, and by proper manipulation can be
distributed in time in any desired manner, — for instance,
evenly, as above supposed.

Since the mining-use has the higher present value, there
is an advantage in selecting it rather than the farm-use
which has the more desirable time-shape; for after the
mining income is converted into the same time-shape as
the farming income, it will be greater in magnitude, in the
ratio of their present values,[2] 9110 : 9000.

---

[1] See Chap. VII, § 4.

[2] This is evident from the principles explained in *The Nature of Capital and Income*, Chap. XIII; for the mining income, after conversion
by investment at 5 per cent., will still have the same present value,
$9110, and the even income of which this is present value is at 5 per
cent., $455.50, instead of the $450 which the farm-use yields. The

Again, it may be that the mine owner prefers, not a steady, but an ascending income-stream, and as in the case just considered, he may secure such an income by modifying the income by means of properly graduated investments of the early parts of the mine's income. He can secure, if he likes, exactly the same time-shape as though he had chosen the forestry use, with the advantage that his income will be larger. Thus, he may invest all of his first two years' income of $2000 and $1800 respectively, $1290 in the third year, $987 in the fourth year, and so on, reducing his annual investments by the proper gradations; and, proceeding at the proper time to "realize" on these investments, he may obtain, as the final result of these operations, an income of precisely the same time-shape as that which he would have obtained from the forestry use. But the size of the income will be larger in the ratio of the present values of the mining and forestry income-streams, 9110 : 8820. The following table exhibits these operations: —

	Receives from Mines	From which he Invests	So that his Income is	As against what the Forest Use would have Yielded
1st year	2000	2000	000	000
2d year	1800	1800	000	000
3d year	1600	1290	310	300
4th year	1400	987	413	400
5th year	1200	684	516	500
6th year	1000	484	516	500
7th year	800	284	516	500
8th year	600	84	516	500
9th year	400	− 116	516	500
10th year	200	− 316	516	500

mine owner needs simply to invest annually the excess of his income above $455.50; namely, $1544.50 in the first year, $1344.50 in the second year, etc. When the ninth year is reached the investment ceases, for the mine then yields only $400. This is then eked out by $55.50 from the amounts previously invested, and the same methods are pursued thereafter.

Since any time-shape may be transformed into any other
no one need be deterred from selecting an income because
of its time-shape, but may choose it exclusively on the
basis of maximum present value.   On the other hand,
were it not for the possibility of modifying the time-shape
of his income-stream by borrowing and lending or buying
and selling, the land owner would not feel free to choose
the one from among the three optional employments of
his land which possessed the highest value, but might be
forced to take one of the others.   We assume in this
chapter that, after the most valuable option has been
chosen, it is possible to borrow and lend or to buy and
sell *ad libitum*.   It will then happen that his income as
finally transformed will be larger than it could have been

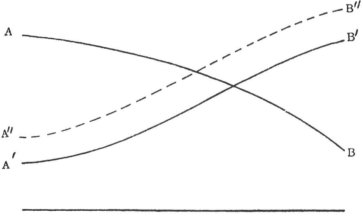

FIG. 16.

if he had chosen some other use which afforded that same
time-shape.

To illustrate this by a diagram, let AB and $A'B'$ in Figure
16 be alternative income-streams, of which the descending
income-stream AB has a larger present value than the ascending income-stream $A'B'$.   The choice will then fall on
AB, even though the individual prefers the time-shape of

174

the other income-stream $A'B'$. He will then lend some of the early receipts from the income-stream AB and receive back some of the later, converting his income AB of undesirable shape into the income-stream $A''B''$ which has the desired shape. Consequently this final income $A''B''$ combines the virtues of both the original alternative incomes AB and of $A'B'$; it possesses the superior shape of $A'B'$ and the superior present worth of AB. As compared with $A'B'$ it has the same shape but a greater size.

We see, then, that the capitalist reaches his final income through the coöperation of two separate kinds of choice of incomes, — first, the choice of the income-stream which has the highest present value, and second, the choice among different possible modifications of this income-stream by borrowing and lending or buying and selling. These two kinds of choice are distinguished from each other by the fact that the first is a selection among optional incomes of *different market values,* and the second is a selection among optional incomes of the *same* market value.

§ 4

Since this double choice, when it is made, results in a perfectly definite income-stream, it might seem that the situation does not materially differ from the case of a rigid income-stream discussed in the preceding chapter. But the two cases differ materially; for in the present case of optional income-streams, the particular choice *depends upon the rate of interest.* A change in that rate may shift the choice of maximum present value to some other alternative. Thus, in the example cited, if the rate of interest should be $4\frac{1}{2}$ per cent. instead of 5 per cent., the order of choice would be changed. The value of the land for forestry use would be $9920, for farming use, $10,000, and for mining use, $9280. The farming use would now be the best choice. Again, if the rate of interest should be 4 per cent. instead of $4\frac{1}{2}$ per cent., the present value of the use of the land for forest purposes would be $11,300, for farming purposes, $11,250, and for mining purposes, $9450.   In this case the forestry use would be chosen.   We see, then, that it pays best to employ the land for mining if the rate of interest is 5 per cent., for farming if it is 4½ per cent., and for forestry if it is 4 per cent.

The various options open to the owner of the land at different rates of interest are summarized in the following table : —

Optional Uses	Present Value at		
	5%	4½%	4%
For forestry . . .	8,820	9,920	11,300
For farming . . .	9,000	10,000	11,250
For mining	9,110	9,280	9,450

Thus a change in the rate of interest results in a change in the choice of income-streams.   A high rate of interest will encourage investment in the quickly returning incomes, whereas a low rate of interest will encourage investment in incomes which yield distant returns.   As the business man puts it, when interest is high he can less afford to wait for a remote return because he will "lose so much interest."

An investor will, therefore, make very different choices according as interest is at one rate or another.   Consequently the existence of optional uses of capital introduces a new variable into the problem of interest-determination. To the individual, the rate of interest will determine the choice among his optional income-streams; but for society, the order of cause and effect is reversed, — the rate of interest will be influenced by the existence of the options. To trace this influence is the purpose of the present chapter.

§ 5

At first sight it may appear that we are reasoning in a circle: the rate of interest depends on individual rates of preference; the rates of preference depend on the time-shapes of individual income-streams; and the choice of these time-shapes of income-streams depend, we have just seen, on the rate of interest itself.

It is perfectly true that the rate of interest depends on a series of factors which finally depend on the rate of interest. Yet this series is not the vicious circle it seems, for the last step is not the inverse of the first.

To distinguish between a true and a seeming example of a circular dependence we may contrast the following two simple problems: We wish to find the height of a father who is known to be three times as tall as his child. To solve this we need to know something about the height of the child. If we are told that the child's height differs from his father's by twice itself, the problem is circular and insoluble, for the last step is reducible to the first, being merely a concealed inversion of it. The problem essentially states that the father's height is three times the child's and the child's one third of the father's, — an obvious circle. But if the dependence of the father's height on the child's were essentially different from that of the child's on its father's, there would be no circle. Thus, suppose as before that the father is three times as tall as the child, but that the child's height differs from the father's by four times the child's, less four feet. This *sounds* as circular as the first problem, — the father's height is expressed in terms of the child's, and the child's in terms of the father's; but here the second expression is not reducible to the first. The heights are entirely determinate, that of the father being six feet and that of the child, two. The mere fact that each of these magnitudes is specified in terms of the other does not constitute a vicious circle.

The same is true in our present problem. Real examples of circular reasoning in the theory of interest are common enough, and many of them have, in fact, been noted in earlier chapters, but the dependence above stated, of interest on the range of options and of the choice among those options on interest, is not a case in point. The logical principle holds true that any problem is determinate if only there are as many determining conditions as there are unknown quantities; it is only necessary that these conditions shall be "independent"; in other words, that no one shall be derivable from the others. That this is mathematically the case under our present hypothesis is shown fully in the Appendix to this chapter. For our present purpose we need only present the matter to the reader's imagination by a series of successive approximations.

To find out the rate of interest on which the market will finally settle, let us try successively a number of different rates. First, suppose a rate of 5 per cent. This rate will determine the choice of income-streams for each individual. The landowner formerly supposed will, as we have seen, choose the mining-use. Every other individual in the market, in like manner, will select that particular use for his capital which will give him the maximum present worth. With these choices made, the different individuals will then enter the market of loans or sales, desiring to modify the time-shapes of their income-streams to suit their particular desires. The amount which the would-be lenders are willing to lend at 5 per cent. out of this year's instalment of their chosen income-stream will be perfectly definite, and likewise the amount which the would-be borrowers are willing to take. This we saw in the preceding chapter. In other words, the demand and supply of loans for the present year *for the given rate of interest*, 5 per cent., will be definite quantities. Should it happen that the demand for loans is less than the supply, it follows that 5 per cent. cannot be the correct solution of the rate of interest, for it is too high to clear the market.

In that case, let us suppose a rate of 4 per cent. Following the same reasoning as before, we find that the landowner will now select the forestry use for his land. Other capitalists will select likewise their definite income-streams, and on the basis of these income-streams there will be the consequent desire to borrow and lend. Should it then happen that the demand and supply of loans, *on the basis of* 4 *per cent.*, are not equal, but that this time the demand exceeds the supply, it is a proof that not 4 per cent. is the true solution, but some higher rate. By again changing our trial rate back toward 5 per cent. we may evidently reach some intermediate point, let us say 4½ per cent., *at which rate not only will all individuals choose definite income-streams, but also, at the same time, the demand and supply of loans engendered by these income-streams will exactly clear the market.*

The introduction, therefore, of flexibility into our income-stream still leaves the problem of interest entirely determinate. Though the income-streams are now a matter of choice, there is one definite choice corresponding to each rate of interest. The particular rate of interest which will solve the problem is that which will both determine the choice among income-streams differing in present value, and also bring it about that individual departures from such income-streams shall mutually cancel each other, — in other words, that the markets for loans and sales shall be cleared.

§ 6

For the determination of the rate of interest we have therefore to modify the various conditions as given in the previous chapter. The modifications which are introduced are, (1) that in place of the single fixed income-stream formerly assumed, there now exists a *given range of choice* between different income-streams; and (2) that whereas formerly the individual had no choice of income-streams, he now chooses out of those available the one which possesses the maximum present value. We therefore have six conditions determining the rate of interest, as follows: (1) There exists for each individual a given series of possible income-streams among which he may choose; (2) Each individual's preference rate depends upon his income-stream, — its size, shape, composition, and probability; (3) The rates of preference of different individuals must be equal to each other and to the rate of interest in the market; (4) Out of all available income-streams, that one is selected which has the maximum present value for the rate of interest finally determined; (5) The rate of interest must be such as will equalize supply and demand, or exactly clear the market; (6) The additions to and deductions from each income-stream, brought about by borrowing and lending or buying and selling, must be such that their net present value is zero.

As to the first condition, viz., the existence of a range of choice, it is worth noting that some of the optional income-streams would never be chosen under any circumstances. These are the income-streams the present value of which could not be the maximum, no matter what the rate of interest might be. We have seen that the land, in our example, would be most profitably employed for farming, for mining, or for forestry, according to the rate of interest. But it would not be employed, let us say, for a quarry, no matter what might be the rate of interest. The optional uses which are thus out of the question may be called *ineligible*. We need consider only the *eligible* options.

§ 7

The six conditions for determining interest just enumerated differ from those given in the preceding chapter chiefly by the introduction of number four, — that the use of capital which yields the maximum present value will

be selected. This additional condition is of so much importance that it should be restated in two other forms.

To illustrate these, let us recur to the example of the
land, which could be used in any one of three ways. We
found that when the rate of interest was 4 per cent., the
use chosen would be forestry, as this possessed the greatest
present value. If we now compare, year by year, the income from the land when used for forestry purposes with
the income which it might have yielded if used in one of
the other ways, — as farming, — we shall see that in some
years there is an excess in favor of the forest use, and in
other years a deficiency, as shown in the following table: —

	ANNUAL VALUE OF USES FOR		DIFFERENCE IN FAVOR OF FOREST USE
	FORESTRY	FARMING	
1st year	——	450	− 450
2d year	——	450	− 450
3d year	300	450	− 150
4th year	400	450	− 50
5th year	500	450	+ 50
6th year	500	450	+ 50
7th year	500	450	+ 50
8th year	500	450	+ 50
9th year	500	450	+ 50
10th year	500	450	+ 50
11th year	500	450	+ 50
Each year after . . .	500	450	+ 50

Here we see that for the first four years there is a comparative disadvantage or sacrifice (amounting to $450, $450,
$150, $50 in successive years) from the use of the land for
forest purposes as compared with farm uses, but that this
disadvantage is made up later by an advantage or return of
$50 per annum. If we now take the total present value,
at 4 per cent., of the deficiencies marked with a minus sign,
we shall obtain $1024, whereas the present value of the
excesses (continuing in perpetuity), indicated by a positive

sign, will be $1070. Thus the present value of the gains exceeds the present value of the sacrifices by the difference between $1070 and $1024. In other words, as reckoned in present estimation, the gains outweigh the sacrifices. We may say, therefore, that, the rate of interest being 4 per cent., forestry is preferable to farming because of a surplus of advantages over disadvantages reckoned in present value. But if the rate of interest were 4½ per cent. we should find the present value of the sacrifices to be $1017, and the present value of the gains, $930, showing a preponderance of the sacrifices. That is, if the rate of interest is 4½ per cent., the sacrifice in using the land for forestry rather than mining outweighs the gains. The land would, therefore, in that case, not be used for forestry purposes.

The general principle is, therefore, that out of the various income-streams at the disposal of the capitalist, he chooses the most advantageous, or, more fully expressed, the one which, compared with any other, offers advantages which, reckoned in present estimation at the given rate of interest, outweigh the disadvantages; and this is evidently merely a new formulation of the original principle that the use chosen will be that which has the maximum present value at the given rate of interest.

§ 8

There is yet a third method of stating this principle. This method may also best be shown by an example. We have seen in the previous illustration that if the rate of interest is 4 per cent., the net advantage is in favor of the forest use; and if the rate of interest is 4½ per cent., the advantage is in favor of the farming use. It is evident that at some intermediate rate of interest the comparative advantages of the two uses would be equal. This intermediate rate is approximately 4.2 per cent. To show the nature and importance of such an equalizing rate, we may vary the example given to the following simple illustration: —

| | ANNUAL VALUE OF USES FOR | | DIFFERENCE IN FAVOR OF FORESTRY |
	FORESTRY	FARMING	
1st year	000	100	− 100
2d year	210	100	+ 110
3d year	100	100	000
4th year	100	100	000
Each subsequent year	100	100	000

In this case the equalizing rate is 10 per cent. If the two income-streams be both discounted at 9 per cent., the forestry use will have the greater present value, $1112, as against $1111 for the farming use. If 11 per cent. is used, the scales are turned and the farming use is the more valuable, being worth $909, as against $908 for the forestry. At the intermediate rate of 10 per cent., the two uses are equivalent in present value, both being worth exactly $1000. Since 10 per cent. is the rate which equalizes the advantages and disadvantages of the two alternatives in present value, it is the rate at which the third column in the table will have a present value of zero. Again, it is the rate which the $110 yields on the − $100, or the rate "realized" to the investor who, by choosing the forestry use, relatively sacrifices $100 this year, but obtains a compensating return of $110 next year. Such a rate is therefore called the *rate of return on sacrifice*. These terms are applied exclusively to the comparative merits of two alternative income-streams. By "sacrifice" is meant the comparative loss from one's income-stream at first, caused by substituting one use of capital for another; and by "return" is meant the comparative gain which later accrues by reason of this same substitution.

To return to the original example and the table in § 7, the equalizing rate was 4.2 per cent. This was the

rate of return on sacrifice of the forestry use when compared with the farming use. It is the rate which makes
the series of future returns, $50, $50, etc., indefinitely,
equivalent in present value to the first sacrifices, $450,
$450, $150, and $50. It follows [1] that if the latter series of
sums were successively deposited at 4.2 per cent. in a savings bank, they would "earn" for the depositor the former
series of sums. In short, 4.2 per cent. is the rate which an
investor "realizes" who in the first four years sacrifices successively $450, $450, $150, and $50, and receives as return
in succeeding years, $50, $50, etc. In general, the rate of
return on sacrifice is a supposed rate of interest which
will make equal the present values of the "sacrifices"
and "returns" involved in comparing one optional
income-stream with another. It is not, of course, to be
confused with the actual rate of interest.

Now if the actual rate of interest is 4 per cent., while
the rate of return on sacrifice which would be realized by
choosing the forestry rather than the farming use is 4.2
per cent., it would evidently be profitable to choose forestry.
As the investor might put it, he would be getting more than
the market rate, — getting 4.2 per cent. instead of 4 per
cent. If, however, the rate of interest in the market is
4.5 per cent., it would not pay to choose the forestry use,
for to do so would, comparatively to the farming use, return only 4.2 per cent. In this case the prospective
investor would evidently prefer to choose the farming use,
and then lend his money at 4.5 per cent. Recurring to the
former table, we see that had he chosen the forest use
instead of the farming use he would have sacrificed during
the first four years successively $450, $450, $150, and $50.
He may, if he likes, put these very sums at interest in
a savings bank and make 4.5 per cent. upon them, whereas,
had he chosen the forest use, he would have received only
4.2 per cent. In other words, when a man can invest at

[1] See *The Nature of Capital and Income,* Chap. XIII.

4.5 per cent. by lending, he will not invest at 4.2 per cent. by choosing forestry rather than farming.

Out of all possible employments of his capital, the capitalist will choose that one which, compared with any other, has advantages worth the disadvantages, — returns worth the sacrifices. This means that the *rate of return on sacrifice will exceed the rate of interest.*

In case the advantages precede the disadvantages, as when the merits of the mining use are compared with those of the farming use, the proposition must be reversed, as follows: The earlier advantage will be chosen only in case the rate of later sacrifice on present return is *less* than the rate of interest. In such a case it would be more convenient, in comparing the two uses, to regard them in the opposite order, that is from the point of view of the advantages, not of the mining use over the farming use, but of the farming use over the mining use. This will make the sacrifices precede the returns. As long as the sacrifices always precede the returns, we need only to consider whether or not the rate of return on sacrifice exceeds the rate of interest. If it does, the optional income-stream which, compared with another, yields such return on sacrifice will be chosen in preference; otherwise it will be rejected.[1]

[1] Of course it is possible to have two alternative uses so related that the sacrifices are not grouped together in one mass and the returns in another, but are intermingled. Thus, the first few years may offer advantages, the following, disadvantages, those following still later, advantages, and so on in alternating succession. In such a case, if the market rate of interest is 4 per cent. and the rate which equalizes the gains and sacrifices is 4.2 per cent., in order to decide which of the optional income-streams ought to be chosen, it would be necessary to consider the effect of a slight variation from the 4.2 per cent. rate used in discounting the comparative advantages and disadvantages. Let the rate change from 4.2 per cent. to 4.1 per cent., *i.e.* toward the actual rate 4 per cent. If the effect of such a change is to make the advantages outweigh the disadvantages, in present value, it is a proof that the income-stream possessing these advantages and disadvantages is preferable to the one being compared with it. In such a case it is much more convenient not to

The condition, therefore, determining the choice between options may be stated in any one of three ways, namely: (1) Out of all options that one is selected which has the maximum present value, reckoned at the market rate of interest; (2) Out of all options that one is selected of which the advantages over any other outweigh, in present value, its disadvantages, when both are discounted at the market rate of interest; (3) Out of all options that one is selected which, compared with any other option, yields a rate of return on sacrifice greater than the rate of interest.

§ 9

Let us now apply the third mode of statement to the case in which the range of choice is not confined to a few options, but extends to an infinite number. This case is really more like the facts of life than the imaginary case of a few options, such as the farming, mining, or forestry uses of land. As a matter of fact, each of these is not a single use, but a whole group of optional uses. Thus, the farmer may cultivate his farm with any degree of intensity; and for each particular degree of intensity he will have a different income-stream. He may, for instance, invest $100 worth of labor in the present, in order that in six months he may have a larger income than otherwise, by $200. If the rate of interest is 4 per cent. (reckoned semi-annually), he would evidently prefer this option; for it diminishes his present income by $100 and increases his income six months later by $200, being 100 per cent. in six months, whereas the interest for that time is only 2 per cent. Another course would be to invest, not $100, but $200, in present cultivation. The extra $100 would add to his returns in a half-year's time something less than the $200 yielded on his

consider at all any equalizing rate, such as 4.2 per cent., but to recur to one of the preceding methods. In practice, however, such perplexities seldom or never arise.

first $100, let us say $150.   This also would be a good investment, yielding him 50 per cent. return when the rate of interest is 2 per cent.   And so each successive choice, compared with its predecessor, shows a *law of decreasing returns for additional sacrifice.*   Thus, if he invests, not $200, but $300, the third $100 thus sacrificed will add to his returns in six months, let us say $120.   Here is a gain of 20 per cent., whereas the rate of interest is only 2 per cent. As another option, he may sacrifice a fourth $100 for the sake of a return of an additional $110; in like manner he may sacrifice a fifth $100 for the return of an additional $105; a sixth $100 for an additional $103; a seventh $100 for $102.   Thus far, each successive option is preferred to its predecessor; for, as compared with its predecessor, each option yields more than 2 per cent., which is the rate of interest for six months.   The next option is to sacrifice an eighth $100 for an additional $101 in six months. Evidently, it will not be to the farmer's interest to take this last step; he will stop at the previous step, at which he gets a 2 per cent. return on the last sacrifice of $100. As we saw in the preceding section, each successive option is chosen as long as the rate of return on sacrifice of that option, compared with the previous option, is greater than the rate of interest, and that use is rejected at which the rate of return on sacrifice becomes less than the rate of interest.   The intensiveness of his farming is thus determined by the rate of interest.   He chooses that degree of intensiveness which gives his income-stream the maximum present value, — which is the same thing as choosing that degree at which the rate of return on sacrifice is equal to the rate of interest.

The various possible income-streams are represented in Figure 17.   Income-stream *A* is large for the first six months, and for the second six months very small.   The next income-stream *B* is $100 smaller than *A* for the first six months, and $200 larger for the last six months. The other options are also indicated.   Income-stream *H* is the one chosen, because, as compared with its predecessor, its disadvantage is $100 for the first six months and its advantage $102 for the second six months — just enough to "compensate for interest."

We therefore reach the conclusion that where the options are indefinite in number, the option chosen, compared with a neighboring option with which it was in competition, yields a rate of return on sacrifice equal to the rate of interest.

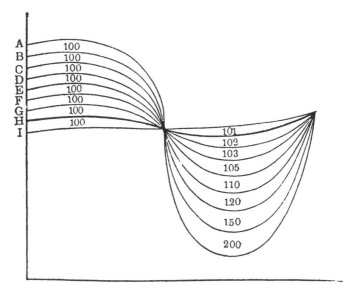

Fig. 17.

This rate of return, computed on the basis of two alternative income-streams closely neighboring upon each other, we shall call the *marginal rate of return on sacrifice*. It follows that, when there is a continuous range of choice, we may substitute for the statement that the choice will fall upon the option of maximum present worth, the better statement that the choice will fall on the option whose *marginal rate of return on sacrifice, reckoned relatively to a neighboring option, is equal to the rate of interest.*

§ 10

We have introduced a new magnitude into our discussion; namely, the rate of return on sacrifice, and especially the particular value of this rate of return called the *marginal* rate of return on sacrifice. This marginal rate of return on sacrifice comes close to being a "natural rate of interest." By means of it we are enabled to admit into our theory the elements of truth contained in some of the claims of the productivity theories, the cost theories,[1] and Böhm-Bawerk's theory of the technique of production.

The example just given of the farmer who selects, out of a series of income-streams, that for which the return on sacrifice is equal to the rate of interest, perfectly exemplifies the theory of John Rae.[2] According to Rae, all instruments may be arranged in an order depending on the rate of return on cost. Some instruments return double the cost of their formation in a year; in other words, the rate of return on sacrifice is 100 per cent. Others return 50 per cent., 20 per cent., and so on in descending order. In any community, Rae says, instruments will be "wrought up" to the point at which the rate of return on sacrifice corresponds to Rae's equivalent for what we have called the "rate of preference," and this, in turn, as we have seen, is equal to the rate of interest. It will be evident to every student of Rae that the preceding discussion accords with Rae's idea that those instruments which most promptly yield returns are formed first, and that the less rapidly returning instruments are successively formed until the margin is reached which corresponds to the rate of interest. The statement of Rae that, for a certain cost of formation, an instrument will yield a certain return, is merely a form of our statement that a certain decrease of present income will be accompanied by a certain increase

[1] See Rae, *The Sociological Theory of Capital*, Chapters IV to VI.
[2] Cf. also Landry, *L'Intérêt du Capital*, 1904, Chapter III; Carver, *Distribution of Wealth*, New York, 1904, p. 230.

in future income. The relation between the immediate
decrease and the future increase will vary within a wide
range, wherein the choice will fall at the point corresponding to the ruling rate of interest.

The subject is one which may be looked upon from many
points of view, and it is important that these points of
view should be thoroughly coördinated. In the example
above given, the farmer was supposed to invest to-day
and receive returns six months afterward. Consider now
a case in which the returns are repeated regularly each
year. Let us suppose that our farmer possesses some
swamp land in a primitive state. He has a large range of
choice as to the method of utilizing this land. He can
allow it to remain a swamp or, by clearing and draining
it, convert it into crop-yielding land, the yield being in
proportion to the thoroughness with which the clearing and
draining are accomplished. Under the first use, let us
suppose that he derives a perpetual net income of $50 a
year, and let us suppose that, at an immediate cost of $100
for clearing and draining, he can secure a perpetual net
income from crops of $75 a year. As between these two
choices, the second involves a decrease of immediate income of $100, and an increase in annual income thereafter,
from $50 to $75, or of $25. In other words, the invest-
ment of $100 will yield him 25 per cent. per annum. Evi-
dently, if the rate of interest in the market is 5 per cent.,
it will pay him to make such an investment. Next suppose that a second $100 invested in improving the swamp
would cause the crop returns to be $90 instead of $75 a year,
or $15 more than before. Evidently, the investment of
the second $100 yields 15 per cent., and is also a lucrative
one, when we consider that the rate of interest is only 5 per
cent. A third $100 may increase the annual crop to $100
instead of $90, an excess of $10 as compared with the
previous investment, or a yield of 10 per cent. A fourth
$100 invested will cause the annual crop to be $105, giving
an increase of $5 and a yield of 5 per cent. A fifth $100 will

cause the crop to increase to $108, giving an increase of $3 and a return of 3 per cent. Evidently it will pay the farmer to invest in draining and improving his swamp up to the fourth $100, but not to the fifth $100. Rather than invest this fifth $100 and receive thereon an annual income of $3 a year, he would prefer to invest $100 in the savings bank and receive 5 per cent. a year.

In other words, the intensity with which he will improve and cultivate his land is determined by the current rate of interest. Should the rate of interest in the market fall from the 5 per cent. just assumed to 2 per cent., it would then pay him to invest the fifth $100. For, evidently, if need be, he could borrow $100 at 2 per cent. and receive from his land a return of 3 per cent. As Rae has so clearly pointed out, in communities where the rate of interest is low, swamps will be more thoroughly improved, roads better made, dwellings more durably built, and all instruments "worked up" to a higher degree of efficiency and a lower marginal return than in a community where the rate of interest is high.

The same illustrations which have been given will serve to set the present theory in line with that of Adolphe Landry in his *Théorie de l'Intérêt*. He states that one of the conditions determining the rate of interest is the "productivity of capital," in the peculiar sense which he gives to this phrase. The process described by Landry by which the productivity is assimilated to whatever rate of interest happens to rule the market, virtually corresponds to the successive selection of income-streams as outlined in the preceding examples.

§ 11

Our next case will serve to show how the element of truth already pointed out in the productivity theory of Del Mar and George fits into the theory here propounded. This theory is that the rate of interest corresponds to the rate of growth of animals and plants. In Chapter III we

191

saw that the time of cutting a forest will be that at which it is growing at a rate equal to the rate of interest. Thus, if nine years from the planting of the forest it contains 900 cords of wood, while in ten years it contains 1000 cords, in eleven years, 1050, and in twelve years, 1071, and if the rate of interest is 5 per cent., the cutting will occur between the tenth and eleventh years. This choice is determined by precisely the same principle that has already been enunciated; namely, that the particular income-stream selected will be that which has the maximum present value; or, in other words, that which is such that the marginal rate of return on sacrifice will be equal to the rate of interest.

To show how this principle applies to the cutting of the forest, let us consider as the first option the cutting of the forest at the end of nine years, when the income-stream consists of the single item, — the production of 900 cords of wood.[1]

The second option is cutting the forest at the end of ten years, and receiving an income item of $1000. The two alternatives may be put in the tabular form previously employed for the case of forestry and farming, as follows: —

OPTIONAL INCOMES FROM FOREST

	10-Year Plan	9-Year Plan	Difference in Favor of 10-Year Plan
1st year	000	000	
2d year	000	000	
9th year	000	900	− 900
10th year	1000	000	+ 1000

[1] Inasmuch as we assume that the income from the forest is all to accrue at one time — the time of cutting — instead of being distributed over a long period, the phrase "income-stream" might here better be replaced by "income item."

The last column shows that the ten-year plan, compared with the nine-year plan, involves a sacrifice of $900 in the ninth year which might be secured by the nine-year plan, but involves a return of $1000 in the tenth year.   The rate of return on sacrifice would thus be a little over 11 per cent.   If the rate of interest in the market is 5 per cent., it would evidently pay to "wait," or to choose the cutting in the tenth year rather than the ninth year.

The next option would be to cut in the eleventh year, which, as compared with the second alternative, would involve a sacrifice of $1000 in the tenth year and a return of $1050 in the eleventh year — in other words, a rate of return on sacrifice of 5 per cent.   Evidently, then, it would be a matter of indifference whether the forest was cut in the tenth or eleventh year, inasmuch as the rate of return on sacrifice in one alternative as compared with the other would be exactly equal to the rate of interest.

Similar reasoning shows that the choice of the next option, that of cutting the forest in the twelfth year, would yield a return of $\frac{21}{1050}$, or 2 per cent.   Inasmuch as 2 per cent. is less than the rate of interest, this alternative would be rejected.   Should, however, the rate of interest fall to 2 per cent., or below, it is clear that the time of cutting the forest would be postponed until the rate of increase in stumpage value was reduced to correspond to the rate of interest.

§ 12

The same example will serve to show the bearing of Böhm-Bawerk's discussion as to the influence of the "roundabout process" upon the rate of interest.   According to him, it is at the option of society to invest to-day's labor in any one of many different processes bringing returns in different lengths of time, let us say, nine years, ten years, eleven years, etc.; and he premises that the returns in these successive years will increase, but at a diminishing rate, let us say, in the order of the numbers already given: $900 for the ninth, $1000 for the tenth, $1050 for the eleventh, $1071 for the twelfth, etc. That use will be selected, as Böhm-Bawerk has pointed out, which has the maximum present value; and also, as he points out, the lower the rate of interest, the remoter will be the "production period" on which the choice will fall. If the rate of interest is 5 per cent., the choice will fall on the tenth or eleventh year; if the rate is 2 per cent., on the eleventh or twelfth year; and the lower the rate of interest the more "roundabout" will be the methods of production.

This is entirely valid under the hypothesis involved; namely, that there is a range of optional returns, each consisting of a definite return at a definite point of time, increasing as the production period increases, but at a decreasing rate. It is also true, as Böhm-Bawerk has pointed out, that not only does a lower rate of interest tend to the choice of remoter returns, but that, contrariwise, the choice of remoter returns tends to check the fall in the rate of interest; the reason, expressed in our own terminology, being that the choice of an income-stream relatively large in the future and small in the present tends to increase the relative valuation of present as compared with future income. The existence of such a range of choice as Böhm-Bawerk assumes, therefore, tends to act as a buffer, checking the variations in the rate of interest. This effect of the operation of a range of choice will be again referred to.

§ 13

Thus, the elements of truth which were found in the productivity theory, in the cost-theory, and in Böhm-Bawerk's technique-of-production theory, all find a place under the head of the choice among optional uses of capital. In some cases, as in the example illustrating the theories of Henry George and Böhm-Bawerk, the selection of one option rather than another involves, as its effect on the income-stream, the mere omission of one item of income and the substitution of another. In other cases, as in the examples illustrating the theory of John Rae and Adolphe Landry, the selection of one option rather than another involves the application of labor, or the incurring of cost of some other sort, for the sake of a future return. But in all cases there is a choice among optional income-streams, — a decision how to adjust the income-stream at different periods, whether or not to decrease it at one time in order to increase it at another. It matters not in what way or at what periods of time the flexing of the income-stream occurs. It may be, as in the case of the farmer contemplating the planting of a crop, that the income is flexed or varied at merely two points of time, as seed time and harvest; or, as in the case of clearing a swamp, there may be a decrease of present income for the sake of an increase of the income of all succeeding years; or there may be any other arrangement of sacrifices and returns. But in all cases we have to deal simply with a range of choice among income-streams of different conformations. If this range of choice were limited to a few options, the best statement of the principle which governs the selection would be that the income-stream having the maximum present worth would be selected. But if there is a varied or continuous range of choice, the preferable method of stating the principle is that the income-stream will be selected which, as compared with the neighboring streams, will yield a rate of return on sacrifice equal to the rate of interest.

To a person who has never tried to connect them, many of the theories of the authors just compared seem to have no vital relation. But they are seen to be connected as soon as we look at them in the light of the concept of an income-stream. The problems of choosing when to cut a forest, of what length to make a production period, to what degree of intensiveness to cultivate land, or how far to improve a piece of land, are all problems of choosing the best out of innumerable possible income-streams. In each problem the rival income-streams present differences as to size, shape, composition, or probability, — especially shape. In respect to shape, they can best be compared by means

Fig. 18.

of diagrams. Figures 18 to 21 show typical ways in which the income-stream may conceivably be subjected to slight

Fig. 19.

variation. The unbroken line in each case indicates the income-stream chosen, and the dotted line a neighboring

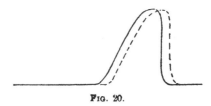

Fig. 20.

possible choice. Figure 18 may be taken as applying to the planting of a crop; Figure 19 to the draining of a swamp;

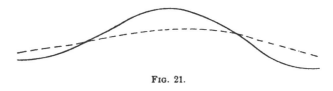

Fig. 21.

Figure 20 to the cutting of a forest; and Figure 21 to a case of alternating sacrifices and returns.

To students of physics, it will be interesting to obesrve
that the identity of the principle of maximum present
value with the principle that the marginal rate of return
on sacrifice is analogous to the identity between the principle of minimum energy and D'Alembert's principle. A
suspension bridge assumes the form which will bring its
center of gravity at the lowest possible point ; this is in
accordance with the principle of minimum energy. It is
clear that the various parts of the structure, so to speak,
compete with each other in the effort each to reach the
lowest possible point. The result is a compromise; no
part reaches the lowest point for itself but is held
above it by the sagging of other parts. If from the
position of equilibrium a slight displacement of any description is imagined, it requires that the depression of
some parts is offset by the elevation of others, the work
being done *by* the one set being equal to that done *upon*
the other set; this is in accordance with the principle of
D'Alembert (principle of virtual displacements). The
income-curve is like the curve of the hanging bridge reversed. The effort is to raise it as high as possible so that
its present value is a maximum. But its various parts
compete with each other in the attempt each to reach the
point highest in present value. The result is a compromise; no part reaches the highest value possible for itself
but is kept from so doing by the other parts. If from the
position of equilibrium a slight displacement of any description is imagined, it requires that the elevation of some
parts is offset by the depression of others, the present
value of the gains being equal to the present value of the
losses. This is equivalent to saying that the rate of return on sacrifice is equal to the rate of interest.

§ 14

Up to this point one complication in the problem of
interest has been carefully kept in the background, not

because it invalidates any of the principles which have been developed, but because it seemed advisable not to distract attention from the essential features of the theory by introducing prematurely a factor which, after all, is more intricate than important. This complication consists in the fact that not only, as we have seen, does the choice between different optional income-streams depend upon the rate of interest, but also that even the *range* of choice depends upon that rate. If the rate of interest is changed, a change is produced not only in the present values of the income-streams but in the income-streams themselves. To recur to the illustration of the land which may be devoted to one of three uses, not only is it true that a change in the rate of interest from 5 per cent. to 4 per cent. will change the relative present values of the income-streams which consist of the farming, mining, and forestry uses of the land, but this change from 5 per cent. to 4 per cent. may also materially affect the three income-streams themselves.

The net income from any instrument of wealth is the difference between the total gross income and the outgo. But many of the elements, both of income and outgo, are materially dependent upon the rate of interest. This is true, whether the items of income and outgo are "final" or merely "intermediate." [1] In the case of intermediate income, or "interactions," a change in the rate of interest affects the income-stream directly, because, as has been shown elsewhere,[2] the valuation of an interaction involves the discount-process and is therefore dependent upon the rate of interest. Thus, the service of planting apple trees will be valued in part by discounting the value of the future apples. Given the value of the apples, it is evident that the value of the planting will be high or low according as the discounting is reckoned at a low or a high rate of interest. But even "final" income — the income secured from the apples, for instance — may be indirectly affected

[1] See *The Nature of Capital and Income*, Chaps. VII–X.
[2] *Ibid.*, p. 317.

by a change in the rate of interest, through a redistribution in the amounts, combinations, and values of the various items constituting final income, and hence in their values.

It would lead us aside from our topic to follow these lines of reasoning to the limit. It will suffice to indicate in brief their application in the case of labor. The labor cost is one of the commonest elements of outgo in the income-account connected with any group of capital. For instance, whether the land is used for farming, mining, or forestry, it must be worked by human beings, and the cost of the work will materially affect the values of the three income-streams. Now the cost of that work is wages, and, to the employer, takes the form of and normally represents the discounted value of the ultimate enjoyable services to which the labor leads. Consequently, if interest varies, wages will vary. Thus, if the land is used for farming, the wages paid for planting crops will be gauged in the estimation of the farmer by discounting the value of the expected crops, and will vary somewhat according as the discounting is at 5 per cent. or 4 per cent. In like manner, the workers engaged in bridge building are paid the discounted value of the ultimate benefits which will accrue after the bridge is built; the wages of those engaged in making locomotives normally represent the discounted value of the completed locomotives, and hence (as the value of a completed locomotive is in turn the discounted value of its expected services) their wages represent the discounted value of the ultimate benefits in the series. In all these cases, the rate of wages is the discounted value of some future product, and therefore tends to decrease as interest increases. But the effects in the different lines will be very unequal. Workers whose product matures rapidly, as in the case of domestic servants and in the case of those engaged in putting the finishing touches on enjoyable goods, will have their wages comparatively little affected by the rate of interest. On the other hand, for laborers who are engaged in work requiring much time, the element of discount applied to their wages is a much more important factor. If a tree planter is paid $1 because this is the discounted value, at 5 per cent., of the $2 which the tree will be worth when matured in fifteen years, it is clear that a change in the rate of interest to 4 per cent. will tend materially to raise the value of such labor. Supposing the value of the matured tree still remains at $2, the value of the services of planting it would be, not $1, but $1.15. On the other hand, for laborers engaged in a bakery or other industry in which the final satisfactions mature early, the wages are almost equal to the value of these products. If they produce final services worth $1, due, let us say, in one year, their wages, being the discounted value of this sum at 5 per cent. per annum, would be 95 cents. Evidently in such a case a change in the rate of interest from 5 per cent. to 4 per cent. would only increase the wages from 95 cents to 96 cents.

But it is clear that such unequal effects coming from a reduction in the rate of interest, as an increase from $1 to $1.15 in one industry, and from 95 cents to 96 cents in another, could not remain permanently. For the laborers engaged in the occupations in which their work matured in a relatively short time, such as the bakers just mentioned, finding that their neighbors engaged in lengthier processes were receiving higher wages, would tend to desert their work for this more remunerative employment. The consequence would be that the amount of labor, and consequently the amount of final enjoyable income, accruing from the shorter processes would be reduced, and that from the longer processes increased. The consequence of this, in turn, would be to raise the value of the earlier enjoyable income and lower that of the later. Therefore, in the end, the change in the rate of interest from 5 per cent. to 4 per cent. would effect a redistribution in the values, not only of intermediate items of income, but in the values of the final items themselves. For the various final elements of income are bound together, as it were, by means of the competition of the preparatory services, such as those of the laborers just mentioned, and the consequent necessity of equalizing the remuneration for these preparatory services.

In short, a change in the rate of interest will affect all income-streams flowing from given instruments of capital whether these streams consist of interactions or of final services. It will affect (1) the value of interactions, like tree-planting or bread-baking. because the rate of interest enters directly into the valuation of all interactions; and (2) the value of final income, enjoyments, because many interactions, as, for instance, the services of laborers, may be used interchangeably in several different directions. The effect of a change in the rate of interest, on the value of the interactions, will naturally be the more pronounced, and will be greater in a country where lengthy processes are usually employed than in one where the shorter ones are common. If, for instance, laborers in a given country are engaged largely in building elaborate works like the Panama Canal, in planting forests, and otherwise investing for the sake of remote returns, a fall in the rate of interest will produce a considerable rise in wages; whereas, in a country where such lengthy processes are unknown and workmen are chiefly employed in tilling the ground and performing personal services, a change in the rate of interest will scarcely affect wages and the values of other preparatory services at all.

§ 15

The complete discussion of this subject would lead us to a statement of the general theory of the "price of labor" and of prices in general. For present purposes, it is only necessary to emphasize the bare fact that the range of choice between different income-streams is somewhat dependent upon the rate of interest. If the modification due to this fact were introduced into the tables previously given for the three different uses of land, we should find that the income-streams from using the land for farming, forestry, and mining would differ according to the rate of interest.

Thus, let us suppose, as before, that for a rate of interest of 5 per cent. the three optional income-streams are: —

	FORESTRY	FARMING	MINING
1st year	000	450	2000
2d year	000	450	1800
3d year	300	450	1600
4th year	400	450	1400
5th year	500	450	1200
6th year	500	450	1000
7th year	500	450	800
8th year	500	450	600
9th year	500	450	400
10th year	500	450	200
Thereafter	500	450	000

In our previous discussion, when we changed the rate of interest from 5 per cent. to 4 per cent., we supposed the figures in this table to remain unchanged. The only change we had then to deal with was the change in their present values. Now, however, we admit the possibility of a change in the table figures themselves. If the rate of interest falls to 4 per cent., the product of forest, farm, and mine will be more nearly equal to the value of the ultimate services to which they lead. The value of lumber will be more nearly equal to the value of the houses it makes, and these to the value of the shelter they give; the value of wheat from a farm will be nearer the value of the bread it will make; and the value of ore from a mine will be nearer the value of the steel it will become, and this, in turn, more nearly equal to the values of those innumerable satisfactions which come through the use of steel. These shiftings forward of the values of the intermediate income of forest,

farm, and mine toward the values of the ultimate satisfactions to which they lead, combined with possible readjustments in the values of these satisfactions themselves
—the values of house shelter, bread consumption, etc.—
will result in a change, say in the figures in the table from
those just given for 5 per cent. to the following for 4 per
cent. : —

	FORESTRY	FARMING	MINING
1st year	000	500	2100
2d year	000	500	1900
3d year	350	500	1700
4th year	450	500	1500
5th year	600	500	1300
6th year	600	500	1100
7th year	600	500	850
8th year	600	500	650
9th year	600	500	450
10th year	600	500	225
Thereafter	600	500	000

If, then, the rate is 5 per cent., the landowner will choose
that use among the three which, computing from the figures
in the *first* table, has the greatest present value; while if
the rate is 4 per cent., he will choose that which, computing
from the figures in the *second* table, has the greatest present
value.   If, then, the rate is 5 per cent., he will choose mining, since, as we saw in § 4, the present values, when we
compute at 5 per cent., are : forestry, $8820; farming, $9000;
mining, $9110; but if the rate is 4 per cent., he will choose
the highest from the present values at 4 per cent., computed
from the second table. These present values now are:
forestry, $13,520; farming, $12,500; mining, $10,100.
Thus the owner will choose forestry. It is true in this
case that the change in the range of choice does not affect
the final result. In § 4 the choice also fell on the
forestry use. The only difference is that the particular

figures of present values in our revised 4 per cent. computation are different from their values in our original 4 per cent. computation. The present values at 4 per cent. for forestry, farming, mining, respectively: —

Under our present hypothesis are	13,520	12,500	10,100
Under our former hypothesis were	11,300	11,250	9,450

But, whatever, the final outcome of all the readjustments, it is evident that the introduction of the influence of the rate of interest on the range of choice does not in any material way affect the reasoning already given in regard to the determination of interest. Since the rate of interest will itself fix the range of choice, it will still be true that, once the range of choice is fixed for a given rate of interest, the individual will choose, as before, that use which has the maximum present value. On the basis of this choice he is then led to borrow or lend in order to modify his income-stream so that his rate of time-preference may harmonize with the rate of interest. If, upon an assumed rate of interest, the borrowing and lending for different individuals actually cancel one another, — in other words, clear the market, — then the rate of interest assumed is clearly the one which solves the problem; otherwise the borrowing and lending will not be in equilibrium, and some other rate of interest must be selected. By successively postulating different rates of interest, and remembering that each rate carries with it its own range of options and its own set of present values of those options, we finally obtain that one which will clear the market.

We therefore conclude by repeating, slightly modified, the formulation of the theory stated in § 6: (1) Each individual has given a specific list of eligible optional income-streams (some of which depend upon the rate of interest); (2) The rate of preference for each individual depends upon the character of his income-stream; (3) All the individual rates of preference are, through the loan or sale market, equalized with one another and with the rate of interest; (4) Each individual selects, out of the range of choice of income-streams available at a given rate of interest, that particular one which has the maximum present value, — in other words, that one whose advantages over any other outweigh (in present value) its disadvantages, — or, in still other words, that one which compared with others makes the rate of return on sacrifice greater than the rate of interest, — or, finally (if the options are infinitely numerous), that one which compared with neighboring options makes the marginal rate of return on sacrifice equal to the rate of interest; (5) The demand and supply of loans must balance for each period of time; and (6) The loans returned must equal the loans obtained, with interest.

§ 16

Having completed the formal statement of the effect of the existence of a range of choice upon the rate of interest, it remains to point out a practical effect of such a range of choice. This effect is to diminish the fluctuations in the rate of interest. In a country where there is a large range of choice between optional income-streams, the rate of interest is apt to be steadier than in one where the income streams are relatively rigid and unalterable. If any cause tends to lower the rate of interest, the immediate effect will be to put a premium on those income-streams the return from which is in the remote future, — for instance, to put a premium on forestry uses rather than mining uses of land. But the decision to choose such income-streams tends to prevent the very fall in the rate of interest which caused the choice. For, by relatively over-supplying the future with income, and undersupplying the present, such uses as forestry will tend to raise the relative valuation of present over future income, and therefore also to raise the rate of interest. The fall, therefore, in the rate of interest which led to the choice of remoter incomes, is checked, and is not so great as it would be if no such options were open.

Conversely, a rise in the rate of interest will favor those options for which the income-streams are relatively immediate, and will bring its own check; for the choice of such an income-stream will relatively impoverish remote income and enrich immediate income, and consequently tend to diminish the premium on the latter.

The existence of a large number of available income-streams, then, acts as a balance wheel which tends to check any excessive changes in the rate of interest. Interest cannot fall or rise unduly; for any such fluctuation corrects itself through the choice of appropriate income-streams. If interest is high, descending income-streams will be chosen which tend to make interest low; while, if it is low, the reverse will be true.

We see here another reason, in addition to those given in Chapter VII, for the fact that interest does not suffer very violent fluctuations. It is not only true, as was then pointed out, that natural processes are regular enough to prevent sudden and great changes in the income-stream; but it is also true that man constantly aims to prevent such changes. Man is not the slave of Nature's income; to some extent he is her master. He has many *options* among which he may choose. He possesses, within limits, the power to flex his income-stream to suit himself. For society the flexibility is due to the adaptability and versatility of capital, — especially human capital commonly called labor; for the individual the flexibility is greater still, since he possesses a double range of choice. He may not only choose among different employments of capital, but he may choose among different ways of exchanging with other people, — he may borrow or lend, buy or sell, invest or spend. This power is virtually the power to trade in income; for under whatever form an exchange takes place, at bottom it is income, and income only, which is exchanged. In making his choice among different employments of capital, he relies on his power to remedy any undesirable time-shape, etc., by recourse to exchange. The result of the double range of choice — that between optional employments of capital and between optional modes of exchanging income — is that his income is flexible and controllable in a high degree. Not only may he select the most valuable income, but also the income which is most desirable in respect to time-shape. He need not even commit himself to a given time-shape for any great length of time, for by changing his expenditures and investments he can alter that time-shape at will.[1]

[1] For further discussion of the subject of this chapter by means of mathematics, see Appendix to Chap. VIII.

CHAPTER IX

§ 1

In order to present a full view of what is meant by "optional employments of capital," it will be worth our while to pause a moment and examine the different classes of options open to the capitalist.

Options are of three chief kinds: (1) options among employments of capital which differ in kind, as, for instance, the options previously cited of using land for mining, farming, or forestry; (2) options among employments of capital which differ in the degree of certainty, as, for instance, the choice of sailing a ship over several routes differing in the constancy of wind and current; and (3) options among employments of capital which differ in size and time-shape.

Options of the first group do not concern the theory of interest so much as the theory of prices, unless, as in the example of the mining, farming, and forestry uses of land, the optional incomes differ in time-shape as well as in the kind of service rendered. This group may be designated as options of versatility. They are most striking in the case of tools and human beings.

Options of the second class may be called options of chance. They concern the theory of insurance and speculation rather than the theory of interest, and, under the hypothesis which has thus far been maintained, that risk is absent, have no need as yet to be considered. This group of options is, however, of great practical importance. Under this head, when the options relate to contractual

178

services, comes the special case of trade options. It is to this class that the term "option" is ordinarily applied by business men, and it has been with some hesitation that it has been given a broader meaning in this book. But no better term seems available; and there is to be said, in favor of the broader use of the word, that it corresponds closely to its popular and untechnical meaning.

The third group of options is the one which specially concerns us here, and will alone engage our attention through the remainder of this chapter.

When, in Chapter VII, we explicitly excluded optional employments of capital, we thereby assumed that the income-stream was fixed both in amount and in the times when it accrued. We may pass from this case of perfect rigidity to the simplest form of option by introducing at first only one degree of flexibility. Let us suppose that the income-stream from any capital is relatively fixed in amount, and that only the time of obtaining it is controllable at will. This species of choice occurs in the case of durable goods for consumption, which neither improve nor deteriorate with time. Wheat and other grains, for instance, may be used at almost any time, with little difference in the efficiency of the use and little cost except for storage. The same is true of coal, cloth, iron, and other durable raw materials, as well as, to some extent, of finished products such as tools and machinery, though usually deterioration from rust or other injury by the elements will set in if the use is too long deferred.

Where such a range of choice exists, the possibility of obtaining an income from the capital in the future instead of in the present will have the effect of preventing the rate of interest from sinking as far as it otherwise would; for if the rate of interest is low, the tendency on the part of the investor will be to defer the use of durable goods, — wheat, for instance, — and such a decision, by increasing future income and diminishing immediate income, will tend to raise the rate of interest, or at least to check its fall. Reversely, the possibility of using such articles at the present time instead of later has the effect of preventing the rate of interest from rising as far as it otherwise would; for, should interest rise, the tendency on the part of the investor will be to more immediate employment of such durable goods as he had set apart for future use, and this decision, by relatively increasing present income and diminishing future income, will tend to reduce the rate of interest, or, at any rate, to check its rise. This is illustrated by wheat speculation. A rise in the rate of interest will check "bull" operations, since the speculator will be less willing to "lose the interest on his money." Reversely, when the rate of interest falls, wheat holding will be encouraged. Likewise land speculation is relatively easy when interest is low and difficult when interest is high.

§ 2

Under the group of options applying to durable instruments, there are many special cases. One of the most instructive is that which we might suppose if the *quantity* of income obtainable from an instrument or number of instruments were definitely fixed, but the *time* at which those services might be obtained were entirely optional. To illustrate this, uncomplicated by the presence of instruments of different types and the consequent necessity to translate the rate of interest into a common monetary standard, let us imagine a community in which the income from *all* capital is of the character just described. This society would then be endowed with a quantum of income as fixed as the quantity of money in a strong box. It could obtain all the income at once, or spread it over any number of years, but could not alter its amount either by increase or decrease, just as the owner of a strong box could take the contents all out at once, or at such times as he pleased, but could not increase or diminish the total amount. Every dollar's worth of income sacrificed from this year's income would eke out next year's income by a dollar and no more; and reversely, every dollar's worth indulged in this year would reduce by a dollar and no more the possibility of future indulgence.

Let us suppose this case realized on a desert island on which some sailors are shipwrecked and left each with 1000 pounds of hardtack and no prospect of ever improving their lot. We will suppose the use of this hardtack to be the only "real income" open to these castaways, and that they have given up hope of ever adding to it by accessions from outside or by cultivating the island (which, by our hypothesis, must be barren), the only possible variation of their income-stream — consisting of hardtack — being that produced by varying the time of its consumption. They have the option of consuming their entire store during the first year, or of spreading its use over two or more years, but in any case they will have the same total income, measured in hardtack. A little reflection will show that in such a community the rate of interest in terms of hardtack would necessarily be zero.[1] For, by hypothesis, the sacrifice of one pound of hardtack unconsumed from this year's income can only result in an equal increase in the income of future years. Therefore the *rate of return on sacrifice* is zero. Since this rate must equal the rates of preference and the rate of interest, these rates must all be zero also.

To illustrate this case by a diagram, we see, as one option, that the entire consumption of hardtack may take place at an even rate OA within the time OB (Fig. 22). The total income will then be represented by the area $OACB$. Another option is that it shall be spread over OB', double the above-mentioned time, and consumed at the rate OA', half the rate first mentioned, so that the same total amount will be represented by the area $OA'C'B'$. The choice of the second use rather than the first implies

[1] Cf. Adolphe Landry, *L'Intérêt du Capital*, p. 49; Carver, *The Distribution of Wealth*, p. 232.

the sacrifice of that part of the immediate income represented by the rectangle *AD*, but the addition of equal future income represented by the rectangle *DB'*. If the

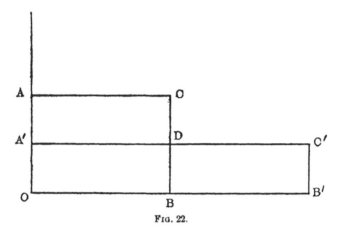

Fig. 22.

hardtack is not consumed at a uniform rate, the optional income-streams will not be represented by rectangles, but

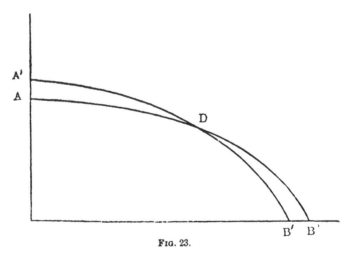

Fig. 23.

by sloping curved figures, as *ADB* and *A'DB'* (Fig. 23), which have the same area. The substitution of the alternative $A'DB'$ for ADB increases immediate income by ADA' and decreases subsequent income by the exactly equal amount BDB'.

The conclusion that the rate of interest under such conditions must be zero, is at first startling; but it is easy to convince ourselves of its correctness if we reflect that the sailors will modify the time-shape of their respective income-stream until any possible rate of preference for a present over a future allowance of hardtack disappears. It would be impossible for any would-be lender to obtain interest on his loan, for the only way in which a borrower could repay a loan would be to pay it out of his original stock of hardtack. He would not be fool enough to borrow 100 pounds to consume to-day and pay back 105 pounds at the end of a year, when he had the option to consume the 100 pounds of his own hardtack, by sacrificing only 100 ·pounds out of his own stock kept for next year. Consequently there could be no interest payable in any exchange of present for future hardtack. It is equally impossible that there should be a negative rate of interest. No one would lend 100 pounds of hardtack to-day for 95 receivable a year later, when he had the option of simply storing away his 100 pounds to-day and taking it out undiminished a year later. Hence, exchanges of present for future hardtack could not exist, except at par. There could be no premium or discount in such exchange.

Nor could there be any rate of preference for present over future hardtack. A pound of this year's hardtack and a pound of next year's hardtack would be equally balanced in present estimation; for, should a man prefer one rather than the other, he would take a pound for the preferred use away from the unpreferred, and this process would be continued until the desirability (in the present) of a pound of immediate hardtack and that of a pound of future hardtack were brought into equilibrium. Thus, if, through insufficient self-control, he foolishly prefers to use his store freely in the present and to cut down his reserve for the

213

future to a minimum, the very scantiness of the provision for the future will enhance his appreciation of its claims, and the very abundance of his provision for the present will diminish the urgency of his desire to indulge so freely in the present. Provided there is some hardtack for *both* uses, the present desire for a pound of each will necessarily be the same. Failure of such equilibrium of desire can only occur when, as in starvation, the desire for the present use is so intense as to outweigh the desire for even the very last pound for future use, in which case there will be none whatever reserved for the future. But whether the hardtack is at first abundant — for instance, enough to insure a long life — or whether starvation will necessarily follow after a year or two, the needs of the present and future will be adjusted on a basis of par price up to a point of time when the income-stream will cease. It is evident that some of the sailors, with a keen appreciation of the future, would plan to consume their stores sparingly. Others would prefer generous rations, even with the full knowledge that starvation would thereby ensue earlier; but none of them would consume all of their stock immediately, for to do so would unduly rob the future, already poorly provisioned. They would, generally speaking, prefer to save, out of such reckless waste, at least something to satisfy the more urgent needs of the future. In other words, a certain amount of saving (if such an operation can be called saving) would take place without any interest at all. This coincides with conclusions expressed by Professor Carver in his *Distribution of Wealth*.[1] It shows also that the preference for present over future goods of like kind and number is not, as some writers seem to assume, a necessary attribute of human nature, but that it depends always on the relative provisioning of the present and the future.

[1] p. 232. See also "The Place of Abstinence in the Theory of Interest," *Quarterly Journal of Economics*, July, 1894, and Fetter's *Principles of Political Economy*, New York (Century), 1904, p. 160.

§ 3

The fact that interest was bound to be zero in the case of the sailors just discussed, was due to the extreme adjustability of the time of receiving the given income. To see this clearly, let us next consider the case of an income-stream which, as before, is of a fixed amount, and the times of receiving which, though capable of being postponed as far as desired, are not capable of being hastened beyond a certain limit; the income, in other words, is fixed and sure, but comes slowly. Approximately such a case is found in mining.[1] The total yield of a mine is practically fixed by the ore deposits which it contains. It is like the chest of money; just so much as it contains can be taken from it, and no more. But it is unlike the chest of money in that its contents cannot be extracted as fast as desired. The ore at the top must be removed before that beneath can be reached. Time for mining operations is required. Nature is slow in yielding up her treasures. This *slowness of Nature*, in view of man's impatience to exploit her, will give rise to a rate of interest.

It is as though the hardtack of our shipwrecked sailors had in some way been stored in a series of storehouses, each provided with a time lock arranged to open at a certain date. There is a definite amount of income, but it is only available at intervals. Under these circumstances, unless the time locks are timed to open as fast as the castaways would have chosen of themselves to eat their stores, the hardtack of to-day and of next year will no longer exchange at par. There will be a premium on present hardtack as compared with future hardtack, the amount of the premium depending on the relative provisioning of the various storehouses, — in short, on the size and time-shape of the

---

[1] Strictly speaking, of course the total product and total expense of exploiting a mine will vary somewhat with the rate of extraction. An animated discussion of the most profitable rate of extraction was carried on in *The Engineering and Mining Journal*, New York, 1904.

income-stream as made available by the time locks. The case will be practically the same as though the income-stream were rigid, as in Chapter VII; for the only option is to postpone the consumption of these provisions, and this option would not, under the circumstances, be exercised.

We see, therefore, that in order that a positive rate of interest shall emerge, it is only necessary that income shall sufficiently hold back its flow. It is not necessary that Nature should be reproductive, as Del Mar and George maintain. Interest would exist even if there were no growing animals and plants, but only a world of minerals and other fixed stores to be extracted by man, provided only Nature were slower than we could wish in admitting us to her stores. In fact, if we were asked to state in a word why there is interest, we should reply, because Nature is slow and keeps man waiting.

§ 4

But while the slowness of Nature is a sufficient cause for interest, her productivity is an additional cause. This brings us to our next class of options, the class, namely, in which, if present income is sacrificed for the sake of future income, the amount of the latter secured thereby is greater than that of the former sacrificed. The income which we can extract from our planet is not, in the aggregate, a fixed quantum, as is that part of it which comes from mines, but is obtainable in larger amounts for the remote future than for the present. Nature is reproductive and tends to multiply. Growing crops and animals make it possible to endow the future more richly than the present. By waiting, man can obtain from the forest or the farm more than he can by premature cutting or the exhaustion of the soil. In other words, not only the slowness of Nature, but also her productivity or growth, has a strong tendency to keep up the rate of interest. Nature offers man, as one of her optional income-streams, the possibility of great future abundance at trifling present sacrifice. This option acts as a bribe to man to sacrifice present income for future, and this tends to make present income scarce and future income abundant and hence also to create in his mind a preference for a unit of present over a unit of future income.

§ 5

We next consider the case of an option the exact reverse of the preceding, — the case in which, if present income is sacrificed, the amount of future income obtained thereby is less than the amount sacrificed to obtain it. This is true of the income from perishable goods.

Suppose our sailors were left, not with a stock of hardtack, but with a stock of figs which deteriorate at the foreknown rate of 50 per cent. per annum. In this case the rate of interest would be necessarily *minus* 50 per cent. per annum, as may be shown by the same reasoning that established the zero rate in the former case. The possibility of such negative interest has been discussed in a previous chapter.[1] When goods are perishable the tendency is to preserve them by cold storage, preservatives, etc., so as to extend their use into the future. This is an effort to create a new optional employment for those goods.

Some goods, then, like grain for food, and cloth, may be indiscriminately applied to the present or future without either loss or gain; others, like grain for seed, breeding animals and plants, gain in income power with time; and still others, like meat and fruit, lose.

The resultant is that, for income as a whole, taking man and Nature as they are, it is impossible to sacrifice future income for present very far without selling one's birthright for a mess of pottage, or, to make use of another phraseology, without killing the goose that lays the golden egg. Thus Nature, by her productivity, stimulates man to self-denial, and by her slowness she compels it. Were the

[1] Chap. V, § 5.

world in which we live neither slow nor reproductive, but simply an open storehouse of wealth, two things would happen which we saw in the case of the shipwrecked sailors. One is that the rate of interest would be zero, and the other is that man, however frugally he consumed his stores, must ultimately perish.

§ 6

In the foregoing cases the options consisted of different employments of instruments of capital which were assumed to retain their physical identities throughout the period of those employments. If now we regard an instrument or group of instruments of capital as retaining its identity through renewals or repairs, we introduce another large and important class of options; namely, the options of making those renewals and repairs, or not making them, or making them in any one of many different degrees. If the repairs are just sufficient for the up-keep they may be called renewals; if more than sufficient, they may be called betterments. We shall include all these alterations wrought upon an instrument in the same category. They are alterations in the form, position, or condition of an instrument or group of instruments which affect the stream of services which that instrument or group will yield. This class of optional employments, when the employment of the capital involves sales, merges imperceptibly into the special case which we originally called the method of modifying an income-stream by buying or selling. Thus, consider a merchant who buys and sells rugs. His stock of rugs is conveniently regarded as retaining its identity, although the particular rugs in it are continually changing. This stock yields its owner a net income equal to the difference between the gross income, consisting of the proceeds of sales, and the outgo, consisting chiefly of the cost of purchases, but including also cost of warehousing, insurance, wages of salesmen, etc. If the merchant buys and sells equal amounts of rugs and at a uniform rate, his stock of rugs will remain constant and its income to be credited to that stock will normally be equal to the interest upon its value. It will be standard income.[1] But the owner has many options. He may choose to enlarge his business as fast as he makes money from it, in which case his net income will be zero for a time, but his stock will increase and his ultimate income will be larger. In this option, therefore, his income-stream is not constant, but ascends from zero to some figure above the "standard income" of the first option. A third option is gradually to go out of business, by buying less rugs than are sold, or none at all. In this case the income at first is very large, as it is relieved of the burden of purchases; but it declines gradually to zero. In the interstices between these three options there are, of course, endless intermediate options. The merchant thus has a very flexible income-stream. If the expenses and receipts for each rug bought and sold are the same whichever option is chosen, and if the time of turnover is also the same, it will follow that all of the options possess the same present value and differ only in desirability. We should then be dealing with that special class of options which we found open even in the case of rigid income-streams, — what we then called modifications of the income-stream through buying and selling. The reason for placing optional employments of capital on a different footing is that they do not all possess the same present value. In actual fact, the rug merchant, and merchants in general, would not find that all the optional methods of proportioning sales and purchases of merchandise possessed equal present values; for if he attempted to enlarge his business too fast he would find that his time of turnover would be lengthened, and if he reduced it too fast he would find that

---

[1] The case of evenly reconstituted capital is emphasized in J. B. Clark's writings, *e.g. The Distribution of Wealth*. New York (Macmillan), 1899; see *The Nature of Capital and Income*, Chap. XIV, § 4.

his selling expenses per unit of merchandise would be increased. There is for each merchant, at any time, one particular line of business policy which is the best; namely, that which will yield him the income-stream having the maximum present value. It is his interest to choose this policy and to relieve himself of any resulting inconvenience in the time-shape of his income-stream by borrowing and lending or by buying and selling. Since, therefore, the various methods of renewing one's capital usually yield income-streams differing in present value, they resemble what we have called optional employments of capital and may be properly classed as such.

§ 7

The propriety of such a classification becomes still more evident when, instead of renewals, we consider repairs and betterments; for it is clear that the income from a farm has a very different present value according as it is tilled or untilled, or tilled in different degrees of intensity; that the income from a house so neglected that a leak in the roof or a broken window pane results in injuring the interior is less valuable than the income it would yield if properly kept up; and that real estate may be under-improved or overimproved as compared with that degree of improvement which secures the best results.

In all cases the best results are secured when that series of renewals, repairs, or improvements is chosen which renders the present value of the prospective income-stream a maximum. This, as we have seen, is tantamount to saying that the renewals, repairs, or improvements are carried up to the point at which the return which they bring is equal to the rate of interest. The owner of a carriage, for instance, will replace a broken spoke, because the cost of doing so will prolong the life of his carriage so far as to earn much more than the interest upon the trifling cost of the spoke. This repair may cost him $1 and may save him $20. But so high a

220

rate of return as these figures imply cannot be expected from every repair, and after the really necessary repairs are made, it soon becomes a question to what extent it is worth while to keep a carriage in repair. Repainting, revarnishing, and resetting the tires are all costly, and though in every case the service of the carriage is increased in quantity and improved in quality, the return grows less and less as the owner strives after increased efficiency. He will spend money on his carriage in repairs and renewals up to that point where the last increment of repairs will secure a return which will just cover the cost with interest; beyond this he will not go.

§ 8

Another case of optional income-streams is found in the choice between different *methods* of production, especially between different degrees of what has been called "capitalistic" production. It is always open to the prospective housebuilder to build of stone, wood, or brick; to the prospective railroad builder to use steel or iron rails; to the maker of roads to use macadam, asphalt, wood, cobble, brick, etc., or to leave the earth unchanged except for a little hardening and rolling. The choice will in all cases depend on the principles which have been already explained.

For another example, the services of a house which has a durability of 60 years will, compared with one which has a durability of 30 years, be equivalent to the services of two houses, one built to-day and lasting 30 years, and the other built at the expiration of that period and lasting 30 years more. The difference between the one long-lived house and the two short-lived houses is thus not in the services, but in the cost of construction. The cost of constructing the 60-year house occurs in the present; that of the two successive 30-year houses occurs half in the present and half at the end of 30 years. In order that the more durable house may have the advantage as to cost, the excess of its cost over the cost of the first of the less durable ones must be less than the present value of the cost of the second, deferred 30 years.

The choice between different instruments for effecting the same purpose may, of course, depend on their relative efficiency, — the *rate* of flow of income, or upon their relative durability, — the *time* of the flow. It is true, however, as John Rae has pointed out,[1] that efficiency and durability usually go hand in hand. A house which will endure longer than another is usually more comfortable also; a tool which will cut better will wear out more slowly; a machine which does the fastest work will generally need to be strong and therefore lasting.

The alternatives constantly presented to most business men are between policies which may be distinguished as temporary and permanent. The temporary involves the use of easily constructed instruments which soon wear out, and the permanent policy involves the construction at great cost of instruments of great durability. When one method of production requires a greater cost at first and yields a greater return afterward, it may, conformably to popular usage, be called the more "capitalistic" of the two. In other words, "capitalistic" methods of employing capital are those which tend toward an ascending income-stream. The title "capitalistic" is not a happy one, although it has some justification in the fact that an ascending income-stream means the accumulation of capital, or "saving," and still more in the fact that only a capitalist can afford to choose a method of production which at first yields little or no income, or even costs some outgo; for without capital no one could subsist, or at any rate subsist with comfort, in the interim. It is clear that the capitalist who thus subsists on his accumulations does so by possessing, or becoming possessed of, a descending income-stream. It is therefore as a possessor of *income* that he is enabled to subsist while waiting for the returns from his new venture.

[1] *The Sociological Theory of Capital*, p. 47.

He is enabled to invest in an ascending or slowly returning income-stream by having at command a descending or
quickly returning income-stream. We may say, therefore,
that a "capitalistic" method is a method requiring an
ascending income-stream, and it is so called because it is
open only to those who have command of other and
descending income-streams, such persons being necessarily
capitalists.

§ 9

The best example of the choice between those uses of
capital affording immediate and those affording remote
returns is found in the case of human capital, commonly
called labor. Man is the most versatile of all forms of
capital, and among the wide range of choices as to the best
disposition of his energies is the choice between using them
for immediate or for remote returns. This choice usually
carries with it a choice between corresponding uses of
other instruments than man. To choose to plant a tree for
the sake of fruit ten years hence, rather than to plant corn
for the sake of next year's crop, is to make choice of different uses of land as well as of labor. But the existence of
optional employments of labor, however inextricably bound
up with optional employments of other instruments,
deserves mention both because of its importance and because it usually supplies the basis for the optional employments of other forms of capital.

It is, in fact, almost exclusively through varying the
employment of labor that the income-stream of society
as a whole is capable of changing its time-shape. The
individual may modify the time-shape of his particular
income-stream through exchange, but in this case the person
who exchanges with him must modify his income-stream in
the opposite manner, and the two modifications cancel each
other in the total of the world's income. But if an income
is modified in time-shape through a change in the exertions

223

of laborers, there is no such offset, since the total social income is actually modified also.

The labor of a community is exerted in numerous ways, some of which bring about enjoyable income quickly, others slowly. The labor of domestic servants is of the former variety. The cook's and waitress's efforts result in the enjoyment of food within a day. Within almost as short a time, the chambermaid and the laundress promote the enjoyment of house, furniture, and clothing. The baker, the grocer, the tailor, are but one step behind the cook and laundress; their efforts mature in enjoyments within a few days or weeks. And so we may pass back to labor increasingly more remote from enjoyable income, until we reach the miner whose work comes to fruition years later, or the laborer on the Panama Canal, whose work is in the service of coming generations.

The proportions in which these various kinds of labor may be assorted vary greatly, and it is through this variation that the income-stream of the community changes its time-shape. If there are at any time relatively few persons employed as cooks, bakers, and tailors, and more as builders, miners, and canal diggers, there will tend to be less immediately enjoyable income and correspondingly more enjoyable income several years later. By withdrawing labor from one employment to another it is in the power of society to determine the character of its income-stream not only in time-shape, but also in size, composition, and uncertainty. This power is exerted through the entrepreneur or "enterpriser" [1] according to his estimate of what return will come from each particular employment taken in connection with the sacrifice involved and the ruling rate of interest. Upon his judgment depends the future of society's income, and — since capital merely represents expected income — its future capital. If his judgment is good and he diverts labor from domestic service and the production

[1] See Fetter, *The Principles of Economics*, New York (Century), 1904, Chap. XXIX.

of commodities for immediate service to the construction
of great engineering projects such as the tunnels to connect
Manhattan Island with the mainland, he is increasing
future income at the sacrifice of immediate income, and
at the same time accumulating capital. If, on the
contrary, he makes opposite choice of the employment of
labor, the opposite results will follow. Should his judgment be at fault in either case, to that extent will the
results stated fail to be achieved. His task is one of much
responsibility and great moment for the welfare of the
world. The great majority whose interests he sup-
posedly serves are almost as much dependent on his good
judgment as are the passengers in a railway train dependent for their safety on the good judgment of the
engineer.

§ 10

Since the choice, for an individual, among different options,
depends on the rate of interest in the manner described
in Chapter VIII, it is clear that a low rate favors the choice
of ascending income-streams, but also that the choice of
such income-streams reacts to raise the rate of interest.
If, on the contrary, the rate is high, the opposites of both
these propositions hold true. Thus, applying these principles to the question of repairs, renewals, and improvements, it is evident that the lower the rate of interest, the
better can the owner afford to keep his carriage in repair,
and the higher the state of efficiency in which it and all
other instruments will be kept. But it is equally clear that
the very attempt to keep instruments up to the highest
level of efficiency tends, in turn, to increase the rate of interest; for every repair means a reduction in present income for the sake of future — a shifting forward in time
of the income-stream — and this will cause a rise in the rate
of interest. Thus, any fall in the rate of interest, by stimulating repairs, renewals, and betterments, will bring its

own correction through oversupplying future income at the expense of immediate income.

Again, it is evident that a choice of the more durable instruments, as compared with those less durable, will be favored by a low rate of interest, and a choice of short-lived instruments will be favored by a high rate of interest. If the rate of interest should fall, there would be a greater tendency to build stone houses as compared with wooden. The present value of the prospective services and disservices of stone houses as compared with wooden would be increased; for although stone houses are more expensive at the start, they endure longer, and their extra future uses, which constitute their advantage, will have a higher present value if the rate of interest is low than if it is high. We find, therefore, as John Rae has so well pointed out, that where the rate of interest is low, instruments are substantial and durable, and where the rate of interest is high they are unsubstantial and perishable. In this case, as in the preceding cases, the low rate of interest leads to a choice which shifts the income-stream forward in time, and thus tends to raise the rate of interest, and *vice versa*.

In general, then, a low rate favors the choice of "capitalistic" methods of production. The construction of a substantial bridge which will never wear out is more likely to pay if the rate of interest is low than if it is high; for the lower the rate of interest, the higher will be the present value of the remote income which the permanent structure commands. Reciprocally, the more "capitalistic" the production, the greater the tendency to raise the rate of interest; so that the existence of numerous options has a regulative effect. Beyond the margin of choice there always lie untouched options ready to be exploited the instant the rate of interest falls. Among these, as Cassel[1] has pointed out, are waterworks of various kinds. Not only the canals of stupendous size but hundreds of less con-

---

[1] *The Nature and Necessity of Interest*, London (Macmillan), 1903, p. 122.

spicuous waterways are subjects of possible investment ; among the lesser ones are the Elbe and the Erie canals; and there might be built numerous others as soon as the rate of interest falls low enough to make the return upon cost equal to the rate of interest. The same is true of the improving, dredging, and deepening of harbors and rivers, the use of dikes and jetties, and the construction of irrigation works for arid lands.

There is still room for much improvement in our railway systems by making them more efficient and more durable, by making the roads straighter, the roadbeds more secure, the rolling stock heavier, the bridges larger and stronger, etc. In a new country where the rate of interest is high and the return on sacrifice precarious or small, the cheapest and most primitive form of railway is first constructed. Very often it is a narrow-gauge road with many curves, costing little to construct, but much to operate. Later, when the rate of interest falls, or the traffic so increases that the rate of return on sacrifice is greater, the broad-gauge comes into use and the curves are eliminated. This is the kind of change which has been proceeding in this country with great rapidity during recent years. There is a transition from relatively small first cost and large running expenses to precisely the opposite type of plant, in which the cost is almost all initial and the expense of operation relatively insignificant.

CHAPTER X

INVENTION

§ 1

EVERY range of choice is of necessity a range of choice among *known* options; consequently the range of choice will change as human knowledge is enlarged and increased through invention and discovery. In the matter of transportation, man originally had no choice but to walk. Afterward, when he learned how to domesticate animals, the use of horses for riding purposes opened a new and more rapid method of locomotion. Still later, owing chiefly to the invention of the wheel, the use of vehicles drawn by horses was introduced, then the construction of rails on which vehicles should run brought a fourth method. And now, with modern technical knowledge, each of the foregoing options is split up into a number of subordinate options; there is the possibility of street transit by surface, elevated, or subway transportation, and the surface transit may be by railway, trolley, automobile, vehicles of various kinds, bicycle, or the primeval method of walking.

When a new invention thus enlarges the range of choice, the new options introduced may be effectual or ineffectual, —generally the latter. The great majority of patents do not pay the cost of procuring them. The reason for this is that when it comes to exploiting the new option, the rate of expected return on cost is found to be less than the rate of interest. Where the opposite is true the invention is effectual, and leads not only to a change in the range of options, but also to a change in the selection among them.

When inventions thus result in a new option—in other words, when it is profitable to exploit them, —the effect necessarily is, for a time, to reduce the immediate income-stream of the community, for the sake of increasing the remoter income-stream.　The deferred increase is expected to yield a return on the immediate sacrifice at a rate sometimes far greater than the rate of interest.　But this high rate of return on sacrifice to the exploiter of the newly discovered method of utilizing capital does not by itself fix the rate of interest at that level.　On the contrary, the valuation of the property is immediately readjusted to the new conditions.　Those who are first to enter the new field, or, in the slang of business, "come in on the ground floor," will obtain a return on their investment far greater than the rate of interest.　But they will immediately value their property in accordance with its expected productivity, and the rate of interest on loan contracts will be but slightly raised.　The effect in raising interest comes merely from the shifting forward of the income-stream, which leaves the immediate income smaller than before, but compensates for this by a still greater increase afterwards. For, as we have seen, when an income-stream is of ascending type, the rate of interest, for contracts connecting the periods of scarce income and those of plentiful income, tends to be high.

§ 2

But, although the effect of the invention is to tilt social income into the ascending form, the individual who exploits the process may, by the methods of borrowing and lending or buying and selling already explained, rectify his distorted income curve.　He may, if he desires, restore his income curve to the very same time-shape that it had before his investment in the new enterprise.　In this case it will be higher than before, all along the line.

Thus, if his original income curve were AB in Figure 24, and the exploitation of the new invention required, for a certain period, a sacrifice tilting his income curve to the position of the dotted line $A''CB''$, he might, by borrowing, obtain the income $A'B,'$ which has the shape of his original income curve AB, but exceeds it all along the line. Thus, the final effect of the investment is to enlarge the income of the investor. Provided he can borrow against the antici- pated returns, not only need he not suffer any temporary

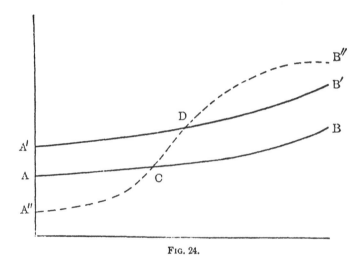

Fig. 24.

reduction in income from the necessity of investing in his new enterprise, but he may even be enabled to enjoy a larger income from the outset.

But if those who exploit the new invention make little or no sacrifices in their immediate income, others must; and these are they whose savings meet the cost of exploi- tation. Since the invention will more than repay this cost (whether or not to those who incur it does not matter), the effect will be to decrease immediate and increase remote income for society as a whole. Borrowing and lending merely distribute the pressure upon those most willing to bear it; but the effect is necessarily, for society, to cause a temporary depression followed by an ascent of the income-stream, and therefore to increase somewhat the rate of time-preference and the rate of interest.   The inventions of Watt and others, which led to the present railway system, are cases in point.   They caused the income-stream of society, from being fairly uniform, to assume a rapidly ascending form.   The earliest investors were compelled to make great sacrifices, and afterwards, when the fruits of their labors began to come in, they were often foregone for the sake of yet greater and more remote returns. Throughout the period of railroad building, social income has been a series of investment, return, and partial reinvestment, and a curve which would depict the actual income enjoyed would show it to be sharply ascending. Numerous other inventions have coöperated to this end. A whole series of new appliances have followed the discovery of electricity.   The elevator and the steel skeleton have revolutionized the art of building.

In consequence of the ascending time-shape of the income-stream, the rate of interest has been kept up.   It is not sufficient, therefore, to say with Rae, that the high rates of return on sacrifice offered by the new inventions have directly raised the rate of interest.   These very high returns were secured only by a few.   They are out of proportion to the rates of interest ruling on loans, or the rates of interest realized to the ordinary investor.   These latter are the rates of interest in the true sense of the word, and they were raised for the ordinary investor, because he was called to the aid of those who were in a position to secure the exceptionally high returns, and had, therefore, temporarily, to sacrifice income.   The result is a general rise in the rate of interest, and in consequence a revaluation of investment securities, and, in fact, of all capital.   The value of capital sinks as the rate of interest rises, assuming that the value of the income from the capital remains the same.

§ 3

This revaluation applies also to the very capital in which the new invention or discovery is embodied.   If it is found that a million dollars invested in a newly discovered gold mine will result in a yield of ten millions a year, that mine will no longer sell for its cost, but for a sum far above it. It is the relation of the income to the new value of the mine, and not its relation to the old value, which will reflect the true rate of interest. So, also, a new machine may at first return an enormous rate of profit on its cost, — far higher than the rate of interest; but soon the price of the machine in relation to the value of its services will be adjusted to the rate of interest.

The same principle holds of all new enterprises. The original investors in The Bell Telephone Company realized returns far beyond the interest on their investment; but the present investor pays a price for Bell Telephone stock commensurate with its dividends.

The effect of a new invention on the rate of interest is therefore registered, not by the original rate of return on sacrifice to the lucky "insiders," but by the rate realized to the investor who comes in later and invests at market prices. These prices, in the case of successful inventions, will be far in excess of the cost.

New devices will also cause a revaluation of the older ones which they have displaced, but in this case the new values are lower than before. The buzz saw rendered nearly valueless the mill plants equipped in the older methods, and the band saw had the same effect with reference to the buzz saw. Hand looms and presses became junk or curiosities after the advent of steam looms and presses, and the first forms of the latter have in turn been superseded.

The reasons for these reductions in value are simple. Each new process produces a larger supply of the particular kind of service rendered. The price of this service — e.g. sawing or printing — is reduced, and consequently the capitalized value of the given amount of such service which can be expected from the older devices is reduced, and often so far reduced as to make the reproduction or even the repair of these older instruments wholly unprofitable.

232

§ 4

The subject of the economic effect of invention, and particularly of its effect upon the rate of interest, has been fully treated by John Rae, and to him the reader of this book is referred for extended study.[1] There is one point, however, which Rae apparently did not observe, certainly did not emphasize, and that is the *temporary* nature of the effect of invention in raising the rate of interest. The effect in raising interest lasts only so long as |the resulting income-stream is sufficiently distorted in time-shape to be of a decidedly ascending type. This period may be called the period of investment or exploitation, during which society is sacrificing present income, or, as it is inaccurately called, "investing capital." Society, instead of confining its productive energies to the old channels and obtaining a relatively immediate return in enjoyable income, as by producing food products, clothing, etc., directs its labor to great engineering enterprises such as constructing tunnels, subways, water works, and irrigation systems, that is, to instruments which cannot begin to contribute a return in inenjoyable income for many years. In contemplation, future income, during this period, is relatively plentiful, and in consequence of these "great expectations," the rate of interest will be high.

Later, however, there will come a time when the income-stream ceases to ascend, when all the necessary investment has been completed, when no further exploitation is possible, and when it is only necessary to keep up the newly constructed capital at a constant level. When this period is reached, the after effect of the invention will be felt. Society will then have a larger income-stream than before, but no longer an ascending one. A mere increase in the *size* of the income-stream, while its *shape* remains constant, has the effect, as we have seen, not of increasing, but of somewhat decreasing the rate of time-preference. Con-

[1] *The Sociological Theory of Capital.*

sequently the after effect of all inventions and discoveries is not to increase but to decrease the rate of interest. Thus, the railway inventions have led to a half century of investment in railways, during which the income-stream of society has been constantly on the increase. To-day, however, the limit of steam railway investment has been nearly reached in some places, and in others the rapidity of investment is perceptibly slackened. Railroads have been an outlet for the investment of savings, and have tended to supply for them a good return. As the necessity for new railroads becomes less, this outlet diminishes, and the rate of interest falls.

But while the after effect of an old invention is to reduce the rate of interest, it may, of course, be true that *new* inventions will be made rapidly enough to neutralize this tendency. It is only when there is a cessation in the world's output of new inventions that the rate of interest is thus apt to fall back, but whenever invention is active it rises. It thus rises and falls according as the introduction or the exploitation of inventions is active or inactive.

The same principles apply not only to invention in the narrower mechanical sense, but also to scientific and geographical discoveries. The unearthing of a new bed of ore, as in Cripple Creek, Alaska, or South Africa, has as its immediate effect the necessity for a considerable depression in the immediate income-stream of those who desire to exploit the new territory, but offers the prospect of very great increase in the future; consequently, the rate of interest in such instances tends to be very high. After the period of exploitation, however, the income curve ceases to rise and begins to fall. Thereupon the rate of preference for present over future income assumes the opposite tendency, and the rate of interest declines.

§ 5

It has not been the purpose of this chapter to investigate the general effect of inventions, but merely their effect on

the rate of interest.   Before leaving the subject, however,
it should at least be stated that invention is the basis of
progress in civilization.   The inventions of fire, the alpha-
bet, and the means of utilizing power — first of animals,
then of wind and water, then of steam and electricity —
and their manifold applications, especially to transportation
and communication, have made it possible for the earth
to support its increasing population, and deferred the
Malthusian pressure upon the means of subsistence; they
have made possible the stable existence of great political
units such as the United States; and they have given opportunity for the presentation, diffusion, and increase of
knowledge in all its forms of art, literature, and science.
And thus it happens that invention is self-perpetuating.
For not only has science sprung from inventions such as the
printing press, the telegraph, and specific scientific instruments for observation, like microscopes and telescopes, or
for measurements, like chronographs, balances, and microme-
ters; but modern science is now in turn yielding new
inventions.   Helmholz's researches in sound led to the
telephone; Maxwell's and Hertz's researches on ethereal
waves led to wireless telegraphy.   Nations like the United
States and Germany will lead in civilization by taking the
greatest advantage of this self-propagating principle of
invention; and nations like China, which give it the least
attention, will lag behind.

The conditions for the most rapid multiplication of inventions are: (1) personal efficiency, dependent on breeding,
hygienic habits, and the education (both general and technical) of the faculties; and for this the Greek motto "a
sane mind in a sane body" is in point; wherefore Galton
seems to show that in Greece genius was far more common than in modern civilization; (2) the ease of diffusion
of knowledge; (3) the size of the population within which
the diffusion occurs, —the larger the population the greater
being the number of inventive geniuses, the greater their
incentive, and the wider their sphere of influence; (4) the

encouragement of invention through patent protection, and more especially through the early discovery and approval of genius. Inventors are at once the rarest and most precious flower of the country. Too often they are crushed by the obstacles of poverty, prejudice, or ridicule. While this is less so to-day than in the days of Roger Bacon or Galileo, it still requires far too much time for the Edisons or the Burbanks to get their start. The decades in which these rare brains are doing their wonderful work are at most few, and it is worth many millions of money for their countrymen to set them to work early. As Huxley says, it should be the business of any educational system to seek out the genius and train him for the service of his fellows; for whether he will or not, the inventor cannot keep the benefits of his invention to himself. In fact, it is seldom that he can get even a small share of the benefits. The citizens of the world at large are the beneficiaries, and being themselves not sufficiently clever to invent, they should at least be sufficiently alive to their own interest to subsidize the one man in a million who can.

CHAPTER XI

THIRD APPROXIMATION TO THE THEORY OF INTEREST
(ASSUMING INCOME UNCERTAIN)

§ 1

UP to this point we have ignored the element of chance, by assuming that the entire future income-stream, or at any rate, such portions of it as need to influence present choice, are foreknown and mapped out in advance. In the preceding chapter, we have assumed inventions to be *surprises*, — sudden enlargements of knowledge coming upon us without previous anticipation. In other words, we have assumed that men disregard future inventions and act as though their knowledge of the future were perfect. This assumption, like the assumption that bodies fall *in vacuo*, in the ordinary presentation of the theory of gravitation, has enabled us to complete our formal statement of the theory more easily, although at the expense of exact conformity to actual historical fact; for, in the concrete world, the most conspicuous characteristic of the future is its uncertainty. Consequently the introduction of the element of risk will give, as by magic, the aspect of reality. The general principles which have been stated, however, will still hold true when we assume uncertainty instead of certainty; they merely require to be supplemented by other principles.

One consequence of changing our assumption as to the certainty of future events is to compel the abandonment of the idea of a single rate of interest. Instead of a single rate of interest representing the rate of exchange between this year and next year, we now find a great variety of rates according to the risk involved. The rate in every loan contract is adjusted on the basis of the degree of security given. Thus, security may be furnished by simple indorsement of reputable persons, in which case the degree of security will be the greater the larger the number of indorsers and the higher the credit which they possess; or it may be by the deposit of collateral securities. The necessity of the latter operation will affect a man's ability to borrow, and limit the extent to which he may modify his income-stream by this means. It will not be possible, as hitherto assumed, for a man to modify his income-stream at will, but only up to the limit of his credit. In consequence of this limitation upon his borrowing power, he may not succeed in modifying his income-stream sufficiently to bring the rate of preference between present and future income down to the rate of interest ruling in the market; and for like reasons, he may not succeed in bringing the rate of return on sacrifice into conformity with the rate of interest.

One feature of this limitation is the fact that the ability to borrow depends, not so much on the amount of capital which the would-be borrower possesses, as on the form in which that capital happens to be. Some securities are readily accepted as collateral, and accepted for a high percentage of their face value, whereas others will pass with difficulty and only for a low percentage. The recent tendency to change the organization of business to the corporate form has had a striking effect in increasing the power to borrow. Whereas formerly many businesses were conducted as partnerships and on a small scale, numerous stocks and bonds have now been substituted for the old rights of partnership and other less negotiable forms of security; hence the possessors of these securities have wider opportunities to deposit collateral, and the tendency to borrow has received a decided impulse. This explains to a large extent the investing and speculative mania which followed the recent widespread consolidation and formation of trusts.

Where the security does not exist in the convenient form of written certificates, there is often considerable difficulty in negotiating a loan.   If commodities are used for security, they must ordinarily be themselves deposited with the lender, — in other words, put in pawn.   Where the borrowing takes place in pawn shops, it is not because of the inadequacy of the security, but because of its inconvenient form, that the rate of interest is usually very high.   The pawnbroker will need to charge a high rate of interest, partly because he needs storage room for the security he accepts, partly because he needs special clerks and experts to appraise the articles deposited, and partly because, in many cases, he needs to find a market in which to sell them when not redeemed.   He is, moreover, able to secure these high rates partly because pawnbroking is in bad odor, and those who go into it therefore find a relative monopoly; and partly because of the fact that the customers usually have, either from poverty or personal peculiarity, a relatively high valuation of present over future income.   The effect of their flocking to the pawn shop is to reduce this high valuation; but it will not reduce it to the general level in the community, because these persons do not have access to the loan market in which the ordinary business man deals.   To them, undoubtedly, the fact that they cannot borrow except at high or usurious rates is often a great hardship; but it has, as one beneficent effect, the discouragement of getting unwisely into debt.   Those who patronize pawn shops to a large extent do so because they possess little foresight and self-control, and the impediment which they find in the shape of a high interest rate in a measure takes the place of the self-control and foresight which they should possess.   Were it possible for this class to borrow at lower rates, many of them would sink even more deeply into debt than they actually do.   Thus, if slavery were legalized and it were possible for a man to mortgage the income from his own labor, it is unfortunately true that many would avail themselves of this privilege, and would drop to the lowest place in the economic scale,— slavery. The fact that such contracts are illegal fixes a limit below which the ordinary ne'er-do-weel cannot fall. At this point his rate of preference for present over future is not in harmony with the rate of interest in the community. When the market rate of interest is 5 per cent., he may feel a rate of preference of 25 per cent.

§ 2

We find, therefore, that the introduction of the element of chance, and the necessity of overcoming it by the giving of security, has as one of its effects the splitting up of the market into a number of sub-markets. Instead of one huge market in which there is a single rate of interest, to which every individual conforms his own rate of preference, we now find a number of separate markets, a number of different rates of interest, and a very imperfect adjustment of the individual rates of preference to those rates.

We need here to emphasize the distinction between a commercial rate of interest which includes risk and a pure or riskless rate of interest.[1] The commercial rates vary widely, although the range of variation for rates on loans easily negotiable is relatively small. In ordinary real estate mortgages in the same market the range of variation is seldom over 1 per cent.

If we pass from explicit interest, or the rate of interest involved in a loan contract, to implicit interest or the rate involved in purchases and sales of property of various kinds, we see again that the greater the risk the higher the "basis" on which a security will sell. A "gilt-edge" security may sell on a 3 per cent. basis, when a less known or less salable security will be selling on a 6 per cent. basis. The element of risk will affect also the value of the collateral securities. Their availability for this purpose will increase their sala-

[1] See Glossary under "Basis"; also *The Nature of Capital and Income,* Chap. XVI.

bility and enchance their price. On the other hand, when, as in times of crises, the collateral is imperatively demanded, it often happens that, for purposes of liquidation, it is sold at a sacrifice.

In the same way that risk causes the rates of explicit interest in a community to diverge from each other, or causes rates of preference to separate from rates of interest, it will cause the rates of implicit interest to diverge. The same individual who would borrow, if he could, at 25 per cent., but who lacks the necessary security, must devote his energies instead to acquiring or producing instruments which will have a return on sacrifice at the 25 per cent. level. Although it would be more economical, if he could only borrow the money, to build durable houses, he will build inferior ones. Hence the anomaly, that even in countries where the rate of interest is low, there will be primitive communities in which the instruments possessed, in the form of dwellings, tools, implements, etc., are far less substantial than is compatible with the low rate of interest.

§ 3

Among other phenomena which follow from the existence of risk are the variations in the duration of loans. Where the future is regarded as safe, loan contracts tend to be longer in time than otherwise. Railway and government securities are thus often drawn for half a century or more. On the other hand, to provide for the uncertainty of the immediate future, the "call loan" is devised. This is a loan which has no specified due date, but can be demanded at the option of the lender whenever some circumstance makes this course advisable. A loan contract of this kind brings the burden of risk on the borrower and relatively relieves the lender, and in consequence, under such conditions, the rate on call loans will usually tend to be low.

The same principles will explain the low rate of implicit interest in many cases. Where a security, because it is well known, or for any other reason, has a high degree of salability, that is, can be sold on short notice without great sacrifice, the price will be higher than otherwise, and the rate of interest it yields will therefore be low. Hence it is that the rate of interest on individual mortgages will be higher than the rate of interest on more marketable securities. It is usually considered an advantage to any stock to be listed on the stock exchange; for, being thus widely known, should the necessity arise to sell it, there will be found a more ready market.

The most salable of all properties is, of course, money; and as Karl Menger has pointed out, it is precisely this salability which makes it money. The *convenience* of being able, without any previous preparation, to dispose of it for any exchange, is itself a sufficient return upon the capital which a man keeps in this form, and takes the place of any rate of interest in the ordinary sense of a money payment.

§ 4

A further consequence of the introduction of the element of risk is the wide divergence between the actual rate of return realized by an investor and the expected rate. When risk was regarded as absent, it was assumed that the expected always happened; but in the actual world this is far from true. Those who invested in some of the mining "bonanzas" many years ago have received a rate of return of many hundred per cent.; and far in excess of the rate of interest which they would have been willing to take for a loan. Reversely, those who invested in the South Sea Bubble found an opposite disparity between their expectations and their realizations. Risk is especially conspicuous at the time of new inventions or discoveries. Almost all prediction is based on a belief in the repetition of past experience; but at these times, past experience is a poor guide. When new inventions are made, uncertainty is introduced, speculation follows, and after that, great wealth or ruin. The history of gold and silver discoveries and of the invention of rubber, steel, and electrical appliances, is filled with tales of thousands of wrecked fortunes, by the side of which tower the fortunes of to-day's *nouveaux riches*.

The rate of interest is always based upon expectation, however little this may be justified by realization. Man makes his guess of the future and stakes his action upon it. In his guess he discounts everything he can foresee or estimate, even future inventions and their effects. In a recent estimate of the value of a copper mine, allowance was made for future economies from inventions which might reasonably be expected. So, also, the buyer of machinery allows not simply for its depreciation through physical wear, but for its being possibly superseded. New investments in steam railroads are to-day made with due regard to the possibility that the road may within a few years be run by electricity. It may easily happen that in a country consisting of oversanguine persons, or during a period when business men are overhopeful, the rate of interest will be higher than the event justifies. It is probable that, in ordinary communities, realization justifies the average expectation; but in the individual case this is not always true, otherwise there would be no risk. Risk is due to partial knowledge. Our present acts must be controlled by the future, not as it actually is, but as it looks to us through the veil of chance.

§ 5

In the preceding section we discussed the effect of risk on the pseudo- or impure rate of interest;[1] that is, the rate on unsafe investments. But even the pure rate of interest, or the rate on safe investments, is affected by risk. The effect is different according to the various conditions which may influence the rate of preference for

[1] See *The Nature of Capital and Income*, Chap. XVI, § 8.

present over future income. Where the risk relates to
human life, the rate of preference for present over future
income is increased.[1] Consequently the rate of interest,
even on safe loans, will be raised by the existence of
such risk. The man who looks forward to a short or
precarious existence will be less likely to make permanent
investments, or, if he makes them, less likely to pay a high
price for them. Only a low price, that is, a high rate of
interest, will induce him to invest. When the risk relates,
however, not to the duration of life, but to the income-
stream, the effect upon the rate of interest will depend
upon which portion of the income-stream is subject to
risk. If the immediately ensuing income is insecure,
whereas the remoter income is sure, the rate of preference
for immediate as compared with remote income will, as was
shown, be high, and consequently the effect of such a risk
upon the rate of interest will be to raise it. But if, as is
ordinarily the case, the risk applies more especially to the
remoter income than to immediate, the effect is the exact
opposite; namely, to lower the rate of interest on a safe
loan. This is, perhaps, the typical case. If a man regards
the income for the next few years as sure, but is in doubt as
to its continuance into the remoter future, he will be more
keenly alive to the needs of that future, and will consequently
have a less keen preference for the present. He will then
be willing, even at a very low rate of interest, to invest, out
of his present assured income, something to eke out the less
sure income of the future. The effect of risk in this case,
therefore, is to lower the rate of interest on safe loans,
though at the same time, as already explained, it will raise
the rate of interest on unsafe loans. Consequently, in times
of great social unrest and danger, we witness the anomalous
combination of high rates where inadequate security is
given, coexistent with low rates on investments regarded
as perfectly safe. In commercial language, when an
investor cannot find many investments into which he may

---

[1] Cf. Carver's *The Distribution of Wealth*, p. 256.

put his money without risk of losing it, he will pay a high price for the few which are open to him. It has been noted in times of revolution that some capitalists have preferred to forego the chance of all interest and merely hoard their capital in money form, even paying for storage charges, which amounts to a negative rate of interest.

§ 6

When risk thus operates to lower the rate of interest on safe investments and to raise the rate on unsafe investments, there immediately arises a tendency to differentiate two classes of securities and two classes of investors, — precarious securities and adventurous investors on the one hand, and safe securities and conservative investors on the other. Risk is inevitable in every business, but is regarded by most people as a burden; hence the few who are able and willing to assume this burden become a separate class. To-day, when any enterprise is organized in corporate form, it is usual to recognize this tendency by dividing the securities into stocks and bonds, the stockholder being the person who assumes the risk and, theoretically at least, guarantees that the bondholder shall be free of all risk. Which persons shall fall into the class of risk takers and which not, is determined by their relative coefficients of caution,[1] as well as by the relative degree of risk which an enterprise would involve for the various individuals. The same enterprise may be perilous to one and comparatively safe to another, because of superior knowledge or other conditions; and the same degree of risk may repel one individual more than another, owing to differences in temperament, or, most important of all, differences in amount of capital.[2]

This shifting of risk from those on whom it bears heavily to those who can best assume it, discloses another motive

[1] See *The Nature of Capital and Income*, Chap. XVI, § 6.
[2] *Ibid.*, Appendix to Chap. XVI, p. 409.

for borrowing and lending besides those which were discussed
in a previous chapter. Lending, in modern finance, often
indicates not simply a difference in time-shape as between
two income-streams, but also a difference of risk. The object
of lending which was emphasized in earlier chapters, before
the risk element was introduced into the discussion, was
to alter the time-shape of the income-stream, the borrower
desiring to increase his present income and decrease his
future, and the lender desiring, on the contrary, to decrease
his present income and add to his future. But the stockholder and bondholder do not differ in this way so much
as in respect to risk. They are both investors, and
stand in a very similar position as to the effect of their
investment on the time-shape of their income. For the
stockholder, however, there is a risk attached to his income-
stream from which the bondholder is relatively free. It
is this difference in risk which is the primary reason for
the distinction between stockholders and bondholders.
The bondholder "commutes" [1] his chance of a high income
for the certainty of a steady income.

The existence of this risk, tending, as we have seen, to
raise the rate of impure interest and lower that of pure
interest, has as its effect the lowering of the price of stocks
and the raising of the price of bonds from what would have
been their respective prices had the risk in question been
absent. On the other hand, the separation of the investors
into stockholders and bondholders reacts upon the prices
of stocks and bonds and tends to lessen the disparity
between them. Were there no bonds, but only stocks, the
price of the stock would have to be lower than it now is,
in order to induce the timid investor to buy. In other
words, the effect of the separation between risky and safe
investments is at once to moderate the lowness of the low

---

[1] Cf. Hadley, *Economics*, p. 270. The rate of interest, however,
is not, properly speaking, the rate of commutation; for the rate of
commutation would be the ratio between the average earnings of the
stockholder and the average earnings of the bondholder, whereas
the rate of interest is the ratio between income and capital.

rate on safe investments and the height of the high rate on the unsafe investments.

The same tendency, to reduce the disparity between the rates of interest on safe and unsafe investments, grows out of the practice of *insurance*. One effect of insurance [1] is to raise the value of capital subject to risk of fire or other insurable risks, by consolidating those risks and thus virtually reducing them. But this rise in the value of capital implies a reduction in the rate of interest which it yields. Again, the effect of *speculation*, by setting aside a certain class of persons to assume the risks of trade, has the effect of reducing these risks by putting them in the hands of those who have most knowledge; for, as we have seen, risk varies inversely with knowledge. In this way the whole plane of business is put more nearly on a uniform basis so far as the rate of interest is concerned.

§ 7

We see, then, that the element of risk introduces disturbances into those determining conditions which were expressed in previous chapters as explaining the rate of interest. To summarize these disturbances, we may apply the risk factor to each of the six conditions which were originally stated as determining interest. We shall find that its effects are as follows: —

1. The condition that each individual has a given range of choice still holds true, but these choices are no longer confined to absolutely *certain* optional income-streams, but include options with risk. That is, each individual finds open to his choice a given set of options which differ in size, time-shape, composition, and *risk*.

2. Rates of preference for present over future goods are of two kinds, according as the goods are comparatively certain or uncertain. The marginal rate of preference for a *certain* present over a *certain* future good, or the *pure* rate

[1] See *The Nature of Capital and Income*, Chap. XVI.

of time-preference, depends upon the character of the total income-stream, — not only its size, shape, and composition, but also and particularly upon the degree of certainty attaching to various parts of it and the degree of certainty of life of the recipient. Again, the preference rate for present *certain* income as compared with future *uncertain* income, or the *impure* rate of time-preference, will, in normal individuals, be greater than if both incomes were certain, and will be the greater, the higher the risk and the higher the caution in assuming it.

3. Pure rates of time-preference (as among *certain* goods) in different individuals tend toward equality by the practice of borrowing and lending, and more generally, buying and selling; but this equality is not in all cases attainable, because of limitations on the freedom to modify the income-stream at will. These limitations grow out of the existence of the element of risk. There are various means of reducing or avoiding risk, — in particular, by the devices of collateral security, indorsement, underwriting, etc., but all of these processes have more or less definite limitations. In consequence, it is not always possible to provide security for as large a loan as would be necessary to change the income-stream enough to reduce the rate of preference of the borrower to the rate of interest. If the security is adequate, the rate of preference will be equalized with the rate of interest; if not, it will remain above it. Where the security introduces impediments which affect the lender as well as the borrower, it will also happen that the rate of interest will be raised, as in the case of pawn shops which hold in pledge their motley assortment of cumbersome merchandise. Thus, instead of one rate for several loans, there will be a number of separate rates and a number of separate markets, according to the nature of the security asked and given.

At the same time there will be a tendency to ask and receive loans with inadequate security. This introduces a pseudo- or impure rate of interest which will be above the pure rate by a margin differing according to risk and caution.

4. When risk was left out of account, it was stated that from among a number of different alternatives the individual would select that one which had the maximum present value, — in other words, that one which, compared with its nearest neighbors, possessed a rate of return on sacrifice equal to the rate of preference, and therefore to the rate of interest. When the risk element is introduced, it will still be true that the maximum present value is selected; but in translating future uncertain income to present cash value, use must now be made of the probability and caution factors. One consequence is that when we express this principle of maximum present value in its alternative form in terms of the "marginal rate of return on sacrifice," we must qualify this expression as the "marginal rate of *anticipated* return on sacrifice." The rate of return on sacrifice which will be actually realized may turn out to be widely different from that originally anticipated.

5. In the former approximations, where the element of risk was considered absent, it was shown that the aggregate modification of the income-streams of individuals for every period of time was zero. What was borrowed equaled what was lent, or what was added by sale was equal to what was subtracted by purchase. The same principle still applies; for what one person pays, another person must receive.

6. In the former approximations, the total present value of the projected modifications of one's income-stream was zero; that is, the present value of the loans equaled the present value of the borrowings; or the present value of the additions and subtractions due to buying and selling balanced each other. In our present discussion, in which future income is recognized as uncertain, this principle still holds true, but only in the sense that the present market values balance at the moment when the future loans or other modifications are planned and decided upon. The

fact that risk is present may lead to a wide discrepancy between the original expectation and the actual realization. In liquidation there may be default or bankruptcy. When the case is not one of a loan contract, but relates merely to the difference in income-streams of two kinds of property bought and sold, the discrepancy between what was expected and what is actually realized may be still wider. But, *viewed in the present*, the estimated value of the future return is still the equivalent of the sacrifice. The present value of a future uncertain event is equal to its mathematical value multiplied by a caution factor,[1] and the mathematical value is equal to the expected value multiplied by a probability factor and discounted according to the rate of preference for present over future income.

§ 8

We thus see that instead of the series of simple equalities which we found to hold true in the vacuum where risk was absent, we have only a *tendency* toward equalities, interfered with by the limitations of the loan market, and therefore resulting in a series of *in*equalities. Rates of interest, rates of preference, and rates of return on sacrifice are only ideally, not really, equal.

We conclude by summarizing in the following table the interest-determining conditions for our three successive approximations: —

[1] See *The Nature of Capital and Income*, Chap. XVI, § 6.

FIRST APPROXIMATION	SECOND APPROXIMATION	THIRD APPROXIMATION
[1. Each individual has a *rigid* and unalterable *certain* income-stream except by exchange.]	1. He has the choice of any one from among a specific list of eligible *certain* income-streams (some of which may depend on the rate of interest).	1. He has the choice of any one from among a specific list of eligible *uncertain* income-streams (some of which may depend on the rate of interest).
2. His preference rate depends on that income-stream as modified by exchange.	2. His preference rate depends on his certain income-stream as (1) selected and (2) modified by exchange.	2. His preference rate depends on his uncertain income-stream as (1) selected and (2) modified by exchange.
3. Preference rates of different individuals become equal to the common rate of interest.	3. Preference rates of different individuals become equal to the common rate of interest.	3. Preference rates of different individuals tend toward a common rate of interest.
[4. The individual, having no choice, accepts the income-stream given.]	4. The individual selects, from the eligible list, the income-stream which possesses the maximum present value. If the alternatives are numerous and vary continuously from each other, this condition is equivalent to the condition that the marginal *rate of return on sacrifice* shall equal the rate of interest.	4. The individual selects, from the eligible list, the income-stream which has in present estimation, whether truly or falsely, the maximum present value. If the alternatives are numerous and vary continuously from each other, this condition is equivalent to the condition that the marginal rate of *estimated* return on sacrifice shall equal the rate of interest.
5. The modifications, through exchange, of the income-streams at the *same* time for *different* individuals mutually cancel one another for each separate time interval.	5. The modifications, through exchange, of the income-streams at the *same* time for *different* individuals mutually cancel one another for each separate time interval.	5. The modifications, through exchange, of the income-streams at the *same* time for *different* individuals mutually cancel one another for each separate time interval.
6. The modifications, through exchange, of the income-stream of the *same* individual through *different* time periods mutually cancel one another in present value.	6. The modifications, through exchange, of the income-stream of the *same* individual through *different* time periods mutually cancel one another in present value.	6. The modifications, through exchange, of the income-stream of the *same* individual through *different* time periods mutually cancel one another in *estimated* present value.

In the first approximation, conditions 1 and 4 are inserted to complete the correspondence with the other two approximations; but they are both really the same condition, and merely reëxpress the hypothesis under which the first approximation was made. It is the remaining four conditions which are of real significance.

The first two approximations were, of course, merely preparatory to the third, which alone corresponds to the actual world of facts. Yet the other two approximations are of equal importance with the third from the point of view of analysis. They tell us what *would* happen *if* future income were (1) fixed and certain, and (2) flexible but certain; and to know what would happen under these hypothetical conditions enables us better to understand what does happen under actual conditions, just as the knowledge that a projectile would follow a parabola if it were in a vacuum, and that it would follow a certain other curve if in a still atmosphere of given density, enables the student of practical gunnery better to understand the actual behavior of his cannon balls. In fact, no scientific law is a perfect statement of what *does* happen, but of what *would* happen *if* certain conditions existed which do not actually exist.[1] Science consists of the formulation of hypothetical sequences, not of historical facts; though by successive approximations the hypotheses may be made nearly to coincide with reality.[2]

[1] See the writer's "Economics as a Science," *Science*, August 31, 1906.
[2] See Appendix to Chap. XI, § 1.

PART IV. Conclusions

CHAPTER XII

§ 1

HAVING shown how the rate of interest is determined, we have reached the goal which we have set ourselves in the present book. But, though this goal marks the end of the present inquiry, it is also the starting-point for other economic inquiries of the greatest importance. We cannot attempt in this book to explore the fields which would thus open out, but in the present chapter we shall indicate briefly what they are.

The rate of interest plays a central rôle in two great branches of economic science, — the theory of prices, and the theory of distribution. The rôle of the rate of interest in the theory of prices applies to the determination of the price of wealth, property, and services.

As was shown in *The Nature of Capital and Income*, the price of any article of wealth or property is equal to the discounted value of its expected future services. If the value of these services remains the same, a rise or fall in the rate of interest will consequently cause a fall or rise respectively in the value of all instruments of wealth. The extent of this fall or rise will be the greater the further into the future the services of wealth extend.[1] Thus, land, from which services are expected to accrue uniformly and forever, will be doubled in value if the rate of interest is halved, or halved in value if the rate of interest is doubled. In the case of dwellings, however, the life of which is limited, if the rate of interest is doubled, the price of

[1] See *The Nature of Capital and Income*, Chap. XIII.

225

dwellings will fall less than half, and if the rate of interest is halved, the price of dwellings will rise to less than double. In the case of furniture the fluctuations in value will be even less extensive, and so through the list of less durable commodities, such as clothing, to those of very perishable types, such as food, the value of which will not be sensibly affected by a variation in the rate of interest.

§ 2

As to the influence of the rate of interest on the price of services, we first observe that services may be intermediate or final.[1] The value of intermediate services or "interactions" is derived from the succeeding future services to which they respectively lead. For instance, the value to a farmer of the services of his land in affording pasture for sheep will depend upon the discounted value of the services of the flock in producing wool. If he rents the land, he will calculate what he can afford to pay for it on the basis of the value of the wool which he would expect to obtain from his flock. In like manner, the value of the wool-output to the woolen manufacturer is in turn influenced by the discounted value of the output of woolen cloth to which it contributes. In the next stage, the value of the production of woolen cloth will depend upon the discounted value of the income from the production of woolen clothing. Finally, the value of the last named will depend upon the expected income which the clothing will bring to those who wear it, — in other words, upon the use of the clothes.

Thus the final services, consisting of the use of the clothes, will have an influence on the value of all the anterior services of tailoring, manufacturing cloth, producing wool, and pasturing sheep, while each of these anterior services,

[1] See *The Nature of Capital and Income*, Chap. IX. The subject has already been referred to in the present volume, Chap. VIII.

when discounted, will give the value of the respective capital which yields them; namely, the clothes, cloth, wool, sheep, and pasture. We find, therefore, that not only all articles of wealth, but also all the *intermediate* services ("interactions") which they render, are dependent upon final enjoyable uses, and are linked to these final uses by the rate of interest. If the rate of interest rises or falls, this chain will shrink or expand. The chain hangs, so to speak, from its final link of enjoyable services, and its shrinkage or expansion will therefore be most felt by the links most distant from these final services. A change in the rate of interest will affect but slightly the price of making clothing, but it will affect considerably the price of pasturing sheep.

A study, therefore, of the theory of prices involves (1) a study of the laws which determine the final services on which the prices of anterior interactions depend; (2) a study of the prices of these anterior interactions, as dependent, through the rate of interest, on the final services; (3) a study of the price of capital instruments and capital property as dependent, through the rate of interest, upon the prices of their services. The first study, which seeks merely to determine the laws regulating the price of final services, is relatively independent of the rate of interest. The second and third, which seek to show the dependence on final services of the anterior services and of the capitals which bear them, involve and depend upon the rate of interest. Under this second study will fall, as a special case, the study of the determination of economic rent, both the rent of land and the rent of other instruments of wealth. Thus, the rent of the pasture referred to, consisting, as it does, of the value of the services of pasturing, is dependent, through the rate of interest, upon the discounted value of the future final services to which the land contributes. It is clear, then, that the rent of the land is partly dependent upon the rate of interest, and that the same dependence applies to the rent of any other instrument.

§ 3

Similar considerations apply to the determination of the rate of wages. So far as the employer is concerned, the payment of wages to a workman represents the value of his services. These services are interactions or intermediate services leading to some future enjoyable service. Thus, the shepherd hired by the farmer to tend the sheep in the pasture renders services the value of which to the farmer is estimated in precisely the same way as the value of the services of the land which he hires. It follows that the rate of wages is dependent upon the rate of interest, and, conformably to the previous reasoning, the dependence of wages on the rate of interest is the more pronounced the more remote are the ultimate services to which the work of the laborer leads. As stated in Chapter IX, in a community where the workmen are largely employed in enterprises requiring a long time, such as digging tunnels and constructing other great engineering works, the rate of wages will tend to fall appreciably with a rise in the rate of interest, and to rise appreciably with a fall in the rate of interest; whereas in a country where the laborers are largely engaged in personal services or in other work which is not far distant from the final goal of enjoyable services, a change in the rate of interest will affect the rate of wages but slightly.

What has been said, however, applies only to wages from the standpoint of the employer. The rate of wages is dependent upon supply as well as demand; that is, upon the willingness of the workman to offer his services, as well as upon the desire of the employer to secure them. From the standpoint of the laborer, wages constitute an incentive to exertion or labor. This exertion is, as we have seen, a final disservice, and its value is not determined by the rate of interest in the manner of services which are intermediate. It is a great mistake to treat the subject of wages, as many authors do, exclusively from the employer's standpoint.

Our purpose here, however, is not to enter into an extended discussion of the theory of wages, but merely to show at what points in that theory the rate of interest enters, and at what points it does not enter.

§ 4

The second great branch of economics to which the rate of interest applies is the theory of distribution. In the classical political economy, the relation of the rate of interest to distribution was entirely misconceived. Distribution was erroneously regarded as a separation of the income of society into "interest, rent, wages, and profits." By "interest" of course was meant, not the rate of interest, but the rate of interest multiplied by the value of the capital "yielding interest." But we have seen that the value of the capital is found by taking the income which it yields and capitalizing it by means of the rate of interest. To reverse this process, and obtain the income by multiplying the capital by the rate of interest, is proceeding in a circle. The result of multiplying capital by the rate of interest, i.e. income, is not really a complex product of two factors, but, on the contrary, is the single original factor, — income. We have seen in this book that it is this income which affords the basis for the determination of the rate of interest, and, through the rate of interest, of capital value. The income-stream of society is the ultimate and basic fact from which the whole economic fabric should be constructed. All of this income springs from capital-wealth, if land and man are included in that term, or if not, from capital and man, or capital, land, and man. It may all be capitalized, and hence, if we follow the definition of capital adopted in this book, it may all be regarded as interest upon the capital-value thus found. Hence "interest" is not a part, but the whole, of income. It includes what is called rent and profits, and even wages; for the income of the workman may be capitalized quite as truly as the income of land or machinery. Thus, so far from having "interest, rent, wages, and profits" as mutually exclusive portions of income, we see that "interest" includes all four. The error of the classical economists and of their modern followers in distinguishing between interest, rent, etc., as separate but coördinate incomes, is partly due to the failure to perceive that whereas all income springs from capital-wealth, yet capital-value springs from income.

Another oversight closely associated with the last is that by which rent and wages were conceived as determined independently of the rate of interest, whereas we have just seen that the rate of interest enters as a vital element into the determination of both.

We shall, therefore, in discussing the theory of distribution, abandon the "classical" point of view entirely. And little regret should be caused by such abandonment, for the concept of distribution which the classical economists have given us is quite incompatible with the ordinary conception of the term. The phrase "distribution of wealth" implies ordinarily, or should imply, the problem of the relative wealth of individuals, — the problem of the rich and the poor.[1] But the separation of the aggregate income into four abstract magnitudes has little to do with the question of how much income the different individuals in society receive. Were it true that society consisted of four independent and mutually exclusive groups, — laborers, landlords, entrepreneurs and capitalists, — the fourfold definition would have some connection with the actual distribution of wealth. But, in fact, the entrepreneur is almost invariably a "capitalist"; *i.e.* is the owner of other capital than land; the "capitalist" is frequently a landlord, or *vice versa;* and even the laborer is to-day often a small capitalist. It is true that a century ago in England the lines of social classification corresponded roughly and to some extent, at least, with the abstract divisions into which

[1] Cf. Edwin Cannan, " The Division of Income," *Quarterly Journal of Economics*, May, 1905.

economists separated income; but this fact is of interest only in explaining historically the origin of the classical theory of distribution.[1]

§ 5

Turning to the true problem of distribution, that of determining the amounts of capital and income possessed by different individuals in society, we find that economists have contributed extremely little to its solution. A statistical beginning has been made by Professor Pareto in his interesting "curves of distribution of income,"[2] in which he shows the surprising result that in all cases where figures are available, the relative distribution of incomes is fairly uniform in different times and places. So far as the philosophical theory of distribution is concerned, the only writer who seems to have contributed materially to the subject is John Rae.[3] He showed that persons who had naturally what we have called in this book a low rate of preference for present over future income tended to grow rich, whereas those who had the opposite trait tended to grow poor.

We saw in a previous chapter that the rates of preference among different individuals were equalized by borrowing and lending or buying and selling. In the case of an individual whose rate of preference for present enjoyment was unduly high, we found that he would contrive to modify his income-stream by increasing it in the present at the expense of the future. We were then intent on studying this phenomenon only on the side of income; but the effect on capital can be easily seen by applying the principles of *The Nature of Capital and Income*, Chapter XIV. If a modification of the income-stream is such as to make the present rate of realized income exceed the "standard"

[1] Cf. Edwin Cannan, *loc. cit.*
[2] *Cours d'Économie Politique*, Vol. II, Lausanne, 1897, Book III.
[3] *The Sociological Theory of Capital*, Chap. XIII.

income, capital must be depleted to the extent of the excess, and the individual will grow poor. This may be brought about by borrowing immediate income and paying future income, or by selling those instruments the income of which is far distant, and buying those which have more immediate returns. Individuals of the type of Rip Van Winkle, if in possession of land and other durable instruments, will either sell or mortgage them in order to secure the means for obtaining enjoyable services more rapidly. The effect will be, for society as a whole, that those individuals who have an abnormally low appreciation of the future and its needs will gradually part with the more durable instruments, and that these will tend to gravitate into the hands of those who have the opposite trait. By this transfer an inequality in the distribution of capital is gradually effected, and this inequality, once achieved, tends to perpetuate itself. The poorer a man grows the more keen his appreciation of present goods is likely to become. When once the spendthrift is on the downward road, he is likely to continue in the same direction. When he has succeeded in losing all his capital except his own person, the process usually comes to an end, because society, in self-protection, decrees that it shall go no further. But where there is no such safeguard, the unfortunate victim may sink into even lower stages of debt servitude, as in Java[1] or Russia. Reversely, when the accumulator is well advanced in his accumulations, his rate of preference for the present diminishes still further, and accumulation becomes still easier. Hence, in some countries the rich and poor come to be widely and permanently separated, the former constituting a hereditary aristocracy and the latter a helpless and degraded peasantry.

Fortunately, however, another factor enters which tends to counteract these tendencies. This is the effect of habit. It has already been noted that one's rate of preference for

[1] See Prof. Clive Day, *The Dutch in Java*, New York (Macmillan), 1904, Chap. X.

present over future income, given a certain income-stream, will be high or low according to the past habits of the individual. If he has been accustomed to simple and inexpensive ways he finds it fairly easy to save and ultimately accumulate a little property. The habits of thrift being transmitted to the next generation result in still further accumulation, until, in the case of some of the descendants, affluence or great wealth may result. Reversely, if a man has been brought up in the lap of luxury he will have a keener desire for present enjoyment than if he had been accustomed to the simple living of the poor. The effect of this factor is that the children of the rich, who have been accustomed to luxurious living and who have inherited only a fraction of their parents' means, will, in attempting to keep up the former pace, be compelled to check the accumulation and even to start the opposite process of the dissipation of their family fortune. In the next generation this reverse movement is likely to gather headway and to continue until, with the gradual subdivision of the fortune and the increasing reluctance of the successive generations to curtail their expenses, in the third or fourth generation there comes a return to actual poverty. It thus often happens that there is a tendency for the accumulation and dissipation of wealth to occur in cycles. If there is the conjunction of favorable circumstances, as thrift, ability, and good fortune, a few individuals will rise from the lower ranks. They accumulate a few thousand dollars, which, under like favoring circumstances, in the next generation or two may become several millions. Then the unfavorable effects of luxury begin, and in an equal number of generations the majority of the heirs have returned to the level at which their ancestors began. An old adage has stated this observation in the form, "From shirt sleeves to shirt sleeves in four generations." This cyclical movement is more apt to occur in countries like the United States, where, owing to the rapidly changing conditions, there is a larger number of opportunities either for rising or falling in the economic scale. Where, as in the older countries of Europe, conditions have become fixed and less favorable to changes of any kind, the tendency of the distribution of wealth is to remain relatively unchanged. This is especially true where, as in England, the customs as to the inheritance of property have tended to keep large fortunes intact in the hands of the eldest son.

§ 6

In the general causation of distribution which has thus been outlined, the central rôle is played by the individual rate of preference for present over future income, which, as we have seen, is the subjective prototype of the rate of interest. The study of the theory of interest, therefore, lays the foundation for a study of the theory of distribution. The objective rate of interest represents the norm to which the individual adjusts his rate of preference for present over future income, and in this adjustment he changes his economic status for better or worse. The existence of this general market rate of interest to which he adjusts his rate of preference supplies an easy highway for the movement of his fortune in one direction or the other. If an individual has spendthrift tendencies, their indulgence is facilitated by access to a loan market; and reversely, if he desires to save, he may do so the more easily if there is a market for savings. The irregularities in the distribution of capital are thus due to the opportunity to effect exchanges of parts of the income-stream separated in time. The rate of interest is simply the market price for such exchange. By means of this market price, both those who wish to barter present for future income and those who wish to do the reverse, may satisfy their desires. The one will gradually increase, and the other decrease, his capital. If all individuals were hermits, it would be much more difficult either to accumulate or to dissipate fortunes, and the distribution of wealth would therefore be much more even.

Inequality arises out of the exchange of income, carrying some individuals toward wealth and others toward poverty. The inequality of wealth is facilitated by the existence of a loan market. In a sense, then, it is true, as the socialist maintains, that inequality is due to social arrangements; but the arrangements to which it is due are not, as he assumes, primarily such as take away the opportunity to rise in the economic scale; they are the contrary arrangements which facilitate both rising and falling, according to the choice of the individual. The improvident sink like lead to the bottom. Once there, they or their children find difficulty in rising. Accumulation is a slow process, and especially slow when the great numbers of the poor have, by competition, reduced the values of their services so low that the initial saving becomes almost impossible.

This is not the place for following out these tendencies and their sociological effects, nor need we stop to answer the many questions which arise in such an inquiry, such as, What is the effect of a change in the rate of interest in stimulating or discouraging the accumulation or dissipation of capital?[1] Or, What is the effect on the poor of the luxurious habits of the rich? Nor are we concerned with the other factors which influence the distribution of wealth, but which do not involve the rate of interest. We are at present content merely to prepare the way for their answer by indicating the nature of the problems and the relation of the theory of interest to them.

[1] See E. C. K. Gonner, *Interest and Saving*, London (Macmillan), 1906.

CHAPTER XIII

APPLICATION TO ACTUAL CONDITIONS

§ 1

WE have now completed the formal statement of our theory of interest. It remains to show in what way this theory may be brought into connection with actual experience. For this purpose we need first to classify the various forms which interest takes.

We have seen that the rate of interest discloses itself in two ways; namely, as explicit and implicit interest. We begin with explicit interest, or the interest in a loan contract. From the standpoint of the borrower, loan contracts may be classified as follows:—

LOANS
- For private purposes
  - To offset misfortune or improvidence.
  - To offset fluctuations in income and outgo.
  - To anticipate improvement in financial condition.
- For public purposes (municipal, etc.)
  - For military purposes.
  - To offset fluctuations in revenue and expenses.
  - For public improvements.
- For business purposes
  - Short or periodic loans
    - Crop liens.
    - Commercial paper.
    - Accommodation paper.
    - Call loans.
  - Long or permanent loans
    - Mortgages on farms.
    - Mortgages on city real estate.
    - Mortgage bonds of corporations.
    - Debentures of corporations.

236

266

Private loans are loans of individuals for personal purposes other than those arising out of business relations.   Of these, loans contracted because of misfortune or improvidence, though to-day constituting a very small fraction of total indebtedness, represent probably the original type of loan. It was against such loans that the biblical, classical, and mediæval prohibitions and regulations were directed, and it is only against them to-day that, in enlightened communities, regulations affecting the rate of interest still survive.   It is such loans that supply most of the business to pawn shops, the patrons of which are usually victims of misfortune or improvidence.   It is clear that the theory of interest which has been propounded applies to this species of loan.   Sickness or death in one's family, or losses from fire, theft, flood, shipwreck, or other causes, make temporary inroads upon one's income.   It is to tide over such a stringency in income that the loan is contracted. It ekes out the less adequate income of the present by sacrificing something from the more adequate income expected in the future.   Similar principles apply to the spendthrift, who, though not a victim of accidental misfortune, brings misfortune upon himself.   He borrows in order to supplement an income inadequate to meet the requirements which he has set himself, while he trusts for repayment to the shadowy resources of a distant future.   It is evident, therefore, that the loans just described are made for the sake of correcting an income curve the time-shape of which is inconvenient or intolerable.

The second class of personal loans comprises those growing out of such fluctuations in income as are not due to misfortune or improvidence.   Many persons receive their money-income in very irregular and unequal instalments, while their money outgo may likewise have an irregular time-schedule.   Unless the two sides of the account happen to synchronize, the individual will be alternately "short" and "flush."   Thus, if he receives his largest dividends in January, but has to meet his largest expenses, let us say taxes, in September, he is likely to borrow at tax time for the ensuing four months, in anticipation of the January dividends. That is, he borrows at a time when his income-stream would otherwise be low, and repays at a time when it would otherwise be high. The effect is to level up the fluctuations of his income.

The third class of personal loans comprises those which grow out of large expected additions to income. Heirs to a fortune sometimes borrow in anticipation of their bequests. A considerable volume of such loans has undoubtedly been contracted, especially in Great Britain. The borrower in this case is evidently trying to enjoy in the present some of the income which is promised for the future; in other words, to alter the time-shape of his income-stream in accordance with his desires. The same motives actuate young men preparing for life, and explain the loans which are often contracted by them for defraying the expenses of education. It was for such persons that Benjamin Franklin left his peculiar bequests to the cities of Philadelphia and Boston in 1790. To each he bequeathed £1000 to be lent out in small sums at 5 per cent. to young married "artificers." The sums repaid were to be added to the fund and again lent.

§ 2

In the case of public loans, we find the same general principles in operation which we have just seen to apply to private loans. By a public loan is meant a loan contracted by a public corporation or association, such as a state, county, municipality, school district, or other administrative unit, as well as such quasi-public institutions as churches, hospitals, and public libraries. Public loans may be subdivided into three classes: (1) those growing out of military exigencies; (2) those growing out of fluctuations in income; (3) those growing out of need for public improvements.

The first class, loans for war and war preparation, corresponds to the case first considered under private loans, —

loans growing out of misfortune.   Ordinarily the expenses
of government are defrayed out of taxes, which constitute
a regular deduction from the incomes of the taxpayers;
but war brings with it extraordinary expenses which must
be met by extraordinary means.   If the cost of war were
wholly defrayed by taxes, the taxpayers would suffer large
and sudden reductions in their incomes for the time being.
They prefer instead to place some of the burden on the
future, — even upon posterity.   This is accomplished by
war loans, to be repaid many years after the war is over.
Thus, so far as the taxpayers are concerned, the expense
of the war is spread over a considerable time, and the immediate reduction in their income-stream, which would
otherwise be caused by the war, is avoided.   But for the
world as a whole this is not true; for others than the taxpayers, namely, the bondholders, must bear the brunt of
the reduction in the world's income-stream which the war
has brought about.   It follows that the issue of bonds has
as its ultimate effect, not a postponement of the cost of the
war, but its shifting from one class to another.   We thus
see that war loans clearly exemplify the theory of loans
which has been elaborated.   The need for such loans grows
out of an impending depression in the income-stream of
the taxpayers.

The second class of public loans, namely, loans due to
fluctuations in public receipts and disbursements, corresponds to the second class of private loans.   A government
receives its income chiefly in taxes, and only once a year,
whereas its outgo occurs day by day and month by month.
It thus happens that a government is alternately accumulating a large surplus and suffering a large deficit.   The inconvenient effects of this have been often commented upon,
especially in this country, where the Treasury for half a
century has been relatively independent of institutions
of credit.[1]   This inconvenience may be largely avoided by

[1] See David Kinley, *The Independent Treasury of the United States*,
Boston (Crowell), 1893.

a business relation between the government and some institutions of credit, as, for instance, in England, between the government and the Bank of England. The government may correct the irregularities in its income-stream either by borrowing for current expenses in anticipation of taxes, or by lending at interest; that is, depositing the taxes when first received, in anticipation of the expenses which follow.

The third class of public loans comprises those for public improvements, such as the erection of government buildings, the improvement of roads, bridges, and harbors, the construction of municipal waterworks or schoolhouses, or the prosecution of other government enterprises. In all such cases it is usual to finance the enterprise by issuing bonds. The reason clearly is that these improvements constitute an extraordinary cost, similar to the expense of a war, which, without the issue of bonds, would cause a temporary depression in income-streams. The taxpayers as a whole cannot afford the first heavy drain, even with the prospect of substantial benefits to follow. They therefore prefer, in place of such a fluctuating income-stream, a more uniform one. To secure this uniformity is evidently the purpose of the loan. We see, therefore, that this class of loans also exemplifies the theory of the relation of borrowing and lending to the time-shape of an income-stream.

§ 3

The third and last general class of loans is that of business loans. Business loans are loans growing out of trade. They are commonly, though not very felicitously, called "productive loans," whereas the loans which have thus far been considered would commonly be called "consumption loans." Business loans constitute by far the most important class of present indebtedness. Mr. George K. Holmes has estimated that at least nine tenths of the existing indebtedness in the United States was incurred for the acquirement of the more durable kinds of property, leaving not more than one tenth, and probably much less, as a "consumption debt," or a debt necessitated by misfortune. No theory of interest would therefore be complete which should fail to apply to business loans.

At first sight it would seem that the theory which has been given, depending as it does on the enjoyable income-stream of an individual, can apply only to consumption loans. Net income, as was shown elsewhere,[1] consists of one's personal satisfactions, — nourishment, clothing, shelter, and other enjoyable services. The loans of business seem too impersonal to be explained by a theory which depends wholly on personal satisfactions. In fact, it has often been said by economists, in treating this subject, that consumption loans are explained on quite other principles than loans contracted in the regular course of commercial transactions. Even Böhm-Bawerk, in his *Positive Theory of Capital*, states that consumption loans are explained by the preference for present enjoyment over future, but that the loans of business are chiefly due to the "technical superiority of present goods," which grows out of the greater productiveness of lengthy processes.

A little consideration will show, however, that business loans are not so different from consumption loans; that they also are used to tide over lean times in anticipation of prosperity; and that they are contracted to rectify the distortion of the income-stream which would otherwise result from business operations. The truth is — and it should never be lost sight of — that business men conduct their business with an eye always to enjoyable income. This is the object of all their operations, though it may be obscured by the interposition of the many intermediate steps, or "interactions." Business operations are not ends in themselves, but means for ultimate personal enjoyment.

[1] *The Nature of Capital and Income*, Chaps. IX, X.

A business man not only conducts his business for what he can get out of it for personal use, but also regulates it so that what thus comes out may accrue not in irregular spurts, but so far as possible in such a stream as will synchronize with the exigencies of his home life. In a sense we may say, therefore, that it is his home that "runs" his business rather than his business that "runs" his home.

§ 4

In order to see how the theory of interest which has been explained applies to business loans, let us consider the two chief classes; namely, short loans, or those growing out of periodic variations, and long loans, or those for relatively permanent investment. The short or periodic loans are those which grow out of the change in the seasons and the ebb and flow of business. These loans are obtained usually but once a year at a specified time. The ultimate cause is the cyclical change in the position of the earth in reference to the sun. This gives rise to the cycle of the seasons, the effects of which are felt not only in agriculture, but in manufacturing, transportation, trade, and banking. The alternate congestion and thinning of the freight business, the alternate stocking and depletion of raw material in factories, the fluctuations of trade activity, both wholesale and retail, the transfer of bank deposits between New York and the West for "moving crops" or for other uses, all testify to the seasonal rhythm which is constantly felt in the great network of business operations. Without some compensating apparatus such as that for borrowing and lending, these seasonal fluctuations would transmit themselves to the final enjoyable income-streams of individuals, and those incomes, instead of constituting an even flow, would accrue by fits and starts, a summer of lavish enjoyment being followed by a winter on short rations.

To show how borrowing and lending compensate for these fluctuations, we may consider first what is perhaps the most primitive type of the short or periodic loan; namely, that contracted by poor farmers in anticipation of crops. In the South among the negroes this takes the form of what is called a "crop lien," the cultivator borrowing money enough to enable him to live until crop time and pledging repayment from the crop. Here, evidently, the purpose of the loan is to eke out the meager income of actual enjoyments. The loan, in other words, is for subsistence. This case, therefore, is covered by the theory of interest which has been given.

We proceed now to show that this same theory of interest applies also to loans contracted in the commercial world at large. A short-time commercial loan is contracted for the purpose of buying goods, with the expectation of repayment after their sale. A common form is what is called "commercial paper." A ready-made clothing house may buy overcoats in summer in order to sell them in the fall. If these operations were conducted on a strictly cash basis, the tendency would be for the income of the clothier to suffer great fluctuations. He could realize but little during the summer, on account of the enormous expense of stocking-in for fall trade, whereas in the fall he could obtain large returns and live on a more elaborate scale. This would mean the alternation of famine and feast in his family. One way to avoid such a result would be to keep on hand a large supply of cash as a buffer between the money-income and personal expenditure. In this case the fluctuations would not reach the stage of personal enjoyment, but would spend their force in fluctuations of the volume of cash. A more effective and less wasteful method for the merchant, of taking the kinks out of his income, is by negotiating commercial paper. The clothier, instead of suffering the large cash expense of stocking-in in summer, will make out a note to the manufacturer of overcoats. After the fall trade, this note is extinguished, having fulfilled its function of leveling the income-stream of the clothier.

Sometimes merchants contract short-time or periodic loans, not for some specific transaction such as the purchase of stock in trade, but for general business purposes, as, for instance, improvement or enlargement. In this case, the extraordinary expense involved may be met by a species of loan called "accommodation paper." Evidently its function is precisely the same; namely, to rectify the time-shape of the income-stream. In Wall Street and other speculative centers a type of loan known as the "call loan" is common, subject to redemption at the pleasure of the lender, and used by the speculator for the purchase of securities. The speculator borrows when he wishes to buy, and repays when he has sold; and by adroitly arranging his loans prevents the sudden draining or flushing of his income-stream which these purchases and sales would otherwise involve.

In all the cases which have been described, the loan grows out of a purchase or group of purchases; and since the tendency of every purchase is to decrease one's income, and of every sale to increase it, it is clear that loans contracted for a purchase and extinguished by a sale have as their function the obliteration of these decreases and increases of the income-stream. It is clear, therefore, that these commercial loans fit into the theory of interest which has been propounded.

§ 5

The second class of business loans is that of long-time loans or "permanent" investments. In this class are placed mortgages, whether on farms or on urban real estate. As shown by Mr. George K. Holmes of the United States Census, more than two thirds of farm mortgages are contracted for the purchase of the property, and the remainder principally for improving it, or for the purchase of farm implements and other durable wealth or property. These purchases or improvements, involving as they do large expenditures, would be difficult or impossible without loans. If the attempt were made to enter into them without recourse to a loan market, they would cause temporary depressions in the income-streams of the farmers. The farmer who attempted to buy his farm without a loan would have to cut down his current expenses to a minimum and suffer a corresponding reduction in his enjoyable income-stream, unless he avoided this result by some other of the methods which have been explained, such as "the method of buying and selling." For instance, he may sell some other capital in order to buy his farm.

Mortgages on city lots are usually for the purpose of improving the property by erecting buildings upon it. Here, again, the expense involved would, if taken out of income, reduce the income of the owner temporarily to very small proportions. He naturally prefers to compensate for such extraordinary inroads by a mortgage which defers this expense to the future, when his receipts will be more adequate to meet it.

We come next to the loans of business corporations and firms, such, for instance, as railroad bonds and debentures, the securities of street railroads, telegraph, and telephone companies, and other "industrials." These loans are usually issued for construction purposes, as in cases in which a railroad wishes to extend its lines, replace iron rails with steel ones, or a curved route by a straighter one. The borrowers in this case are the stockholders. They may be said to contract the loan in order not to have the expenses of the improvement taken out of their dividends. Sometimes, where the dividends are large and the stockholders few, dividends are applied, in part or wholly, to the making of improvements. But ordinarily the reduction in the stockholder's income-stream is avoided by the device of inviting the bondholders to cancel the outgoes connected with the improvement, in consideration of receiving a part of the increased income which will later follow from these improvements.

§ 6

We see, therefore, that business loans, or loans growing out of a purchase and sale, are as truly for the purpose of reshaping the income-streams as are private and public loans. The reasons that business loans are usually regarded by economists as on a different footing from private and public loans appear to be three: —

1. The proceeds of business loans are usually spent, not for the borrower's bread and butter, but for durable capital; consequently the loan seems not to be connected with income, but rather with capital. A spendthrift who borrows $1000 in order to pay for wines is certainly to be distinguished from a merchant who borrows the same sum in order to pay for new stock in trade. Yet in either case the loan adds $1000 to immediate income beyond what the income would have been *without the loan but with the expense for the wines or the stock in trade.*

To make the comparison as simple as possible, let us suppose that the two men were each enjoying an income of $10,000 a year. This represents the value of their nourishment, clothing, shelter, etc., which constitute true income. In the year (say 1901) of the proposed loan, each man has two courses open to him: (1) he may meet the expenditure for wines or stock in trade by sacrificing one-tenth of his $10,000 worth of nourishment, clothing, shelter, etc., or (2) he may meet it by borrowing. If the spendthrift follows the first course and meets the expenditure by skimping out of his $10,000 income, he will not suffer any change in the value of his income, but will obtain $1000 worth of wine drinking, at a sacrifice of $1000 worth of other pleasures. His income for the year 1901 will still be $10,000. Nor will there be any necessary change in the income of subsequent years. He merely changes the composition of this year's enjoyable income partly into wine-drinking, but his income remains $10,000 a year. The merchant, however, who skimps out of his $10,000 income in 1901 in order to pay for stock in trade, will actually reduce his enjoyed income of 1901 by $1000; for this stock in trade, unlike wine, will not give any immediate satisfaction. It serves only as a means of securing future satisfactions, so that, let us say,

$1100 may be enjoyed in 1902. The income of the mer-
chant will thus be, not $10,000 each year, as was that of
the spendthrift, but $9000 in 1901 and $11,100 in 1902.

Having seen what effect the expenditures would have in
the two cases *without recourse to borrowing*, we next ask
what will be the effect in the two cases of borrowing $1000
in 1901 and repaying, let us say, $1050 in 1902.   The spend-
thrift who borrows to get his $1000 worth of wine will have,
in 1901, that much more of enjoyed income, making a total
enjoyed income in that year of $11,000, and in 1902, when
called upon to pay his debt of $1050, he will have to sacrifice
just so much out of his income of $10,000 for 1902.   His
resulting enjoyed income will therefore be in 1902 only
$8950.   As to the merchant, he will be able to buy his
stock in trade in 1901 without the necessity of any sacrifice
out of his $10,000 for that year, so that his income in 1901
will be $10,000.   In the following year he will pay the
$1050 for his loan out of the $11,100 for 1902.   (Of the
$11,100, $10,000 was the original income, and $1100 what
we have assumed to be the returns from his stock in
trade.)   He will thus have $10,050 left as his real income
for that year.

Comparisons are shown in the following tables: —

INCOME OF SPENDTHRIFT
WHO BUYS $1000 WORTH OF WINE

	1901	1902
Without loan	$10,000	$10,000
With loan	11,000	8,950

INCOME OF MERCHANT
WHO BUYS $1000 WORTH OF STOCK IN TRADE

	1901	1902
Without loan	$ 9,000	$11,100
With loan	10,000	10,050

It is clear that in each case the effect of the loan is to add $1000 to the income of 1901 and subtract $1050 from that of 1902. There is absolutely no difference between the two men in this respect. The difference between them is chiefly that the spendthrift is making a foolish and the merchant a wise addition to his income of 1901 at the expense of that of the year following, and this difference is only one of degree, due to the fact that the final satisfactions by means of the wine come earlier than the satisfactions obtained by means of the stock in trade.

2. But the example given of the "consumption"-loan is not the only one possible, and no doubt it will still seem to some readers that there must be another difference between production- and consumption-loans. Suppose the case of a victim of misfortune, such as illness. To tide him over his emergencies he is compelled to borrow, using the proceeds of his loan merely to meet his grocer's and butcher's bills. Here is indeed a case of a "consumption"-loan which is not foolish, and yet is surely different from the loan of the merchant to buy stock in trade.

The effect of business loans is to enable a merchant to embark on an enterprise, while personal loans merely relieve needs. Let us examine this difference. It is not a difference which invalidates the principle that both loans are additions to present income at the expense of future income. The unfortunate, *with* his misfortune, but *without* his loan, would have, let us say, an income of $9,000 in 1901 and $11,100 in 1902, which are the same figures we assumed for the merchant *with* his investment but *without* his loan. *With* the loan, therefore, the unfortunate and the merchant would be in the same situation. Both would have $10,000 in 1901 and $10,050 in 1902. The effect of the loan in the two cases is thus identical so far as their income-streams are concerned. The difference is that the unfortunate, if deprived of his loan, could not escape from his income-stream of $9,000 in 1901 and $11,100 in 1902, whereas the merchant, if deprived of his loan, could, if he chose, give up the investment in new stock altogether.   If the merchant did not have this option, the two cases would be so similar that not even a stickler for the distinction between consumption-loan and productive-loan would assert any essential difference.   For, suppose the merchant has already been committed, sometime previously, to buy the goods for his stock in trade, not, perhaps, realizing that he would be unable to pay for them without borrowing or skimping. When the time arrives that he must *of necessity* buy the goods and pay for them, he finds that a loan is badly needed to avoid pinching himself in income.   He will now think of the loan, not as enabling him to buy stock in trade, for that must be done anyway, but as enabling him to buy his bread and butter.   In short, his loan, like the unfortunate's, is a necessity-loan.   It is because ordinarily the merchant is *not* thus constrained to buy the goods that the loan is connected, in his mind, with their purchase rather than with his private necessities.   It still serves to relieve that income, but he has another method of relief, — not to buy the goods at all.   The contrast, then, between him and the unfortunate is simply that he has a third possible course which the latter does not have.   This is shown in the following tables: —

INCOME OF MERCHANT

	1901	1902
A Without loan and without investment .	$10,000	$10,000
B Without loan but with investment . .	9,000	11,100
C With loan and with investment . . .	10,000	10,050

INCOME OF UNFORTUNATE

	1901	1902
B Without loan	$ 9,000	$11,100
C With loan	10,000	10,050

We see here that the unfortunate has two options, B and C, and the merchant three possible options, A, B, and C. It is the existence of this third option A which makes the chief real difference between the merchant borrower and the borrower in misfortune. So far as the other two options are concerned, the two men are similarly situated. That this fact is overlooked is due to the unconscious substitution, in considering the case of the merchant, of the third option, A, for the second, B. That is to say, when the effect of a merchant's loan is considered, this effect is measured with reference to his situation without the loan *and without the purchase of the goods*, instead of with reference to his situation without the loan but *with the purchase*. The latter method measures the effect of the loan in the sense that it shows the difference produced by its presence or absence, *other things being equal*. It treats the merchant's loan in the same way that the unfortunate's loan is treated, and thus puts the two on the same basis. The true sequence of thought then is: Of the two options A and B, the merchant selects B (buying the goods) because it has the greater present value (or, what amounts to the same thing, because the rate, 10 per cent., of the return of \$1100 on the sacrifice of \$1000 is greater than the rate of interest, 5 per cent.); then he selects C (borrowing money), which has the same present value as B, but a more desirable time-shape. This description takes account of the whole series of operations, and corresponds to the principles propounded in Chapter VIII.

3. It is the third option A which gives rise to the contention that the loan produces a profit not possible or easy without it, and that it is, therefore, "productive." We have just seen that the loan phenomena are resolved into two separate steps, the rejection of A in favor of B, and the rejection of B in favor of C. Yet since it may often happen, as shown in Chapter VIII, that the first step (choice of options) would not be taken unless the second step (loan) were already in contemplation, it is true that, in a sense,

280

the choice of the loan includes the choice between the options A and B. Looked at in this way, the effect of the loan is measurable by comparing C with A, such comparison including both the steps stated. In this sense, and in this sense alone, is the loan "productive." It is productive in that it enables the merchant to buy the goods. He thus chooses an option (B) which has an advantage (over A) in present value, or yields a rate of return on sacrifice (10 per cent.) greater than the rate of interest. The reason that the loan is regarded as "productive," then, is that it gives the merchant the opportunity to make 10 per cent. instead of 5 per cent. But obviously it is not the *loan* (choice of C rather than B) which yields the 10 per cent., but the *choice of options without the loan* (B rather than A). The profit is the advantage of B over A; but the loan merely substitutes C as a more desirable equivalent of B. It does not add to the profit, though it changes the form in which it appears. After the loan, the profit appears in the accounts for 1902 in the form of $50 more income for C than for A.

If, after all has been said and understood, any one still prefers to call such a loan "productive," no objection is offered, provided always that it is made wholly clear what is meant by the term "productive." The essential point is that our theory of interest is not restricted in its application to personal and public loans, but includes the loans of business. These business loans come into the same theory as the other loans, and differ only in the existence of a wider range of choice in income-streams.

§ 7

We have seen that the theory of interest which has been propounded is adequate to explain the motives which lead to borrowing and lending in the actual business world. The purpose of loans in all cases may be said to be to modify the shape of income-streams so as to suit the particular

requirements of the case, — to increase present income at
the sacrifice of future, and to eke out present scarcity
in anticipation of future abundance.   As Jevons stated,
capital is required to enable one to support himself while
engaged in undertakings which require time.

The foregoing classification is made from the standpoint
of the borrower.   From the standpoint of the lender, loans
do not need to be so minutely classified.   The lender is
usually either one who wishes to invest permanently, or one
who wishes to invest temporarily.   The former may lend
on mortgage, or he may buy the securities of companies,
governments, or municipalities, or he may be a depositor in a
savings bank.   In all cases the lender is evidently sacrificing
what he might enjoy in present income, in order that he may
have a still larger income in the future.   In other words, he
is modifying the time-shape of his income curve in a manner
opposite to that which the borrower pursues.   When he
invests for short times, this course is generally due to a
periodic fluctuation in his income-stream, the large present
flow being precedent to a shortage in the not far distant
future.   Business men and institutions are in this way
constantly investing for short periods funds which otherwise
would exist in the form of idle cash.   The government
or individual which we supposed to have borrowed at the
time of deficit in anticipation of surplus may, instead, follow the reverse policy of investing the surplus at interest,
in order to provide better for the payment of expenses at the
time of anticipated deficit.

§ 8

The same person may be alternately borrower and lender,
according to the exigencies of his income-stream.   When the
same person is *simultaneously* borrower and lender, he becomes a broker for managing credit operations for other
persons.   This is usually the function of institutions such
as banks of discount and deposit, savings banks, trust companies, exchange brokerage firms, and mortgage companies.

It is through such firms that borrowers and lenders usually reach each other, rather than directly; but whether directly or by means of such intermediaries, the borrowers and lenders are constantly playing into each other's hands. This is particularly evident in the case of periodic fluctuations; for it usually happens that the same cycle of operations which makes one man's income alternately large and small will make another man's alternately small and large. Thus, when the clothing manufacturer sells to the retailer of ready-made clothing, not only does this operation tend to make inroads in the income-stream of the latter, but it also tends to bring to the former an accession of income inconveniently concentrated. For this reason the manufacturer may decide to keep the commercial note which the clothier makes to him, rather than to discount it at a bank.

The manner in which fluctuations in income-streams mutually compensate among borrowers and lenders is well seen in the South, where cotton planters have long been accustomed to borrow of the banks in springtime, to repay in the fall after the cotton is sold. Until recently the banks which supplied these loans found difficulty in leveling the consequent irregularities produced in their own income-streams. They were forced to do so largely by keeping an idle stock of cash, or investing it at low rates in Northern banks. But recently cotton mills have settled in the South, with a cycle of income exactly the reverse of that of the planters. They buy their crops in the fall, manufacture through the winter, and sell in the spring. The consequence is that they come to the banks for loans in the fall, which is just the time when the banks are receiving their pay from the planters, and liquidate these loans in the spring, at just the time when the banks are in need of funds to lend to the planters. In this way the irregularities in the income-streams of both planters and manufacturers are leveled, virtually by mutual cancellation, but actually through the intermediation of the banks.

§ 9

Hitherto we have considered loans only with reference to the time of issue and repayment.   But it frequently happens that loans are transferred at points intermediate between these two dates.   In that case they pass by sale like other property, and affect the income-streams of those who buy and sell in precisely the same way as if they lent and borrowed. The buyer of a security is in the same position as a lender, — he parts with present income for the sake of future. The seller of a loan security is in the same position as a borrower, — he is securing present income and foregoing the future interest he would otherwise receive.   The price at which such loan securities are sold will determine the rate of interest realized and borne by the buyer and seller respectively.   The effects caused by the transfer of loans may be negatived by later transactions.   The seller of a bond may not really use the proceeds to swell a large income, but may reinvest in some other security, and the buyer may not hold the security until maturity, but may sell again at the next turn of the market.

What has been said of loan securities applies also to every form of property which may be regarded in the same light. The buyer of railway stock is not very different from the buyer of railway bonds, or the lender.   He also is sacrificing present income for future, so far as this particular purchase is concerned, even though, as just shown, the effect may be negatived by some other transaction. Likewise the seller of railroad stock is similar to the seller of bonds, or the borrower.   The only distinction is that in the case of buying and selling stock the rate of interest is implicit rather than explicit.

§ 10

Explicit and implicit interest really differ, however, in degree rather than in kind.   An income bond, while nominally yielding explicit interest, may actually, if the income is inadequate, yield quite a different interest, and the price of sale takes into account the latter contingency quite as much as the former. Preferred stock, likewise, while nominally involving the risk of non-payment, often represents a case more nearly like that of explicit interest. It is quite as possible, on the basis of the purchase price and the practical certainty of a definite fixed income, to calculate the rate of interest to be realized to the investor, as in the case of the bond buyer. In the case of ordinary stock, however, in order to calculate the interest to be realized, it becomes necessary to make a forecast of the probable dividends. It is where the element of chance thus enters that implicit interest really differs from explicit. Where the ownership of an article of wealth is total instead of partial, the element of chance is always present. In fact, bonds, so far as they escape from the universal reign of chance, do so only by carving out of the fluctuating income arising from a mass of capital-wealth a certain definite part, small enough not to absorb the whole even at its lowest ebb. But while the rate of interest is somewhat difficult to calculate in advance in the case of other property than loan securities, it may be approximately estimated, and from the rate which has been actually realized in the past it may sometimes even be exactly calculated. In the case of land, it is not uncommon to reckon the value of so many years' purchase of the crop returns, on the assumption that the same value of the crop returns will continue indefinitely.

The element of risk, which is so dominant in actual business relations, has also been considered in the theory of this book. The buying and selling of property serve to modify not only the *time-shape* of the income-stream, but also the *degree of certainty*. The investor who wishes to take chances may invest in stock, and he who does not, in bonds. Risk constitutes the real difference between them, and the reason for the existence of the two types of securities. Both are investors, and both sacrifice present income for future; but one assumes a future income with risk and the other receives one without risk, or at any rate, with no large degree of risk. That stockholders and bondholders are both investors is not inconsistent with the fact already emphasized that the stockholder is a borrower of the bondholder as a lender. In dealing with each other they are on opposite sides of the market, the bondholder being a buyer or investor and the stockholder a seller or borrower. But in dealing with "the company," they are on the same side of the market; both are buyers of securities, or investors.

Thus by borrowing and lending, or by buying and selling, an individual regulates the character of his income-stream to suit his individual needs and idiosyncrasies. This adjustment involves comparisons of risk and of futurity, and in the latter case involves a rate of interest, implicit or explicit. This rate is utilized by individuals to enable them to increase or decrease the flow of their income at different periods of time, and it is through their efforts to do so, by bargaining with each other, that the rate of interest is itself determined. The theory of its determination applies to the actual loans of business, loans of necessity, improvidence, or purchase, loans of persons, corporations, and loan brokers, and applies also to cases in which there are no contract loans at all, but only the buying, selling, and valuing of property, in which transactions the rate of interest is always implicitly contained.

CHAPTER XIV

INDUCTIVE VERIFICATION (MONETARY)

§ 1

No study of the principles governing the rate of interest would be complete without verification by facts. In this chapter those facts will be presented which bear on the problem discussed in Chapter V, the problem of *appreciation and interest*. The object will be to ascertain the extent to which, in the actual world, the appreciation or depreciation of the monetary standard is foreseen by borrowers and lenders, and provided for in the rates of interest upon which they agree.

At the outset the question arises, How can a merchant be said to foresee the appreciation of money? Appreciation is a subtle concept. Few business men have any clear ideas about it. Economists disagree as to its definition, and statisticians as to its measurement. If we ask a merchant whether or not he takes account of appreciation, he will say that he never thinks of it, that he always "regards a dollar as a dollar." In his mind, other things may change in terms of money, but money itself does not change. Yet it may be true that he does take account of a change in the purchasing power of money, under guise of a change in the prices of other things. In our daily life we seldom think of the earth as moving; nevertheless we take account of its rotation whenever we speak of "sunrise" or "sunset." During a period of paper-money inflation the ordinary man conceives the premium on gold as a rise of gold bullion, not a fall of the paper money; but he arrives at the same practical results. Appreciation of money, whether in reference to gold bullion, commodities, or labor, is in effect taken account of in the practical man's forecast of

257

all the economic elements which concern him, — the prices of his product, the cost of his living, the wages of his workmen, and so forth. Moreover, he takes account of the relative importance of these factors as affecting himself, and not of their relative importance in the elaborate averages of the statistician, — averages which may emphasize some particular commodity or labor whose fluctuations have no interest for him. His own aim is not to predict the index numbers of Sauerbeck or of the United States Bureau of Labor, but to foresee those price changes which affect his own economic future. To foresee a rise or fall of a particular price is to that extent to foresee a change in the purchasing power of money. Such forecasts enable a man to make reasonably correct decisions, and in particular to contract a loan with intelligence. If gold appreciates in such a way or in such a sense that he expects for himself a shrinking margin of profit, he will be cautious about borrowing unless interest falls; and this very unwillingness to borrow, lessening the demand in the "money market," will bring interest down. On the other hand, if inflation is going on, he will see rising prices and rising profits, and will be stimulated to borrow capital unless interest rises; moreover, this willingness to borrow will itself raise interest.

Foresight is clearer and more prevalent to-day than ever before. Multitudes of trade journals and investors' reviews have their chief reason for existence in supplying data on which to base prediction. Every chance for gain is eagerly watched for. An active and keen speculation is constantly going on which, so far as it does not consist of fictitious and gambling transactions, performs a well-known and provident function for society. Is it reasonable to believe that foresight, which is the general rule, has an exception as applied to falling or rising prices?

§ 2

Appreciation and depreciation in this book are used in a purely relative sense. If gold appreciates relatively to silver, then necessarily silver depreciates relatively to gold. Any standard appreciates 1 per cent. relatively to another standard if a certain amount of it now commands 101 units in this other standard, when previously it commanded only 100 units.

General evidence that an expected appreciation or depreciation of money has an effect on the rate of interest in that money can be obtained from several sources.   During the free-silver agitation of 1895–6, it was observed that municipalities could often sell gold bonds at better terms than "currency" or "coin" bonds.   There was a strong desire on the part of lenders to insert a gold clause in their contracts, and they were willing to yield something in their interest to secure it.   The same tendency was strikingly shown in California [1] during the inflation period of the Civil War.   For a time, gold contracts could not be enforced, and in consequence interest rates were exceptionally high.

During a period of progressive paper inflation the rate of interest in contracts drawn on a paper basis is high. This was true during the Civil War, and also during the currency troubles in the thirties.   Raguet wrote: [2]   "In the six months before the suspension of '37, although the amount of the currency was greater than it had ever been before in the United States, yet the scarcity of money was so great that it commanded from 1 per cent. to 3 per cent. per month."   It would be unsafe to found much inference on these facts; their significance may be partly or wholly different.   But they raise a presumption that anticipation of further depreciation of currency tends to increase the rate of interest.

A definite test must be sought where two standards are simultaneously used.   An excellent case of this kind is

[1] Bernard Moses, "Legal Tender Notes in California," *Quarterly Journal of Economics*, October, 1892, p. 15.

[2] *Currency and Banking* (1839), p. 139; also Sumner, *History of Banking*, New York (1896), p. 264.

supplied by two kinds of United States bonds, one payable in coin and the other in currency. From the prices which these bonds have fetched in the market it is possible to calculate the interest realized to the investor. The currency bonds were known as currency sixes and matured in 1898 and 1899. The coin bonds selected for comparison were the fours of 1907. The following table gives the rates of interest realized in the two standards, together with the premium on gold.

RATES OF INTEREST REALIZED FROM DATES MENTIONED TO MATURITY [1]

	Coin	Currency	Price of Gold		Coin	Currency
Jan., 1870	6.4	5.4	119.9	Jan., 1879	3.7	4.5
July, 1870	5.8	5.1	112.2	Jan., 1880	3.8	4.0
Jan., 1871	6.0	5.3	110.8	Jan., 1881	3.3	3.4
July, 1871	5.8	5.0	113.2	Jan., 1882	3.0	3.5
Jan., 1872	5.3	4.9	109.5	Jan., 1883	2.9	3.3
July, 1872	5.6	5.0	113.9	Jan., 1884	2.6	2.9
Jan., 1873	5.7	5.1	111.9	May, 1885	2.7	2.7
July, 1873	5.4	5.0	115.3	Jan., 1886	2.6	2.6
Jan., 1874	5.0	5.0	110.3	Jan., 1887	2.3	2.6
July, 1874	5.1	4.9	110.7	Mar., 1888	2.3	2.9
Jan., 1875	5.0	4.7	112.6	Jan., 1889	2.2	2.6
July, 1875	5.1	4.4	117.0	May, 1890	2.1	2.6
Jan., 1876	4.7	4.4	112.9	July, 1891	2.4	3.0
July, 1876	4.5	4.2	112.3	Jan., 1892	2.6	3.1
Jan., 1877	4.5	4.4	107.0	Mar., 1893	2.8	3.1
July, 1877	4.4	4.3	105.4	Nov., 1894	2.7	3.5
Jan., 1878	5.0	4.6	102.8	Aug., 1895	2.8	3.6
July, 1878	3.9	4.4	100.7	Aug., 1896	3.2	4.3

[1] This table has been obtained by the aid of the usual brokers' bond tables. In the case of currency bonds, it was only necessary to deduct accrued interest (if any) from the quoted price and look in the table for the interest which corresponds to the price so found and the number of years to maturity. In the case of coin bonds,

Several points in this table deserve notice. In 1870 the investor made 6.4 per cent. in gold but was willing to accept a return of only 5.4 per cent. in currency. This fact becomes intelligible in the light of the theory which has been explained. It meant the hope of resumption. Because paper was so depreciated there was a prospect of a great rise in its value. It was not until 1878, when the prospect of a further rise disappeared, that the relative position of the two rates of interest was reversed. After resumption in 1879 the two remained very nearly equal for several years, until fears of inflation again produced a divergence. The quotations for 1894, 1895, and 1896 show a considerably higher rate of interest in the currency standard than in the coin standard, as well as a higher rate in both standards than in previous years. The difference is between 2.7 per cent. and 3.5 per cent. in 1894, and between 3.2 per cent. and 4.3 per cent. in 1896. Both the increase and the wedging apart of the two rates are explainable as effects of the free-silver proposal and its incorporation (July, 1896) in the platform of the Democratic party.

§ 3

We see, therefore, that the facts agree with the theory previously laid down. But it is necessary further to inquire *how close* is this agreement. For this purpose the figures just given are of little value. They represent the rates of interest realized for the periods between the dates named and the times at which the bonds matured; but as these

since the quotations are given in currency, it is necessary to divide the quoted price by the price of gold in order to obtain their price in gold (*i.e.* "coin"), and then proceed as above indicated. The quotations of prices of bonds and gold are the "opening" prices for the months named, and are taken from the *Financial Review* (Annual Summary of the *Commercial and Financial Chronicle*), 1895, *The Commercial and Financial Chronicle*, the (New York) *Bankers' Magazine*, and the *Bankers' Almanac*. After 1884, January quotations were not always available.

periods are not the same for the two bonds, the two corresponding series of interest rates are not entirely comparable. Such a rate of interest is a sort of average of the rates of interest for the individual years of the periods in question.[1] Thus, in the foregoing table, the rate of interest in currency placed opposite January, 1870, is 5.4 per cent. This is the rate realized between 1870 and 1899. It is a sort of average of, say, the rate of interest for the period

RATES OF INTEREST REALIZED FROM DATES MENTIONED TO JANUARY 1, 1879 (DATE OF RESUMPTION)[2]

| | Coin j | Currency i | Appreciation of Currency in Gold | |
			"Expected" a	Actual
Jan., 1870 . .	7.1	6.3	.8	2.1
July, 1870 . .	6.2	5.7	.5	1.4
Jan., 1871 . .	6.7	6.3	.4	1.3
July, 1871 . .	6.4	5.7	.7	1.8
Jan., 1872 . .	5.9	5.7	.2	1.3
July, 1872 . .	6.2	5.7	.5	2.1
Jan., 1873 . .	6.5	6.2	.3	2.0
July, 1873 . .	6.2	6.0	.2	2.8
Jan., 1874 . .	5.6	6.1	− .5	2.1
July, 1874 . .	5.7	5.8	− .1	2.4
Jan., 1875 . .	6.0	5.4	.6	3.1
July, 1875 . .	6.1	4.2	1.9	4.9
Jan., 1876 . .	5.4	4.1	1.3	4.3
July, 1876 . .	5.2	2.4	2.8	4.9
Jan., 1877 . .	5.5	4.0	1.5	3.5
July, 1877 . .	5.7	3.1	2.6	3.6
Jan., 1878 . .	8.2	6.0	2.2	2.8
July, 1878 . .	4.8	2.6	2.2	1.4

[1] For the nature of this average, see *The Nature of Capital and Income*, Appendix to Chap. XII, § 5.

[2] Since the figures in this table represent the rates of interest which will render the "present value," at the date of purchase, of all the future benefits up to January, 1879, equal to the purchase price, they can be calculated by Horner's method as indicated in § 9

between 1870 and 1879 (which, as we shall see, was 6.3 per cent.) and that for the period between 1879 and 1899 (which was 4.5 per cent.). For a true comparison between coin and currency rates, we must seek rates relating to the *same* period in each case. This is the method in the following table. In it, the periods selected all terminate on January 1, 1879, the date of resumption of specie payments. The rates of interest in this table are the rates which would be realized by investors who should buy the bonds at the dates mentioned and sell them on January 1, 1879.

of the Appendix to Chap. V. But the method which has been adopted is less laborious, as it enables us to use the bond tables. It can best be explained by an example. The opening price, January, 1870, of currency sixes was 109¼, and in January, 1879, the price was 119¼. These prices require no correction for accrued interest. Our problem is, if a man spends $109¼ in 1870 and receives $119¼ in 1879 with $6 per annum (semiannually) in the meantime, what rate of interest does he realize? Now it is clear that the answer is the same if all the benefits and sacrifices involved are doubled or halved or increased or decreased in any common ratio. Let us then divide them all by 1.19¼. Then we would have $91.3 paid in 1870 for $100 due in 1879, and $5.02 per annum in the meantime. That is, the rate of interest realized is exactly as if the bond were a 5.02 per cent. bond maturing in 1879 and bought at 91.3 in 1870. This rate can readily be obtained from the bond tables by interpolating between the figures for a 5 per cent. and a 5½ per cent. bond purchased at 91.3 with 9 years to run. For a 5 per cent. bond we obtain 6.28 per cent. and for a 5½ per cent. bond, 6.81 per cent. Hence for a 5.02 per cent. bond the result is 6.30 per cent.

The third column gives what may be called the expected rate of appreciation of currency in terms of gold; that is, that rate of appreciation which would have made the two interest rates equally profitable. It is therefore the difference between the two rates of interest.

Finally, the last column gives the actual rate of appreciation between the dates mentioned and January 1, 1879. This is calculated from the quoted prices of gold. Thus the opening price of gold January, 1870, was 119.9, and January, 1879, 100. Hence currency appreciated in nine years in the ratio of 100 to 119.9, which is at the rate of 2.1 per cent. per annum. If the appreciation proceeded uniformly, this method would be strictly correct. As it is, a more elaborate method would be required, in accordance with the principles explained in § 9 of the Appendix to Chap. V, to take account fully of the fluctuations of the annual appreciation. But for our present purposes, and for results worked out to but one decimal place, the simpler method here adopted is sufficiently correct.

From this table we see that the rates of interest realized for the period, January, 1870 to January, 1879, were in coin, 7.1 per cent., and in currency, 6.3 per cent., the difference [1] between which is .8 per cent., the rate of appreciation which would equalize the investments in the two bonds. This may be called the "expected appreciation." The actual rate of appreciation was 2.1 per cent. That is, the estimated appreciation was about two-fifths of the appreciation as it really turned out. Those who held currency sixes therefore had the better investment during 1870–1879. In fact, it is well known that many speculators grew rich by exchanging gold bonds for currency bonds about this time. The table shows that there was the same underestimate of future appreciation in July, 1870, January, 1871, and July, 1871. From that time to July, 1874, the table shows that the outlook for resumption grew gloomy, due no doubt to the strong greenback sentiment. The inflation bill of 1874 actually produced a prospect of negative appreciation; *i.e.* depreciation. This bill was vetoed by President Grant, and in December of that year the bill for resumption was passed by the Senate. Accordingly, January, 1875, opened with a more hopeful estimate. The bill became a law on the 14th of January, and there was an immediate rise in the "expected appreciation" which from that time forward averaged 2 per cent. But during the same period the actual ap-

---

[1] The formula used is therefore simply $j = i + a$. (j represents the rate of interest in coin, i the rate of interest in currency, a the expected rate of appreciation — that is, the rate of appreciation of the currency standard with respect to the coin standard). As shown in Appendix to Chap. V, § 3, this formula applies strictly only when the rates of interest and of appreciation are "reckoned continuously." But practically it applies to all cases with which we have to deal, as the interest periods are seldom over half a year. Even when the interest is payable only annually, and, in consequence, the correct formula is $1 + j = (1 + i)(1 + a)$, (see Appendix to Chap. V, § 2), the value of a calculated by this formula will seldom differ perceptibly from its value calculated by the simpler formula $j = i + a$, here employed.

preciation from the dates named to January, 1879, averaged 3.6. per cent., so that even after the government promised resumption, investors and speculators did not put implicit confidence in that promise, the "expected appreciation" being only a little more than half the actual appreciation. This corresponds to the well-known fact that the resumption act was looked upon as a political maneuver, likely to be repealed.[1]

§ 4

Having compared the rates of interest in paper and coin, we may next compare them in gold and silver. The comparison, to be of value, must be between gold and silver contracts in the same market and with the same security. Such contracts are fortunately available in the London market of government securities. The loans of India

---

[1] It should be observed that the method employed to determine the rate of interest realized is open to one danger. It correctly represents the rate of interest actually realized between two dates, but, unless the later of the two dates is maturity, it does not necessarily represent the rate of interest *expected* at the first date. The investor could not know in January, 1870, what the price of bonds would be in January, 1879, unless the bonds matured at that time. To accurately compare, in 1870, the relative advantages of coin and currency bonds for the period 1870–1879, a forecast would have been necessary, not only of the relation of currency to gold, but also of the prices of the two bonds in 1879. These prices, in turn, depend on a new forecast made in 1879. It follows that a mistake in this forecast of 1879 and embodied in the prices of that year would affect the rate of interest realized between 1870 and 1879 in the same manner as a mistake of the opposite kind in the forecast of 1870.

But in most cases the method given is sufficiently exact. For, although in 1870 it would have been impossible to predict exactly the prices of the two bonds in 1879, yet it can usually be depended upon that any great change in price is apt to affect both alike, and thus eliminates itself for the most part in the comparison. The reason that the errors in predicting what the prices of the two bonds would be in 1879 are nearly equal is that the two bonds selected were approximately of the same term. The coin bonds matured in 1907, the currency bonds in 1898 and 1899. The eight or nine years between them would be almost immaterial in 1879. It is for this reason that the coin bonds of 1907 were chosen in preference to those of 1881.

have been made partly in gold and partly in silver, and both forms of securities are bought and sold in London.[1] The interest on the silver, or rather rupee, bonds is paid by draft on India. The sums actually received in English money depend on the state of the exchanges. The rate of interest in the silver standard is calculated in the same way as was shown[2] for coin bonds in § 3. The results are contained in the following table: —

RATES OF INTEREST REALIZED FROM DATES NAMED
TO MATURITY OR IN PERPETUITY[3]

	Rupee	Gold	Differ-ence	Exchange on India Pence per Rupee
1865	4.3	4.1	.2	23.2
1868	4.3	4.0	.3	23.0
1870	4.3	4.0	.3	23.6
1871	4.1	3.8	.3	23.2
1872	3.9	3.7	.2	22.6
1873	3.9	3.7	.2	22.4
1874	3.9	3.8	.1	22.2

[1] The silver bonds or "rupee paper" were issued to raise loans in India, but they have also been enfaced for payment in England, and in 1893–1894 some Rs. 25,000,000 were on the London books. — Burdett's *Official Intelligencer* (1894), p. 75.

[2] Thus in 1880 the average price paid in London for "rupee paper" of face value Rs. 1,000 yielding 4 per cent., or Rs. 40 per annum, was £79. In order to find the rate of interest realized by the investor, we must translate £79 into silver. The average rate of exchange in 1880 was 20d. per rupee. Hence £79 were equivalent to 948 rupees. That is, speaking in terms of silver (or, more exactly, in terms of exchange on India), the price of a 4 per cent. bond was 94.8, which, if the bond be treated as a perpetual annuity, yields the investor 4.3 per cent. In the same year, an India gold bond yielded 3.6 per cent.

[3] This table is formed from averages of (usually ten) quotations distributed through each year, taken from the *Economist*, the *Investor's Monthly Manual*, and the (London) *Bankers' Magazine*. The fourth column is founded on the table in the *Report of the Indian Currency Committee* (1893), p. 27, but is corrected to apply to calendar instead of official years.

RATES OF INTEREST REALIZED FROM DATES NAMED
TO MATURITY OR IN PERPETUITY — *Continued*

	Rupee[1]	Gold[2]	Differ-ence	Exchange on India Pence per Rupee
1875	4.0	3.6	.4	21.9
1876	4.1	3.7	.4	20.5
1877	4.1	3.7	.4	20.9
1878	4.2	3.9	.3	20.2
1879	4.4	3.7	.7	19.7
1880	4.3	3.6	.7	20.0
1881	4.0	3.4	.6	19.9
1882	3.9	3.5	.4	19.5
1883	4.1	3.4	.7	19.5
1884	4.1	3.3	.8	19.5
1885	4.1	3.5	.6	18.5
1886	4.1	3.5	.6	17.5
1887	4.1	3.4	.7	17.2
1888	4.1	3.1	1.0	16.5
1889	4.1	3.0	1.1	16.5
1890, 1st half	4.0	3.0	1.0	17.6
1890, 2d half	3.9	3.1	.8	19.3
1891	3.8	3.1	.7	17.1
1892	3.9	3.1	.8	15.3
1893	3.9	3.0	.9	15.0
1894	3.9	3.0	.9	13.5

[1] The quotation from which the interest was computed for 1895 and succeeding years is for 3½ per cent. rupee paper. All previous quotations are for 4 per cent.'s. The 4 per cent.'s were repayable on three months' notice; this notice was given in 1894, and the bonds redeemed or converted into 3½ per cent.'s before the close of the year. To obtain the rate of interest realized, the London quotations in pounds sterling are first converted into rupees at the current rates of exchange, and then the bonds are treated as perpetual annuities. The results differ from those given in the *Investor's Monthly Manual*, because the rupee is there converted at a conventional value, not the market value.

[2] From 1865 to 1880 inclusive the figures refer to 4 per cent.'s, repayable October, 1888, or later; those of 1881–1884 are for 3½ per cent.'s maturing in 1931, and those for 1885–1906 are for 3 per cent.'s maturing in 1948.

RATES OF INTEREST REALIZED FROM DATES NAMED
TO MATURITY OR IN PERPETUITY — *Concluded*

	RUPEE	GOLD	DIFFER-ENCE	EXCHANGE ON INDIA PENCE PER RUPEE
1895	3.4	2.8	.6	13.4
1896	3.3	3.1	.2	14.3
1897	3.5	3.1	.4	15.1
1898	3.7	3.2	.5	16.0
1899	3.6	3.2	.4	16.1
1900	3.7	3.4	.3	16.0
1901	3.7	3.5	.2	16.0
1902	3.6	3.5	.1	16.0
1903	3.5	3.5	.0	16.0
1904	3.6	3.7	− .1	16.1
1905	3.6	3.6	.0	16.1
1906	3.6	3.2	.4	16.0

From this table it will be seen that the rates realized to investors in bonds of the two standards differed but slightly until 1875, when the fall of Indian exchange began. The average difference previously to 1875 was .2 per cent., while the average difference from 1875 to 1892 inclusive was .7 per cent., or more than three times as much. Within this period, from 1884 exchange fell much more rapidly than before, and the difference in the two rates of interest rose accordingly, amounting in one year to 1.1 per cent. Inasmuch as the two bonds were issued by the same government, possess the same degree of security, are quoted side by side in the same market, and are similar in all other respects except in the standard in which they are expressed, the results afford substantial proof that the fall of exchange (after it once began) was discounted in advance and affected the rates of interest in those standards. Of course investors did not form perfectly definite estimates of the future fall, but the fear of a fall predominated in varying degrees over the hope of a rise.

The year 1890 was one of great disturbance in exchanges, the average for the first six months being 17.6 and for the last six months 19.3. The gold price of the silver bonds rose from an average for the first six months of 73.8 to 83.5 for the last six months, but the rise in their silver price was only from 100.6 to 103.7, showing that the increase of confidence in the "future of silver" was not great, and in fact only reduced the disparity in the interest from 1.0 to .8 per cent.

This great rise in exchange and the slight revival in silver securities occurred simultaneously with the passage of the Sherman Act of July, 1890, by which the United States was to purchase four and a half million ounces of silver per month. There can be little doubt that the disturbance was due in some measure to the operation or expected operation of that law.

This is not the only case in which the relative prices of rupee paper and gold bonds were probably affected by political action. One of the smallest differences in the two rates occurs in 1878, which was the year of the Bland Act and the first international monetary conference.

After the closure of the Indian mints on June 26, 1893, exchange rose from 14.7 to 15.9, the gold price of rupee paper from 62 to 70, and consequently its rupee price from 101.2 to 105.7. From this point the exchange again dropped, much to the mystification of those who had predicted an established parity between gold and silver at the new legal rate of 16d. per rupee. There was much discussion as to the reasons for the failure of the legal rate to become operative. The reason seems to have been that the closure of the mints to silver attracted into the circulation silver from other channels, especially old Native hoards. Within a few years, however, this source of supply was dried up so that the legal par was reached in 1898 and has been maintained ever since, subject only to the slight variations of exchange due to the cost of shipping specie. But until the par was proved actually stable by two or

299

three years' experience, the public refused to have confidence that gold and the rupee were once more to run parallel. Their lack of confidence was shown in the difference in the rates of interest in gold and rupee securities during the transition period, 1893–1898, and the two or three succeeding years. From 1893 to 1900 inclusive the two rates averaged .5 per cent. apart. From 1901 to 1906 inclusive, the average difference was only .1 per cent.[1]

§ 5

We shall next attempt to apply the theory of appreciation and interest to periods of rising and falling prices. We are met, however, by the difficulty that comparison can only be made between *successive* periods. We can learn what the rate of interest *has been* during a price movement, but we cannot know what it *would have been* if that price movement had not taken place. Without this missing term of comparison, it is difficult to measure the influence of the rise or fall in price level. No two periods are so alike industrially that we can say they differ only in the state of the monetary standard. Other influences innumerable affect the "value of money." In spite of these difficulties, however, certain general conclusions can be established.

It must be borne in mind that we are studying the effects of rising, not high, prices, and of falling, not low, prices. *Falling* prices are as different from *low* prices as a waterfall is from sea level. Our study is not of price *levels*, but of the *slopes* between price levels.[2]

---

[1] The preceding comparisons serve only to establish the influence of the divergence between the standards on the rates of interest, but afford no measure of that influence. In order to measure the extent to which the fall of silver was allowed for by investors, it would be necessary to examine the rates realized during specific periods, as in the case of coin and currency bonds considered in § 3. A somewhat unsatisfactory attempt to do this was made in "Appreciation and Interest," but is not reproduced here. The case is unlike that of the United States coin and currency bonds, since in the case now under discussion, the two kinds of bonds, rupee and gold, did not have approximately the same date of maturity.

[2] De Haas appears to have fallen into the confusion between high

It was once predicted by Mr. H. H. Gibbs,[1] formerly a director of the Bank of England, that the progressive scarcity of gold would raise the rate of interest. He reasoned that such scarcity would make a stringency in the money market, and that the banks, each struggling to attract reserves from the others, would raise their rates. This prophecy, however, was not fulfilled. The theory that appreciation raises interest has been frequently affirmed, and has even received the stamp of approval of Mr. Robert Giffen. But it is utterly at variance with facts.[2]

When prices are rising or falling, money is depreciating or appreciating *relatively to commodities*. Our theory would therefore require high or low interest according as prices are rising or falling, provided we assume that the rate of interest in the commodity standard does not vary. This assumption would be thoroughly justified only in case the two periods were alike in all respects except in the expansion or contraction of credit and currency.

In the following table for London the periods are selected to correspond with the main movements of prices. Thus, the period 1826–1829 was a period of falling prices, so that money appreciated in terms of commodities at the average rate of 4.2 per cent. per annum. This is indicated in the third column by the figure + 4.2. In the period 1836–1839 prices rose so that money fell at the rate of 2.3 per cent. per annum, indicated by − 2.3. The fourth and last column indicates the rate of interest which is *virtually* paid in commodities. It is the rate of commodity-interest equivalent to the market rate of money-interest actually paid, and therefore is, in each case, the sum of the two items of the two preceding columns.

and rising prices, both in his criticism of Jevons and in his treatment of statistics. See "A Third Element in the Rate of Interest," *Journal of the Royal Statistical Society*, March, 1889.

[1] *The Bimetallic Controversy*, London (Wilson), 1886, pp. 19, 231 245–249, 373.

[2] See "Appreciation and Interest," p. 57.

LONDON RATES OF INTEREST IN RELATION TO RISING AND FALLING PRICES [1]

	Bank	Market	Appreciation of Money in Commodities	Virtual Interest in Commodities (Market)
		i	a	j
1826–1829	4.4	3.5	+ 4.2	7.7
1830–1835	4.0	3.2	0.0	3.2
1836–1839	4.7	4.2	− 2.3	1.9
1840–1844	4.2	3.5	+ 5.9	9.4
1845–1847	3.7	4.2	− 3.0	1.2
1848–1852	2.9	2.5	+ 1.2	3.7
1853–1857	4.1	5.3	− 2.4	2.9
1858–1864	4.4	4.2	− 3.0	1.2
1865–1870	3.8	3.6	+ 1.1	4.7
1871–1873	3.9	3.7	− 6.2	− 2.5
1874–1879	3.2	2.7	+ 4.3	7.0
1880–1887	3.3	2.6	+ 3.8	6.4
1888–1890	3.8	2.9	− 1.4	1.5
1891–1896	2.5	1.5	+ 3.4	4.9
1897–1900	3.2	2.6	− 6.6	− 4.0
1901–1906	3.6	3.1	− 1.5	1.6

[1] This table is constructed from the data given in the Appendix to this chapter. The third column is based on index numbers (Jevons' for 1826–1852, and Sauerbeck's for the remaining years). The index numbers for two dates, as 1826 and 1829, being given, their inverse ratio gives the relative value of money (in commodities) at those two dates. From these it is easy to calculate the average annual change in its value. The method is the same as that employed for finding the rate of interest by which $1, by compounding, will amount to a given sum in a given time. Theoretically, since the loans here included run usually perhaps thirty to ninety days, the quotations of rates of interest averaged should begin at the first of the two dates, and cease, say, sixty days before the second. But the index numbers are not always for definite points of time, nor can the interest quotations be subjected to such minute corrections without an immense expenditure of labor. Hence, the method adopted has been to average the rates for all the years of a period; e.g. for the four years, 1826–1829. The "appreciation" is reckoned between those dates. If the index numbers represent the price levels at the middle of 1826 and 1829, then the average interest rates ought in theory to include only the last six months of 1826, and the first four months of 1829. But it seems better to include too much at both ends than to omit the averages for 1826 and 1829 altogether, for the reason that an average is the more valuable the greater the number of terms included.

If this table be examined, it will be found that if, in comparing one period with the next, the rate of interest *falls*, the "appreciation" usually *rises*, or if the rate *rises*, the "appreciation" *falls*. The comparison of each period with the one following may be designated as a "sequence." In twelve out of fifteen sequences for bank rates and in eleven out of fifteen for market rates, interest is high or low according to the degree in which prices are rising or falling. Attention is called particularly to the period 1853–1857, during which prices rose very fast simultaneously with, and presumably because of, the great gold production. The market rate of interest averaged 5.3 per cent., which was far higher, not only than in any subsequent, but also than in any previous period.

§ 6

The following table for Berlin displays the same connection between price movements and interest : —

BERLIN RATES OF INTEREST IN RELATION TO RISING AND FALLING PRICES [1]

	Bank i	Market $\imath$	Appreciation of Money in Commodities a	Virtual Interest in Commodities (Bank) j	Virtual Interest in Commodities (Market) j
1851–1852	4.0	—	− 1.5	2.5	—
1853–1857	4.7	—	− 3.3	1.4	—
1858–1864	4.3	3.7*	− 2.2	2.1	1.5
1865–1870	4.7	4.0	0.0	—	4.0
1871–1873	4.5	4.1	− 4.1	—	0.0
1874–1879	4.3	3.2	+ 3.1	—	6.3
1880–1883	4.3	3.4	− 0.1	—	3.3
1884–1888	3.6	2.5	+ 2.9	—	5.4
1889–1891	4.0	3.1	− 1.4	—	1.8
1892–1895	3.4	2.2	+ 5.2	—	7.4
1896–1899	4.2	3.6	− 6.8	—	− 3.2
1900–1902	4.2	3.2	5.4	—	8.6
1903–1905	3.9	3.0	− 1.4	—	1.6

[1] This table is constructed from the data in the Appendix. The average in the second column marked (*) is for the years 1861–1864,

In the foregoing table the relation between appreciation and interest is observed in seven out of twelve sequences for bank rates (two being neutral) and in eight out of ten, for market rates.

For France, index numbers covering a wide range of articles are not available. Using those given in the "Aldrich Report" for sixteen articles, we have : —

PARIS RATES OF INTEREST IN RELATION TO RISING
AND FALLING PRICES [1]

	Bank	Market	Appreciation of Money in Commodities
1861–1864	5.1		− 8.1
1865–1870	3.2		+ 3.6
1871–1873	5.3	4.6*	− 4.5
1874–1879	3.1	2.6	+ 4.3
1880–1886	3.2	2.8	+ 2.3
1887–1890	3.1	2.6	− 5.1
1891–1895	2.6	2.0	

Here the same connection is observed in five out of six sequences for bank rates and three out of four for market rates.[2]

It will be noted that the course of prices and interest has been very much the same in England, Germany, and France.

For New York we have the following table : —

not 1858–1864. The "appreciation" to 1891 is calculated from the figures of Soetbeer and Heinz, as given in the "Aldrich Report" of 1893 of the U. S. Senate on Wholesale Prices. The figures for the later years are taken from The *London Economist* and from A. Soetbeer's tables in the *Journal of the Royal Statistical Society*, Vol. LXVII, Part I, pp. 85, 89.

[1] This table is constructed from the data in the Appendix. The average in the second column marked (*) is for the years 1872–1873, not 1871–1873.

[2] Assuming that prices fell, 1891–1895.

NEW YORK RATES OF INTEREST IN RELATION TO
RISING AND FALLING PRICES[1]

	CALL	60 DAYS i	PRIME TWO NAME 60 DAYS i	APPRECIA-TION OF MONEY IN COMMOD-ITIES a	VIRTUAL INTEREST IN COMMODITIES (60 Days) j	VIRTUAL INTEREST IN COMMOD-ITIES (Prime) j
1849–1857	6.2	9.2	—	− 3.8	5.4	—
1858–1860	5.0	7.4	—	+ 6.4	13.8	—
1861–1865	5.9	8.4	6.8	− 20.2	− 11.8	− 13.4
1866–1874	5.4	8.4	7.5	+ 4.7	13.1	12.2
1875–1879	—	—	5.1	+ 7.9	—	13.0
1880–1884	—	—	5.4	+ 0.6	—	6.0
1885–1891	—	—	5.1	− 0.2	—	4.9
1892–1897	—	—	4.6	+ 5.6	—	10.2
1898–1906	—	—	4.6	− 3.5	—	1.1

We find here the same association of appreciation and interest in all of the three sequences for call loans, in two of the three cases for 60-day paper (the third being neutral), and in three of the six cases for "prime" paper (one being neutral).

Perhaps the most remarkable feature of this table is the extremely low rate for 1875–1879. The extraordinary change in interest rates beginning in 1875 has been observed before; but its connection with the resumption act (as it seems to the writer) has been misconstrued.[2]

[1] This table is constructed from the data in the Appendix. The rates of appreciation are calculated from Falkner's figures for prices and wages in the "Aldrich Report."

[2] Thus William Brough, referring to that act, says: "The mere announcement of our intention to put our money on a sound metallic basis had brought capital to us in such abundance that the resumption was not only made easy, but the normal rate of interest was reduced. . . . This remarkable reduction . . . is explainable only on the ground of a large reflux of foreign capital." (*Natural Law of Money*, New York, 1894, p. 124.) If this explanation were correct, we would expect a still lower rate of interest after resumption had been accomplished; but the facts are the opposite.

305

§ 7

The preceding statistics apply to gold standard countries. The following table gives the rates of interest and appreciation for silver standard countries—India, Japan, and China:—

RATES OF INTEREST IN RELATION TO RISING AND FALLING PRICES IN CALCUTTA, TOKYO, AND SHANGHAI [1]

		BANK	MARKET	APPRECIATION IN COMMODITIES
Calcutta,	1873–1875	5.3		+ 2.6
	1876–1878	6.8		− 11.0
	1879–1885	5.9		+ 3.8
	1886–1889	6.0		− 2.6
	1890–1893	4.3		− 4.7
Tokyo,	1873–1877	14.0	12.0	− 0.2
	1878–1881	16.3	12.2	− 13.3
	1882–1886	12.8	10.3	+ 10.4
	1887–1893	9.3	9.4	− 2.8
	1894–1899	9.7	11.2	− 5.8
	1900–1902	11.0	12.4	0.0
Shanghai,	1874–1881	9.1		− 1.4
	1882–1888	7.5	5.8*	+ 1.3
	1889–1893	7.0	5.8	− 0.9

Here we find the theory confirmed in three out of four cases for India, three out of five for bank rates in Japan, and three out of five for market rates; one out of two for bank rates in China, while the one case for market rates is neutral.[2]

[1] This table is constructed from the data given in the Appendix. The entry marked (*) is for 1885–1888, not 1882–1888.

[2] See also " Price Movements and Interest in India," by the writer, in *Yale Review*, May, 1897, p. 80.

Summarizing the cases for the seven countries examined we find 64 favorable and 22 unfavorable to the theory, distributed as follows: —

	Eng-LAND	Ger-MANY	France	United States	India	Japan	China	Total
Favorable	23	15	8	8	3	6	1	64
Unfavorable	7	5	2	2	1	4	1	22

The favorable cases are about three times as numerous as the unfavorable cases. This is a large preponderance, especially when we consider that there are so many causes affecting the rate of interest besides the mere appreciation or depreciation of the monetary standard. We therefore conclude with great confidence that, "other things being equal," *the rate of interest is relatively high when prices are rising and relatively low when prices are falling.*

§ 8

The question now arises whether, on the average, the rate of interest *fully* adjusts itself to price-movements. This question cannot be answered with perfect certainty in any individual case, for the reason that we have no means of knowing what the rate in commodities *would have been* had it been possible to have contracts drawn in "commodities" or in a monetary standard which was stationary with respect to commodities. We have, however, computed the "virtual" interest in commodities by adding to the rate of interest in money the rate of appreciation of money *in commodities.* Thus in London for 1826–1829 the rate of interest in money was 3.5 per cent., but money was appreciating relatively to commodities 4.2 per cent., so that the "virtual interest," or interest actually paid, translated in terms of commodities (the forty commodities averaged by Jevons), was 7.7 per cent. It will be seen from the tables that the virtual rate of interest reckoned in commodities

307

usually varies inversely with the rate reckoned in money.
For 1853–1857, money interest was 5.3 per cent., and for
1874–1879, 2.7 per cent.; but commodity-interest for 1853–
1857 was 2.9 per cent. and for 1874–1879, 7 per cent. There
are two possible explanations for this inverse relation. One
is that when prices are rising the cause may not be monetary
but may lie in a progressive scarcity of commodities produced and exchanged; and, reversely, when prices are falling,
the cause may lie in progressive abundance. From the
theory of interest maintained throughout this book it
follows that a progressive scarcity of commodities, implying
as it does a progressive descending income curve, tends to
make the rate of interest low; and reversely, progressive
abundance, implying an ascending income curve, tends to
make interest high. When, therefore, general price-movements represent changes in the income-stream of enjoyable
services, the rate of "commodity interest" would naturally
be high when prices were falling and low when prices were
rising, whatever might be true of "money-interest."

The second possible reason that commodity-interest and
money-interest vary inversely during price-movements is
that these movements are often *imperfectly foreseen*. The
high or low rate in commodities is then an abnormal
phenomenon. It is, as it were, a trick played by money
on those who put too much faith in its stability. Thus,
during 1898–1905 the increase of prices in the United
States is known to have been due largely to the increase of gold production. There is no evidence that
commodities were getting scarce and incomes decreasing,
but rather the reverse. There seems, therefore, no reason
which would justify the low commodity-rate of interest
of 1.8 per cent. which we found to have been virtually paid
during that period. This low rate must, in all probability,
have been due to inadvertence. The inrushing streams of
gold caught merchants napping. They should have stemmed
the tide by putting up interest, not only to 4.6 per cent., as
they did, but two or three per cent. higher.

Doubtless both of the causes play a part in the explanation of particular cases. Sometimes commodity-interest is low during rising prices because it is foreseen that the real income-stream is then drying up, sometimes because it is *not* foreseen that monetary inflation is taking place, and sometimes for both reasons; and reversely, commodity-interest is high during falling prices, sometimes because of a foreseen increase of the income-stream, sometimes because of unforeseen contraction of the currency, and sometimes both.

It is impossible to decide what part these two factors — foreseen changes in real income and unforeseen changes in their monetary measure —may play in each individual case. We are too ignorant of the actual conditions behind the scenes. Nevertheless there is internal evidence to show that in general the latter factor —unforeseen monetary change — is the more important. This evidence consists in the fact that commodity-interest fluctuates so widely, in some cases even becoming negative. The following table shows that the mean variability or "standard deviation" from the mean, which is the best measure of the fluctuations of any variable, is far greater for the calculated or "virtual" rate of interest than for the actual money rate of interest:—

	No. Periods	Variability (Standard Deviation)	
		Market Interest	Virtual Interest
London	16	.88	3.42
Berlin	11	.56	2.93
New York . . .	7	1.06	8.43

The virtual interest in commodities is from four to eight times as variable as the market interest in money.

All these facts suggest — indeed, practically demonstrate —that money-interest was not adequately adjusted to the changes in purchasing power of money. It is, of course, not to be assumed that commodity-interest ought

309

to be absolutely invariable; but it is practically certain that
its variations could not be three and a half times the
variations in money-interest, unless the price-movements
were inadequately predicted. If any doubts were possible
on this point they must disappear when we find that for
1871–1873 commodity-interest in London was *minus* 2.5
per cent. This shows that money lenders would have been
better off had they simply bought commodities in 1871 and
held them until 1873. As it was, they actually *lost* something, measured in commodities, as a consequence of
lending money. Such losses are especially apt to appear
in short periods. Thus if we take the period 1824–1825,
we find that the market rate was 3.7 per cent., the rate of
appreciation was *minus* 14.5 per cent., and the virtual rate
of interest in commodities, *minus* 10.8 per cent. !

In New York during the inflation period, 1861–1865,
commodity-interest sank to the ridiculously low figure of
minus 13.4 per cent. This shows in a striking way how
thoroughly the greenback inflation upset all business calculations, and how little the investing public realized in
advance the serious rise in prices of those fateful years.
That foresight was actually misguided at this time is amply
confirmed if we examine the predictions as to the termination of the war and the reduction of the gold premium,
which were recorded from month to month in the "Notes
on the Money Market" in the (New York) *Bankers' Magazine*. In all probability such errors of prediction are
common in periods of paper money inflation. Our tables
in § 7 show it for the Japanese inflation of 1878–1881.

§ 9

We can now understand why a high rate of interest need
not retard trade nor a low rate stimulate it. These facts
have puzzled many writers. For instance, Robert Baxter
wrote: [1] —

[1] *Journal of the Royal Statistical Society*, June, 1876.

"Public inquiry has been of late strongly directed to the reasons for the very low rate of interest upon loanable capital in the year 1875, the more especially as ten years ago the very high rates then prevailing created equal surprise."

And Jevons wrote:[1] —

"The effect of such and many more changes effected during the last twenty years or so is seen in a general increase in wealth and of mercantile industry and profits. Thus only can be explained the extraordinary high rate at which the interest of money has in the last ten years often stood. During 1854–1857 the rate of interest was only for a few months below 5 per cent., but for many months above it. For more than half a year it stood at 6 and 7 per cent., and in the end of 1857 it remained for nearly two months at 10 per cent. Again, in 1861, interest rose to 6 and 8 per cent., and all this, *to the surprise of the elder generation, without the general stoppage of trade, the breach of credit, and the flood of bankruptcy, which has hitherto attended such rates of interest.* It is certainly not to increasing scarcity of capital we should attribute such rates, but rather to a greatly extended field for its profitable employment."

But were these rates high? If we turn to our table for London rates, we find that the average market rate for 1853–1857 does appear to be the highest in the table; but, unmasking it of the money element, we find it is equivalent to a commodity-interest of 2.9 per cent. This is a very low rate. Merchants with increasing prices and money profits would find it easy to repay loans on such a basis.

Professor Bonamy Price,[2] writing at a time of very low interest rates, says: —

"Every one remembers the agitations associated with 7 per cent., the trepidation of merchants, the apprehension of losses in business. . . . If only a moderate rate could be reckoned on as steady, how happy would every one have been! . . . Yet what are the facts and feelings to-day? Is every merchant, every manufacturer rejoicing in the pleasant terms on which he obtains the accommodation so necessary for his business? . . . Alas! no such sounds meet our ears. . . . Commercial depression is the universal cry, depression probably unprecedented in duration in the annals of trade, except under the disturbing action of a prolonged

[1] *Investigations in Currency,* p. 95. (The italics are the present writer's.)

[2] "One per cent," *Contemporary Review,* April, 1877. (The italics are the present writer's.)

war. . . . In the export figures, the writer still fails to see any signs of the long-looked-for revival of trade. Both quantities and values continue to shrink in all save a few cases. . . . What, then, is the cause? *The explanation will certainly not be found in gold nor in any form of currency whatever . . . nor has any one said anything so ridiculous.* . . . That cause is one and only one: overspending."

If we turn back to the London table we find, however, that for 1874–1879 the commodity-rate of interest, so far from being low, was 7 per cent.! It would be astonishing if trade did *not* shrink under such a burden.

All these writers mistook high or low nominal interest for high or low real interest. Tooke apparently did the same. In his *History of Prices*, Vol. II, p. 349, he names as the last of six reasons for the fall of prices for 1814-1837, "a reduction in the general rate of interest." This is probably not only an inversion of cause and effect, but also, when the veil of money is thrown off, a misstatement of fact. The commodity-interest for 1826–1829 was 7.7 per cent. Tooke, Price, and Jevons all overlooked the fact that interest, unlike prices, is not an instantaneous but essentially a *time* phenomenon.

§ 10

When long periods of price-movements are taken, the influence of appreciation on interest is more certain. The following table shows this for England. It consists of four periods, of 10, 12, 22, and 11 years respectively:—

LONDON MARKET RATES OF INTEREST IN RELATION
TO RISING AND FALLING PRICES

	Market Interest i	Appreciation of Money in Commodities a	Virtual Interest in Commodities j
1826–1835	3.4	+ 1.2	4.6
1853–1864	4.6	− 0.9	3.7
1874–1895	2.4	+ 2.4	4.8
1896–1906	2.9	− 2.9	0.0

In averages covering so many years we may be sure that accidental causes are almost wholly eliminated. We find that during the period of falling prices, 1826–1835, the average rate of interest was only 3.4; that during the following period of rising prices, 1853–1864, it was higher (4.6 per cent.); that during the next period, 1874–1895, when prices were again falling, the rate was again low (2.4 per cent.); and finally that in 1896–1906, with prices rising, interest again recovered. In every case interest is high when prices are rising and low when they are falling. For these long periods, therefore, we find the facts in agreement with the theory in every case. It is also a noteworthy fact that the commodity-interest in this table of long periods is far less variable than for short periods. The variability, as shown by the "standard deviation" of the four figures in the above table is, for London, .82 for the market rate, and 1.94 for the virtual rate. *The adjustment of (money) interest to long price-movements is more perfect than to short price-movements.*

The following table gives the long time averages for New York. The war period is omitted:—

NEW YORK RATES OF INTEREST IN RELATION TO RISING AND FALLING PRICES

	Interest Prime Two Name 60 Days i	Appreciation of Money in Commodities a^1	Virtual Interest in Commodities j^1
1849–1857	8.2[1]	− 3.8	4.4
1875–1896	5.1	+ 2.6	7.7
1897–1906	4.5	− 3.4	1.1

We find that the money rate in the second period, when money was appreciating, was, as our theory requires,

[1] The average of Elliott's figures (which are not for "prime" paper) is 9.2, but 1.0 has been deducted from this average in order that it may be properly compared with the average of Robbins's figures for 1875–1891. This correction is based on the fact that 1.0 was the average excess of Elliott's figures over Robbins's during the fifteen years, 1860–1874. See Appendix to Chap. XIV, § 1.

lower than that in the first, when money was depreciating, but that the rate in the third period, when money was again depreciating, was, unfavorably to our theory, lower than that in the second when money was appreciating. Here we also see that the variability of the virtual interest in terms of commodities is less than for short periods, and more nearly like the variability for the market rate of interest in terms of money. The variability, as measured by the "standard deviation," of the rates of interest for the three periods in the above table are for market rate of interest in terms of money, 1.6; for virtual interest in terms of commodities, 2.3.

§ 11

Three general facts have now been established: (1) Rising and falling prices and wages are directly correlated with high and low rates of interest; (2) The adjustment of interest to price-movements is inadequate; (3) This adjustment is more nearly adequate for long than for short periods.

These facts are capable of a common explanation expressing the manner in which the adjustment referred to takes place. Suppose an upward movement of prices begins. Business profits (measured in *money*) will rise; for profits are the difference between gross income and expense, and if both these rise, their difference will also rise. Borrowers can now afford to pay higher "money-interest." If, however, only a few persons at first see this, the interest will not be fully adjusted,[1] and borrowers will realize an

[1] It seems scarcely necessary to add as an independent cause of maladjustment the accumulation (or in the opposite case, depletion) of bank reserves, for this is but another symptom of maladjustment due to imperfect foresight. An increase of gold supply, as in 1852–1853 (see Tooke and Newmarch, *History of Prices*, Vol. V, p. 345), may first find its way into the loan market instead of into circulation. But if foresight were perfect, this would not happen, or if it did happen, borrowers would immediately take it out (or increase the liabilities against it) to avail themselves of the double advantage of low interest and high prospective profits from the rise of prices about to follow.

extra margin of profit after deducting interest charges. This raises an expectation of a similar profit in the future and this expectation, acting on the demand for loans, will raise the rate of interest. If the rise is still inadequate, the process is repeated, and thus by continual trial and error the rate approaches the true adjustment.

When a fall of prices begins, the reverse effects appear. Money profits fall. Borrowers cannot afford to pay the old rates of interest. If, through miscalculation, they still attempt to do this, it will cut into their real profits. Discouraged thus for the future, they will then bid lower rates.

Since at the beginning of an upward price-movement the rate of interest is too low, and at the beginning of a downward movement it is too high, we can understand not only that the averages for the whole periods are imperfectly adjusted, but that the delay in the adjustment leaves a relatively low interest at the beginning of an ascent of prices, and a relatively high interest at the beginning of a descent. And this is what we find to be true. That the adjustment is more perfect for long periods than for short seems to be because, in short periods, the years of non-adjustment at the beginning occupy a larger relative part of the whole period.

§ 12

What has been said bears directly on the theory of "credit cycles." In the view here presented, periods of speculation and depression are the result of *inequality* of foresight. If all persons underestimated a rise of price in the same degree, the non-adjustment of interest would merely produce a transfer of wealth from lender to borrower. It would not influence the volume of loans (except so far as the diversion of income from one person to another would itself have indirect effects, such as bankruptcy). Under such circumstances the rate of interest would be below the normal, but as no one would know it, no borrower would borrow more and no lender lend less because of it. In the actual world however, foresight is very unequally distributed. Only a few persons have the faculty of always "coming out where they look." Now it is precisely these persons who largely make up the borrowing class. Just because of their superior foresight, there is delegated to them the management of capital; they become "captains of industry." It therefore happens that when prices are rising, borrowers are more apt to see it than lenders. Hence, while the borrower is willing to pay a higher interest than before for the same loan, lenders are willing to loan for the same interest as before. This disparity has as its effect that the rate of interest will not rise as high as if both sides saw the conditions equally well. It will also cause an increase of loans and investments.[1] This constitutes part of the stimulus to business which takes place in times of rising prices.

When prices fall, on the other hand, borrowers see that they cannot employ "money" productively except on easier terms, but lenders do not see why the terms should be made easier. In consequence, "enterprisers" borrow less, trade languishes, and, though interest falls in consequence of decrease in demand, it does not fall enough to keep the demand from decreasing.[2]

We see, therefore, that while *imperfection* of foresight transfers wealth from creditor to debtor or the reverse, *inequality* of foresight produces overinvestment during rising prices and relative stagnation during falling prices.

[1] That this and the corresponding statement in the next paragraph are borne out by facts appears to be confirmed, so far as bank loans and discounts are concerned, by Sumner, *History of Banking in the United States* (New York, 1896), and Juglar, *Crises Commerciales* (Paris, 1889).

[2] President Andrews, in *An Honest Dollar*, p. 3, writes: "Interest is low . . . not because money is abundant as before, but because it is not, its scarcity having induced fall of prices, and so paralysis in industry." But, it should be added, the cause of the fall of interest is primarily the *expectation* of small profits.

In the former case society is trapped into devoting too much investment of productive energies for future return, while in the contrary case, underinvestment is the rule. It does not seem possible to decide the question which of the two evils is the greater.[1]

§ 13

The facts which have been shown in this chapter are important in two respects. They prove, first, that men do actually, even if unaware of so doing, contrive to offset the effects of changes in the monetary standard by adjusting the rate of interest; and, secondly, that this adjustment is far from adequate. In consequence of the inadequacy of the interest-adjustment, a large amount of wealth is continually and unintentionally transferred from the creditor- to the debtor-class, and *vice versa*. The bimetallists were partially right in their claim that the creditor-class were gainers during the period of falling prices in the two decades 1875–1895. The situation has been the exact opposite during the decade 1896–1906. We must not make the mistake, however, of assuming that the enrichment of the debtor-class during the last decade atones for the impoverishment of that class during the previous two decades; for the personnel of social classes changes

[1] For arguments on both sides, see Professor Marshall's evidence, *Report on Depression of Trade* (1886), p. 422. See also his *Principles of Economics*, Vol. I (3d ed., 1895), p. 674: "When we come to discuss the causes of alternating periods of inflation and depression of commercial activity, we shall find that they are intimately connected with those variations in the real rate of interest which are caused by changes in the purchasing power of money. For when prices are likely to rise, people rush to borrow money and buy goods, and thus help prices to rise; business is inflated, and is managed recklessly and wastefully; those working on borrowed capital pay back less real value than they borrowed, and enrich themselves at the expense of the community. When afterwards credit is shaken and prices begin to fall, every one wants to get rid of commodities and get hold of money which is rapidly rising in value; this makes prices fall all the faster, and the further fall makes credit shrink even more, and thus for a long time prices fall because prices *have* fallen."

rapidly.   Nor must we make the mistake of assuming that
the debtor-class consists of the poor.   The typical debtor
to-day is the stockholder, and the typical creditor, the
bondholder.   What is actually going on to-day in consequence of a steadily cheapening dollar is a vast transfer
of advantage from bondholders to stockholders.   It is this
transfer which has produced many of our latest millionaires.   Their millions have been silently abstracted from
the pockets of the unsuspecting "safe" investors in bonds,
depositors in savings banks, and the salaried classes.   The
fault, however, is not of those who thus profit, but of the
monetary conditions which permit the ceaseless ebb and
flow of price-levels.   The problem of a stable monetary
standard is of vital importance.   We are apt to forget its
importance during a period of "prosperity," and we are
apt also to forget that much of what is called prosperity
is delusive.   It is delusive for two reasons: First, it is
often not general prosperity, but prosperity of the debtor
or stockholding or entrepreneur classes, who are always
much in evidence, at the expense of the creditor, bond-
holding, salaried classes, who bear their losses silently
behind the scenes; secondly, so-called prosperity is often
another name for reckless wastefulness, for which there must
be a day of reckoning in the form of a commercial crisis.[1]

[1] See *The Gold Supply and Prosperity*, edited by Byron W. Holt
(The Moody Corporation), New York, 1907.

CHAPTER XV

§ 1

In the last chapter we found statistical evidence of the influence of changes in the monetary standard upon the rate of interest. We now proceed to a similar inductive study of the economic — as distinct from the monetary — influences upon the rate of interest.

In a study so broad, it would be useless to attempt any exhaustive verification by statistics; the facts at hand are too meager, and not such as to enable us to isolate the separate causes at work. It will usually happen in any given case that some of the economic causes tending to make interest high are combined with others which tend to make it low. The fact, therefore, that interest is either high or low in such a case will not, of itself, be decisive in favor of any theory. The best that we can expect is to show that the facts as we find them are at any rate consistent with the theory maintained. For practical purposes, such a showing is enough, both because the theory should stand on its own merits as an analysis, without the bolstering of statistical verification; and because, if the analysis were really incorrect, a very cursory examination of the facts would probably suffice to refute it.

In our study of facts it is well to remember that the causes tending to make interest high or low sometimes work out their effects, partly or wholly, in other ways. For instance, the economic causes which, in the United States, have tended to make interest high, have also tended to bring in loans from other countries, such as Great Britain, where the rate of interest was low. The introduction of the loans prevented interest from being as high as it otherwise would.

289

In general it is true that a cause which would tend to make interest high in a community may simply result in increasing the loans contracted by that community, provided there exists another community in which the rate of interest is lower. If recourse to borrowing is not practicable, other methods of adding to present at the expense of future income — of "tipping forward" the income curve — may be found. If this "tipping forward" goes far enough it will show itself in a dissipation of capital; if not, in a slower accumulation. Contrariwise, the causes which work toward lending may, if lending is impracticable, result in some other form of "tipping back" the income curve and may show itself in a more rapid accumulation of capital or a less rapid dissipation. Finally, the same economic causes which tend to make interest high will tend also to encourage the production of the less substantial and durable instruments, whereas those causes which tend to make interest low will favor the production of instruments of the more durable and substantial types.

In short, in our collection of facts we should ascribe very similar significance to the four sets of phenomena — *high interest, borrowing, dissipation of capital, and perishability of instruments;* any causes back of these phenomena, which, according to our theory, should produce any one of the four, will tend also to produce the other three. Likewise we should ascribe similar significance to the four opposing phenomena — *low interest, lending, accumulation,* and *durability of instruments.*

§ 2

Briefly stated, the theory we are testing is that the rate of interest expresses human preference for present over future goods, as that preference works itself out from the nature of the individual and the character of his income-stream. We shall begin by considering the manner in which the nature of the individual influences the rate of interest.

In a previous chapter we enumerated the causes which, in the nature of man, tend to make interest high or low. It was there maintained that foresight, self-control, and regard for posterity tend to make interest low. We may therefore expect to find, in a community possessing these qualities, one or more of the four interequivalent phenomena already mentioned — low interest, lending to other communities, accumulation of capital, and construction of substantial instruments; and to find, in a community lacking these qualities, one or more of the four opposite conditions.

No extended study is needed to show that precisely these opposing sets of phenomena are actually found in the two opposite conditions mentioned. The communities and nationalities which are most noted for the qualities mentioned — foresight, self-control, and regard for posterity — are probably Holland, Scotland, England, France, and the Jews, and among these peoples interest has been low. Moreover, they have been money lenders, they have the habit of thrift or accumulation, and their instruments of wealth are in general of the substantial variety. The durability of their instruments is especially obvious in their buildings, both public and private, and in their ways of transportation — carriage roads, tramways, and railroads. Thus in England the railways have expended an average of $165,000 per mile, which is from two to three times the corresponding expenditure in most countries.[1] The difference, though partly explainable by a difference in methods of accounting, seems largely due to the lower rate of time-preference in England.

John Rae observes of Holland: —

"The Dutch seem, of all European nations, hitherto to have been inclined to carry instruments to the most slowly returning orders. The durability given to all the instruments constructed by them,

[1] See Dorsey, *English and American Railroads Compared*, New York (Wiley), 1887; Price Howell, *Journal of the Royal Statistical Society*, Vol. LXII, p. 83; *Commercial and Financial Chronicle*, Vol. LXXIV, p. 1224.

the care with which they are finished, and the attention paid to preserving and repairing them, have been often noticed by travelers. In the days when their industry and frugality were most remarkable, interest was very low, government borrowing at 2 per cent., and private people at 3." [1]

On the other hand, among communities and peoples noted for lack of foresight and for negligence with respect to the future are China, India, Java,[2] the negro communities in the Southern states, the peasant communities of Russia,[3] and the North and South American Indians, both before and after they had been pushed to the wall by the white man. In all of these communities we find that interest is high, that there is a tendency to run into debt and to dissipate rather than accumulate capital, and that their dwellings and other instruments are of a very flimsy and perishable character.

It may well be that there are other causes at work to produce these results. We are here merely noting the fact that lack of foresight is one factor present.

Of China, Rae states: —

"The testimony of travelers ascribes to the instruments formed by the Chinese a durability very inferior to similar instruments constructed by Europeans. The walls of houses, we are told, unless of the higher ranks, are in general of unburnt bricks of clay, or of hurdles plastered with earth; the roofs, of reeds fastened to laths. We can scarcely conceive more unsubstantial, or temporary fabrics. Their partitions are of paper, requiring to be renewed every year.

A similar observation may be made concerning their implements of husbandry and other utensils. They are almost entirely

---

[1] *The Sociological Theory of Capital*, pp. 128–129.

[2] My colleague, Professor Clive Day, informs me that the rate of interest in Java is often 40 per cent.

[3] See Bloch, *The Future of War*, p. 205. It appears that the peasant will sell a promise to labor a short time in the future at one third the current wages! See also E. B. Lanin (pseud.), "Russian Finance," *Fortnightly Review*, February, 1891, Vol. LV, pp. 188, 190, 196, for typical and extreme cases. Inostranietz, "L'Usure en Russie," *Journal des Economiste*, 1893, Ser. 5, Vol. XVI, pp. 233–243, states that the rates paid by poor peasants to well-to-do peasants are frequently 5 per cent. *per week!*

of wood, the metals entering but very sparingly into their construction; consequently they soon wear out, and require frequent renewals." [1]

"European travelers are surprised at meeting . . . little floating farms, by the side of swamps which only require draining to render them tillable. It seems to them strange that labor should not rather be bestowed on the solid earth, where its fruits might endure, than on structures that must decay and perish in a few years. The people they are among think not so much of future years as of the present time." [2]

"The Father Parennin, indeed, asserts, that it is their great deficiency in forethought and frugality in this respect, which is the cause of the scarcities and famines that frequently occur. 'I believe,' he says, 'that, notwithstanding its great number of inhabitants, China would furnish enough grain for all, but that there is not sufficient economy observed in its consumption, and that they employ an astonishing quantity of it in the manufacture of the wine of the country, and of raque.'" [3]

"In China, we are told by Barrow, that the legal rate of interest is 12 per cent., but that, in reality, it varies from 18 to 36." [4]

Simcox writes of China as follows:—

"The legal maximum is 3 per cent. per mensem, and the usual rate, as already mentioned, 30 per cent., per annum." [5]

Even on the seacoast where Englishmen have settled, the rate of interest is high, and its reduction, such as has occurred, is only because of the equivalent economic phenomenon, loans from abroad. These facts are seen in the Appendix, [6] where the rates of interest in China are given. It is interesting to observe how the economic conditions in China which at first produced high interest afterward led gradually to loans from England and a fall in the rate of interest. The bank rate in Shanghai as given in the table was at first (1866) 13 per cent., and gradually fell to 6 per cent. as investments of English capitalists were made.

[1] *The Sociological Theory of Capital*, pp. 88–89.   [2] *Loc. cit.*, p. 92.
[3] *Loc. cit.*, pp. 89–90.   [4] *Loc. cit.*, p. 128.
[5] *Primitive Civilizations*, London (Swan Sonnenschein), 1894, Vol. II, p. 327.
[6] See Appendix to Chap. XIV, § 1.

Of the North American Indians, Rae observed : —

"Upon the banks of the St. Lawrence, there are several little Indian villages. They are surrounded, in general, by a good deal of land from which the wood seems to have been long extirpated and have, besides, attached to them, extensive tracts of forest. The cleared land is rarely, I may almost say never, cultivated, nor are any inroads made in the forest for such a purpose. The soil is, nevertheless, fertile, and were it not, manure lies in heaps by their houses. Were every family to inclose half an acre of ground, till it, and plant in it potatoes and maize, it would yield a sufficiency to support them one half the year. They suffer too, every now and then, extreme want, insomuch that, joined to occasional intemperance, it is rapidly reducing their numbers. This, to us, so strange apathy proceeds not, in any great degree, from repugnance to labor; on the contrary, they apply very diligently to it, when its reward is immediate." [1]

Of the South American Indians in Paraguay Rae tells of the difficulties which the Jesuits found in persuading the natives to provide for the future : —

" . . . if these [the Jesuits] gave up to them the care of the oxen with which they plowed, their indolent thoughtlessness would probably leave them at evening still yoked to the implement. Worse than this, instances occurred where they cut them up for supper, thinking, when reprehended, that they sufficiently excused themselves by saying they were hungry." [2]

In regard to the negro and the Russian we may cite the statistics of George K. Holmes [3] and the observations of N. T. Bacon. [4]

§ 3

In many if not all of the cases which have been cited there are, of course, other elements which would tend to explain the facts besides mere mental characteristics. Thus, the high rate of interest among the negroes and the Russian peasants is undoubtedly due in part to their pov-

---

[1] *The Sociological Theory of Capital*, pp. 71–72.
[2] *Loc. cit.*, p. 76.   [3] Census of 1890.
[4] *Yale Review*, Vol. XII, pp. 141, 239; Vol. XIII, p. 51.

erty, though their poverty is in turn largely due to the mental characteristics. There is here in operation the vicious circle which has been noted in Chapter XII. Where there is too little appreciation of the needs of the future, capital tends to disappear; and the pressure of poverty tends to enhance still further the demands of the present and to press down its victims from bad to worse.

But there are not wanting cases in which even persons who have wealth, but who nevertheless lack foresight and self-control, exhibit the same facts, especially by running into debt. This is characteristic of a considerable number of the spoiled sons of rich English noblemen. The type is well described in some of Stevenson's novels. These persons are found living in Australia and elsewhere in virtual exile on a stipend provided by their families at stated intervals. This stipend is sometimes provided on condition that they remain away from their original environment with its temptations to extravagance. One such individual known to the writer had inherited a large fortune. The precaution had been taken to leave it in trust so that he could draw only the income. Yet this man contrived to contract large debts on chattel mortgages at high rates of interest, and was noted for his wasteful, short-sighted erection of temporary dwellings in the various communities among which he continually flitted. The same characteristics are often found among wealthy students at universities, who have acquired, through improper home training, an exaggerated idea of the needs of the moment and little appreciation of those of the future. These men become the victims of money lenders, and are frequent patrons of the pawn shops.

Not only do we find examples of a high rate of preference for present over future goods among the prodigally rich, but we often find the opposite example of a low rate of preference for present over future goods among the thrifty poor. Examples are especially frequent among the Jews, whose propensity to accumulate and to lend money even

325

in the face of misfortune and social ostracism, is too well
known to require extended comment.

§ 4

The factor which has been designated as "regard for posterity" deserves special attention.   Perhaps the most conspicuous example of extreme disregard for posterity is
found in Rome during the time of its decline and fall.   The
following quotations from Rae contain important testimony : —

"It were needless," he says, "to enlarge on a subject so well
known as that of the general corruption of Roman manners, from
the time of the first Cæsar.   Venality and licentiousness may be
said to have been universal.   I shall confine myself to one particular, as marking sufficiently the declension of those principles on
which the strength of the effective desire of accumulation mainly
depends.   I allude to the decay of the family affections, of which
evidence everywhere meets us.   The men did not wish to be fathers,
scarcely did the women wish to be mothers. . . .   They lived, not
in others, or for others, but for themselves, and sought their good
in enjoyments altogether selfish.   It was their aim to expend on
their own personal pleasures whatever they possibly could.   It
would seem as if the majority, could they have foreknown the
exact limits of their lives, would have made their fortunes and
them terminate together.   As they could not do so, the fortunes
of many ended before their lives, as the fortunes of others held out
beyond their lives.   To reap, however, themselves, while alive,
all possible benefit from what they might chance to leave others
to enjoy after their death, they encouraged some of the members
of a despicable class who seem to have constituted no inconsider-
able part of Roman society.   Parasites ready to minister to every
pleasure, and to perform every possible service, waited on the man
of wealth, in the hope and expectation of enjoying a portion of it
after his death.   They were more desirable than children, both
because they were able to give something more than mere unsubstantial affection and esteem, and because they were willing to
give it. . . .   It gave occasion to the law compelling parents
to leave their children a certain part, a fourth, of their property.
Its prevalence may be judged of by the wording of the enactments
increasing the children's share. . . .   The general selfishness of
the principles guiding the conduct of individuals may be gathered

from the prevailing proverb, "When I die let the world burn." . . .
Pasture took place of tillage; corn was brought from the provinces;
and when the supply failed famine ensued. Even the construction of ships for the transport of this, and other merchandise, would
seem to have been an effort to which the accumulative principle
was scarcely equal. It was found necessary to encourage it by
rewarding those who prosecuted that branch of industry. Sometimes land formerly cultivated was allowed to lie entirely waste,
and passed altogether out of the class of instruments. The forest
and wilderness gained on the Romans, as they would now, for
similar reasons, on an Indian population, were some of these tribes
put in possession of the domains, anciently the property of their
race, at present yielding abundantly to the provident industry
of the whites. Had there been no interruption of the barbarians,
the Empire must have perished, more slowly perhaps, but as certainly, from the operation alone of these internal causes of decay.
They were occasioning a progressive diminution of the capacity
which materials formerly possessed. Thus, it is to the Romans
themselves as much as to the barbarians, that the destruction of
the public edifices is to be ascribed. The stones were applied to
private purposes." [1]

"Thus, among the Roman writers, the heir is always represented
in an invidious light, and to save for him is represented as a folly.
The writings of Horace, and the contemporary poets, throughout,
exemplify the prevalence of this feeling." [2]

"In ancient Rome, interest was in reality exceedingly high, from
12 to 50 per cent." [3]

These rates doubtless refer to the degenerate days.
Previously, at the time of the end of the republic, the rate
was as low as 4 to 6 per cent. [4]

§ 5

The characteristics of foresight, self-control, and regard
for posterity seem to be partly natural and partly acquired
within the lifetime of the individual. Among the cases

---

[1] *Loc. cit.*, pp. 95–99.   [2] *Loc. cit.*, p. 64.

[3] *Loc. cit.*, p. 129.   Rae's authority is Boucher's *Histoire de L'Usure*,
Paris, 1819, p. 25.

[4] See Seligman's *Principles of Economics*, New York (Longmans),
1905, p. 404.

327

which have been given are conspicuous examples of both, although it is difficult here, as always, to disentangle the influence of nature from that of environment. We are accustomed, for instance, to ascribe to the Jews a natural racial tendency to accumulate, though this characteristic is certainly reënforced by, if not entirely due to, the extraordinary influence of Jewish tradition. Of the Scotch, it would be difficult to say how much of their thrift is due to nature and how much to training handed down from father to son. The American negro is regarded by nature as a happy-go-lucky creature; but recent experience with industrial schools has demonstrated the fact that these characteristics can be largely reversed by training, if in fact they have not been entirely created by the lack of training under conditions of slavery. There is now accumulating much testimony [1] to show that there is more error than truth in the common opinion as to the relatively great importance of heredity as compared with environment.

When postal savings banks were first introduced in England, it was objected that the habits of the English poor, for whom they were intended, were such that they would never make use of them. But Gladstone insisted that habits were an arbitrary matter, and that the fashion of spending could be displaced by the fashion of saving as soon as the principle of imitation had had time to operate. The experience with English postal savings banks has justified his prediction.[2]

In fact, it would be a serious mistake to assume that the characteristics of man as to foresight, self-control, and regard for his own and his children's future are fixed racial or national qualities. The part which nature may play in

[1] For instance, the reports of the Children's Aid Society of New York; the child-saving work of Dr. and Mrs. J. H. Kellogg at Battle Creek; the evidence of the British Interdepartmental Committee on School Children, etc.

[2] See *The Development of Thrift*, by Mary W. Brown, New York (Macmillan), 1900.

these matters is as yet far from being understood; but however great that part may be, it is certainly true that the influence of training is also great, and therein lies the possibility and hope of social reform in these matters.   It should be one of the distinct aims of any intelligent modern education, whether in the home or the school, to inculcate foresight, self-control, and a due regard for the needs of future years and even of future generations.   It goes without saying that individuals and nations with these characteristics have therein a more secure and permanent claim for success in all directions.

§ 6

But, as has been emphasized in previous chapters, the rate of preference for present over future goods is not a question of mere personal characteristics, but depends also upon the character of one's income-stream; namely, on its size, shape, composition, and probability.   In respect to *size*, our theory maintains that the larger the income, *other things such as foresight and self-control being equal*, the lower the rate of preference for present over future goods.   If this is true, we should expect to find poverty and riches associated respectively with a high and a low rate of interest, or with borrowing and lending, or with spending and saving, or with perishable and durable instruments.   That this characterization is in general correct is not likely to be denied. It is true of course that the *amount* loaned to the poor is small because each individual loan is necessarily small; but the *number* of these loans is very great, and the desire of the poor to borrow, when it exists, is very intense.   The many conspicuous exceptions to these rules are explainable on other grounds.   It not infrequently happens that the poor, instead of being borrowers, are lenders; but in this case either they have unusual foresight, self-control, regard for their children, and other qualities tending in the same direction, or else their income-stream has such a time-shape

as to encourage lending rather than borrowing. Reverse
conditions apply likewise to the case of many wealthy men,
viz. those who are borrowers rather than lenders. Whether
from wrong training or other causes, they lack foresight, self-
control, regard for posterity, etc. But disregarding these
factors and confining our view to the direct influence of the
size of income, it is true, in a general way, that the poor
are more eager borrowers than the rich, and will often patronize pawn shops and other agencies in which the rate
of interest is inordinately high; also that their dwellings
or other structures are often of a very unsubstantial character, such as would not "pay" except to those who put
a very high estimate on present as compared with future
goods. The deeper the poverty, the higher the rates which
the borrowers are compelled to accept. Even pawnbroking is not available for the extremely poor, but is
patronized rather by the moderately poor. Those who are
extremely poor cannot give the kind of security which the
pawnbroker requires. On this account they become the
victims of even higher rates of interest, pledging their
stoves, tables, beds, and other household furniture for the
loans they contract. These loans are repaid in installments
such that the rate of interest is seldom lower than 100 per
cent. per annum.[1]

Turning from classes to countries, it is noteworthy that
in the countries in which there are large incomes we find low
interest, a tendency to lend rather than borrow, accumulate
rather than spend, and to form durable rather than perishable instruments, whereas in countries where incomes are
low the opposite conditions prevail. Thus, incomes are
large and interest is low in Holland, France, and England,
whereas the reverse conditions hold in Ireland, China, India,
and the Philippines. In Ireland, for instance, especially

---

[1] For details as to thirteen typical loans of this character, see
U. S. Bureau of Labor Bulletin, No. 64, May, 1906, pp. 622–633.
Thus, "loan 1," 143 per cent., "loan 3," 224 per cent., "loan 7," 156
per cent.

in the early part of the nineteenth century, the rate of interest was high.   The cottier was always in debt, and his hut and other instruments were of the most unsubstantial variety.[1]   Again in the Philippines the rates of interest on good security are often 2, 5, and even 10 per cent. a month.   "The Chinese money lender frequently takes advantage of the Filipino's poverty."[2]   Many of these cases may be wholly or partly explained by other causes such as have been mentioned in the last section.   The possibility of more than one explanation shows that in this field we can scarcely hope to adduce any complete proof of an inductive nature.   But since any of the possible explanations fit in with our theory, we are safe in saying that the facts do not at any rate contradict that theory.

§ 7

As to the influence of the *composition* of income, it is even more difficult to obtain any statistical confirmation of value.   In a previous chapter it was shown that variations in the amount of that income which takes the form of food would have an effect on the rate of interest similar to the effect of variations in the total income itself.   Scarcity of food should therefore cause high interest, and abundance of food, low interest.   Certain presumptive evidence is found in the observation of Jevons on the relation between the price of wheat and the rate of discount.[3]   Wheat being the most typical food in England, it may be assumed with considerable probability that its price varies inversely with the amount of food consumed.   Jevons found that a

[1] See Longfield, "The Tenure of Land in Ireland," in Proloyn's *Systems of Land Culture*, London (Cassell, Petter, and Galpin), 1876, p. 16.

[2] From a letter to the author from Professor E. W. Kemmerer; see also his article in *The Business Monthly*, Pittsburg, April, 1907, p. 2.

[3] See *Investigations in Currency and Finance*, 1884, p. xiv; also, Robert Goodbody, in Byron W. Holt's *Gold Supply and Prosperity*, p. 166.

high price of wheat corresponded to high rates of interest,
and *vice versa*.   This would almost amount to saying that a
relative scarcity of food was associated with high interest,
and *vice versa*.   During the siege of Paris the rate of interest was high, although other causes than the scarcity of
bread were doubtless accountable for the fact.

§ 8

As to the influence of *risk*, we encounter similar difficulties.   But evidence as to our main contention, namely,
that in general risk tends to raise the commercial rate of
interest but to lower pure interest, is forthcoming.   The
first part of this proposition is a matter of so common observation that no special collection of facts is necessary.
Every lender or borrower knows that the rate of interest
varies directly with risk.   A bird in the hand is worth
two in the bush.   The principle applies not only to the
explicit interest in loan contracts, but to the implicit
interest which goes with the possession of all capital.
Where there is uncertainty whether capital saved for the
future will ever be of service, but there is certainty that
it can be of service if used immediately, the possessor
needs the possibility of a very high future return in order
to induce him to save the capital for future use.   It is noteworthy that in time of war there is a ruthless destruction
of crops and a tendency among the possessors of consumable
wealth to enjoy it while they may.   The same conditions
are characteristic of communities which are in a perpetual
state of uncertainty.[1]   " The rate of interest is everywhere
proportional to the safety of investment.   For this reason
we find in Korea that a loan ordinarily brings from 2 to
5 per cent. per month.   Good security is generally forthcoming, and one may well ask why it is so precarious to

[1] On the uncertainties of Indian life, see *The Sociological Theory
of Capital*, pp. 69, 70.

lend.   The answer is not creditable to Korean justice.
. . . In a land where bribery is almost second nature,
and private rights are of small account unless backed up
by some sort of influence, the best apparent security
may prove a broken reed when the creditor comes to lean
upon it." [1]

There remains the second part of the proposition in regard to risk; namely, that while risk tends to increase the
rate of interest on risky loans, it tends at the same time to
decrease that on safe loans.   This proposition is not familiar
to most persons.   It has usually caused surprise when,
during a time of political stress and danger, the rates of
interest on perfectly safe loans were found to be so small.
Many such instances may be cited.   At certain periods
during the Civil War, when the greatest uncertainty
prevailed, loans with good security were contracted at
nominal rates, and bank deposits tended to accumulate
for lack of sufficient outlet in secure investments.   Times
when public confidence is shaken are characterized not only
by high rates on unsafe loans, but by efforts on the part
of timid investors to find a safe place for their savings, even
if they have to sacrifice some or all of the interest upon it.
They will even hoard it in stockings and safe deposit vaults,
or leave it idle on deposit in bank.   ". . . In 1903 . . .
the public took alarm and began to hoard their capital
in the form of banking credits, instead of bidding with it
for securities.   In the meantime, the scarcity of free capital
in the market enabled the banks, which held the money
of the public, to exact 5 and 6 per cent." [2]   We may even
occasionally find cases in which the desire to obtain a safe
method of using capital is so keen and so difficult to satisfy
that the rate of interest is negative.   The investor is then
in the position of the user of a safe deposit vault, thankful
enough to receive the assurance that his capital, by being

[1] H. B. Hurlbert, *The Passing of Korea*, New York, 1906, p. 283.
[2] Charles A. Conant, "How the Stock Market reflects Values,"
North American Review, March, 1905, pp. 346–359.

intrusted to another, will not be diminished, to say nothing of being increased.[1]

§ 9

We still need to verify the most essential part of our theory; namely, that the rate of interest depends upon the *time-shape* of the income-stream. If the theory is correct, we should find, other things being equal, that when, in any community, the income-streams of its inhabitants are increasing, the rate of interest will be high; that when they are decreasing, the rate of interest will be low; and that when they alternate from one condition to the other, the rate of interest will also alternate according to the period of the loan.

The most striking examples of increasing income-streams are found in new countries. It may be said that the United States has almost always belonged to this category. Were it possible to express by exact statistics or diagrams the size of American incomes, they would undoubtedly show a steady increase since colonial days. Statistics almost equivalent to these desiderata are available (though not very accurate) in the form of the United States Census figures of "per capita wealth," as well as statistics of production and consumption of staple commodities and of exports and imports. These, combined with common observation and the statements of historians, lead to the conclusion that American incomes have been on the increase for two hundred years. It is also true that during this period of rising incomes, the rate of interest has been high. The simplest interpretation of these facts is that Americans, being constantly under the influence of great expectations, have been always ready to promise a relatively large part of their abundant future income for a relatively small addition to their present, just as he who expects soon to

[1] See Bagehot, *Lombard Street*, Chap. VI; also, Macaulay, *History of England*, Chap. XIX.

come into a fortune wishes to anticipate its realization by contracting a loan.

Not only has the rate of interest been high in America as compared with other countries during this period of ascending incomes, but some of the other conditions equivalent to a high rate of interest have also been in evidence. Thus, the country has been conspicuously a borrowing country, in debt to other countries. The proceeds of such loans have shown themselves in increased imports and diminished exports, creating a so-called unfavorable balance of trade. These phenomena have usually been expressed as a "demand for capital"; but, while it is quite true that the exploitation of our natural resources required the construction of railways and other forms of capital, this fact is better and more fully expressed in terms of income. We wanted, not the railways and machinery themselves, but the future enjoyable products to which this apparatus led. The construction of these instruments necessarily diminished the immediate enjoyable income of the country and added to that of the expected future. It was to even up this disparity of immediate and remote income that loans were contracted. It does not matter whether the loans from the foreigner were received in the form of machinery and other instruments of production, or in the form of the comforts of life to support us while we ourselves constructed the instruments. In either case the essential fact is the transformation of the income-stream, and not the "need of capital," which is merely one of the means thereto. Import statistics show that, as a matter of fact, we received our loans from the foreigner in both forms.

Not only have we witnessed the phenomena of high rates of interest and of borrowing during this period of American development, but it is also true that the character of the instruments created was for the most part of the unsubstantial and "quickly returning" kinds. Our highways, as John Rae pointed out, were little more than the natural surface of the earth after the removal of trees and rocks; our railways were lightly ballasted, often "narrow gauge," and crooked to avoid the necessity of excavations and tunnels; our earliest buildings were rude and unsubstantial. Everything was done, not in a permanent manner with reference to the remote future, but in order to save a large first cost.

During the last two decades these conditions have been reversed. The rates of interest in America have fallen greatly, as the statistics in the Appendix will show.[1] We have ceased to be a borrowing nation, and are buying back our securities from abroad. This repayment of debts is accomplished through the export of our now abundant products, and creates a so-called favorable balance of trade. Again, the character of the instruments which have been now for some time in process of construction is of the most substantial kind. Steel rails have long since taken the place of iron rails, "broad gauge" of "narrow gauge"; railways have been straightened by expensive tunnels, by bridges, and by excavations;[2] dwellings and other buildings have been made more substantial; macadamized roads are gradually coming into vogue; and in every direction — industrial, agricultural, and domestic — there is an evident tendency to invest a large first cost in order to reduce future running expenses.

§ 10

Thus in America we see exemplified on a very large scale the truth of the theory that a rising income-stream raises and a falling income-stream depresses the rate of interest, or that these conformations of the income-stream work out their effects in other equivalent forms. A similar causation may be seen in particular localities in the United States, es-

[1] See Appendix to Chap. XIV, § 1.
[2] It is estimated that Western railways in the United States have actually under way or in contemplation improvements amounting to $1,000,000,000. *Wall Street Journal*, December 19, 1905.

pecially where changes have been rapid, as in mining communities.   In California, in the two decades between 1850 and 1870, following the discovery of gold, the income-stream of that state was increasing at a prodigious rate, while the state was isolated from the world, railroad connection with the East not being completed until 1869.   During this period of isolation and ascending income, ". . . opportunities for investment were innumerable. Hence the rates of interest were abnormally high. The current rates in the 'early days' were quoted at $1\frac{1}{2}$ to 2 per cent. a month. . . .   The thrifty Michael Reese is said to have half repented of a generous gift to the University of California, with the exclamation, 'Ah, but I lose the interest,' a very natural regret when interest was 24 per cent. per annum." [1]   After railway connection in 1869, Eastern loans began to flow in. The decade, 1870–1880, was one of transition during which the phenomenon of high interest was gradually replaced by the phenomenon of borrowing from outside.   The rate of interest consequently dropped from 11 per cent. to 6 per cent. [2]   "Since 1880 the economic history of California, or at least of San Francisco and vicinity, has not differed so very much from that of the rest of the country." [3] During recent years the rate on mortgages in San Francisco, up to the time of the earthquake and fire, has been 4 to $4\frac{1}{2}$ per cent. exclusive of the state tax.

The same phenomena of enormous interest rates were also exemplified in Colorado and the Klondike.   There were many instances in both these places during the transition period from poverty to affluence, when loans were contracted at over 50 per cent. per annum, and the borrowers regarded themselves as lucky to get rates so "low." It was also conspicuously true that the first buildings and apparatus constructed in these regions were very unsub-

[1] Carl C. Plehn, "Notes concerning the Rates of Interest in California," *Quarterly Publications of the American Statistical Association*, September, 1899, pp. 351–352.

[2] *Ibid.*, p. 353.   [3] *Ibid.*, p. 353.

stantial. Rude board cabins were put up in a day. Thus, high interest, borrowing, and unsubstantial capital were the phenomena which attended these communities when undergoing their rapid expansion.

In Nevada in the seventies, when the mines were increasing their product and the income of its inhabitants was tending upwards, the rate of interest was high and the people in debt. The bonded state debt itself amounted to $500,000 and drew 15 per cent. interest.[1] In the next decade all these conditions were reversed. The mines were on the decline,[2] the rate of interest fell, and the state and territorial debts were largely paid off.[3] The fall of the rate of interest in this case could not have been due to the introduction of loans from outside, except so far as old debts were refunded at lower rates; fresh loans were seldom made, as the state had ceased to be a good place for new investments. In the last few years new Nevada mines in the gold-field region have been opened. Loans are again entering the state, and the same cycle of history as above described is about to be repeated.

Lumbering communities often go through a somewhat similar cycle. The virgin forests when first attacked tend to increase rapidly the income-streams of those who exploit them. Then comes a period of decrease. Thus in Michigan two or three decades ago the lumber companies found a profitable investment, and borrowed in order to exploit the Michigan forests. After the exploitation was complete and the forests had been (often unwisely) exhausted, those regions ceased to be a desirable place for investment, and their owners came into the position, not of receiving, but of seeking, investments.

After the trunk lines of railway were completed, connecting the Mississippi Valley with the East, there arose a great demand for loans to exploit the rich farming lands in that

---

[1] See "Message of the Governor of the State of Nevada," 1879.
[2] *Mines and Quarries*, 1902. Special *Report* U. S. Census, p. 255.
[3] See later, "Messages of the Governor of the State of Nevada."

section of the country.   The rate of interest frequently was
10 and 12 per cent., and even higher.   During much of this
time the Northwestern Mutual Life Insurance Company,
up to 1880, made an average rate on all its mortgage
loans, $10,000,000 in amount, of nearly 10 per cent.
Another striking proof of the demand for loans in the
Middle West is shown in the experience of the New York
and Connecticut life insurance companies.   New York,
up to 1880, had a law prohibiting the life insurance companies in that state from loaning on real estate outside of
New York.   Connecticut had no restriction in this regard,
and her companies loaned extensively in the West.   The
result is seen in the rates of interest realized on mortgage
loans of companies in the two states.   Taking the period
1860 to 1880 as a whole, the Connecticut companies realized
$1\frac{2}{10}$ per cent. more than did the New York companies.
Since 1880, the Middle West has developed rapidly, and
loans on farming lands are now made at low rates.   During
the past two years, certain of the insurance companies have
been making mortgage loans in Illinois at $4\frac{1}{2}$ per cent.[1]
A similar history has recently been enacting itself in the
northwest region of the United States.   During the period
of exploitation while the Great Northern and other railways
were developing this territory, the phenomena of high
interest and borrowing were almost universal.   But latterly, much to the surprise of many Easterners, it has been
found that the rates of interest in these states have been
at times lower even than in most American cities, and that
the inhabitants have actually been seeking to lend to the
East instead of to borrow from it.

§ 11

Australia furnishes another example of a country which,
through improvement in the means of transportation,

[1] See Zartman, *The Investments of Life Insurance Companies*,
New York (Holt), 1906, pp. 89–91.

created a great demand for loans. The rate during the fifties on safe securities was rather low. This rate increased until, during the seventies, 7, 8, and 9 per cent. were usual. Since 1880 the rates have declined.[1]

England may perhaps be cited as exemplifying the same phenomena which we have seen in the case of Nevada, though in a less degree. Thus, as Nevada has exhausted its mines of precious metals, so England is on the road toward exhaustion of its coal and iron supplies. This fact has been noted with considerable alarm by many economists, especially Jevons. It does not necessarily indicate that the economic power of Englishmen will be greatly or even at all lessened. Its significance shows itself in the tendency of England to become an investing country. It is the part of those who have property in mines not to use all of the product as income, but to reinvest in order to maintain the capital. This the Englishmen have done and are doing; and being unable to make satisfactory investments at home, they have placed their loans all over the world. The income-stream produced for them by their native island is destined, perhaps, to decline, certainly not greatly to increase; but by saving from this declining income and investing in South America, Australia, South Africa, and other regions where the natural resources are on the increase instead of on the wane, the Englishmen may still maintain their capital intact or even increase it. It is said, with how much accuracy I do not know, that Englishmen own an area in the United States as large as Ireland. The figures given by Giffen show that the national income increased for several decades, but that the rate of increase slackened[2] for the decade 1875–1885 compared with 1865–1875; that whereas in the earlier decades there was a general increase in all directions, in the later

[1] Zartman, *The Investments of Life Insurance Companies*, p. 103.

[2] Giffen, *Growth of Capital*, London (Bell), 1889. See also articles by Giffen in continuation of the same subject in *Journal of Royal Statistical Society*.

decade there were many items of decrease,[1] the most notable being of mines and ironworks;[2] and finally, that among the greatest increases was that of foreign investments.[3]

We thus see that the rate of preference for present over future goods, in its various manifestations — such as a high or low rate of interest, more or less lending and accumulation of capital, and the character of the instruments formed — depends upon the time-shape of the income-stream of a community, as determined by its natural resources; that in virgin countries like the United States in the last two centuries, Australia and South Africa, rich in timber, untouched ore, and raw materials generally, the income-stream is of the ascending type and produces a high rate of preference, whereas in older countries like England and Holland, in which the natural resources have been fully developed, and are even declining, the rate of preference tends to be low; such a country either uses up its income and thereby reduces its capital, or seeks economic salvation in foreign investment.

§ 12

The time-shape of an income-stream is, however, determined in part by other causes than natural resources. Among these causes, misfortune holds a high place in causing temporary depressions in the income-stream, that is, giving to it a time-shape which is first descending and afterwards ascending. The effect of such temporary depression is to produce a high valuation of immediate income during the depression period as compared with the valuation of the income expected after the depression is over. It is a matter of common observation in private life that loans often find their source in personal misfortune. The above-mentioned investigation of the conditions of borrowing among the poor[4] shows that the chief causes

---

[1] *Ibid.*, p. 44.   [2] *Ibid.*, p. 35.   [3] *Ibid.*, pp. 40–42.
[4] U. S. Bureau of Labor Bulletin, No. 64, May, 1906, pp. 622 ff.

for borrowing are a death or birth in the family, or protracted illness, the expense of which, even when amounting to only $10 or $20, would, without the loan, make serious inroads on the daily necessities.

We may see the operation of the same principle on a larger scale in the case of the San Francisco earthquake, which, had it not been for the succor rendered by the whole country, would have cut down the income-stream of the city to the starvation point. In addition to the aid of many millions of dollars of gifts, there were needed also heavy loans. Whether these loans were used to produce sustenance, which is direct income, or to offset the cost of rebuilding the city, which is outgo, the effect is the same, —they were for the purpose of salving over a temporary injury to the income-stream. The effect on the rate of interest was slight, because of the opportunity to borrow heavily from outside. Had the city not had this opportunity, the depression in its income-stream could not have been mitigated, and the rate of interest would inevitably have risen to a level comparable with that which prevailed in the same region a half century ago during the gold fever.

In much the same way is the income-stream of a nation affected by war. The effects in this case, however, are more complex, owing, first, to the element of uncertainty which the war introduces until peace is declared; and, secondly, to the fact that wars are apt to be more protracted than most other misfortunes. The effect, according to previous explanations, should be that at the beginning of the war the rates of interest on risky loans would be high. This would be especially true of the loans the periods of which are short, or not long enough to outlast the war. On the other hand, the rate of interest on safe loans would be lowered for short-term loans, and raised for long-term loans. A short-term loan relates to a descent in the income curve if repayable at a time when the income-stream is apt to be still further reduced. This descent in the income-stream, together with the element of uncertainty, tends, as has been seen, to lower the rate of interest on safe loans.   On the other hand, for long-term loans intended to outlast the war, the rate of interest is apt to be high, for the income-stream at the time of repayment may be expected to exceed the income-stream at the time of contract.

At the close of the war, after peace is declared and the element of uncertainty introduced by it has disappeared, the rate of interest, even on short-term loans, will be high; for then the country is, as it were, beginning anew, and the same causes operate to make interest high as apply in the case of all new countries.   The situation at this period is exemplified by the recent peace loan for Japan.

When the effects of the war include the issue of depreciated paper money, the rate of interest is affected in a somewhat more complex manner, being then subject to the influence of depreciation, according to the principles explained in Chapter V, and statistically verified in Chapter XIV.

Among the most powerful causes which affect the time-shape of income-streams has been noted the effect of invention.   That the claims which have been made for the effect of invention are verified in fact can scarcely be doubted when we consider the history of railway transportation. The very fact that during the last half century the chief outlet for investors' savings has been in the creation of new railways, is sufficient testimony.   What is true in the case of this single invention or group of inventions is more signally true when a large number of inventions is being made. The effect of the activity of the inventive faculty must have materially contributed to keep up the rate of interest in the United States, and during the last generation in Germany.

The striking way in which the rate of interest in Germany has been maintained during the past century is shown by the experience of the Gotha Mutual Life Insurance Company, the largest in Germany.   From 1829 to 1838, this company made an average rate of 3.9 per cent.   During the years

1850-1852, the rate realized was 3.9 per cent. In 1874, the rate had risen to 4.8, influenced partly by the same causes that had affected the interest rate all over the world, and partly by the great industrial progress which Germany was making. In 1885, the rate had fallen to 4.2 per cent., and in 1902 to 3.9 per cent., a rate the same as that which had been realized three quarters of a century before![1]

§ 13

We have considered the effect on the rate of preference of those changes in the income-stream due to the growth or waning of natural resources and to the temporary influence of misfortunes and inventions. There remain to be considered those regular changes in the income-stream of a rhythmic or seasonal character. Though most persons are not aware of the fact, it can scarcely be doubted that the annual succession of seasons produces an annual cycle in the income-stream of the community. This is especially true of agriculture. Grains, fruits, vegetables, cotton, wool, and almost all the organic products flow from the earth at an uneven rate, and require for their production also an uneven expenditure of labor from man during different seasons of the year. Statistics of consumption show that the income enjoyed conforms in general to a cycle. Food products are usually made available in the warm months when crops ripen; logs are hauled out of the woods in winter, floated to mills in spring, and made into lumber in summer.

But the tendency to a cycle is modified by the existence of stocks of commodities to tide over the periods of scarcity. The ice of winter is stored for summer, and the fruits of summer are canned and preserved for winter. Only so far as such storage and preservation are difficult and expensive, or impair the quality of the goods thus held over, or, because of the perishable nature of the goods, are im-

[1] See Zartman, *The Investments of Life Insurance Companies*, pp. 105–106.

practicable, does there remain any cyclic change in enjoyed income.   The cycle is different for different industries and for different classes of the population.   The farmer is perhaps the most typical for the country as a whole.   For him the lowest ebb is in the fall, when gathering and market-ing his crops cause him a sudden expenditure of labor, or of money for the labor of others.   To tide him over this period he may need to borrow.   A whole group of other industries, particularly those connected with transporta-tion, experience a sympathetic fluctuation in the income-stream.   In the parlance of Wall Street, "money is needed to move the crops."   The rate of interest tends upward, as the following table shows:[1] —

MONTHLY DISCOUNT RATES FOR PRIME TWO–NAME 60 TO 90 DAYS' PAPER IN NEW YORK CITY
(Average for 10 years, 1896–1905)

January	4.3
February	4.1
March	4.4
April	4.4
May	4.1
June	3.9
July	4.2
August	4.7
September	5.2
October	5.2
November	4.8
December	4.8

In a community dominated by some other industry than farming the cycle would be different.   Even in the above table the rates are of course a composite in which the cycles of the manufacturer and of other elements are superimposed upon the cycle of the farmer.   The manufacturer's cycle is a little later than the farmer's and shifts the high rates from fall toward winter.

Accordingly in England, which is more dominated by the manufacturer, the cycle, though similar to that just observed

[1] Compiled from daily rates given in *The Financial Review*.

for the United States, is shifted forward, as the following table shows:[1] —

MONTHLY AVERAGES OF MINIMUM RATE OF DISCOUNT OF BANK OF ENGLAND FOR YEARS 1845–1900

January	4.0
February	3.6
March	3.5
April	3.4
May	3.6
June	3.4
July	3.3
August	3.4
September	3.4
October	3.9
November	4.2
December	4.1

§ 14

The facts as presented in this chapter harmonize with the theory as presented in previous chapters. According to the theory, if there is a high degree of foresight, self-control, and regard for posterity, or if income-streams are large or plentiful in the food-element, or have a descending time-shape, then, other things being equal, the rate of interest will be low, or capital will be accumulated, or the community will lend to other communities, or the instruments it creates will be durable. We find these results present in actual fact where the antecedent conditions enumerated are also present. Reversing the conditions, we find reversed results. Of course this inductive verification is very rough, since we never can assert that "other things are equal," and thus isolate and measure any one particular factor, as in the more exact inductions of physical science. Yet the inductive study is worth something, even if it be only in the fact that it does not contradict the theory; for a false theory usually encounters facts with which it cannot be reconciled.

[1] See Palgrave's *Bank Rate and the Money Market*, New York (Dutton), 1903, p. 97.

CHAPTER XVI

§ 1

It would be impracticable, even if it were worth while, to array before the tribunal of facts all the rival theories of interest which have been presented. We must rest our case largely on the statement of principles which has already been made. It was shown, for instance, that the common theory, that interest varies inversely with the quantity of money, was superficial, since money is merely a means for obtaining capital. It was also shown that the theories commonly given in economic text-books, that the rate of interest depends on "quantity of capital," are only a little less superficial, since capital itself is merely a means to income. We cannot reach the ultimate regulator of interest until we reach income; and it is only because of the lack of an adequate theory of income that economists have been content with analyses so incomplete.

It is often true that up to a certain point facts may be adduced even in support of a false theory. It could doubtless be shown, for instance, that interest was often high when capital was scarce, and *vice versa*. The crucial test, however, comes when an income-stream of an ascending type occurs where capital is plentiful, or of a descending type where capital is scarce. If incomes are rising, though capital be plentiful, interest will be high, as in the United States recently; and if incomes are falling, though capital be scarce, interest will be low. As soon as economists think in terms of income, and give up thinking in terms of capital, which is merely an expression for contemplated income, there can be no difficulty in reaching a correct view of the problem, without the necessity of confuting all previous theories by special facts.

317

The only theory for which its adherents will demand a test by facts is the theory, believed by many business men, that the rate of interest varies inversely with the quantity of money. This theory, in spite of having been refuted by economists for over a hundred years, is still dominant among many if not most business men. The business man prides himself on reasoning by facts, and it is only by misreading facts, and not by any analysis of the problem, that he inclines to the money-theory of interest. It follows that only by facts can he be convinced of his error. As *Moody's Magazine* well says: [1] —

"Slowly but surely the great financial, commercial, and business men of the world are reaching the conclusion . . . that an increased supply of gold means higher, rather than lower, interest rates. Most converts, however, are converts from the force of facts, rather than from reason and logic."

§ 2

So far as the matter of appreciation in its relation to interest goes, facts have already been adduced in sufficient numbers in Chapter XIV. At present we are to consider the theory that high rates of interest are associated with scarce money, and low rates with plentiful money. Since in general it is true that plentiful money means high prices, and scarce money low prices, if this theory were correct, we should expect to find that during those years when prices were high, rates of interest would be low, and *vice versa*.

In the following table we see that there is no such inverse correlation between prices and interest as this theory calls for. The columns of the table relate respectively to different decades. Two rates of interest are given for each decade. The first, written opposite "high prices," is the average rate for those years of the decade whose price-levels, as shown by an index-number, were above the average price-level for the whole decade; the second is the average rate for the years whose prices were below the general average : —

[1] August, 1906.

MARKET RATES OF INTEREST IN RELATION TO HIGH AND LOW PRICES[1]

		1824 to 1831 incl.	1832 to 1841 incl.	1842 to 1851 incl.	1852 to 1861 incl.	1862 to 1871 incl.	1872 to 1881 incl.	1882 to 1891 incl.
London,	High prices . .	3.8	4.4	3.6	5.4	5.1	3.7	3.0
London,	Low prices . .	3.2	3.2	2.6	3.0	2.6	2.5	2.5
New York,	High prices . .	.	.	.	.	9.1	7.4	7.0	5.3
New York,	Low prices . .	.	.	.	.	9.1	6.7	5.1	5.1
Berlin,	High prices . .	.	.	.	.	.	4.6	3.7	3.3
Berlin,	Low prices . .	.	.	.	.	.	3.4	3.2	2.7
Paris,	High prices . .	.	.	.	.	.	.	4.1	2.6
Paris,	Low prices . .	.	.	.	.	.	.	2.4	2.6
[2] Calcutta,	High prices . .	.	.	.	.	.	.	6.2	5.4
Calcutta,	Low prices . .	.	.	.	.	.	.	5.6	6.2
[3] Tokyo,	High prices . .	.	.	.	.	.	.	12.3	10.1
Tokyo,	Low prices . .	.	.	.	.	.	.	12.0	10.1
[4] Shanghai,	High prices . .	.	.	.	.	.	.	.	6.0
Shanghai,	Low prices . .	.	.	.	.	.	.	.	5.7

Of the 21 comparisons contained in this table, 17 show higher rates for high-price years than for low-price

[1] This table is constructed from the data given in the Appendix to Ch. XIV. For New York, the rates for the first decade are averaged from the column in the Appendix headed "60 days," and are not to be compared with those for the remaining decades, which are averaged from the column headed "Prime two-name 60 days." The index-numbers of prices which have been employed are those of Jevons (1824–1851), and Sauerbeck (1852–1891) for England, Soetbeer and Heinz for Germany, the Aldrich Senate report for the United States and France, and the Japanese report for India, Japan, and China. (See Appendix to Ch. XIV, § 3.)

[2] For Calcutta the rate for the bank of Bengal is employed, no "market" rate being available. The first column is for 1873–1881 instead of 1872–1881, for the reason that no index-number for 1872 is available.

[3] For Tokyo the first column is for 1873–1881 for the same reason.

[4] For Shanghai the period is 1885–1893 instead of 1882–1891, for the reason that the available rates begin in 1885 and the index-numbers end in 1893.

years, one shows the opposite condition, and 3 show
equal rates in the two cases. As the table covers 68 years
for London, 40 for New York, 30 for Berlin, 20 for Paris,
19 each for Calcutta and Tokyo, and 9 for Shanghai, or
205 years in the aggregate, the result may be accepted with
great confidence that high and low prices are usually associated with high and low interest respectively.

There are two probable reasons for this connection. One
is that a high price-level is often due to a temporary scarcity of enjoyable commodities, as in a beleaguered city, in
San Francisco after the earthquake and fire when bread was
a dollar a loaf, or in the Klondike during the gold fever.
In such cases the rate of interest is high for economic,
not monetary, reasons, — because, in fact, of the relative
scarcity of present real income.

The second reason is that the years of high prices are
usually the culminations of periods of rising prices, during
which the rate of interest has been rising through the depreciation of money, in accordance with the principles explained in Chapters V and XIV. If the tables given in the
Appendix are examined, it will be found that prices usually
rise to a point, and then often break suddenly after a crisis.
The high-price years in this case evidently belong more often
to the period of rising than to the period of falling prices.

§ 3

Whatever be the correct explanation, the facts give no
countenance to the theory that the rate of interest depends
upon the supply of money.

It may be said that the preceding table is not conclusive,
owing to the fact that the correlation it shows is one of
prices and interest, and not directly of *quantity of money*
and interest. But this objection can be readily met by
constructing another table in which per capita circulation
of money is stated in conjunction with the rates of
interest : —

RATES OF INTEREST IN RELATION TO PER CAPITA CIRCULATION

	Per Capita Money in Circulation in U.S. July 1	Interest Rate in N.Y. (Prime Two-Name 60 Days)
1871	18.10	6.1
1872	18.19	8.0
1873	18.04	10.3
1874	18.13	6.0
1875	17.16	5.5
1876	16.12	5.2
1877	15.58	5.2
1878	15.32	4.8
1879	16.75	5.0
1880	19.41	5.2
1881	21.71	5.2
1882	22.37	5.7
1883	22.91	5.5
1884	22.65	5.2
1885	23.02	4.1
1886	21.82	4.7
1887	22.45	5.7
1888	22.88	4.9
1889	22.52	4.8
1890	22.82	6.0
1891	23.42	5.7
1892	24.56	4.3
1893	24.03	7.1
1894	24.52	3.4
1895	23.20	3.8
1896	21.41	5.8
1897	22.87	3.4
1898	25.15	3.8
1899	25.58	4.2
1900	26.94	4.4
1901	27.98	4.4
1902	28.43	4.9
1903	29.42	5.5
1904	30.77	4.2
1905	31.08	4.3

An examination of this table will show that the per capita circulation goes up and down quite independently of the fluctuations of the rate of interest. If the money theory were true we should expect that when money shrank, interest would rise, and reversely. The two should vary inversely. But as a matter of fact, out of the thirty-four pairs of consecutive years, we find that interest varied about as often directly as it did inversely with the per capita circulation. To be exact, it varied inversely in 15½ and directly in 18½ cases.[1] Thus it happened to move a little oftener in the manner opposed to the money theory than in the manner favorable to that theory.

A statistical study of the rates of interest and the production of the precious metals made by B. R. G. Levy leads to the same conclusion, that the rate of interest is not related to the quantity of money.[2]

§ 4

The preceding facts must convince any one open to conviction that the rate of interest is not inversely correlated to the quantity of money. But business men familiar with banking will not be satisfied until some place is found in our theory of interest for the common observation that if money in general does not, certainly bank reserves do vary inversely with the rate of interest. That this observation is correct is not questioned. It is the established policy of large banks, like the Bank of England, to protect their reserve by raising the rate of interest. From these facts the conclusion is drawn that the scarcity of bank reserves produces a high rate of interest. But the facts fit in with the present theory of interest quite as well as

---

[1] When the rate remained the same in two consecutive years, it was counted as one half a variation both ways.

[2] "Du taux actuel de l'intérêt et de ses rapports avec la production des métaux précieux et les autres phénomènes economique." B. R. G. Levy, *Journal des Économistes*, March, 1899, p. 334; April, 1899, p. 28.

with the fallacious money theory of interest.   A low bank reserve is merely a symptom of a general ebb tide in the income of the community.   A bank of discount and deposit stands between those who have surplus income to deposit and those who wish to eke out a lean income by borrowing. Those persons whose income is larger than they need to-day are the ones who swell the deposits of a bank.   When a farmer receives for his crops more money than he cares at once to turn into enjoyable income, he deposits some of it in a bank or trust company — with interest if possible, without it if necessary.   On the other hand, the same farmer, before his crop is sold, may wish to discount a note at the bank in order to pay off his help.   Bank deposits grow, as compared with loans, when men's incomes are temporarily flush, that is, when their income-curves are descending; loans grow as compared with deposits when their incomes are temporarily scant, that is, when their income-curves are ascending.   The banker must keep in equilibrium between the two classes of customers, those who discount and those who deposit.   If the loans increase too much, the banker's reserve will be endangered; if the deposits accumulate, it will be idle.   He regulates his reserve by adjusting the rate of discount, raising it if his reserve is low, or lowering it if it is high.   To him, his action appears in the light of protecting and utilizing his reserve; but the banker is not the prime factor.   Back of the reserve are the real causes, — the state of the incomes of his customers.   If ascending incomes are predominant, the reserve will need more "protection" than in the contrary case.   A rise of the discount rate is therefore due, in the last analysis, to the predominance of ascending incomes, and a fall, to the predominance of incomes of the opposite type.   The reserve is merely the football between the two sets of persons, those who deposit and those who loan.   The business man regards the rate of interest too much from the banker's point of view.   A banker or broker is merely an intermediary.   To regard him, or the gold that happens to be in his vaults, as primary influences on the rate of interest is as erroneous as to regard the operations of a grain broker as primary influences upon the price of wheat, or those of a real estate agent as primary influences upon the price of land. The banker enables the lenders and borrowers to find each other; they, and not he, in the end fix the rate of interest.[1]

The theory of interest which does not look beyond the bank coffers is almost as crude as the theory which would ascribe the weather to the thermometer. In a Western town a servant was being instructed to prepare a bath at a particular temperature, and was shown the point recorded by the thermometer when the bath was at the right temperature. To the consternation of the housekeeper, when the servant had prepared the bath the next day its temperature was found to be far too cold. The servant explained that she had used the "conjure stick," referring to the thermometer, but that it didn't seem to heat the water at all! Many persons have a similar superstition that money is a sort of "conjure stick" potent to regulate the rate of interest, whereas in fact it is only a thermometer to faithfully record the variations of that rate. When there is "plenty of money in Wall Street," interest is low, and *vice versa;* but the causes which have influenced interest are the causes which have put the money on loan in Wall Street.

§ 5

The money-theory comes nearest to scoring a point when applied to panics, for during a time of panic it is true that *money* loans are sought to be used as solvents of debts. This fact has often puzzled economists who, while disbelieving the money-theory of interest in general, have felt that in this case at least it was true.[2] It is clear, how-

[1] Cf. George Clare, "*A Money Market Primer,*" London (Effingham Wilson), 1905, pp. 134–135.
[2] See Mill, *Principles of Political Economy*, Book 3, Chap. XXIII, § 4.

ever, that even a panic loan, from Peter to pay Paul, is a case of an effort to maintain the even flow of one's income-stream. The alternative, if one does not borrow, is to sell some of one's goods, necessitating the sacrifice of the income which they are designed to bring. The choice between the loan and the sale is between the necessity of repaying the loan when due, and the necessity of losing the income from the goods, — a choice between two bits of income different in amount, or kind, or distribution in time. The loan substitutes one of these bits of income for the other, and is therefore in this respect exactly similar to any other loan. If one's solvency is in question, the same exchange occurs in a somewhat different form; the loan is then undertaken in preference to the deformation of the income-stream which insolvency involves.

It is true, however, that money, as money, is more vitally related to panic loans than to any other. In ordinary loans, money enters merely as a *convenient* medium for securing something else — capital, and through that capital, income; in a panic loan, however, the money enters as a *necessary* medium for the legal discharge of a debt. Again, in an ordinary loan, the borrower is free to adjust the amount borrowed according to the rate of interest; in a panic loan, on the other hand, there is no such elastic choice. The borrower must borrow that fixed amount necessary to discharge his debt, even if the rate of interest is exorbitant. If physical money is not sufficient to allow debtors to discharge their debts, the rate of interest will be high and there can be no escape from it as in ordinary times. In this case it may be truly said that scarcity of money has made interest high. Money of any kind brought into the market will relieve the stringency and lower the rate of interest. The United States has accomplished this by prepaying interest on bonds, and the clearing house has accomplished it by issuing clearing-house certificates. It is therefore important, in order not to have violent changes in the rate of interest, that the currency should be *elastic*.

A panic is always the result of unforeseen conditions; and among those unforeseen conditions, and partly as a consequence of other unforeseen conditions, is *scarcity of money on loan*.   Under ordinary and normal conditions, money on loan is so automatically adjusted as to make it a mere transmitter through the medium of which borrowers and lenders act upon the rate of interest, just as a smooth-running gear transmits power from one wheel to another, without exerting any independent force itself.   But when the gear gets out of order it may stick and offer a resistance of its own to the wheels with which it is in contact.

It is therefore not asserted that money plays no rôle in determining the rate of interest.   But its rôle is a minor one, and very different from that often assigned to it. Its rôle normally is to efface itself and merely facilitate the frictionless working of economic machinery.   Under the abnormal conditions of a panic, the dearth of it may create friction and enhance interest at that particular point.

Finally, as we have seen in previous chapters, a *change* in the monetary standard will affect the *number* by which the rate of interest is expressed, increasing it if the monetary standard is depreciating, and decreasing it if the standard is appreciating.

With these reservations, we may say that the rate of interest is not affected by the quantity of money.

CHAPTER XVII

SUMMARY

§ 1

WE have seen that the rate of interest is subject to both a nominal and a real variation, the nominal variation being that connected with changes in the standard of value, and the real variation being that connected with the other and deeper economic causes. As to the nominal variation in the rate of interest, we found that, theoretically, an appreciation of 1 per cent. of the standard of value in which the rate of interest is expressed, compared with some other standard, will reduce the rate of interest in the former standard, compared with the latter, by about 1 per cent.; and that, contrariwise, a depreciation of 1 per cent. will raise the rate by that amount. Such a change in the rate of interest, however, is merely a change in the number expressing it, and not in any sense a real change. Yet the appreciation or depreciation of the monetary standard does produce a real effect on the rate of interest, and that a most vicious one. This effect is due to the fact that the rate of interest does not change enough to fully compensate for the appreciation or depreciation. Thus, if the monetary standard is appreciating at the rate of 3 per cent. per annum and the rate of interest falls only 2 per cent., the deficiency of 1 per cent. shows that the rate of interest has not really fallen, but risen. This rise of 1 per cent. is abnormal, being the result of an error in prediction. Had the debtors and creditors concerned foreseen fully the change in the monetary standard, they would have forestalled it fully. Their failure so to do results in an unexpected loss to the debtor, and an unexpected gain to the creditor. What

327

usually happens, therefore, as a consequence of an appreciation in the monetary standard, is that the rate of interest *nominally* falls, but *really* rises, whereas in the contrary case, if the monetary standard is depreciating, the rate of interest *nominally* rises, but *really* falls. It is consequently of the utmost importance, in interpreting the rate of interest statistically, to ascertain in each case in which direction the monetary standard is moving, and to remember that the direction in which the rate apparently moves is apt to be precisely the opposite of that in which it really moves.

§ 2

Turning from the nominal to the real variation in the rate of interest, we see that the rate of interest, considered independently of fluctuations in the monetary standard, is determined by six causes, namely: (1) The extent of the effective range of choice of different incomes which are open to each individual; (2) the dependence of "time-preference" upon prospective income — its size, shape, composition, and probability; (3) the tendency of the rates of time-preference for different individuals to become equal to each other and to the rate of interest, through the loan market, or through buying and selling property; (4) the tendency of the various "rates of return on sacrifice" to become equal to each other and to the rate of interest, through the operation of free choice among available options; (5) the fact that supply and demand are equal, that the modifications in the income-streams of individuals through buying and selling or borrowing and lending mutually offset each other for each interval of time considered, — that what is lent must equal what is borrowed, and what is gained by one in each year's income, by buying and selling, is lost by some one else; (6) the fact that, for the same individual, the estimated present values of the changes he elects to make in his prospective income-stream

mutually offset each other; that is, the estimated present
value of what he borrows is equal to the estimated present
value of what he returns, or, more generally, the estimated
present value of an addition to his immediate income is
equal to the present value of the consequent reduction in
his future income.

Of these six conditions, many are so inflexible that they
have little influence on any variation in the rate of interest.
The last four are of this relatively fixed type. We have
remaining the first two as the only causes subject to important variations.   The fluctuations in these causes explain
for the most part the changes in the rate of interest, as
actually experienced.   We shall now concentrate attention
upon these two, — the range of known choice and the law
of time-preference.

§ 3

As to the range of choice, each individual may, as assumed
in our "first approximation," be possessed of one given income which is *rigid* (except as it may be altered by borrowing and lending); or, as assumed in the other approximations and as found in actual fact, he may be possessed of a
given range of choice of many different income-streams.
The range of choice actually open to any individual will
depend principally upon the amount and character of the
capital-property which he possesses.   It follows that,
for society as a whole, the range of choice of incomes will
depend upon, first, the existing capital of the country; that
is, its "resources," or the amount and character of the
different capital-instruments existing within it at the instant of time considered; and, secondly, the distribution
of ownership of these capital-instruments throughout the
community.   In this statement it is intended, of course,
to include under capital-instruments the individuals themselves who constitute the community, for they are the
source, through their personal exertions, of much of the

income which they enjoy. In short, then, the available range of choice will depend upon capital and its distribution. If the capital-instruments of the community are of such a nature as to offer a *wide* range of choice, we have seen that the rate of interest will tend to be *steady*. If the range of choice is *narrow*, the rate of interest will be comparatively *variable*. If the range of choice is relatively rich in the *remotely future* income as compared with the more immediate income, the rate of interest will be *high*. If the range of choice tends to favor *immediate income* as compared with remote future income, the rate of interest will be *low*. Thus, for the United States during the last century, its resources were of such a character as to favor a remote future income. This is true, for a time at least, in every undeveloped country, and, as we have seen, gives the chief explanation of the fact that the rate of interest in such localities is usually high.

The range of choice in any community is subject to many changes as time goes on, due chiefly to one of three causes. First, a progressive increase or decrease in resources; second, the discovery of new resources or means of developing old ones; and third, change in political conditions. The impending exhaustion of the coal supply in England which has been noted by Jevons and other writers will tend to make the income-stream from that island decrease, at least in the remote future, and this in turn will tend to keep the rate of interest there low. The constant stream of new inventions, on the other hand, by making the available income-streams rich in the remote future, tends to make the rate of interest high. This effect, however, is confined to the period of exploitation of the new invention, and is succeeded later by an opposite tendency. During the last half century the exploitation of Stephenson's invention of the locomotive, by presenting the possibility of a relatively large future income at the cost of comparatively little sacrifice in the present, has tended to keep the rate of interest high. As the period of railroad building is drawing to a close, this effect is becoming exhausted, and the tendency of the rate of interest, so far as this influence is concerned, is to fall. As to the political conditions which affect the rate of interest, insecurity of property rights such as occurs during political upheaval tends to make the pure or "riskless" rate of interest low. At the same time it adds an element of risk to most loans, thereby diminishing the number of safe and increasing the number of unsafe loans. Hence the "commercial" rate of interest in ordinary loans during periods of lawlessness is apt to be high. Reversely, during times of peace and security, the "riskless" rate of interest is comparatively high while the "commercial" rate tends to be low.

§ 4

We turn now to the second factor determining interest; namely, the dependence of time-preference of each individual on his selected income-stream. We have seen that the rate of preference for immediate as compared with remote income will depend upon the character of the income-stream selected; but the manner of this dependence is subject to great variation and change. The manner in which a spendthrift will react to an income-stream is very different from the manner in which the shrewd accumulator of capital will react to the same income-stream. We have seen that the manner in which the time-preference of an individual depends upon his income will vary with five different factors: (1) His foresight and self-control; (2) his love of offspring or regard for posterity; (3) the prospective length and certainty of his life; (4) habit; (5) fashion. It is evident that each of these circumstances may change. The causes most likely to effect such changes are, first, education and training in thrift, whether accomplished through the home, the school, charitable organizations, or banks for small savings, building and loan associations, and other similar institutions calculated to have an educational influence; second, the tendency toward or away from a spirit of extravagance and ostentation through social rivalry;[1] third, the changes in the character of the institutions of marriage and the family which, in one direction or the other, will profoundly affect the love of offspring and regard for the welfare of posterity; fourth, the development of the science of hygiene which may tend to make human life longer and more certain; fifth, the causes which tend to make the distribution of wealth either more concentrated or diffused, and also those which tend to make the existing economic stratification of classes fixed and stereotyped or elastic and variable. These various factors will act and react upon each other, and will affect profoundly the rate of preference for present over future income, and thereby influence greatly the rate of interest. Where, as in Scotland, there are educational tendencies which instill the habit of thrift from childhood, the rate of interest tends to be low. Where, as in ancient Rome, there is a tendency toward reckless luxury and competition in ostentation, and a degeneration in the bonds of family life, there is a consequent absence of any desire to prolong income beyond one's own term of life, and the rate of interest tends to be high. Where, as in Russia, wealth tends to be concentrated and social stratification to be rigid, the great majority of the community on the one hand, through poverty and the recklessness which poverty begets, tends to have a high rate of preference for present over future income; whereas, at the opposite end of the ladder, the inherited habit of luxurious living tends, though in a different way, in the same direction. In such a community the rate of interest is apt to be unduly high.

§ 5

From the foregoing enumeration, it is clear that the rate of interest is dependent upon very unstable influences,

[1] See Rae, *The Sociological Theory of Capital.* Cf. the writer's "Why has the Doctrine of Laissez Faire been Abandoned?" *Science*, Jan. 4, 1907.

many of which have their origin deep down in the social fabric and involve considerations not strictly economic. Any causes tending to affect intelligence, foresight, self-control, habits, the longevity of man, and family affection, will have their influence upon the rate of interest. The most fitful of the causes at work is probably fashion. This at the present time acts, on the one hand, to stimulate men to save and become millionaires, and, on the other hand, to stimulate millionaires to live in an ostentatious manner. Fashion is one of those potent yet illusory social forces which follow the laws of imitation so much emphasized by Tarde,[1] Le Bon,[2] Baldwin,[3] and other writers. In whatever direction the leaders of fashion first chance to move, the crowd will follow in mad pursuit until the whole social body will be moving in that direction. Sometimes the fashion becomes rigid, as in China, a fact emphasized by Bagehot;[4] and sometimes the effect of a too universal following is to stimulate the leaders to throw off their pursuers by taking some novel direction — which explains the constant vagaries of fashion in dress. Economic fashions may belong to either of these two groups, — the fixed or the erratic. Examples of both are given by John Rae.[5] It is of vast importance to a community, in its influence both on the rate of interest and on the distribution of wealth itself, what direction fashion happens to take. For instance, should it become an established custom for millionaires to consider it "disgraceful to die rich," and believe it *de riguer* to give the bulk of their fortunes for endowing universities, libraries, or other public institutions, the effect would be, through diffusion of benefits, to lessen the dis-

[1] *Social Laws*, by G. Tarde, English translation, New York (Macmillan), 1899. Also *Les Lois de l'Imitation*.

[2] *The Psychology of Socialism*, English translation, London (T. Fisher Unwin), 1899. Also *The Crowd*.

[3] *Social and Ethical Interpretations in Mental Development*, New York (Macmillan), 4th ed., 1906.

[4] *Physics and Politics*, Chap. III.

[5] See *The Sociological Theory of Capital*.

parities in the distribution of wealth, and also to lower
the rate of interest.

§ 6

From what has been said it is clear that in order to estimate the possible variation in the rate of interest, we may,
broadly speaking, take account of the following three groups
of causes: (1) The thrift, foresight, self-control, and love of
offspring which exist in a community; (2) the progress
of inventions; (3) the changes in the purchasing power
of money. The first cause tends to lower the rate of interest; the second, to raise it; and the third to affect only
the nominal rate of interest, though practically it usually
produces also a dislocation in the real rate of interest.

Were it possible to estimate the strength of the various
forces thus summarized, we could base upon them a prediction as to the rate of interest in the future. Such a
prediction, however, to be of much value, would require
more painstaking attention than has ever been given to
existing historical conditions. Without such a careful investigation, any prediction is hazardous. We can say,
however, that the immediate prospects for a change in the
monetary standard are toward its gradual depreciation;
that a change in thrift, foresight, self-control, and benevo-
lence, if it occurs, is for the most part likely to intensify
these factors and thus to lower the rate of interest; and
that the progress of discovery and invention seems apt
to slacken in speed, both so far as industrial processes are
concerned, and, what has hitherto been of more consequence, so far as the discovery of exploitable areas is concerned. It is true that the new chemical agriculture has
the same effect as the discovery of new land. It is conceivable, perhaps, that the future development of these
methods may be as potent as was the discovery and exploitation of the American, Australian, and African conti-
nents, which has tended to keep the rate of interest high.

Yet this result can scarcely be regarded at present as probable. America and Australia have been already exploited to a large degree, and within another generation almost the same degree of exploitation is apt to occur in Africa. If we look forward, then, beyond the present lifetime, unless some invention or set of inventions comparable to those of steam and electricity are still in store for us, we see that the probable improvement in thrift, foresight, self-control, family affection, etc., and the slackening in the activity or economic importance of inventive processes, are all in the direction of lowering the rate of interest. It may of course happen that counter currents will prove the stronger. There is certainly danger that the spirit of extravagance and display, a spirit which we have seen leads to reckless loans and high interest, will become a national disease as it did during the decline of the Roman Empire. Only time can tell us whether or not we shall escape this danger.

So far as the effect of the monetary standard on the rate of interest is concerned, the prospect of depreciation of gold tends, on the one hand, *nominally* to raise the rate of interest, but practically to make the rate of interest *really* not only low, but lower than it otherwise would be. With the influx of gold from Colorado, Alaska, California, Australia, and latterly Nevada, and with the resumption of mining in South Africa, there cannot be much question that gold will depreciate.[1] This result will tend to be intensified by the fact that there are few if any large nations left which have not already adopted the gold standard or which are at all likely to do so, and thereby mitigate the fall of gold. The rate of interest is now, on ordinarily safe loans in civilized communities, in the neighborhood of 4 per cent., expressed in money. We may surmise that

[1] See "Symposium," *Moody's Magazine*, December, 1905; Byron W. Holt, *The Gold Supply and Prosperity*, N. Y. (Moody), 1907; also "The Depreciation of Gold," by Professor J. P. Norton, *Yale Review*, November, 1906.

through much of the present century this rate will nominally continue, but that the rate of interest in terms of "commodities" will be 1 or 2 points lower. The effect of these conditions on trade and on the relative fortunes of stockholders and bondholders has been stated in Chapter XIV. The rate will not remain perfectly constant but will tend gradually to rise until the stringency thus produced culminates in a commercial crisis. After such a period of liquidation, the same process of rising prices with high nominal but low real interest will begin anew.

A discrepancy of 1 or 2 points between the rate of interest as it is and as it should be is therefore of no trifling importance. Its cumulative effects, although seldom realized, are serious. It is commonly assumed that the rate of interest is a phenomenon confined to money markets and trade centers, and the public approval or disapproval of the rate usually takes its cue from the sentiments of the borrower. If "money is easy," he is content.

The truth is that the rate of interest is not a narrow phenomenon applying only to a few business contracts, but permeates all economic relations. It is the link which binds man to the future and by which he makes all his far-reaching decisions. It enters into the price of securities, land, and capital goods generally, as well as into rent, wages, and the value of all "interactions." It affects profoundly the distribution of wealth. In short, upon its accurate adjustment depend the equitable terms of all exchange and distribution.

GLOSSARY

[Consisting of definitions of technical terms used in this book. Most of these definitions are more fully discussed in *The Nature of Capital and Income*, to which specific references are therefore made.]

BASIS. — The rate of interest yielded by a property when sold at a specified price. *Capital and Income*, Ch. XVI, § 9.

commercial, of a security. — The basis corresponding to the commercial value of the security. *Capital and Income*, Ch. XVI, § 8.

mathematical, of a security. — The basis corresponding to the mathematical value of the security. *Capital and Income*, Ch. XVI, § 8.

riskless, of a security. — The basis corresponding to the riskless value of the security. *Capital and Income*, Ch. XVI, § 8.

CAPITAL. — Abbreviation for *Capital goods*, and *Capital value*. *Capital and Income*, Ch. V, § 1.

instruments. — (See *Capital Wealth*.)

property. — A stock (or fund) of property existing at an instant of time. *Capital and Income*, Ch. V, § 1.

wealth. — A stock (or fund) of wealth existing at an instant of time. (Syn. *Capital instruments*.) *Capital and Income*, Ch. V, § 1.

value. — The value of a stock of wealth or property at an instant. It is found by discounting (or "capitalizing") the value of the income expected from the wealth or property. *Capital and Income*, Ch. V, § 1.

CAPITALISTIC METHOD. — A method of production requiring a temporary reduction in the income from specified capital. Ch. IX, § 8.

CAUTION, *coefficient of*. — The ratio of commercial value to mathematical value. *Capital and Income*, Ch. XVI, § 6.

CHANCE, *of any event*. — The ratio of the number of cases in which that event may occur to the total possible number of cases, when all the cases are equally probable. Any two cases are equally probable (to any particular person at any particular time) if the person has no inclination to believe one rather than the other to be true. (Syn. *Probability*.) *Capital and Income*, Ch. XVI, § 2.

commercial value of. — The value which the chance will actually

337

command in the market. It is equal to the mathematical value multiplied by the coefficient of caution. *Capital and Income*, Ch. XVI, § 6.

mathematical value of. — The product of the value of the price at stake multiplied by the chance of winning it. *Capital and Income*, Ch. XVI, § 5.

COEFFICIENT, *of caution.* — The ratio of commercial value to mathematical value. *Capital and Income*, Ch. XVI, § 6.

of probability. — The ratio of mathematical value to riskless value. *Capital and Income*, Ch. XVI, § 6.

of risk. — The ratio of commercial value to riskless value; hence the product of the coefficient of caution multiplied by the coefficient of probability. *Capital and Income*, Ch. XVI, § 6.

COMMERCIAL *value of a chance.* — (See *Chance.*)

COMMODITIES. — Movable instruments not human beings. *Capital and Income*, Ch. I, § 2.

CONSUMPTION. — (See *Services, enjoyable objective.*)

DESIRABILITY, *of goods* (wealth, property, or services). — The intensity of desire, for those goods, of a particular individual at a particular time under particular circumstances. (Syn. *Utility.*) *Capital and Income*, Ch. III, § 2.

marginal, of a specified aggregate of goods. — Approximate definition: The desirability of one unit more or less of that aggregate, or the difference between the desirability of that aggregate and another aggregate one unit larger or smaller. *Capital and Income*, Ch. III, § 4.

Exact definition: The limit of the ratio of the increment (or decrement) of desirability to the increment (or decrement) of the aggregate when the last-named increment (or decrement) approaches zero. (Syn. *Marginal utility.*) *Capital and Income*, Appendix to Ch. III, § 1.

DISCOUNT CURVE. — A curve so constructed that, if one of its ordinates represents any given sum, any later ordinate will represent the "amount" of that sum at a time later by an interval represented by the horizontal distance between the ordinates; consequently a curve such that any earlier ordinate will represent the "present value" of that sum at a time earlier by an interval represented by the horizontal distance between the ordinates. *Capital and Income*, Ch. XIII, § 1.

DISCOUNTED VALUE. — (See *Value, present.*)

DISSERVICE. — A negative service. An instrument renders a disservice when, by its means, an undesirable event is promoted or a desirable event prevented. *Capital and Income*, Ch. II, § 2; VIII, § 1.

DISUTILITY. — Negative utility. (Syn. *Undesirability.*) *Capital and Income,* Ch. III, § 2.

EARNINGS. — (See *Income, earned.*)

EXCHANGE. — The mutual and voluntary transfer of goods (wealth, property, or services) between two owners, each transfer being in consideration of the other. *Capital and Income,* Ch. I, § 4; II, § 3.

FLOW. — The quantity of any specified thing undergoing any specified change during any specified period of time. *Capital and Income,* Ch. IV, § 1.

FUND. — A stock of wealth or property or its value. *Capital and Income,* Ch. IV, § 1.

GOODS. — A term to include wealth, property and services. *Capital and Income,* Ch. III, § 1.

INCOME. — Abbreviation for *Income services* and *Income value.* *Capital and Income,* Ch. VIII, § 1.

account. — Statement of specified income and outgo, whether from capital or to a person. *Capital and Income,* Ch. VIII, § 2.

earned, by any capital. — Income realized plus appreciation of the capital (or minus its depreciation); *i.e.* that income which a given capital can yield *without alteration* in its value. If interest be assumed invariable and all future income foreknown, this definition is equivalent to another; viz. the *uniform and perpetual* income which a given capital might yield; but the equivalence ceases if interest varies (see *Capital and Income,* Appendix to Ch. XIV, § 1) or if future income is unknown. (Syn. *Earnings, Standard income.*) *Capital and Income,* Ch. XIV, § 4.

enjoyable. — Income which consists of enjoyable services. *Capital and Income,* Ch. VII, § 6.

gross. — Sum of all positive income elements. *Capital and Income,* Ch. VII, § 1.

individual. — The income from the entire capital of an individual. *Capital and Income,* Ch. VII, § 7.

money. — Income which consists of the receipt of money. *Capital and Income,* Ch. VII, § 7; IX, § 5.

natural. — Income which consists of services not obtained by exchange. *Capital and Income,* Ch. VII, § 7; IX, § 5.

net. — The difference between gross income and outgo. *Capital and Income,* Ch. VIII, § 1.

psychic. — Agreeable conscious experiences. (Syn. *Subjective income.*) *Capital and Income,* Ch. X, § 3.

realized, from any capital. — Its actual income, *i.e.* the value of its actual services. *Capital and Income,* Ch. XIV, § 4.

services, of any capital. — The flow of services from that capital through a period of time. *Capital and Income*, Ch. VIII, § 1.

social. — The income from the entire capital of society. *Capital and Income*, Ch. VII, § 7.

standard. — (See *Income, earned.*)

stream. — Synonym of Income. Employed to emphasize its duration in time.

subjective. (See *Income, psychic.*)

value, from any capital. — The value of its income-services. *Capital and Income*, Ch. VIII, § 1.

INSTRUMENT. — An individual article of wealth. *Capital and Income*, Ch. I, § 1.

INTERACTION. — An event which is a service of one capital and at the same time a disservice of another. (Syn. *Interacting service, Intermediate service, Preparatory service, Coupled service.*) *Capital and Income*, Ch. IX, § 2.

INTERACTING *services.* — (See *Interaction.*)

INTERMEDIATE *services.* — (See *Interaction.*)

INTEREST. — The product of the rate of interest multiplied by the capital-value. *Capital and Income*, Ch. XIV, § 4.

explicit, rate of. — A rate of interest explicitly contracted for (in contradistinction to implicit interest). Ch. II, § 1.

implicit, rate of. — The rate of interest realized on any investment, the exact return of which is not explicitly contracted for, but is left to be determined by circumstances. Ch. II, § 1.

rate of. — Many meanings are given below. The standard meaning used in this book is that called "rate of interest in the premium sense reckoned annually." *Capital and Income*, Ch. XII, § 4.

rate of. — *In the price sense:* The ratio between the annual rate of a perpetual annuity and the equivalent capital-value. *Capital and Income*, Ch. XII, § 2.

The rate of interest is said to be reckoned *annually* if the annuity is payable in annual installments; it is said to be reckoned *semiannually* if the annuity is payable in semiannual installments; *quarterly*, if in quarterly installments; *continuously*, if payable continuously.

rate of. — *In the premium sense:* The excess above unity of the rate of exchange between the values of future and present goods taken in relation to the time interval between the two sets of goods. (Syn. *rate of interest in the agio sense.*) *Capital and Income*, Ch. XII, § 4.

The rate of interest is said to be reckoned *annually* if the two sets of goods are one year apart. This is the standard meaning of the "rate of interest" as used in this book. It is said to be reckoned *semiannually*, if they are a half-year apart; *quarterly*, if three months apart; *continuously*, if infinitesimally apart.

rate of. — *In agio sense:* (See *in premium sense.*)

rate of. — *Reckoned annually, semiannually, quarterly, continuously:* See under *rate of interest in price sense* and *rate of interest in premium sense.*

total. — The difference between any sum and its "amount." *Capital and Income*, Appendix to Ch. XIII, § 7.

INVESTING. — Purchasing the right to remote income. Ch. VII, § 4.

LABOR. — Outgo in the form of human exertion. *Capital and Income*, Ch. X, § 6.

LAND. — Wealth which is part of the earth's surface. *Capital and Income*, Ch. I, § 2.

MATHEMATICAL *value of a chance.* — (See *Chance.*)

OPTION. — Any one of a number of income-streams among which an individual may choose. Ch. IX, § 1.

OUTGO. — Negative income. *Capital and Income*, Ch. VIII, § 1.

PREPARATORY SERVICES. — (See *Interaction.*)

PRICE. — A ratio of exchange. *Capital and Income*, Ch. I, § 4.

money. — The quotient found by dividing the money exchanged for goods by the quantity of the goods themselves. *Capital and Income*, Ch. I, § 4.

PRINCIPAL. — The final payment on a bond or note, supposed to be (but not always in fact) equal to the original sum "lent." *Capital and Income*, Ch. XIII, § 7.

PROBABILITY. — (See *Chance.*)

PRODUCTION. — (See *Transformation.*)

PRODUCTIVE PROCESS. — (See *Transformation.*)

PRODUCTIVITY, *physical.* — The ratio of the *quantity* of services of capital per unit of time to the *quantity* of the capital. *Capital and Income*, Ch. XI, § 2.

PRODUCTIVITY, *value.* — The ratio of the *value* of services of capital per unit of time to the *quantity* of the capital. *Capital and Income*, Ch. XI, § 2.

PROPERTY (or property rights). — Rights to the chance of future services of wealth. *Capital and Income*, Ch. II, § 3.

right, complete. — The exclusive right to all the services of an instrument. *Capital and Income*, Ch. II, § 10.

right, partial. — The right to part of the services of an instrument, other parts belonging to other owners. *Capital and Income*, Ch. II, § 10.

RETURN. — When used alone, "return" signifies the value of the advantage of one income-stream compared with another during any particular portion of its course. Ch. VIII, § 8.

RETURN, *physical.* — The ratio of the *quantity* of services of capital to the *value* of the capital. *Capital and Income*, Ch. XI, § 2.

on sacrifice, rate of. — That rate of interest, reckoning by which the discounted value of the "return" equals the discounted value of the "sacrifice." Ch. VIII, § 8.

value. — The ratio of the *value* of services of capital to the *value* of the capital. *Capital and Income*, Ch. XI, § 2.

RISK, *coefficient of.* — The ratio of commercial value to riskless value. It is equal to the product of the coefficient of probability multiplied by the coefficient of caution. *Capital and Income*, Ch. XVI, § 6.

RISKLESS, *value.* — The value which a thing would have if risk were eliminated. *Capital and Income*, Ch. XVI, § 6.

SACRIFICE. — The value of the disadvantage of one income-stream compared with another during any particular portion of its course. Ch. VIII, § 8.

SERVICE. — An instrument renders a service when, by its means, a desirable event is promoted or an undesirable event prevented. (Syn. *Use.*) *Capital and Income*, Ch. II, § 2.

SERVICES, *coupled.* — (See *Interaction.*)

enjoyable objective. — Services received directly by human beings, and not (like interactions) merely received for human beings by other (objective) capital. (Syn. [not well chosen] *Consumption.*) *Capital and Income*, Ch. X, § 1.

intermediate. — (See *Interaction.*)

preparatory. — (See *Interaction.*)

SPENDING. — Purchasing the right to immediate enjoyable income. Ch. VII, § 4.

STANDARD INCOME. — (See *Income, earned.*)

STOCK. — The quantity of any specified thing at any instant. (Syn. *Fund.*) *Capital and Income*, Ch. IV, § 1.

TIME-PREFERENCE, *rate of.* — The excess above unity of the ratio between the marginal utility (to a given person, under given conditions, *at a given time*) of (say) a dollar's worth of enjoyable income available at any time and a dollar's worth of enjoyable income available one year later. It follows that it is also the excess above unity of the ratio between the quantity of the later income and the quantity of the early income which will exchange for each other (both being expressed in the same standard, as dollars). Ch. VI, § 1.

TIME-SHAPE, *of an income-stream.* — The distribution in time of a given income-stream as expressed by the relative amounts of the income accruing at specified periods. Ch. VI, § 6.

TRANSFORMATION. — An interaction which is a change of form or condition of wealth. (Syn. *Production, Productive process.*) *Capital and Income*, Ch. IX, §§ 2, 3.

UNDESIRABILITY. — Negative desirability. (Syn. *Disutility.*) *Capital and Income*, Ch. III, § 2.

UTILITY OF GOODS. — (See *Desirability.*)

VALUE. — The value of goods (wealth, property, or services) is the product of their quantity multiplied by their price. *Capital and Income*, Ch. I, § 6.

commercial, of a chance. — (See *Chance.*)

discounted. — (See *Value, present.*)

mathematical, of a chance. (See *Chance.*)

money. — The quantity of goods multiplied by their money price. *Capital and Income*, Ch. I, § 6.

present. — The present value of any given future goods is the quantity of present goods which will exchange for those future goods. (Syn. *Present worth, Discounted value.*) *Capital and Income*, Ch. XIII, § 1.

riskless, of a chance. — (See *Chance.*)

WEALTH (in its broader sense). — Material objects owned by human beings. *Capital and Income*, Ch. I, § 1.

(in its narrower sense). — Material objects owned by human beings and external to their owners. *Capital and Income*, Ch. I, § 2.

article of. — A single object of wealth. (Syn. *Item of Wealth, Instrument.*) *Capital and Income*, Ch. I, § 1.

item of. — (See *Wealth, article of.*)

WORTH, *present.* — (See *Value, present.*)

APPENDICES

APPENDIX TO CHAPTER II

Productivity Theories

§ 1 (to Ch. II, § 6)

Mathematical Proof that the Rate of Net Income from Reconstituted Capital is equal to the Rate of Interest employed in valuing the Elements of which that capital is composed.

That the ratio of the net income from the machines to their capital-value is equal to the rate of interest used in calculating the value of each individual machine is a necessary truth and may be shown mathematically as follows: —

For simplicity, let us assume that each machine yields its income in a single item at the end of each year. If a machine when new is to last m years and yields a certain annuity of a dollars each year, the value (v_1) of this machine is found by discounting the terminable annuity of a dollars for m years at a rate of interest i. This value will be

$$v_1 = \frac{a}{1+i} + \frac{a}{(1+i)^2} + \cdots + \frac{a}{(1+i)^{m-1}} + \frac{a}{(1+i)^m}. \tag{1}$$

The gross annual income of a plant consisting of m machines will be ma. The net income of the plant, assuming that one machine wears out and is replaced annually, will be found by deducting from this gross income the cost, v_1, of a new machine. This annual net income $= ma - v_1$.

The value of the plant of m machines can now be found by discounting the future income which the plant will yield. Let us assume that the plant is "kept up" for n years, after which it is allowed to run down until exhausted. The period of running down will be m years, the life of the newest machine. We assume, of course, that whether kept up or running down, the plant yields for each machine a dollars annually. Under these conditions the value of the plant is the discounted value of two series of income: (1) n years of income of $ma - v_1$ per year, while the plant is kept up, and (2) m years of income which gradually shrinks from ma the first year

347

when all the machines are in use, to $(m-1)a$ the second year, after one machine has dropped out, $(m-2)a$ the third, etc., to a in the mth year, after which time the plant will cease to exist. We have, then, the present value of $ma-v_1$ for each of n years, and the present value for m more years of ma, $(m-1)a$, $(m-2)a, \cdots a$. The present value of these successive sums is evidently

$$\left[\frac{ma-v_1}{1+i}+\frac{ma-v_1}{(1+i)^2}+\cdots+\frac{ma-v_1}{(1+i)^n}\right]+$$
$$\left[\frac{ma}{(1+i)^{n+1}}+\frac{(m-1)a}{(1+i)^{n+2}}+\cdots+\frac{a}{(1+i)^{n+m}}\right],$$

which may also be written

$$(ma-v_1)\left[\frac{1}{1+i}+\frac{1}{(1+i)^2}+\cdots+\frac{1}{(1+i)^n}\right]+$$
$$\left(\frac{a}{(1+i)^n}\right)\left[\frac{m}{1+i}+\frac{m-1}{(1+i)^2}+\cdots+\frac{1}{(1+i)^m}\right]. \qquad (2)$$

Of the two terms of which this expression consists, the first is the more important if the rate of interest, i, has a finite positive value, but the second is the more important if that rate is zero. In the former case, the longer the plant is kept up (i.e. the larger n is) the smaller will the second term become; for the divisor of this second term, $(1+i)^n$, will increase indefinitely and the other factors, a and the square bracket, remain constant. Hence, as n increases indefinitely, this second term becomes more and more negligible and approaches zero as a limit. That is, the value of a plant whose up-keep is indefinitely maintained is equal to the first of the two terms. This first term becomes, when n is indefinitely great,[1]

$$(ma-v_1)\frac{1}{i}, \qquad (3)$$

which expresses the value of the plant. In other words, the value of the plant is the capitalization of its annual net income, $ma-v_1$. Or, again, the annual income $ma-v_1$ divided by the value of the plant $(ma-v_1)\frac{1}{i}$ will equal the rate of interest i.

[1] For proof, see *The Nature of Capital and Income*, Appendix to Ch. XIII, § 3.

The same result applies to a plant which contains more or less machines than m, since the size of the plant will affect both income and capital alike.

§ 2 (TO CH. II, § 7)

Discussion of the Case of Zero Interest as Applied to the Valuation of Reconstituted Capital.

The case of a zero rate of interest offers a peculiarity not presented under ordinary circumstances. In all other instances of perpetual up-keep, the net income capitalized gives the entire capital-value. This was shown in § 1 of this Appendix. But in the case of zero interest the proposition is not true, as may best be shown by mathematics. In § 1 of this Appendix the expression for the value of a plant of m machines to be kept up for n years and then allowed to run down during m years was found to be

$$\left[\frac{ma - v_1}{1 + i} + \frac{ma - v_1}{(1 + i)^2} + \cdots + \frac{ma - v_1}{(1 + i)^n}\right] +$$

$$\left[\frac{ma}{(1 + i)^{n+1}} + \frac{(m-1)a}{(1 + i)^{n+2}} + \cdots + \frac{a}{(1 + i)^{n+m}}\right].$$

In the previous section it was assumed that i was finite and positive, from which it followed that when n was indefinitely great the second square bracket became negligible. But under our present assumption that i is zero, the term is not negligible; on the contrary, it is the first square bracket which now vanishes. To show this we observe that formula (1) of § 1, giving the value of each machine, reduces, when $i = 0$, to

$$v_1 = \frac{a}{1} + \frac{a}{1^2} + \cdots + \frac{a}{1^m},$$

$$= ma,$$

whence

$$ma - v_1 = 0.$$

Hence the first term in equation (2), being the product of $ma - v_1$ (zero) by a finite number, is zero.

The second term of (2) reduces, when $i = 0$, to

$$\frac{a}{1^n}\left[\frac{m}{1} + \frac{m-1}{1^2} + \cdots + \frac{1}{1^m}\right] \text{ or } a\left[\frac{m(m + 1)}{2}\right].$$

which, since the first term is zero, represents the entire value of the m machines. The result is now independent of n. If $m = 10$, this expression becomes $55\,a$. The value of such a plant is then fifty-five times the annual yield of each machine. If this yield is \$100, its value is \$5500, which agrees with the calculation in the text.

APPENDIX TO CHAPTER IV

Böhm-Bawerk's Theory

§ 1 (to Ch. IV, § 2)

Nature of Various Means — Arithmetical, Geometrical, Harmonical, etc.

In general, a mean, $\bar{a}$, of a number of magnitudes, a_1, a_2, a_3, etc., is defined by an equation connecting these magnitudes and $\bar{a}$ in such a manner that if all of the magnitudes, a_1, a_2, a_3, etc. are equal to each other, the value of $\bar{a}$ given by the equation will be equal to each of them. That this concept applies to the arithmetical, geometrical, and harmonical means is evident. These means may be defined by the following formulæ, where, for convenience, the number of elements, a_1, a_2, etc., averaged is restricted to three. This restriction, which may be very readily removed, is adopted solely for brevity.

(1) Arithmetical, $\bar{a} + \bar{a} + \bar{a} = a_1 + a_2 + a_3$ or $\bar{a} = \dfrac{a_1 + a_2 + a_3}{3}$

(2) Geometrical, $\bar{a}\, \bar{a}\, \bar{a} = a_1\, a_2\, a_3$ or $\bar{a} = \sqrt[3]{a_1\, a_2\, a_3}$

(3) Harmonical, $\dfrac{1}{\bar{a}} + \dfrac{1}{\bar{a}} + \dfrac{1}{\bar{a}} = \dfrac{1}{a_1} + \dfrac{1}{a_2} + \dfrac{1}{a_3}$ or $\bar{a} = \dfrac{3}{\dfrac{1}{a_1} + \dfrac{1}{a_2} + \dfrac{1}{a_3}}$

The weighted arithmetical mean is given by the formula

$$w_1\bar{a} + w_2\bar{a} + w_3\bar{a} = w_1 a_1 + w_2 a_2 + w_3 a_3 \text{ or } \bar{a} = \frac{w_1 a_1 + w_2 a_2 + w_3 a_3}{w_1 + w_2 + w_3}$$

where the "weights" are the coefficients w_1, w_2, w_3. This is the mean employed by Böhm-Bawerk in the example given, the elements averaged, a_1, a_2, a_3, etc., being the different ages of the labor, 10 years, 9 years, 8 years, 7 years, etc., and the weights being the amount of labor, \$20, \$20, \$5, \$5, etc. The formulæ for both the geometrical and the harmonical averages may also be modified by introducing "weights."

351

By varying the formula we may evidently invent an infinite number of new kinds of means. Thus the formula

$$\bar{a} + \frac{\bar{a}}{1 + \sqrt{\bar{a}}} = a_1 + \frac{a_2}{1 + \sqrt{a_3}}.$$

defines $\bar{a}$ as a sort of mean, though a complicated (and unsymmetrical) one, of a_1, a_2, a_3.

§ 2 (to Ch. IV, § 2)

Case Illustrating Futility of Measuring Average Production Period.

Böhm-Bawerk's chosen concept, which was doubtless adopted purely for convenience, that a given application of labor will yield its return in a single sum all at once, is far too simple to cover the facts as actually found. On the contrary, both the labor of forming instruments and their return are spread over a considerable period of time. This distribution in time may take any form, and some of its forms would render useless the simple arrangement of Böhm-Bawerk of production periods into a series of varying duration.

Suppose, to take an extreme case, that a particular application of labor issues in two items of income, namely: $5 ten years after date, and $100 one hundred years after date; while another application of labor issues in only a single item worth $15 in twenty-five years. In this case it becomes impossible to call one of the production periods longer than the other; for whereas the second is definitely 25 years long, the first may be measured as any period between 10 and 100 years, according to the method employed for averaging 10 and 100. Moreover, it is not true that one of the alternatives will be chosen if the rate of interest is high, and the other if the rate of interest is low, as would be the case if they were subject to Böhm-Bawerk's series. The application of labor which issued in the $5 and $100 would, oddly enough, be the most economical if the rate of interest were either very high or very low, whereas the other alternative would be chosen in case the interest were at a more moderate rate. Thus, if the rate of interest were 5%, the present value of the $15 due in 25 years would be $4.43, and that of the two items, $5 in 10 years and $100 in 100 years, would be $3.83. On the other hand, if the rate of interest were 1%, the value of the $5 and $100 alternative would be $11.70 and of the $15 alternative $41.28.

Again, if the rate of interest were 25 %, the value of the $5 and $100 would be $0.06 and of the $15 alternative, $0.54. Hence, if the rate of interest is 5%, the $15 alternative will be preferable, whereas if the rate of interest is either 1 % or 25 %, the other alternative will be chosen.

§ 3 (TO CH. IV, § 3)

Showing how Periods of Production which are Relatively Long but Unproductive are Eliminated.

That long processes (assuming their length to be measurable) are more productive than short processes is, as Böhm-Bawerk says, a general fact, not a necessary truth. The reason lies in *selection*. It is not true that, of all *possible* productive processes, the longest are the most productive; but it is true that, of all productive processes *actually employed*, the longest are also the most productive. No one will select a long way unless it is at the same time a better way. All the long but unproductive processes are weeded out. The following illustration will make the process clear:

Suppose that by means of 100 days' labor invested to-day we can obtain a product of 100 units one year hence, or of 250 two years hence, of 50 three years hence, of 300 four years hence, of 250 five years hence, of 320 six years hence, of 100 seven years hence, of 300 eight years hence, etc., — a series which we take quite at random. Out of this series of choices there will be eliminated those of 3, 5, 7, and 8 years, for each of these is outclassed by preceding choices. Thus, the 5-year period yielding 250 will be overshadowed by the 4-year period yielding 300; for this prospective return, being not only larger but earlier, will have a higher present value. Eliminating, then, these ineligible cases, we have left, to choose from, the 1, 2, 4, and 6 year periods. Of these, that one will be chosen of which the return will have the highest present value; and the present value will depend on the rate of interest. If interest is at 5 %, it will be profitable to invest the 100 days' labor so as to mature in four years. *AB* is the discounted value of 300 at 5 % for four years, it being found by the discount-curve *BC* drawn at 5 % from *C*. Since this curve passes above the tops, *C'*, *C''*, *C'''*, of all the other vertical lines, this present value (at 5 %) of 300 in four years will be the maximum of the present values of all the returns,

100, 250, 50, etc. But if the rate of interest sinks to 2 %, as indicated by the discount-curve $B'C'$, the point of maximum return is shifted forward to six years; for the discount-curve $B'C'$ at 2 % drawn through C' now passes above the tops (C, C'', C''', etc.) of all other lines, hence a six-year period will be chosen. If, on the other hand, the rate of interest were 10 %, a similar construction would show that the two-year period would be selected, as the highest discount-curve would then pass through C''. But in no case will the highest discount curve touch the top of one of the short lines, 100, 50, 250, 100.

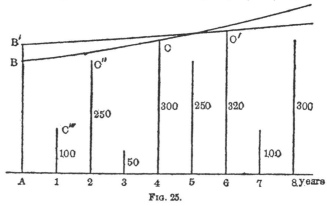

FIG. 25.

§ 4 (to Ch. IV, § 4)

Mathematical Refutation of Böhm-Bawerk's Claim as to Ground of Preference for Present over Future Investment of Labor.

Let the products obtainable by processes of 1, 2, 3, etc. years be p_1, p_2, p_3, etc., and the "marginal utilities reduced in perspective" beginning in 1888 be u_1, u_2, u_3, etc. Then,

A MONTH'S LABOR AVAILABLE

For the economic period	In 1888 yields			In 1889 yields		
	Units of product	Marginal utility reduced in persp.	Amount of value of entire product	Units	Marg. utility	Value
1888	p_1	u_1	p_1u_1	—	u_1	—
1889	p_2	u_2	p_2u_2	p_1	u_2	p_1u_2
1890	p_3	u_3	p_3u_3	p_2	u_3	p_2u_3
1891	p_4	u_4	p_4u_4	p_3	u_4	p_3u_4
etc.	etc.	etc.	etc.	etc.	etc.	etc.

We shall show that the labor available in 1888 is more valuable than that in 1889, provided only $u_1 > u_2 > u_3 > u_4$, etc.; that is, that the maximum of the first series of pu's, relating to 1888, is greater than the maximum of the second series, relating to 1889 (assuming of course that maxima exist). To prove this, select the maximum of the second series. Suppose it to be p_3u_4. This is necessarily less than p_3u_3 in the first series; for since $u_4 < u_3$ by hypothesis, it follows that $p_3u_4 < p_3u_3$. That is, there necessarily exists in the first series a term greater than the greatest term in the second series. *A fortiori* must the *greatest* term in the first series exceed the greatest in the second series. In other words, the value for 1888 exceeds that for 1889, provided only the marginal utilities descend, whether or not the productivities ascend.

APPENDIX TO CHAPTER V

APPRECIATION AND INTEREST

§ 1 (to Ch. V, § 2)

History of Theory of Appreciation and Interest

Investigation shows that the present writer was by no means the first to conceive the relation between appreciation and interest. Apparently the earliest was the anonymous author[1] of a remarkable pamphlet entitled: "A Discourse Concerning the Currencies of the British Plantations in America," Boston, 1740 (reprinted in the *Economic Studies* of American Economic Association, 1897). He writes: —

" *The Arguments current amongst the Populace in favour of Paper Money*, are,

"I. In most of the Paper Money Colonies one of the principal Reasons alleged for their first Emissions ; was, *to prevent Usurers imposing high Interest upon Borrowers, from the Scarcity of Silver Money.* It is true, that in all Countries the increased Quantity of Silver, falls the Interest or Use of Money ; but large Emissions of Paper Money does naturally rise the Interest to make good the sinking Principal : for Instance, in the Autumn, *A.* 1737, Silver was at 26 s. to 27 s. per Ounce, but by a large *Rhode Island* Emission, it became in Autumn 1739, 29 s. per Oz. this is 7 per Cent. Loss of Principal, therefore the Lender, to save his Principal from sinking, requires 13 per Cent. natural Interest (our legal Interest being 6 per Cent.) for that Year. In Autumn *A.* 1733, Silver was 22 s. per Oz. by large Emissions it became 27 s. in the Autumn, *A.* 1734 ; is 22 per Cent. loss of Principal ; and the Lender to save his Principal ; requires 28 per Cent. *natural Interest* for that Year. Thus *the larger the Emissions, natural Interest becomes the higher ;* therefore the Advocates for Paper Money (who are generally indigent Men, and Borrowers) ought not to complain, when they hire Money at a dear nominal Rate.

"If Bills were to depreciate after a certain Rate, Justice might be done to both contracting Parties, by imposing the Loss which the Principal may sustain in any certain Space of Time (the Period of Payment), upon the Interest of a Bond or Price of Goods : but as Depreciations are uncertain, great Confusions in Dealings happen."

[1] Now identified as the physician, William Douglass.

356

John Stuart Mill expressed the same view,[1] as have also Robert Goodbody,[2] Jacob de Haas,[3] and Professor John B. Clark.[4] A principle which apparently has been independently discovered by each of these economic students and quite possibly by others,[5] is likely to be of some importance.

The present writer published in 1896 a monograph[6] in which he worked out the relation between interest and appreciation in quantitative form, its application to special cases, its statistical verification, as well as its significance in the theory of interest and in the practical problem of regulating the standard of deferred payments. The major part of the material contained in this monograph is reproduced in Chapter V, Chapter XIV, and this Appendix.

That the appreciation or depreciation of money does actually

---

[1] *Principles of Political Economy*, Book 3, Ch. 23, § 4. [A single paragraph.]

[2] Mr. Robert Goodbody, Broker, New York, has for years in his trade-letters maintained the doctrine that the rate of interest is high when money is depreciating, and low when money is appreciating. This he discovered about 1876, when the decline in silver was attracting attention. He was then much interested in the higher mathematics, and as he expressed it, "accident or something caused me to differentiate the equation of imports and exports of any country, not with respect to time, but with respect to the variation of the standard of value. The result was that I found that the fraction formed by the ratio of *call* money as numerator and *time* money as denominator was smaller when the money standard was falling and larger when it was rising."

[3] "A Third Element in the Rate of Interest," *Journal of the Royal Statistical Society*, March, 1889. [An extended discussion, with statistics.]

[4] "The Gold Standard in the Light of Recent Theory," *Political Science Quarterly*, September, 1895. [Applied to the bimetallic controversy.]

[5] Mr. Byron W. Holt has cited other cases in which the relation between appreciation and interest has been recognized. In his paper entitled "Interest and Appreciation" (*Sound Currency*, Vol. V, No. 22, 1898) he mentions Senator Jones of Nevada, Professor T. N. Carver, now of Harvard, David I. Greene of Hartford, and Professor H. H. Powers, formerly of Leland Stanford.

[6] "Appreciation and Interest: a study of the influence of monetary appreciation and depreciation on the rate of interest, with applications to the bimetallic controversy and the theory of interest." *Publications of the American Economic Association*, 1896, Vol. XI, No. 4, pp. 331–442.

influece the rate of interest is now well recognized by those who have given attention to the subject.[1]

§ 2 (to Ch. V, § 3)
Formula Connecting the Rates of Interest in two Diverging Standards.

In order to state the general relation between the rates of interest and appreciation or depreciation, let wheat fall in gold price (or gold rise in wheat price) so that the quantity of gold which would buy one bushel of wheat at the beginning of the year will buy $1 + a$ bushels at the end, a being therefore the rate of appreciation of gold in terms of wheat.

Let the rate of interest in gold be i, and in wheat be j, and let the principal of the loan be D dollars or its equivalent B bushels.

Our alternative contracts are then : —

For D dollars borrowed, $D + Di$ or $D(1 + i)$ dollars are due in 1 yr.

For B bushels borrowed, $B + Bj$ or $B(1 + j)$ bushels are due in 1 yr.

and our problem is to find the relation between i and j, which will make the $D(1 + i)$ dollars $\backsim$ the $B(1 + j)$ bushels.[2]

At first, D dollars $\backsim B$ bu.

At the end of the year, D dollars $\backsim B(1 + a)$ bu.

Hence at the end of the year $D(1 + i)$ dollars $\backsim B(1 + a)(1 + i)$ bu.

Since $D(1 + i)$ is the number of dollars necessary to liquidate the debt, its equivalent $B(1 + a)(1 + i)$ is the number of bushels necessary to liquidate it. But we have already designated this number of bushels by $B(1 + j)$.

---

[1] See Professor Marshall's testimony, *Indian Currency Report*, 1899, Pt. II, p. 169; Graziani, *Studi sulla teoria dell' interresse*, Turin, 1898, pp. 120–29; and Joseph F. Johnson, *Money and Currency*, Boston (Ginn), 1905, p. 158. But the subject has as yet attracted little attention in the business journals. See *The Bond Record*, April, 1896 ; also the first number of *Moody's Magazine*, 1905, in which the " Symposium " and editorial on the effects of increasing the supply of gold are partly devoted to the relation between monetary depreciation and the rate of interest. The same material together with much else of importance is assembled in *The Gold Supply and Prosperity*, by Byron W. Holt, New York (Moody Publishing Co.), 1907. See also J. P. Norton, "The Depreciation of Gold," *Yale Review*, 1906–7, pp. 293–306.

[2] The symbol $\backsim$ signifies " equivalent to."

Our result, therefore, is : —

at the end of one year $D(1+i) \backsimeq B(1+j) = B(1+a)(1+i)$, (1)
which, after B is canceled, discloses the formula : —

$$1 + j = (1 + a)(1 + i), \qquad (2)$$
or $$j = i + a + ia. \qquad (3)$$

or in words : *The rate of interest in the relatively depreciating standard is equal to the sum of three terms, viz. the rate of interest in the appreciating standard, the rate of appreciation itself, and the product of these two elements.*

Thus, to offset the appreciation, the rate of interest must be lowered by slightly more than the rate of appreciation.[1]

We may introduce depreciation in a similar manner. Instead of saying gold appreciates at the rate a, relatively to wheat, we may say, wheat depreciates at the rate d, relatively to gold.[2] This means that wheat has sunk in terms of gold in the ratio 1 to $1 - d$, and reasoning similar to the foregoing shows that

$$1 + i = (1 - d)(1 + j). \qquad (4)$$

Equations (2) and (4) may be conveniently combined, thus :

$$\frac{1+j}{1+i} = \frac{1+a}{1} = \frac{1}{1-d}. \qquad (5)$$

Since $\frac{1+a}{1}$ is the ratio of the value of gold at the end of the year to its value at the beginning (all in terms of wheat), that is, the ratio of divergence of the two standards expressed in wheat, while $\frac{1}{1-d}$ is the same ratio of divergence expressed in gold, and since $1 + i$ is the "amount" of \$1 put at interest for one year, while $1 + j$ is the "amount" of one bushel; we may state equation (5) as follows : —

[1] Professor Clark (*Political Science Quarterly*, September, 1895) implies that 1 % appreciation is offset by *less* than 1 % reduction of interest. But in making his calculation he has failed to "compound." The numerical illustrations of the eighteenth century pamphleteer (*supra*) are also erroneous. *E.g.* instead of 28 % the figure should be 29.32 %. Professor Marshall (*Principles of Economics*, Vol. I, 3d ed., p. 674) gives a correct example, designed to show the losses from a fluctuating currency.

[2] The relation between d and a is $(1 + a)(1 - d) = 1$, which is evident from equation (5), or may be easily shown independently.

The ratio of divergence between the standards equals the ratio between their " amounts."

This is, perhaps, the simplest mode of conceiving the relation, and stress is laid upon it, because it brings into prominence the " amount," or ratio of future payment to present loan, a magnitude which in most questions of interest plays a more important rôle than the rate of interest itself.

Equation (5) gives the relation between i and j in terms of a or d.   From it follows the value of j in terms either of i and a or of i and d, and also the value of i in terms either of j and a or of j and d, thus : —

$$\frac{1+j}{1+i}=\frac{1+a}{1}\quad=\frac{1}{1-d}, \tag{5}$$

whence
$$j = i + a + ia = \frac{i+d}{1-d}. \tag{6}$$

or
$$i = j - d - jd = \frac{j-a}{1+a}. \tag{7}$$

It follows that j exceeds i by more than the rate of appreciation, which in turn is more than the rate of depreciation (*i.e.*, $j - i > a > d$).

§ 3 (to Ch. V, § 4)

Formulæ, when Rates of Interest and of Appreciation are Reckoned oftener than Yearly.

In case we take the half-year instead of the year as the interval for compounding the rates of interest and of appreciation, it may readily be shown that the formula

$$1 + j = (1 + i)\ (1 + a)\ \text{gives place to}$$
$$1 + \frac{j}{2} = \left(1 + \frac{i}{2}\right)\left(1 + \frac{a}{2}\right),$$

whence it also follows that instead of $j = i + a + ia$, we have the relation

$$j = i + a + \frac{ia}{2}$$

In case the interest and appreciation are compounded quarterly, the formula becomes

$$j = i + a + \frac{ia}{4},$$

and so on. At the limit, when the rates of interest and appreciation are reckoned continuously, the last term vanishes and the formula becomes simply $j = i + a$.

§ 4 (to Ch. V, § 5)

Case of Partial Payments.

First, consider the case in which no interest is paid until the end of the term of years. Let us suppose, for instance, a savings bank which receives $100, gold standard, and repays the depositor in five years at 5 % compound interest. Let there be an alternative standard, say wheat, worth, at the beginning of the loan, $1 per bushel; but suppose that, in terms of wheat, gold is known to appreciate constantly by 1 % per annum. What would be the rate of interest in terms of wheat? If the repayment were to be made in one year, the equivalent of the 5 % would be a rate of interest in terms of wheat of $6\frac{1}{20}$ %, since the "amount" of a dollar of gold put at interest one year would be $1.05, and this would be worth, in bushels of wheat, 1.05 multiplied by 1.01, or $1.06\frac{1}{20}$ bushels.

This result, $6\frac{1}{20}$ %, is as true for a series of years as for one year. This may be seen by separating the contract into several contracts of one year each. If we imagine deposited to-day in separate savings banks $100 in gold, and its equivalent, 100 bushels of wheat, they will amount in one year respectively to $1.05 at 5 %, and its equivalent, 106.05 bushels at $6\frac{1}{20}$ %. We may now regard these equivalent amounts as withdrawn, but immediately redeposited for one year. Then, with the same rate of interest in gold and the same relative appreciation, we shall obtain the same rate of interest in wheat, so that $105 and its equivalent, 106.05 bushels, will amount in one year respectively to $110.25 at 5 %, and its equivalent, 112.47 bushels at $6\frac{1}{20}$ %. In this way each successive pair of "amounts," including the last, will be equivalent.

For simplicity we have considered only the case in which the debt is allowed to accumulate to the end. The most general case, however, is one in which the repayments are in installments.

Suppose, as before, that the interest in gold is 5 % and that gold is known to appreciate 1 % per annum relatively to wheat. A farmer mortgages his land for $1000, or its then equivalent,

1000 bushels of wheat, and agrees to pay annually the interest and such parts of the principal as he can save, making the repayment complete in seven years. Our problem is to find that rate of interest in wheat which will make the contracts in gold and wheat equivalent in every respect.

The solution is precisely the same as before, viz. $6\frac{1}{20}\%$. For, at the end of one year, the farmer's debt amounts to \$1050 or its then equivalent 1060.50 bushels. Let us suppose that he finds himself able to pay, not only the interest, \$50, but also \$50 of the "principal," that is, \$100 all together. The equivalent of this in wheat is 101 bushels. Hence he can either

pay \$100 on   \$1050.00   leaving \$950.00
or   101 bu. on   1060.50 bu. leaving   959.50 bu.

and, since the "amounts" \$1050 and 1060.50 bu. are equivalent and the deductions \$100 and 101 bu. are equivalent, the remainders \$950 and 959.50 bu. must also be equivalent; in fact, this may be seen directly, since, with gold appreciating 1%, \$950, originally worth 950 bu., becomes worth 1% more or 959.50 bu.

Thus the farmer's remaining debt at the end of the first year is the same whether measured in wheat or gold, and since the same reasoning applies to the second year, third year, etc., the equivalence remains to the end of the contract.

It is worth noting here that the \$100 payment in gold would be regarded as consisting of half "interest" and half "principal," whereas the equivalent payment in wheat, 101 bu., will be regarded as 60.50 bu. "interest," and 40.50 bu. "principal."

The liquidation of the contract during the seven years may thus be supposed to take place in either of the following equivalent ways: —

GOLD STANDARD (dollars)

	Interest	Amount	Payment	Principal Remaining
At beginning				1000.00
In 1 year	50.00	1050.00	100.00	950.00
In 2 years	47.50	997.50	97.50	900.00
In 3 years	45.00	945.00	145.00	800.00
In 4 years	40.00	840.00	150.00	690.00
In 5 years	34.50	724.50	174.50	550.00
In 6 years	27.50	577.50	277.50	300.00
In 7 years	15.00	315.00	315.00	0.00

WHEAT STANDARD (bushels)

	Interest	Amount	Payment	Principal Remaining
At beginning				1000.00
In 1 year	60.50	1060.50	101.00	959.50
In 2 years	58.05	1017.55	99.46	918.09
In 3 years	55.54	973.63	149.39	824.24
In 4 years	49.87	874.11	156.09	718.02
In 5 years	43.44	761.46	183.40	578.06
In 6 years	34.97	613.03	294.57	318.46
In 7 years	19.27	337.73	337.73	0.00

In these two tables, every entry in one is equivalent to the corresponding entry in the other except those in the interest columns.

We thus see that the farmer who contracts a mortgage in gold is, *if the interest is properly adjusted,* no worse and no better off than if his contract were made in a "wheat" standard.

This principle, that debts in different standards are *equivalent* if the rates of interest in the two standards are properly adjusted, holds true, of course, no matter whether the "partial payments" are large, small, or none at all; no matter whether the interest payments are made in full, in part, or not at all. The principals in the two standards are not equivalent, except at the beginning, nor are the annual interest sums equivalent; but the excess of the burden of interest in one standard is accompanied by a deficiency in the burden of the principal, and *vice versa.*

§ 5 (to Ch. V, § 5)

Formulæ for Cases of Compound Interest and Partial Payments.

The general case is precisely similar. If a debt in either of two alternative standards is to accumulate at compound interest, the rates of interest in the two standards must, in order that the contracts in each shall be equivalent, conform to the formula, $1 + j = (1 + a)(1 + i)$, which we found in the simpler case of a one-year debt.

To show this, resolve the contract into a series of one-year contracts. For the first year we have, by formula (1) of § 2 above,

Dollars due	Bushels due	Bushels due

$$D(1+i) \backsim B(1+j) = B(1+a)(1+i)$$

In the second year the same formula applies except that in place of D, the principal is now $D(1+i)$, and in place of B, $B(1+j)$ or $B(1+a)(1+i)$. Making these substitutions in the formula, we obtain

$$D(1+i)^2 \backsim B(1+j)^2 = B(1+a)^2(1+i)^2.$$

And similarly the third year,

$$D(1+i)^3 \backsim B(1+j)^3 = B(1+a)^3(1+i)^3,$$

and so on. Each of the results evidently yields the formula

$$1+j = (1+a)(1+i).$$

If a debt in either of two alternative standards is to be liquidated in " partial payments," the rates of interest in the two standards must, in order that the contracts in each may be equivalent, conform to the same formula.

The reason is simply that equivalent payments subtracted from equivalent " amounts " will leave equivalent remainders. The payment in any year forms the same fractional part of the " amount " in the two standards. We may designate this fraction at the end of the first year by f, the second year by f', etc., and we have the following results :—

End of First Year

	Dollars	Bushels	Bushels
Amount,	$D(1+i) \backsim$	$B(1+j) =$	$B(1+a)(1+i)$
Payment,	$fD(1+i) \backsim$	$fB(1+j) =$	$fB(1+a)(1+i)$
Remainder,	$(1-f)D(1+i) \backsim (1-f)B(1+j) =$		$(1-f)B(1+a)(1+i)$

In like manner the unpaid remainder at the end of the second year can be shown to be

$$\overset{\text{Dollars}}{(1-f')(1-f)D(1+i)^2} \backsim \overset{\text{Bushels}}{(1-f')(1-f)B(1+j)^2}$$

$$\overset{\text{Bushels}}{= (1-f')(1-f)B(1+a)^2(1+i)^2,}$$

and so on for any number of years. Each result again yields the formula $(1+j) = (1+a)(1+i)$. Similar reasoning applied to each succeeding year yields the same formula.

The case in which there are no partial payments is met by putting f, f', equal to zero.

§ 6 (to Ch. V. § 5)

Case of Separate Payments of Interest and Principal in one of the
Two Standards and Equivalent Payments in the Other.

Suppose alternative contracts in gold at 5% and wheat at
$6\frac{1}{20}$%, and suppose that the interest in the gold contract is
annually paid and the principal redeemed in ten years. The
following tables will show what are the equivalent operations
in the wheat standard.

LIQUIDATION IN GOLD STANDARD, CONSISTING OF ANNUAL INTEREST ($50)
AND FINAL PRINCIPAL ($1000).

	INTEREST	AMOUNT DUE	PAYMENT	PRINCIPAL REMAINING
At beginning (Dollars)	—	—	—	1000.00
In 1 year	50.00	1050.00	50.00	1000.00
In 2 years	50.00	1050.00	50.00	1000.00
In 3 years	50.00	1050.00	50.00	1000.00
In 4 years	50.00	1050.00	50.00	1000.00
In 5 years	50.00	1050.00	50.00	1000.00
In 6 years	50.00	1050.00	50.00	1000.00
In 7 years	50.00	1050.00	50.00	1000.00
In 8 years	50.00	1050.00	50.00	1000.00
In 9 years	50.00	1050.00	50.00	1000.00
In 10 years	50.00	1050.00	1050.00	0.00

EQUIVALENT LIQUIDATION IN WHEAT STANDARD; ANNUAL PAYMENTS
ARE LESS THAN INTEREST (60.50 BU.) AND FINAL PAYMENT MORE
THAN PRINCIPAL (1000 BU.).

	INTEREST	AMOUNT DUE	PAYMENT	PRINCIPAL REMAINING
At beginning (Bushels)	—	—	—	1000.00
In 1 year	60.50	1060.50	50.50	1010.00
In 2 years	61.10	1071.10	51.00	1020.10
In 3 years	61.72	1081.82	51.52	1030.30
In 4 years	62.32	1092.62	52.03	1040.59
In 5 years	62.96	1103.55	52.55	1051.00
In 6 years	63.59	1114.59	53.08	1061.51
In 7 years	64.22	1125.73	53.61	1072.12
In 8 years	64.86	1136.98	54.14	1082.84
In 9 years	65.51	1148.35	54.68	1093.67
In 10 years	66.17	1159.84	1159.84	0.00

If we suppose, conversely, that interest in the wheat standard is annually met and the principal redeemed in ten years, the equivalent operations in the gold standard will be as shown below.

LIQUIDATION IN WHEAT STANDARD, CONSISTING OF ANNUAL INTEREST (60.50 BU.) AND FINAL PRINCIPAL (1000 BU.).

	INTEREST	AMOUNT DUE	PAYMENT	PRINCIPAL REMAINING
At beginning (Bushels)	—	—	—	1000.00
In 1 year	60.50	1060.50	60.50	1000.00
In 2 years	60.50	1060.50	60.50	1000.00
In 3 years	60.50	1060.50	60.50	1000.00
In 4 years	60.50	1060.50	60.50	1000.00
In 5 years	60.50	1060.50	60.50	1000.00
In 6 years	60.50	1060.50	60.50	1000.00
In 7 years	60.50	1060.50	60.50	1000.00
In 8 years	60.50	1060.50	60.50	1000.00
In 9 years	60.50	1060.50	60.50	1000.00
In 10 years	60.50	1060.50	1060.50	0.00

EQUIVALENT LIQUIDATION IN GOLD STANDARD; ANNUAL PAYMENTS ARE GREATER THAN INTEREST ($50) AND FINAL PAYMENT LESS THAN PRINCIPAL ($1000).

	INTEREST	AMOUNT DUE	PAYMENT	PRINCIPAL REMAINING
At beginning (Dollars)	—	—	—	1000.00
In 1 year	50.00	1050.00	59.90	990.10
In 2 years	49.50	1039.60	59.31	980.29
In 3 years	49.01	1029.30	58.72	970.58
In 4 years	48.53	1019.11	58.14	960.97
In 5 years	48.05	1009.02	57.56	951.46
In 6 years	47.57	999.03	56.99	942.04
In 7 years	47.15	989.19	56.43	932.76
In 8 years	46.63	979.39	55.87	823.52
In 9 years	46.17	969.69	55.32	914.37
In 10 years	45.71	960.08	960.08	0.00

§ 7 (TO CH. V, § 5)

Case of Separate Payments of Interest and Principal in both Standards.

Let us next compare the liquidations in the two standards by the simple annual payment of interest in each (*i.e.* $50 in the gold standard and 60.50 bu. in the wheat standard, not inter-equivalent) and in ten years, final payment of principal ($1000 and 1000 bu. not inter-equivalent).

In this case the individual payments in the two cases do not correspond, but the *present values* of the debts, reckoned at any date whatever, are always identical. Thus, the present value, at the date of contract, of the interest and principal, separately computed, at 6 % and $6\frac{1}{20}$ % in the two standards respectively, will be : [1] —

	Dollars	Bushels
Present value of all interest payments,	386.09 <	444.24
Present value of principal due in 10 years,	613.91 >	555.76
Present value of total,	1000.00 ⇌	1000.00

If the present values were computed five years after the date of the contract, and the "amounts" of past interest were computed for the same point of time, the items would be: —

	Dollars	Bushels
Interest (present value and amounts),	492.75 <	595.88
Principal (present value),	783.53 >	745.50
Total,	1276.28 ⇌	1341.38

The two sums here, though not equal numbers, are equivalent magnitudes; for whereas at the outset $1 of gold and 1 bushel of wheat were equivalent, now, after five years of annual appreciation of gold relatively to wheat at the rate of 1 %, we shall find $1 worth $(1.01)^5$ bushels, or 1.051 bu., whence $1276.28 will be worth 1341.38 bushels.

We thus see that it would be just as much of a hardship to pay the higher interest in wheat during the whole period as to pay the more onerous principal in gold at last.

§ 8 (to Ch. V, § 5)

Case of Perpetual Annuity.

The case of a perpetual annuity may be given special consideration. As is well known, the present value of a perpetual annuity is its "capitalized" value. Thus, if the rate of interest is taken at 5 %, the present value of a perpetual annuity of $50 per annum is $1000. Applying the same principle to the

---

[1] The symbol < is here used for " is less than the equivalent of," and > for " is more than the equivalent of."

wheat annuity of 60.50 bushels and extending the previous reasoning, we find that the two annuities are equivalent.

At first sight this seems impossible, since $6\frac{1}{20}\%$ is a higher rate of interest than 5%. This is true, numerically, and it is also true that the early payments of 60.50 bushels are actually more valuable than \$50. But after a certain time (in this particular case 19 years) the reverse is true. The 19th payment of \$50 in gold is worth 60.40 bushels, while the 20th is worth 61.01 bushels. That is, the recipient of the wheat annuity has *at first* a slight advantage over the recipient of the gold annuity, which ceases and becomes a slight disadvantage after 19 years.

To derive the formula for the time at which the relative values of the two annuities become reversed, let the rate of interest in gold be i, in wheat j; let the two annuities be Di and Bj, their capitalized values being D and B, ($D \approx B$ at the beginning), and let x be the number of years in which Bj is as valuable as or more valuable than Di. Then

	Bushels Dollars
At the end of x years,	$Bj \gtreqless Di$
At the end of $x+1$ years,	$Bj < Di$

and since we know that in x years $D \approx B(1+a)^x$, and hence $Di \approx Bi(1+a)^x$; and likewise in $x+1$ years, $Di \approx Bi(1+a)^{x+1}$, we see that the previous inequalities become:—

	Bushels Bushels
At the end of x years,	$Bj \geq Bi(1+a)^x$
At the end of $x+1$ years,	$Bj < Bi(1+a)^{x+1}$

which may be combined in the formula:—

$$i(1+a)^x \leqq j < i(1+a)^{x+1},$$

or
$$x \leqq \frac{\log j - \log i}{\log(1+a)} < x+1. \tag{8}$$

That is, x is the integral part of the number
$$\frac{\log j - \log i}{\log(1+a)}.$$

Thus, if $i = .05$, $a = .01$, and hence also $j = .0605$, then
$$\frac{\log j - \log i}{\log(1+a)} = \frac{\bar{2}.7818 - \bar{2}.6990}{.0043} = \frac{.0828}{.0043} = 19.3.$$

Hence $x = 19$.

§ 9 (to Ch. V, § 5)

Case in which the Rate of Appreciation changes each Year.

In this case the rate of interest in one or both of the two standards will change also.

Beginning with a numerical illustration, let us suppose that a syndicate offers the United States government an alternative loan in gold or silver. Let it be known that 100 gold dollars will remain at par throughout the first year, but in two years will be worth 150 silver dollars, that is, gold will "appreciate," in the second year, 50 % relatively to silver; also that in the third and fourth years it will appreciate 10 % and 5 % respectively. We shall suppose that the rate of interest, if the contract be in gold, is 3 % for each year of the contract.

Our problem is to discover what will be the rate of interest in silver. It is perhaps already evident that there will be a different rate for each year. If the contract were made for one year only, the rate of interest in silver would also be 3 %, since silver remains this year at par with gold. If the contract (or any unpaid part of it) were then renewed for a second year the rate of interest would be, by formula (3) : —

$$j = i + a + ai$$
$$= .03 + .50 + .015$$
$$= .545$$
$$= 54\tfrac{1}{2}\%.$$

In like manner, we may deduce the rate of interest in each year, with the following results : —

	Gold Standard	Appreciation	Silver Standard
1st year	3%	0%	3%
2d year	3%	50%	54½%
3d year	3%	10%	13$\frac{3}{10}$%
4th year etc.	3%	5%	8$\frac{15}{100}$%

The question arises, can a single "average" rate of interest be substituted for the above irregular series of rates in the silver standard ?

We answer that such an average is not possible if the debtor has the option of arbitrary partial payments. If, for instance, the average were 20 %, and the government could pay off at any time, it would evidently be tempted to refund the debt at the end of the second year, to which the lender would not agree. If, however, the conditions as to repayment are stipulated for in advance, an average can easily be computed on the principle of present values.

Suppose the borrower agreed to extinguish the debt in four years by paying at the end of successive years 20, 40, 30, and 10 millions (these to include "interest"). The present value of these sums is 66.321 millions, which is therefore the amount of the loan received from the syndicate. This sum is obtained by adding the present values of several payments. The present value of 20 millions, due one year hence, is

$$\frac{20}{1.03} = 19.418 \text{ millions,}$$

and of 40 millions, due two years hence, is

$$\frac{40}{(1.03)\,(1.545)} = 25.136 \text{ millions;}$$

for evidently if this be put at interest for one year at 3 %, and for the next at $54\frac{1}{2}$ %, it will amount to 40 millions. Likewise the third and fourth payments have present values of

$$\frac{30}{(1.03)\,(1.545)\,(1.133)} = 16.639 \text{ millions;}$$

$$\frac{10}{(1.03)\,(1.545)\,(1.133)\,(1.0815)} = 5.128 \text{ millions.}$$

The sum of these four present values is 66.321 millions. Now if we compute the present values of the four payments on the basis of a uniform "average" rate of 20.26 % interest, we obtain the same sum, thus: —

$$\frac{20}{(1.2026)} = 16.631 \text{ millions}$$

$$\frac{40}{(1.2026)^2} = 27.659 \text{ millions}$$

$$\frac{30}{(1.2026)^3} = 17.250 \text{ millions}$$

$$\frac{10}{(1.2026)^4} = 4.781 \text{ millions}$$

Total $= 66.321$ millions

The separate present values are here fictitious, that is, no one of them is the actual present selling price of the future payment to which it refers, but the deviations so offset each other that their *sum* is the actual present selling price of the whole set of future payments. It follows from principles already stated that the debt, 66.321 millions, can be liquidated by precisely the same payments (20, 40, 30, and 10 millions) whether the interest is reckoned separately at 3, $54\frac{1}{2}$, $13\frac{3}{10}$, and $8\frac{15}{100}\%$, or uniformly at 20.26 %. In fact the details of the bookkeeping in the two cases are: —

	At 3, $54\frac{1}{2}$, $18\frac{3}{10}$, $8\frac{15}{100}\%$				At 20.26% uniformly			
	(In Millions)				(In Millions)			
Date	Interest	Amount	Payment	Principal	Interest	Amount	Payment	Principal
	—	—	—	66.32	—	—	—	66.32
In 1 year	1.99	68.31	20.00	48.31	13.44	79.76	20.00	59.76
In 2 years	26.33	74.64	40.00	34.64	12.11	71.87	40.00	31.87
In 3 years	4.61	39.25	30.00	9.25	6.45	38.32	30.00	8.32
In 4 years	.75	10.00	10.00	0.00	1.68	10.00	10.00	0.00

We thus see that 20.26 % is the "average" of 3, $54\frac{1}{2}$, $13\frac{3}{10}$, and $8\frac{15}{100}\%$, in the sense that, reckoning interest by this "average," the same payments will cancel the same debt as if the separate rates were used. It is not identical with the arithmetical average, which is 19.74 %.

To express the law of such an average symbolically, let us suppose that the rate of appreciation of one standard in terms of the other is foreknown to be a_1 the first year, a_2 the second year, a_3 the third year, and so on; also, to be as general as possible, that the rates of interest in both standards are variable, being in the appreciating standard i_1 the first year, i_2 the second, etc., and in the depreciating standard, $j_1, j_2,$ etc. Let the final settlement occur in n years. Then, as above, we may regard the contract as equivalent to a series of one-year contracts successively renewed in whole or in part, the only difference being that the terms are all made in advance. As equation (2) of § 2 applies to each of these contracts, we have

$$1 + j_1 = (1 + a_1)(1 + i_1)$$
$$1 + j_2 = (1 + a_2)(1 + i_2)$$
$$\cdots \cdots \cdots$$
$$1 + j_n = (1 + a_n)(1 + i_n) \tag{9}$$

To obtain an expression for the average rate of interest in either standard, i.e., i_a (or j_a), we require a given series of payments, D_1, D_2, ... D_n, in the one standard (or their equivalent B_1, B_2, ... B_n, in the other standard). The aggregate present value of these payments, reckoned by the separate rates of interest, i_1, i_2, ... i_n (or j_1, j_2 ... j_n) is

$$\frac{D_1}{1+i_1} + \frac{D_2}{(1+i_1)(1+i_2)} + \cdots + \frac{D_n}{(1+i_1)(1+i_2)\ldots(1+i_n)}$$

(or the corresponding expression in terms of B's and j's). Now the "average" rate i_a must be such that if applied to the same set of payments it will produce the same sum of present values; that is, i_a is determined by

$$\frac{D_1}{1+i_a} + \frac{D_2}{(1+i_a)^2} + \cdots + \frac{D_n}{(1+i_a)^n} = \tag{10}$$
$$\frac{D_1}{1+i_1} + \frac{D_2}{(1+i_1)(1+i_2)} + \cdots + \frac{D_n}{(1+i_1)(1+i_2)\cdots(1+i_n)},$$

and j_a is determined by the corresponding formula in B's and j's.

This equation has only one real and positive root or value of i_a. It can readily be obtained by Horner's method.[1] We may call i_a and j_a the "present-worth-average" of i_1, i_2, ... i_n and j_1, j_2, ... j_n respectively.[2]

We may define the average rate of appreciation of one of the two standards in terms of the other as that rate which would connect the two average interest rates if the latter were actual (instead of averages of actual) rates.[3] That is, if the

[1] For, by substituting for $\frac{1}{1+i_a}$ the single letter x, and for $\frac{1}{1+i_1}, \frac{1}{1+i_2}$, etc., the letters x_1, x_2, etc., the equation becomes :
$$D_1 x + D_2 x^2 + \cdots + D_n x^n = D_1 x_1 + D_2 x_1 x_2 + \cdots + D_n x_1 x_2 \cdots x_n.$$
In the example given previously the equation becomes : —
$$20\,x + 40\,x^2 + 30\,x^3 + 10\,x^4 = 66.321,$$
the required root of which is $x = .83155$,
which, applied to $x = \frac{1}{1+j_a}$, gives $j_a = .2026$.

[2] $1 + i_a$ becomes the "geometrical average" of $1 + i_1$, $1 + i_2$, etc., when $D_1 = D_2 = \cdots = D_{n-1} = 0$.

[3] It may be proved that this definition of a_a satisfies the general condition of an average, viz. that a_a reduces to a_1, a_2, etc., when the latter are all equal, whether i_1, i_2, etc. (and j_1, j_2, etc.), be all equal or not. The proof is left to the reader.

average rates of interest are i_a and j_a, the average appreciation, a_n, is given by the equation

$$1 + j_a = (1 + i_a)(1 + a_a);$$

or, $$a_a = \frac{j_a - i_a}{1 + i_a}.$$

Thus, as in the example given above, suppose the average silver interest is 20.26 % and gold interest 3 %, so that

$$a_a = \frac{.2026 - .03}{1 + .03} = .1676,$$

or 16.76 %. This average is not identical with the arithmetical average of 0, 50, 10, and 5 %, which would be 16.25 %, nor is it identical with that rate which, if uniform, would result in four years in the same divergence between silver and gold as was produced by the four successive rates 0, 50, 10, and 5 %; this would be 14.70 %.

APPENDIX TO CHAPTER VII

First Approximation

(This Appendix should be read as a whole after Chapter VII.)

§ 1

As the preliminary statement of the theory of interest enunciated in Chapter VII contains the kernel of our theory, it will be worth our while, before proceeding to introduce the various complications necessary to complete it, to give the first approximation a full mathematical expression. This mathematical statement will serve to make the preceding results clearer and more sharply defined. It will also serve to demonstrate the important fact that the number of determining conditions is exactly equal to the number of unknown quantities, and therefore is adequate for fully determining those unknown quantities.

Inasmuch as the equations are necessarily numerous and complicated, it will aid the reader in following them if we break the argument up into two steps, first considering an artificially simple case where there are only two years of income to be considered, and then passing to the general case where there are any given number of years.

Let us suppose, therefore, that the rate of preference for this year's income over next, in the case of each individual, can be expressed as dependent alone on the amount of this year's and next year's income, the incomes of all the future years being regarded, for the sake of argument, as fixed. Suppose also that the income of each year is concentrated at one point, say the middle of the year, making the two such points just a year apart, and that borrowing and lending are so restricted as to affect only this year's and next year's income.

Let f_1 represent the rate of preference for this year's over next year's income, for individual No. 1, and let his original endowment of income for the two years be respectively c_1' and c_1''. This original income-stream, c_1', c_1'', is modified by borrowing this year and repaying next year. The sum bor-

374

rowed this year is x_1', the value of which is yet to be determined. This sum is therefore to be added to the present income c_1'. Next year the debt is paid, and consequently the income c_1'' for that year is *reduced* by the sum paid. For the sake of uniformity, however, we shall regard both modifications algebraically as *additions*, the addition x_1' to the first year's income being a positive quantity, and the addition, which we shall designate by x_1'', to the second year's income being a negative quantity. Thus, if \$100 is borrowed this year and \$105 repaid next year, x_1' is $+100$ and x_1'' is -105. Thus the first year's income is changed from c_1' to $c_1' + x_1'$ and the second year's from c_1'' to $c_1'' + x_1''$. By this notation we avoid the necessity of employing minus signs. Then the first condition determining interest, namely, that the rate of preference for each individual depends upon his income-stream, is represented by the following equation: —

$$f_1 = F_1(c_1' + x_1', \; c_1'' + x_1''),$$

which expresses f_1 as a function of the income of the two years. In case the individual lends instead of borrows, the same equation may be taken to represent the resulting relation between his rate of preference and his income-stream as modified by *lending;* the only difference is that in this case the particular value of x' is negative and of x'', positive.

In like manner, for individual No. 2 we have the equation

$$f_2 = F_2 \, (c_2' + x_2', \; c_2'' + x_2'').$$

For the third individual,

$$f_3 = F_3 \, (c_3' + x_3', \; c_3'' + x_3''),$$

and so on up to the last or nth individual, for whom the equation will be

$$f_n = F_n \, (c_n' + x_n', \; c_n'' + c_n'').$$

These n equations therefore express the first of the four conditions mentioned at the close of Chapter VII.

The second condition, that the marginal rates of preference of the n different individuals for present over future income shall be equal to each other and equal also to the rate of interest, is expressed by the continuous equation: —

$$f_1 = f_2 = f_3 \cdots = \cdots = f_n = i.$$

405

These equations hold true, as we saw in Chapter VI, because if a particular f should be greater than its corresponding i, the individual would become a borrower, and if f should be less than i, he would become a lender. In the former case the effect of his borrowing would be to reduce his f until it became equal to i. In the latter case the effect of his lending would be to increase his f until it became equal to i likewise. We have, then, as a result of borrowing or lending, the equation $f = i$, and as the same applies to every individual, all the f's are equal to i and therefore to each other also.

The third condition, namely, that the market must be cleared, or that the loans and borrowings must be equal, is expressed by the following two equations: —

$$x_1' + x_2' + \cdots + \cdots + x_n' = 0,$$
$$x_1'' + x_2'' + \cdots + \cdots + x_n'' = 0.$$

That is, the total of this year's borrowings is zero (lendings being regarded as negative borrowings), and the total of next year's returns is likewise zero (payments being regarded as negative returns).

The fourth and last condition, that for each individual this year's loans and next year's returns discounted are equal, is fulfilled in the following equations, each corresponding to one individual: —

$$x_1' + \frac{x_1''}{1 + i} = 0,$$

$$x_2' + \frac{x_2''}{1 + i} = 0,$$

$$x_3' + \frac{x_3''}{1 + i} = 0,$$

. . .

. . .

$$x_n' + \frac{x_n''}{1 + i} = 0.$$

§ 2

We now proceed to compare the number of equations with the number of unknowns. There are evidently n equations in the first set, n in the second, 2 in the third, and n in the fourth, making in all $3n + 2$ equations. The unknown quantities are

$$f_1, \quad f_2, \quad f_3, \quad \cdots, \quad \cdots, \quad f_n, \quad \text{or } n \text{ unknowns,}$$
$$x_1', \quad x_2', \quad x_3', \quad \cdots, \quad \cdots, \quad x_n', \quad \text{or } n \text{ unknowns,}$$
$$x_1'', \quad x_2'' \quad x_3'', \quad \cdots, \quad \cdots, \quad x_n'', \quad \text{or } n \text{ unknowns,}$$

and finally, i,   1 unknown,

making in all $3n + 1$ unknowns.

We have, then, one more equation than necessary. But examination of the equations will show that they are not all independent, since any one equation in the third and fourth sets may be determined from the others of those sets. Thus, to determine the first equation of the third set, add together all the equations of the fourth set. The addition gives

$$(x_1' + x_2' + x_3' + \cdots + \cdots + x_n') + \frac{x_1'' + x_2'' + x_3'' + \cdots + \cdots + x_n''}{1 + i} = 0.$$

In this equation we may substitute zero for the numerator of the fraction, as is evident by consulting the second equation of the third set. Making this substitution, the above equation becomes

$$x_1' + x_2' + x_3' + \cdots + \cdots + x_n' = 0,$$

which is identical with the first equation of the third set. Since we have here derived the first equation of the third set from all the other equations of the third and fourth sets, the equations are not all independent. It follows, therefore, that of the $3n + 2$ equations, one may be dispensed with (namely, any one of the equations of the third or fourth sets), so that there are left only $3n + 1$ *independent* equations, which are therefore exactly equal in number to the unknown quantities to be determined. There are, therefore, just sufficient equations to determine those unknown quantities, namely, the f's, or rates of preference for different individuals, the x''s and x'''s, or the loans and their repayments, and finally, i, the rate of interest.

§ 3

In order to obtain an explicit expression for i, we may "solve with respect to i" all of the preceding equations that can be so treated.   Thus, to take one of the equations from the third set, namely, $x_1' + \dfrac{x_1''}{1+i} = 0$, it is evident that, solving for i, this equation may be written

$$i = \frac{-x_1''}{x_1'} - 1.$$

To interpret this, we recall that x_1' is a sum *borrowed* this year (say \$100) and thus added to this year's income, and x_1'', being the sum "added" next year, and hence a negative quantity (say -105), it follows that $-x_1''$ is the positive quantity (as 105) returned.   Hence $\dfrac{-x_1''}{x_1'}$ is the ratio $\left(\text{as }\dfrac{105}{100}\right)$ of the sum returned to the sum borrowed, or the ratio of exchange between this year's and next year's goods, and $\dfrac{-x_1''}{x_1'} - 1$ $\left(\text{as }\dfrac{105}{100} - 1, \text{ or } 5\,\%\right)$ is the *premium* above par of the rate of exchange.   Since this premium is the definition of the rate of interest, the equation $i = \dfrac{-x_1''}{x_1'} - 1$ is merely an equation of definition.

The results of the proposed transformations may be summarized as follows : —

$$\begin{aligned}
i &= f_1 & &= f_2 & &= \cdots = f_n \\
&= F_1(c_1' + x_1',\, c_1'' + x_1'') &&= F_2(c_2' + x_2',\, c_2'' + x_2'') &&= \cdots = F_n(\text{etc.}) \\
&= \frac{-x_1''}{x_1'} - 1 && = \frac{-x_2''}{x_2'} - 1 && = \cdots = \frac{-x_n''}{x_n'} - 1.
\end{aligned}$$

These three equations give the value of i, subject to the additional condition : —

$$x_1' + x_2' + \cdots + \cdots + x_n' = 0,$$

the other equation of the same type as the last being omitted as the one superfluous equation.   The equation above written could be itself dispensed with by substituting in the previous equations the value of x_1' derived from it, namely,

$$-x_2' - \cdots - x_n'.$$

These equations state that the rate of interest, under the conditions of the problem, will be equal to the rates of time-preference for all the individuals, as well as equal also to a certain definite function of the income-streams as finally determined by the loans and to the premium of exchange of this year's income in terms of next year's income. These conditions, taken together with the condition that the sums lent must be equal to the sums borrowed—that is, that the rate of interest must be such as just to clear the market —will yield a complete determination of the rate of interest, which is the object of our search.

It may be remarked in passing that the first of the three continuous equations given above is closely analogous to the third; in fact, the first may be called the subjective prototype of the third, which may, in like manner, be called the objective expression of the first. The third equation states the definition of the rate of interest as the premium in the ratio of exchange between this year's and next year's income, and the first states that the rate of interest is equal to the premium in the relative desirability of the two. It is not difficult to express the analogy algebraically by putting the f's equal to the excess above unity of the ratio between the marginal desirability of this year's income and the marginal desirability of next year's income.

If we desire only to obtain the simplest expression for determining i, the above equations may be condensed still further. The first continuous equation may be omitted altogether. For, to omit it will evidently rid us of as many unknown quantities as equations, namely, n. Again, since the third continuous equation is evidently nothing more than a definition of the rate of interest, we may, if we choose, omit the letter i and employ the expression $-\dfrac{x_1''}{x_1'}-1$ in its place. We shall then have, instead of the three continuous equations above expressed, simply the following continuous equation:—

$$-\frac{x_1''}{x_1'}-1 = -\frac{x_2''}{x_2'}-1 = \cdots = -\frac{x_n''}{x_n''}-1$$
$$= F_1\left(c_1'+x_1',\, c_1''+x_1''\right)$$
$$= F_2\left(c_2'+x_2',\, c_2''+x_2''\right)$$
$$\cdot \quad \cdot \quad \cdot \quad \cdot \quad \cdot \quad \cdot \quad \cdot$$
$$= F_n\left(c_n'+x_n',\, c_n''+x_n''\right).$$

This equation, together with the equation for clearing the market, $x_1'+x_2'+\cdots+x_n'=0$, will fully determine the rate of interest. But, as was shown, the equation for clearing the market may be omitted, if we first obtain from it the value of one of the unknowns it contains, say, x_1', and substitute this value in the previous continuous equation. The continuous equation, so amended, will then of itself yield a complete solution of our problem.

§ 4

In the preceding solution, the loan transactions were supposed to extend over two years only. This restriction was made in order that the mathematics might be as simple as possible in our first formulation. We shall now remove this restriction and proceed to the case in which more than two years (let us say m years) are involved. We shall assume, as before, that the x's, representing loans or borrowings, are to be considered of positive value when they represent additions to income, and of negative value when they represent deductions. The equations in the first set will now be in several groups, of which the first is:

$$f_1' = F_{1\cdot}(c_1' + x_1',\ c_1'' + x_1'',\ c_1''' + x_1''',\ \cdots c_1^{(m)} + x_1^{(m)}),$$
$$f_2' = F_{2\cdot}(c_2' + x_2',\ c_2'' + x_2'',\ c_2''' + x_2''',\ \cdots c_2^{(m)} + x_2^{(m)}),$$
$$\cdots \cdots \cdots \cdots$$
$$f_n' = F_{n\cdot}(c_n' + x_n',\ c_n'' + x_n'',\ c_n''' + x_n''',\ \cdots c_n^{(m)} + x_n^{(m)}).$$

These equations express the rates of preference of different individuals (f_1' of individual No. 1, f_2' of individual No. 2, etc.) for the *first year's* income compared with the next. To express their preference for the *second* year's income compared with the next there will be another group of equations, namely:

$$f_1'' = F_{1\cdot}(c_1'' + x_1'',\ c_1''' + x_1''',\ \cdots c_1^{(m)} + x_1^{(m)}),$$
$$f_2'' = F_{2\cdot}(c_2'' + x_2'',\ \cdots \cdots \cdots \cdots c_2^{(m)} + x_2^{(m)}),$$
$$\cdots \cdots \cdots \cdots$$
$$f_n'' = F_{n\cdot}(c_n'' + x_n'',\ \cdots \cdots \cdots \cdots c_n^{(m)} + x_n^{(m)}).$$

For the *third* year there will be still another group, formed by inserting "$''''$" in place of "$'''$", and so on to the $m-1$st year; for the $m-1$st year is the last one which has any exchange relations with the next, since the next is the mth or last year. There will therefore be $m-1$ groups of equations, and since each of these $(m-1)$ groups contains n separate equations, there are all together $n(m-1)$ equations in the entire set.

Turning to the second set, we first observe that we are now compelled to assume a separate rate of interest for each year. The rate of interest connecting the *first* year with the next will be called i', that connecting the *second* year with the next, i'', and so on up to $i^{(m-1)}$.

Under these conditions we shall find, as before, that the rates of time-preference for each year will be reduced to a uniform level for all the different individuals in the community, — a level equal to the rate of interest. Algebraically expressed, this condition is contained in several continuous equations, of which the first is

$$i' = f_1' = f_2' = f_3' = \cdots = f_n'.$$

This expresses the fact that the rate of time-preference of the first year's income compared with next is the same for all the individuals, and is equal to the rate of interest between the first year and the next. A similar continuous equation may be written with reference to the time-preferences and interest as between the second year's income and the next, namely : —

$$i'' = f_1'' = f_2'' = f_3'' = \cdots = f_n''.$$

Since the element of risk is supposed to be absent, it does not matter whether we consider these second-year ratios as the ones which obtain in the minds of the community to-day, a year in advance, or those which will obtain next year; under our assumed conditions of no risk, these are necessarily identical.

A similar set of continuous equations applies to time-exchange between each succeeding year and the next, up to that connecting the $m - 1$st and the mth year. There will therefore be $m - 1$ continuous equations. Since each continuous equation is evidently made up of n constituent equations, there are in all $n(m - 1)$ equations in the second set of equations.

The third set of equations, which expresses the "clearing of the market," will be as follows : —

$$
\begin{aligned}
x_1' + x_2' + \cdots + x_n' &= 0, \\
x_1'' + x_2'' + \cdots + x_n'' &= 0, \\
&\cdots \cdots \cdots \\
x_1^{(m)} + x_2^{(m)} + \cdots + x_n^{(m)} &= 0.
\end{aligned}
$$

There are here m equations.

411

The fourth set of equations, expressing the equivalence of loans and repayments, or more generally, the fact that for each individual the total "additions" to his income-stream, algebraically considered, will have a present value equal to zero, as expressed in the following equation: —

$$x_1' + \frac{x_1''}{1+i'} + \frac{x_1'''}{(1+i')(1+i'')} + \cdots + \frac{x_1^{(m)}}{(1+i')(1+i'') \cdots (1+i^{(m-1)})} = 0.$$

Similar equations will hold for each of the n individuals: —

$$x_2' + \frac{x_2''}{1+i'} + \cdots = 0,$$

$$x_3' + \frac{x_3''}{1+i'} + \cdots = 0,$$

$$\cdot \quad \cdot \quad \cdot \quad \cdot \quad \cdot \quad \cdot \quad \cdot \quad \cdot$$

$$x_n' + \frac{x_n''}{1+i'} + \cdots = 0,$$

making in all n equations.

We therefore have as the total number of equations the following: —

$n(m-1)$ equations of the first set
$n(m-1)$ equations of the second set
m equations of the third set
n equations of the fourth set
$\overline{}$
$2\,mn + m - n$ equations in all.

We next proceed to count the unknown quantities. First as to f's: for individual No. 1 these will be $f_1', f_1'', \cdots, f_1^{(m-1)}$ the number of which is $m-1$, and as there are an equal number for each of the n individuals there will be in all $n(m-1)$ unknown f's.

As to x's, there will be one for each of the m years for each of the n individuals, or mn. As to i's, there will be one for each year up to the next to the last, or $m-1$. In short there will be

$n(m-1)$ unknown f's,
mn unknown x's,
$m-1$ unknown i's,

or $2\,mn + m - n - 1$ unknown quantities in all. Comparing this with the number of equations, we see that there is one more equation than the number of unknown quantities. This is due to the fact that not all the equations are independent.

This may be shown if we add together all the equations of the fourth set, and substitute in the numerators of the fractions thus obtained their value as obtained from the third set, namely, zero. We shall then evidently obtain the first equation of the third set. Consequently we may omit any one of the equations of the third and fourth sets. There will then remain just as many equations as unknown quantities, and our problem is exactly determined.

In the preceding analysis, we have throughout assumed a rate of interest between two points of time a year apart. A more minute analysis would involve a greater subdivision of the income-stream, and the employment of a rate of interest between every two successive elements. This will evidently occasion no difficulty except to increase the number of equations and unknowns.

§ 5

The elaborate system of equations which is involved when m years instead of two years are considered introduces very few features of the problem not already contained in the simpler set of equations first given. The new feature of chief importance is that, instead of only one rate of interest to be determined, there are now a large number of rates. It is too often assumed, in theories of interest, that the problem is to determine "the" rate of interest, as though one rate would hold true for all time. But in the preceding equations we have $m-1$ separate magnitudes, i', i'', i''', ... $i^{(m-1)}$. Is there any tendency at work to make these rates of interest equal? Is the rate of interest which expresses the ratio of exchange between this year's and next year's income normally equal to, or nearly equal to, the rate of interest which expresses the ratio of exchange between next year's income and the year after? Böhm-Bawerk[1] put this question, and answered it affirmatively, stating that a species of arbitrage transactions tended to produce this result. If, however, we examine his reasoning closely, we shall see that the only proposition he has proved is that, *if* the rate of interest expressing the premium on the goods of 1888 as compared with 1889 is equal to the premium of 1889 over 1890, then a contract for the exchange of the goods of 1888 for those of 1890 will take place at this same rate. But what is really needed

[1] *Positive Theory of Capital*, p. 280.

is to know whether (as Böhm-Bawerk *assumes*) the rate of interest connecting the years 1888 and 1889 *is* the same as the rate of interest connecting the years 1889 and 1890, and if so, why?

Under the hypothesis of a rigid allotment of future income among different time intervals, there is nothing to prevent great differences in the rate of interest from year to year, even when all factors in the case are foreknown. This is clear from the fact that, by a suitable distribution of the values of c_1, c_2, etc., there may be produced any differences in the values of i', i'', i''', etc. If the total enjoyable income of society should be foreknown to be, in the ensuing year, 10 billion dollars, in the following year one billion, and in the third year 20 billion, and there were no way of avoiding these enormous disparities, it is very evident that the income of the middle year would have a very high valuation compared with either of its neighbors, and therefore that the rate of interest connecting that middle year with the first year would be very low, whereas that connecting it with the third year would be very high. It might be that the members of such a community would be willing to exchange $100 of their plentiful 10 billions for the first year, for only $101 out of their scarce one billion of next year, but would be glad to give, out of the third year's still more plentiful 20 billions, $150 for the sake of $100 in the middle and lean year. The reason that, in actual fact, such abrupt and large variations in the rate of interest as from 1% to 50% are not more frequently encountered is that the supposed sudden and abrupt changes in the *income-stream* seldom occur. The causes which prevent their occurrence are: —

(1) The fact that history is constantly repeating itself. For instance, there is regularity in the population, so that at any point of time the outlook toward the next year is very similar to what it was at any other point of time. The individual may grow old, but the population does not. As individuals are hurried across the stage of life, their places are constantly taken by others, so that, whatever the tendency in the individual life to make the rates of preference go up or down, it will not be cumulative in society. Relatively speaking, society stands still.

Again, the processes of nature recur in almost ceaseless regularity. Crops repeat themselves in a yearly cycle. Even when there are large fluctuations in crops, they are seldom world-wide, and a shortage in the Mississippi valley may be compensated for by an unusually abundant crop in Russia or Asia. The resultant regularity of events is thus sufficient to maintain a fair uniformity in the income-stream for society as a whole.

(2) The fact that the income-stream is not fixed, but may be modified in other ways than by borrowing and lending. The nature of these modifications are considered in Chapter VIII.

§ 6

Let us now return, for fuller discussion, to the second condition, that the rates of preference of the different individuals are equal to each other and to the rate of interest.

It was shown in Chapter VII that when the individual determined his income stream so that his marginal rate of preference for present over future income was equal to the rate of interest, he thereby maximized his present " total desirability." The two statements, that his preference rate is equal to the interest rate, and that his " total desirability " is a maximum, are thus interequivalent, and either may be deduced from the other. Mathematically this may be shown either by geometry or by algebra. We shall begin with the algebraic method.

Assume at first that only two years are considered. The fact that total desirability depends on the amount of income this year and next year may be represented by the equation

$$U = F(c' + x', \ c'' + x''),$$

where U represents total desirability or utility of an individual, and the equation represents this U as a " function " of his income-stream consisting of $c' + x'$ this year and $c'' + x''$ next year. As we shall here consider only one individual, we omit the subscript numbers, 1, 2, etc., previously used to distinguish different individuals. The individual will attempt to adjust x' and x'' so as to maximize U. By the theory of differential equations, the condition that U shall be a maximum, is that the " total differential " of U or of its equal $F(c' + x', \ c'' + x'')$ shall be zero, thus

$$dU = \frac{\delta F(\ )}{\delta x'} dx' + \frac{\delta F(\ )}{\delta x''} dx'' = 0,$$

415

where the δ's represent the "partial differentials" with respect to x' and x'', and the blank parentheses stand for

$$(c' + x'', \; c'' + x'').$$

From this equation it follows that

$$-\frac{dx''}{dx'} = \frac{\delta F(\;)}{\delta x'} \Big/ \frac{\delta F(\;)}{\delta x''}.$$

The *left*-hand member is $1 + i$, as may be seen by differentiating the equation of the loan as originally stated, viz.:

$$x' + \frac{x''}{1+i} = 0. \quad \text{This differentiation yields} \quad -\frac{dx''}{dx'} = 1 + i.$$

The *right*-hand member, being the ratio of this year's marginal desirability to next year's marginal desirability, is by definition equal to $1 + f$. Substituting the new value for the right and left members, we have

$$1 + i = 1 + f,$$

whence it follows that $i = f$.

The same reasoning, applied to three or more years, may now be expressed. The total desirability for any individual is a function of the total future income-stream. In other words,

$$U = F(c' + x', \; c'' + x'', \; c''' + x''', \; \text{etc.}).$$

The individual tries to make this magnitude a maximum. In terms of the calculus, this is equivalent to making the first total differential equal to zero, namely,

$$dU = \frac{\delta F(\;)}{\delta x'} dx' + \frac{\delta F(\;)}{\delta x''} dx'' + \frac{\delta F(\;)}{\delta x'''} dx''' + \text{etc.} = 0.$$

This total differential equation is equivalent to a number of subsidiary equations obtained by making particular suppositions as to the different variations. Let us, for instance, suppose that only x' and x'' vary in relation to each other and that x''', x^{iv}, etc., do not vary. Then in the above equation all terms after the second disappear and the equation reduces to

$$-\frac{dx''}{dx'} = \frac{\delta F(\;)}{\delta x'} \Big/ \frac{\delta F(\;)}{\delta x''}.$$

In other words, $1 + i' = 1 + f'$, and therefore $i' = f'$.

416

This expresses the relation between the first and second years. If we wish in like manner to express the corresponding connection between the second and third years, let us assume that x' is constant and x^{iv}, etc., constant. Then the first term of the equation disappears and all after the third term, and the equation reduces to

$$-\frac{dx'''}{dx''} = \frac{\delta F(\ )}{\delta x''} \bigg/ \frac{\delta F(\ )}{\delta x'''}.$$

In other words, $1 + i'' = 1 + f''$, or $i'' = f''$; and so on for each succeeding year. We therefore see in mathematical language that the point of maximum desirability is also the point at which the marginal rate of preference for each year's income over the next year's income is equal to the rate of interest connecting these two years.

§ 7

We turn now to the geometrical interpretation. In Figure 26, let the point P be found such that its coördinates are c_1'

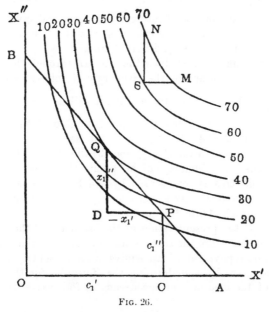

FIG. 26.

and c_1'', the values of this year's income and next year's income respectively, c_1' being laid off along the horizontal axis

OX^1, and c_1'' being laid off vertically. In the same way any other income-stream may be represented by another point, the coördinates of which represent the values of this year's and next year's income respectively. By borrowing or lending, the income-stream P is changed to another point Q to be determined. We shall assume, as before, that the modification of this income-stream, c_1', c_1'', through borrowing and lending or buying and selling applies only to the first and second years; all subsequent years are therefore omitted from our calculations. The income-stream that is the combination of the two magnitudes c_1', c_2'', — the fixed income with which the individual is supposed to be endowed, — is represented by the point P. But this income-stream, c_1', c_1'', he modifies by adding algebraically x_1', through borrowing (or lending, if x_1' has a negative value) this year, and adding next year, when the loan is paid, the sum x_1'', which is equal to x_1' put at interest, but of opposite sign; in ot herwords, $x_1'' = - x'(1+i)$ or $x_1' + \dfrac{x_1''}{1+i} = 0$. It is first proposed to determine x_1' and x_1'', assuming that the rate of interest is a fixed and given magnitude. The new income-stream, $c'+x'$, $c''+x''$, will be represented by a new point, Q, different from P.

To find this point, Q, draw the line AB through the point P at a slope determined by the given rate of interest, namely, so that $\dfrac{OB}{OA} = 1+i$. Then the new point will lie somewhere upon this straight line. For (1) the present value of the modified income-stream $c_1'+x_1'$, $c_1''+x_1''$ is the same as that of the original income-stream c_1', c_1''; and (2) the straight line AB is the "locus" or assemblage of all points the present values of the income-streams represented by which are the same as the present value of the income-stream represented by the point P through which AB is drawn.

That (1) the present values of the original and the modified income-streams are the same is due to the fact that the loan x_1' and its repayment x_1'' are equivalent in present value. This may be seen by transforming the formula for the present value of the modified income-stream, as follows : —

$$c_1' + x_1' + \frac{c_1'' + x_1''}{1+i} = c_1' + \frac{c_1''}{1+i} + \left(x_1' + \frac{x_1''}{1+i} \right) = c_1' + \frac{c_1''}{1+i},$$

since the magnitude in parenthesis is zero by the original hypothesis as to x_1' and x_1''.

That (2) the line AB locates all points of present value $c_1' + \dfrac{c_1''}{1+i}$ is evident from analytical geometry, and may be shown, among other ways, as follows:—

The present value of the original income-stream c_1', c_1'' is equal to the length OA. For

$$OA = OC + CA$$
$$= c_1' + \frac{c_1''}{1+i},$$

for $OC = c_1'$ by construction and $CA = \dfrac{c_1''}{1+i}$ by the similar triangles ACP and AOB, whose proportional sides give $\dfrac{c_1''}{CA} = \dfrac{OB}{OA} = 1+i$, or $CA = \dfrac{c_1''}{1+i}$.

Similar reasoning applied to any other point on the line AB will show, in like manner, that the present value of the income represented by that point is also OA. Hence *every* point on the straight line AB represents an income-combination or income-stream having the same present value, OA, as that of the income-stream c', c'' represented by P. Similar reasoning shows that no point out of AB represents an income-stream of this present value. Therefore the individual who is possessed of the income-stream represented by P, and who modifies this income-stream by borrowing and lending, merely shifts the point representing his income-stream *along the line* AB, as from P to Q. Which of all the points on this line open to his choice will he select? Evidently he will select that one which will give, for him, the maximum present desirability. In order to determine this point, let us suppose that the desirability corresponding to every point upon the plane is indicated by a number attached, and that through the points which have equal desirability, lines of equal desirability, like isothermal lines on a weather map, are drawn.[1] These may be called iso-desirability lines. If any two points

[1] Cf. the writer's " Mathematical Investigations in the Theory of Value and Prices," Part II, *Transactions of Conn. Academy*, New Haven, 1902, p. 68.

on one and the same iso-desirability curve be compared, it will
be seen that one of them represents an income richer this year
and poorer next year than the income represented by the
other; the superiority of the former income over the latter
this year exactly compensates for its inferiority next year, so
that, all considered, the two incomes are equally desirable.
It is clear that these iso-desirability lines will constitute a
"family" of curves, each approaching the axes OX' and OX'',
and that the numbers attached increase in magnitude as the
curves recede from the origin O. The curve drawn nearest
the axes is labeled "10" at each end, to signify that all
points upon that curve have a desirability to the individual
represented by 10. The point P evidently has a desirability
between 10 and 20. As we proceed from P toward B along
the line AB, it is evident that the desirability first increases
and then decreases, reaching the maximum at Q, where the line
AB is tangent to one of the family of curves. This point Q is
therefore the point sought, and represents the income-combination which has the maximum present desirability. Thus, for
the individual, the solution of the problem of how much to
borrow or lend is determined geometrically by drawing through
the point P, representing his fixed original income-endowment,
a straight line at the slope $\dfrac{OB}{OA} = 1 + i'$, and finding the point
Q upon this line at which it is tangent to some one of the numberless curves of equal desirability. Q differs from P in
having one of its coördinates larger (by x_1'') and the other
smaller (by $-x_1'$).

The fact that the iso-desirability curves at the right slope
less than 45° interprets the fact, which should not be lost sight
of, that if this year's income is sufficiently abundant or next
year's income sufficiently scarce, or both, that this year's
goods may exchange for next year's on less than even terms;
that is, that the rate of time-preference may be negative.

§ 8

Not only is it true that Q represents the point of maximum
desirability, but also that at the point Q the rate of preference
f_1 is equal to the rate of interest. First we observe that the
rate of preference for present over future income at any point
depends upon the slope of the iso-desirability curve which

passes through that point. To make this clear, let us consider, on any of the iso-desirability curves, such as 70–70, the point M and an adjacent point N. The substitution of the income-combination represented by N for that represented by M involves the sacrifice of an amount of this year's income represented by MS, which may be called $-\Delta x'$, for the sake of an addition to next year's income represented by NS, or $\Delta x''$. If the points M and N are indefinitely near together, we may represent MS by $-dx'$, and NS by dx''. The loss in desirability by surrendering MS is represented by the difference in number between the iso-desirability curves through M and S, namely, $70-60$, or 10. Likewise, the gain in desirability by the addition of SN to next year's income is represented by the difference between the numbers corresponding to iso-desirability curves through S and N, also $70-60$, or 10. In other words, the loss in desirability through the surrender of MS is equal to the gain in desirability through the addition of SN, or, the desirability of the loss of MS of this year's income equals the desirability of the gain of NS of next year's income. Since, therefore, SM and SN, or $-\Delta x'$ and $\Delta x''$, are the amounts of income for the two respective years which possess equal desirability, it is evident that the degree of desirability *per unit* of income for this year and next year will be in the inverse proportion. Thus, if SM is two hundred and SN is three hundred dollars' worth of income, this means that, for the particular individual for whom the figure is drawn, having an income-stream represented by the point M, \$200 taken from this year's income would be exactly compensated for in present estimation by the addition of \$300 to next year's income. Hence the desirability per dollar of the present income is $1\frac{1}{2}$ times the desirability per dollar of next year's income.

Symbolically these relations are:—

Desirability of $\Delta x'$ + desirability of $\Delta x''$ $= 0$.

Or $\dfrac{\text{desir. } \Delta x'}{\Delta x'} \Delta x' + \dfrac{\text{desir. } \Delta x''}{\Delta x''} \Delta x''$ $= 0$,

or $\dfrac{\Delta u}{\Delta x'} \Delta x' + \dfrac{\Delta u}{\Delta x''} \Delta x''$ $= 0$,

or $\dfrac{\Delta u}{\Delta ''} : \dfrac{\Delta u}{x' \Delta x} = \Delta x'' : -\Delta x' = NS : MS$

That is, the desirability of an additional present dollar is to that of an additional dollar next year, as NS to MS, or the slope of the line joining M and N. If the points M and N are indefinitely near together, the slope will be the slope of the iso-desirability curve through M. Thus the *slope* of any of the curves in the diagram at any point is the geometrical representation of the relative valuation of present and future income which the individual feels when in possession of the income-stream represented by that point. We have already specified that the slope of the straight line AB represents the ratio of exchange of this and next year's income. Thus the slope of the curves represents the subjective, and the slope of the line the objective, ratio of equivalence for the two years. The former slope, the ratio of the marginal desirability of this year's income to the marginal desirability of next year's income, is, by our previous definition, $1 + f_1$, just as the latter slope is $1 + i$.

Applying these ideas to the particular point Q, it is clear that the slope of the iso-desirability curve through Q is equal to the slope of the straight line BA. But the slope of the desirability curve is $1 + f_1$, and the slope of the straight line AB is $1 + i$, therefore, for any individual,

$$1 + f_1 = 1 + i,$$

or
$$f_1 = i.$$

Hence the individual who modifies his income from P by a loan at the rate i will shift it to a point Q, such that his subjective rate of preference f_1 which corresponds to that point will be equal to the objective rate of interest i, — or, speaking geometrically, so that the "slope" of his curves will be made equal to the "slope" of the market.

We have presented the geometrical method in considerable detail, in the belief that it is well worth mastering. It will be found especially helpful when extended so as to apply to the more complicated problem discussed in the Appendix to Chapter VIII.

§ 9

If we proceed from the consideration of two years to that of three, we may still represent our problem geometrically by using three dimensions. Let us consider three mutually perpendicular axes OX', OX'', OX''', and represent the income-

combination or income-stream for the particular individual by
the point P, whose coördinates c', c'', and c''' are the three
years' income-installments with which the individual is initially
endowed. Then through the point P draw, instead of the
straight line in the previous representation, a *plane ABC* cutting the three axes in A, B, and C. This plane has a slope
with reference to the two axes OX' and OX'' of $\dfrac{OB}{OA}$ equal to
$1+i'$, and has a slope with reference to the axes OX'' and
OX''' represented by $\dfrac{OC}{OB}$ equal to $1+i''$. The letters i' and
i'' here represent, as before, the rate of interest in the exchange of this and next year's goods, and of next year's and
the year after. Now suppose the space between the axes to
be filled with iso-desirability *curved surfaces* like the coats of
an onion, such that for all points on the same surface the total
desirability of the income-stream represented by those points
will be the same. These surfaces will be such as to approach
the three axes and the planes between them, and also such that
the attached numbers representing their respective total desirabilities shall increase as they recede from the origin O. The
plane ABC drawn through P at the slope fixed by the rates of
interest, as just indicated, will now be tangent to some one of
the iso-desirability surfaces at a point Q, which is the point at
which the individual will fix his income. For every point on
the plane ABC will have the same present value, and every point
on this plane is available to him by borrowing and lending (or
buying and selling) at the rates i' and i'', but not all of them
will have the same desirability. He will select that one which
has the maximum desirability, and this will evidently be the
point Q, at which the plane is tangent to one of the family of
iso-desirability surfaces. Reasoning similar to that given for
two dimensions will show that this point will be such that
$f_1' = i'$ and $f_1'' = i''$.

To proceed beyond three years would take us beyond the
limitations of space; for we should then need in our representation more than three dimensions. Such a representation is
of little meaning except to mathematicians, since it cannot be
fully visualized. For the practical purpose of visualization,
the simple geometrical representation in *two* dimensions,
though limited to two years, is the most helpful.

§ 10

Having shown the geometrical representation as applied to a particular individual, we now proceed to show how the rate of preference is determined for a series of individuals. To recur to the geometrical representation in Fig. 26, where only two variables are considered, the problem is as follows : —

Given a number of different individuals, each with his own separate point P and his own separate set of iso-desirability curves, we are required to draw through these points straight lines parallel to each other at such a slope as to "clear the market," in other words, such that the sum of the x''s for the different individuals shall be zero, and, as implied thereby, that the sum of the x'''s shall also be zero.

It is evident that, according as the slope of the lines AB changes, the points of tangency, the Q's, for the different individuals will vary, which means that the amount borrowed or lent, namely, x' and x'', will change. We have then a swarm or group of fixed points, the P's, and another swarm of variable points Q's. By rotating the lines each about its pivot P, and so that all remain parallel to each other, we can evidently shift the position of the second swarm of points, the Q's. The solution is found by fixing upon such a slope of the lines that the center of gravity of the Q swarm is brought into coincidence with the fixed center of gravity of the P swarm. The slope of the lines AB which will accomplish this result is the rate of interest which will just clear the market; for the horizontal deviations, x_1', x_2', etc., between the P and Q for each different individual will then be self-canceling, their algebraic sum being zero, and the same is true for the vertical deviations x_1'', x_2'', etc.

For three dimensions, we have precisely similar determinations. The problem of the rate of interest is here solved by finding such an orientation for the various *planes* through the points called P's as will bring the center of gravity of the tangential points, the Q's, into coincidence with the fixed center of gravity of the P's.

APPENDIX TO CHAPTER VIII

SECOND APPROXIMATION

(This Appendix should be read as a whole after Chapter VIII.)

§ 1

In the Appendix to Chapter VII we found that the number of equations available for determining the rate of interest was equal to the number of unknown quantities, and therefore that the rate of interest and the other associated variables were determinate under the assumption there made. This assumption was that all income-streams were unalterable, except as they could be modified by borrowing and lending, or buying and selling. We now introduce, in place of such a fixed income-stream, the hypothesis of a range of choice between different income-streams. This, however, does not destroy the determinateness of the interest problem; for along with the new variables introduced, we find an equal number of new equations.

Let us, then, state and count the equations which, under our several hypotheses, determine the rate of interest. The income-stream, we must remember, no longer consists of known and fixed elements, c_1', c_1'', c_1''', etc., as assumed in Chapter VII, elements which can be modified only by exchange; it now consists of unknown and variable elements which we shall designate by y_1', y_1'', y_1''', etc. This elastic income-stream may be modified in two ways: by the variations in these y's, as well as by the method which we found applicable for rigid income-streams, namely, the method of exchange — borrowing and lending or buying and selling. The alterations effected by the latter means we shall designate as before by x_1', x_1'', x_1''', etc., for successive years. These are to be algebraically added to the original income-items (the y's), deductions being included in this addition by assigning negative values. The income-stream as finally determined is therefore expressed by the installments, $y_1' + x_1'$, $y_1'' + x_1''$, $y_1''' + x_1'''$, etc.

One of the determining conditions stated in Chapter VII is that the individual rates of preference are functions of the income-streams. Algebraically stated, this condition gives the equations : —

$$f_{1'} = F_{1'}(y_1' + x_1', \; y_1'' + x_1'', \; \cdots \; y_1^{(m)} + x_1^{(m)}),$$
$$f_{2'} = F_{2'}(y_2' + x_2', \; y_2'' + x_2'', \; \cdots \; y_2^{(m)} + x_2^{(m)}),$$
$$\cdot \quad \cdot \quad \cdot \quad \cdot \quad \cdot \quad \cdot \quad \cdot \quad \cdot$$
$$f_{n'} = F_{n'}(y_n' + x_n', \; y_n'' + x_n'', \; \cdots \; y_n^{(m)} + x_n^{(m)}).$$

These equations express the individual rates of preference for the *first* year's income compared with the next. To express the preference for the *second* year's income compared with the next, there will be another set of equations, namely : —

$$f_{1''} = F_{1''}(y_1'' + x_1'', \; y_1''' + x_1''', \; \cdots \; y_1^{(m)} + x_1^{(m)}),$$
$$f_{2''} = F_{2''}(y_2'' + x_2'', \; \cdots\cdots\cdots\cdots\cdots \; y_2^{(m)} + x_2^{(m)}),$$
$$\cdot \quad \cdot \quad \cdot \quad \cdot \quad \cdot \quad \cdot \quad \cdot \quad \cdot$$
$$f_{n''} = F_{n''}(y_n'' + x_n'', \; \cdots\cdots\cdots\cdots\cdots \; y_n^{(m)} + x_n^{(m)}).$$

For the third year, as compared with its successor, there would be another similar set, with " ''' " in place of " '' ", and so on to the next to the last or $(m - 1)$ year as compared with the last. Since each of these $m - 1$ groups of equations contains n separate equations, there are all together $n(m - 1)$ equations in the entire set.

The next condition, that the rates of preference and of interest will be equal, is the same as in the first approximation,[1] and is represented by the same $n(m-1)$ equations, namely : —

$$i' = f_1' \qquad = f_2' \qquad = \cdots\cdots\cdots = f_n',$$
$$i'' = f_1'' \qquad = f_2'' \qquad = \cdots\cdots\cdots = f_n'',$$
$$\cdot \quad \cdot \quad \cdot \quad \cdot \quad \cdot \quad \cdot \quad \cdot$$
$$i^{(m-1)} = f_1^{(m-1)} \cdots = f_2^{(m-1)} = \cdots\cdots\cdots = f_n^{(m-1)}.$$

The two sets of equations which express the "clearing of the market" and equivalence of loans and repayments will also be the same as before, and represented by the same m equations : —

$$x_1' + x_2' + \cdots + x_n' = 0,$$
$$x_1'' + x_2'' + \cdots + x_n'' = 0,$$
$$\cdot \quad \cdot \quad \cdot \quad \cdot \quad \cdot \quad \cdot \quad \cdot$$
$$x_1^{(m)} + x_2^{(m)} + \cdots + x_n^{(m)} = 0 ;$$

[1] See Appendix to Ch. VII, § 4.

and the same n equations :

$$x_1' + \frac{x_1''}{1+i'} + \frac{x_1'''}{(1+i')(1+i'')} + \cdots + \frac{x_1^{(m)}}{(1+i')(1+i'')\cdots(1+i^{(m)})} = 0,$$

$$x_2' + \frac{x_2''}{1+i'} + \cdots \qquad\qquad + \frac{x_2^{(m)}}{(1+i')(1+i'')\cdots(1+i^m)} = 0,$$

$$\cdot \quad \cdot \quad \cdot \quad \cdot \quad \cdot \quad \cdot \quad \cdot \quad \cdot \quad \cdot \quad \cdot \quad \cdot \quad \cdot \quad \cdot \quad \cdot \quad \cdot$$

$$x_n' + \cdots \qquad\qquad\qquad\qquad\qquad\qquad\qquad = 0.$$

§ 2

These four sets of equations are the same in number as the corresponding sets given in the Appendix to Chapter VII, namely, $2mn + m - n$, or, for reasons there given, only $2mn + m - n - 1$ *independent* equations. These equations differ from the equations of the preceding Appendix only in the first set, which contain y's in place of c's. The c's were constants, but the y's are unknown quantities. Consequently, the number of unknowns is greater than the number in the first approximation, whereas the number of equations thus far expressed is the same. We therefore need to seek for new equations to supply the deficiency. These additional equations are found from the condition that the choice among the optional income-streams will fall upon that one which possesses the maximum present value.

The range of choice, *i.e.* the complete list of optional income-streams, will include many which are ineligible. By an ineligible income-stream is meant one which would not be selected whatever might be the rate of interest, — whether zero or one million per cent., — being smaller for every year than some other stream on the list. Excluding these ineligibles, the remaining options constitute the *effective range of choice*. This effective range of choice is subject to the "technical" limitations of productive conditions, and constitutes the technical conditions which influence the rate of interest. If this list of options be assumed, for convenience of analysis, to consist of an infinite number of options varying from one to another, not by sudden jumps, but continuously, the complete list can be expressed by those possible values of y_1', y_1'', ... $y_1^{(m)}$ which will satisfy an empirical equation

$$\phi_1\,(y_1', y_1'' \,\cdots\, y_1^{(m)}) = 0,$$

the form of which depends on the particular technical conditions to which the capital of individual No. 1 is subjected,

427

whether dependent on his personal characteristics or on the physical and technical conditions of his business. Thus the form of the function ϕ_1 will be one thing if the capital of the individual, which yields the y's, consists largely of mines which are failing, and quite another if it consists of forests recently planted. In the former case, the equation will be satisfied only by values of the y's such that the earlier y's (as y'_1 or y_1'') are comparatively large and the latter y's (as $y_1^{(m-1)}$ or $y^{(m)}$) are comparatively small; whereas in the latter case the series of y's must conform to the opposite condition. The equation, therefore, while it admits of an infinite number of arrays of y's, does not admit of their variation *ad libitum*. It represents the limitations to which the variation of the income-stream must conform. Each set of values of y_1', y_1'', ... $y_1^{(m)}$ which will satisfy this equation represents an optional income-stream. Out of this infinite number of options, that particular one will be selected of which the present value is a maximum.

Now the present value V_1 of any income-stream y_1', y_1'', ... $y_1^{(m)}$, of individual No. 1, is evidently

$$V_1 = y_1' + \frac{y_1''}{1+i'} + \frac{y_1'''}{(1+i')(1+i'')} + \text{etc.}$$

The condition that this expression shall be a maximum is that the first differential quotient shall be zero. That is

$$dV_1 = dy_1' + \frac{dy_1''}{1+i'} + \frac{dy_1'''}{(1+i')(1+i'')} + \text{etc.} = 0.$$

This last equation expresses the relations which must exist between dy_1', dy_1'', dy_1''', etc., in order that the income-stream y_1', y_1'', y_1''', etc., may have the maximum present value. This condition contains within itself a number of subsidiary conditions. To derive these, let us consider a slight variation in the income-stream, affecting only the income-installments of the first two years, y_1' and y_1'' (the remaining installments, y_1''', etc., being regarded as invariable), and let us denote the values of dy_1', dy_1'', under this assumption of restricted variation, by $\delta y_1'$, $\delta y_1''$. Then, remembering that, under the supposed condition, dy_1''', dy_1^{iv}, etc., will be zero, the above equation becomes

$$\delta y_1' + \frac{\delta y_1''}{1+i'} = 0,$$

from which it is evident that

$$-\frac{\delta y_1{}''}{\delta y_1{}'} = 1 + i'.$$

But the left-hand member of this equation is evidently the marginal rate of return on sacrifice as between next year's income and this year's income, or the ratio of the increase which may be effected in next year's income by a given sacrifice in this year's income. If we call the *premium* in this ratio of return $r_1{}'$, we may express $-\dfrac{\delta y_1{}''}{\delta y_1{}'}$ as $1 + r_1{}'$, and write the above equation thus: —

$$1 + r_1{}' = 1 + i',$$

or thus: —
$$r_1{}' = i'.$$

In other words, the *condition that the marginal rate of return on sacrifice is equal to the rate of interest follows as a consequence of the general condition that the present value of the income-stream must be a maximum.* This proposition and its proof correspond to those in regard to desirability, which have already been discussed in Appendix to Chapter VII, § 6, that the condition of maximum desirability is equivalent to the condition that the marginal rate of preference is equal to the rate of interest.

The same reasoning may be applied to successive years. Thus, if we assume variations in y'' and y''', without any variations in the other elements of the income-stream, y', y^{iv}, etc., the original differential equation becomes

$$\frac{\delta y_1{}''}{1 + i'} + \frac{\delta y_1{}'''}{(1 + i')(1 + i'')} = 0,$$

or
$$-\frac{\delta y_1{}'''}{\delta y_1{}''} = (1 + i''),$$

or
$$1 + r_1{}'' = 1 + i'',$$

or
$$r_1{}'' = i''.$$

Corresponding analysis applied to each successive year will show that the annual successive marginal rates of return on sacrifice are equal to the annual successive rates of interest.

All this reasoning implies that there is a possibility of continuous variation, and that at the margin it is possible to make slight variations in any two successive years' incomes without disturbing the incomes of other years. The values of $1 + r_1'$, $1 + r_1''$, etc., or $-\dfrac{\delta y_1''}{\delta y_1'}$, $-\dfrac{\delta y_1'''}{\delta y_1''}$ (the rate at which the second year's income may be increased by decreasing the first year's income, and the rate at which the third year's income may be increased by decreasing the second year's income, etc.), may be found in terms of y_1', y_1'' $\cdots$ $y_1^{(m)}$ by differentiating the equation for the effective range of choice, $\phi_1(y_1', y_1'', \cdots y_1^{(m)}) = 0$. This differentiation gives

$$-\frac{\delta y_1''}{\delta y_1'} = \psi_{1''}(y_1', y_1'', \text{etc.}),$$

$$-\frac{\delta y_1'''}{\delta y_1''} = \psi_{1''}(y_1', y_1'', \text{etc.}),$$

etc.

Writing together the equations of partial differentiation, we have, as our new set of equations: —

$$1 + i' = 1 + r_1' = \psi_{1''}(y_1', y_1'', \text{etc.})$$
$$= 1 + r_2'' = \psi_{2''}(y_2', y_2', \text{etc.})$$
$$\cdot \quad \cdot \quad \cdot \quad \cdot$$
$$= 1 + r_n' = \psi_{n'}(y_n', y_n'', \text{etc.}).$$

These equations, $2\,n$ in number, relate to the rates of interest and return-on-sacrifice only as between the first and second years. The following similar $2\,n$ equations relate to the rates between the second and third years: —

$$1 + i'' = 1 + r_1'' = \psi_{1''}(y_1'', y_1''', \text{etc.})$$
$$= 1 + r_2'' = \psi_{2''}(y_2'', y_2''', \text{etc.}),$$

etc.

Exactly similar equations apply to each year as related to its successor, until we reach the final set, which connects the next to the last year with the last, viz.: —

$$1 + i^{(m-1)} = 1 + r_1^{(m-1)} = \psi_{1^{(m-1)}}(y_1'', y_1''', \text{etc.}).$$

As there are here $(m-1)$ sets of equations and $2\,n$ in each set, the total number of equations in these sets is $2\,n\,(m-1)$. These equations, together with the n equations of effective range of choice for the different individuals, viz.: —

$$\phi_1(y_1', y_1'', \text{etc.}) = 0,$$
$$\phi_2(y_2', y_2'', \text{etc.}) = 0,$$
$$\cdot \quad \cdot \quad \cdot \quad \cdot$$
$$\phi_n(y_n', y_n'', \text{etc.}) = 0,$$

give therefore $2n(m-1)+n$ or $2mn-n$, the total number of new equations in addition to those repeated or adapted from Appendix to Chapter VII. The number of independent equations thus repeated or adapted from the previous Appendix was $2mn+m-n-1$. Hence we have:—

> number of old equations, $2mn+m\quad -n-1$,
> $+$ number of new equations, $2mn\qquad -n$,
> $=$ number of total equations, $4mn+m-2n-1$.

Examination will show that the number of unknowns will also be $4mn+m-2n-1$. For all of the $2mn+m-n-1$ unknowns previously used (in Appendix to Chapter VII) are here repeated, and in addition, the new unknowns, the y's and the r's, are introduced. There is one y for each individual for each year, the total array being

$$y_1', y_1'', \ldots y_1^{(m)},$$
$$y_2', y_2'', \ldots y_2^{(m)},$$
$$\cdot \quad \cdot \quad \cdot \quad \cdot \quad \cdot$$
$$y_n', y_n'', \ldots y_n^{(m)}.$$

The number of these y's is evidently mn.

There is one r for each individual for each pair of successive years, i.e. first and second, second and third, etc., and next to last and last, the total array being

$$r_1', r_1'', \ldots r_1^{(m-1)},$$
$$r_2', r_2'', \ldots r_2^{(m-1)},$$
$$\cdot \quad \cdot \quad \cdot \quad \cdot \quad \cdot$$
$$r_n', r_n'', \ldots r_n^{(m-1)}.$$

The number of these r's is evidently $n(m-1)$.

In all, then, the number of *new* unknowns, additional to those of the previous Appendix, is $mn+n(m-1)$ or $2mn-n$. Hence we have:

> number of old unknowns, $2mn+m\quad -n-1$,
> number of new unknowns, $2mn\qquad -n$,
> total number of unknowns, $4mn+m-2n-1$,

which total is the same as the number of independent equations. Therefore the problem of the rate of interest and related magnitudes is determinate under the conditions prescribed.

The complication mentioned in Chapter VIII, § 14, that the

income-stream itself depends upon the rate of interest, does not affect the determinateness of the problem. It leaves the number of equations and unknowns unchanged, but merely introduces the rate of interest into the set of equations expressing the influence of the technique of production. These now become

$$\phi_1(y_1', y_1'', \text{etc.}, i', i'', \text{etc.}) = 0,$$

etc., and their derivatives, the ψ functions, are likewise altered.

§ 3

The intricate system of equations just stated may be better understood by means of a geometrical representation.

First we shall represent the *range of choice*. Let us suppose, for simplicity, that only two years need to be considered, so

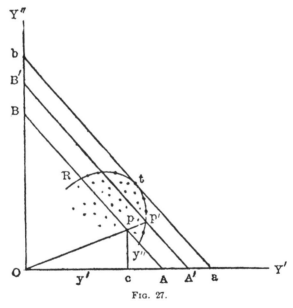

Fig. 27.

that the only unknown y's or income-installments are y' and y'', all the y's for succeeding years being regarded as fixed. In other words, let us suppose the case of a farmer who is considering the choice between different methods of cultivating his farm for this and next year, but does not take into consideration any possible variations in the income from his farm for succeeding years. He has the options of allowing his land to lie fallow both the years; or to lie fallow the first year and yield an income the second year; or to yield an income the first year and lie fallow the second; or to cost him a net loss this year in order to add to the income next year; or to yield him something both years, — from nothing up to the maximum possible, though the maximum for one year would be incompatible with the maximum for the other. The farmer has here a choice among an indefinite number of income-streams.

Let us in Fig. 27 measure y' along the axis OY', and y'' along the axis OY''. Then the point p has for its coördinates y' and y'', that is, for its abscissa $Oc = y'$, and for its ordinate, $cp = y''$. This point thus represents one of the optional income-streams. In like manner we may represent all other options by a series of other points, as shown by the dots in the diagram. Out of this swarm of points, each representing a particular option, only one will of course be chosen. The point to be selected will, as we know, be that which corresponds to the maximum present value. To find it we do not need to consider all the points in the entire swarm, for some of them are evidently out of the question. Thus, if through the point p we draw the line Op and prolong it to p', it is evident that the combination or option represented by the point p' will have a higher present value than that represented by p, no matter what the rate of interest may be; for p' evidently has both of its coördinates y' and y'' larger than the coördinates of p. In other words, p' represents an income-stream which is larger than p both this year and next year, and must consequently have a larger present value, whether the rate of interest be 1 % or 100 %. Consequently, of all the points along the line Op we may disregard all except the one point (p') remotest from the origin O, or *on the boundary* of the entire mass of points. In like manner, by drawing other lines from O we may see that the only points which need to be considered are the points lying *on the boundary $p'tR$* of the entire mass of points. These are, so to speak, the only *eligible* points. Among them, the one which represents the final choice will differ according to the rate of interest; but whatever the rate of interest, the choice will always fall on a point in the designated perimeter. Therefore the perimeter $p'tR$, etc., the boundary of the swarm, alone represents the *effective* range of choice.

The effective range of choice includes only the convex portions of the boundary, the portions which would be points of tangency t of a straight line such as ab, touching and not cutting the boundary, and revolving about the boundary as an "envelope." We may still further restrict the portions of the boundary to be included by limiting the position of the revolving line ab to the vertical position at the right and to the 45° position at the left. Any further rotation to the left would imply a negative rate of interest, which need not be considered.

The configuration of this boundary line is the geometrical representation of those technical conditions which limit the income-stream available from capital. This boundary line representing the effective range of choice will be quite different for different times and places. It will be different according to whether the capital of the individual considered consists largely of land, of machinery, or of other forms of wealth. It is at this point, then, that the technical conditions of industry enter into our problem, and show their influence upon the rate of interest.

In order to find what point on the boundary will be selected as the final choice, let us draw the line AB such that all points upon it will represent options possessing a fixed present value OA. AB will then be a straight line of which the slope is $1 + i'$, depending on the rate of interest.[1] We know that the present value of the income-stream represented by the point p is given by the formula

$$V = y' + \frac{y''}{1 + i'} + \text{constant terms,}$$

in which equation, as in those which follow, the subscripts "₁", etc., are omitted for convenience, as it will readily be remembered that the equations and diagrams always refer to a particular individual. The constant terms represent the discounted income of the years beyond the second year, the income-installments of which are by hypothesis fixed. If now we give to V a fixed value, and transpose to the left-hand member the

---

[1] It may be worth observing that, of its intercepts OA and OB, OA is equal to the value of the income-stream y_1', y_1'', as reckoned by discount in advance, and OB is equal to that value multiplied by the factor $1 + i'$. Hence OB is the value of the same income-stream reckoned by accumulation next year. See *The Nature of Capital and Income*, Appendix to Ch. XIII, § 13.

"constant terms," the left-hand member may be represented by a constant K, and the equation becomes

$$K = y' + \frac{y''}{1 + i'}.$$

This is evidently the equation of the straight line AB drawn so that OA is equal to K and OB is equal to $K(1 + i')$.[1]

We see, therefore, that all points on the line AB drawn in the manner described represent *optional income-streams of equal present values*. The line $A'B'$, parallel to AB, drawn somewhat more remote from the origin O, will in like manner represent the assemblage (or "locus") of all points which have a present value equal to OA' larger than OA.[2]

§ 4

We see at once that to select the point, among the entire swarm of points, which has the maximum present value, we need simply find that point which will be on a line parallel to AB and removed as far as possible from the origin O. Evidently such a line is ab, tangent at t to the boundary line $p'tR$. It is evident, therefore, that t is the point which possesses the maximum present value out of the entire mass. If the rate of interest rises, the slope of the line ab will be steeper and the point of tangency t will shift toward the right. In other words, the option now chosen will be one which has a larger y' but a smaller y''; that is, a larger income for the present year and a smaller one for next year. On the other hand, if the rate of interest falls, the slope of the line ab will be more nearly horizontal and the point of tangency will rise, making y'' larger and y' smaller.

Not only is it true that t is the point at which the present value of the income is a maximum, but it is also true that at this point the "marginal rate of return on sacrifice" will be equal to the rate of interest. We have seen that the slope of

[1] See preceding footnote.

[2] That $A'B'$ will be parallel to AB is evident from the rule for construction, for OA' must equal a constant K', and OB' must equal $K'(1 + i')$, therefore it is evident that, comparing the similar construction for AB,

$$\frac{OB}{OA} = 1 + i' = \frac{OB'}{OA'}.$$

Consequently $A'B'$ is parallel to AB.

the line ab represents the ratio of exchange between next
year's and this year's income, namely $1 + i'$. In like manner
the slope, at any point, of the boundary line $p'tR$ represents
the ratio of the return on sacrifice, or $1 + r'$. This may be
seen clearly from Fig. 28, where a slight variation from t'' to t'
produces in y' a small increase kt', but in y'' a small decrease
kt''. kt' may be designated by $\delta y'$, and kt'' by $-\delta y''$, and we

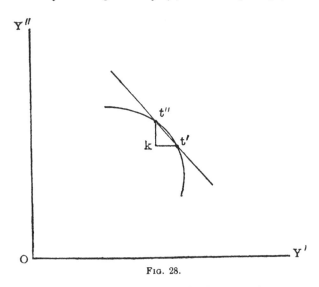

Fig. 28.

may state that $\delta y'$ represents a slight increase in this year's
income, and $-\delta y''$ the consequent slight decrease in next year's
income. The ratio of these two, namely $\dfrac{-\delta y''}{\delta y'}$, is what was
called the marginal ratio of return to sacrifice, or $1 + r'$; that is,

$$\frac{-\delta y''}{\delta y'} = 1 + r'.$$

Returning to Fig. 27, it is evident that at the point of
tangency t the slope of the straight line ab will be identical
with that of the curve $p'tR$. In other words,

$$1 + i' = 1 + r'.$$

Whence it follows that $i' = r'$.

We see, then, from the diagram: (1) that the point t for a particular individual, with a particular rate of interest, is determinate, and (2) that the point t is the one which corresponds with the choice of maximum present value, where $r' = i'$.

§ 5

We shall now proceed to the consideration of the case of three years instead of two. A geometrical representation may still be used, by employing three dimensions and three mutually perpendicular axes, OY', OY'', OY'''. Any point P will indicate a possible income-stream for the three years; for its coördinates y', y'', y''' may be taken to indicate the income-installments for the first, second, and third years respectively. Representing the various options by various points, we have a mass of points occupying three dimensions, like a swarm of bees, and we wish to select from this series of points that one which has the maximum present value. It is evident that we need not consider as eligible every point in the swarm, but need only consider its boundary, or outside surface. For, if any point P be joined to the origin O and prolonged beyond P to the remotest point P' in the mass, it is evident that P', having all of its three coördinates larger than the coördinates of P, will have necessarily a larger present value. Therefore, the only point on the line OP which needs to be considered is P' farthest from the origin O, or on the surface bounding the swarm. Having restricted ourselves, therefore, to the bounding surface as including the *effective* range of choice, we next ask, what point on this surface has the maximum present value. To answer this question we observe that the assemblage or locus of all points or options which have a given present value V is found by drawing a plane cutting the three axes OY', OY'', and OY'''. The expression for the present value of the income-stream is evidently

$$V = y' + \frac{y''}{1 + i'} + \frac{y'''}{(1 + i')(1 + i'')} + \text{constant terms.}$$

If we transpose "constant terms" to the left, and remember that V is for the moment regarded as itself constant, we may call the entire left-hand member a constant K, and have the equation

$$K = y' + \frac{y''}{1 + i'} + \frac{y'''}{(1 + i')(1 + i'')}.$$

This is, in analytical geometry, the equation of a plane which cuts the Y' axis at a distance K from the origin, and cuts the Y'' axis at a distance $K(1 + i')$ from the origin, and the Y''' axis at a distance $K(1 + i')(1 + i'')$ from the origin.

Similar considerations will show, just as in the case of the previous representation in two dimensions, that the farther the plane is from the origin O, the larger the present value of the choices represented by points in this plane. Our problem, therefore, consists merely in finding that point on the bounding surface which is also on the plane farthest from O among the parallel planes just drawn. This is evidently the point of tangency, and may be called t as before. It is also clear that a change in the rates of interest i' or i'' will change the slope of the tangent plane, and therefore the point of tangency t.

The algebraic interpretation of this case will be similar to the algebraic expression already given for two variables.

When we proceed to consider four or more years instead of simply two or three years, the geometrical representation fails us, since the mind has difficulty in picturing spaces of 4, 5, ... and m dimensions.

§ 6

In order to show how the new equations which have just been expressed enter into the determination of the problem of interest, we construct Fig. 29, applying to the case only two unknown quantities y' and y''. The incomes for the third and succeeding years are regarded for the moment as fixed. The diagram refers to a particular individual, and shows (1) the curve *WPZ*, giving the *effective range of choice* among different options open to him, and (2) a series of curves for total utility or desirability, as explained in the Appendix to the preceding chapter. The line *AB* is drawn at a slope equal to $1 + i$ and tangent to the curve *WZ* at the point P. This line will be tangent to one of the family of desirability curves at some point Q. P represents, out of all the options, the particular income-stream chosen by the individual. This income-stream P is, of course, as yet unmodified by borrowing and lending or buying and selling. The point Q represents the income-stream as finally thus modified. The coördinates of P are y' and y'', and the coördinates of Q are $y' + x'$, $y'' + x''$, where x' and x'' are the (algebraic) additions to the income y',

y'' by borrowing and lending or buying and selling. P and Q thus represent graphically the double choice explained in Chapter VIII. We saw there that the individual first chooses, among the various eligible income-streams of different present values, that which is of maximum present value. WZ now represents the series of eligible income-streams, and P the income-stream of maximum present value. Also, we saw that after the individual had chosen this income-stream he modified it by selecting another income-stream of the same present value but of maximum desirability. Q now represents this final choice.

It is worth our while in passing to emphasize that the individual would not follow out this program unless the final step

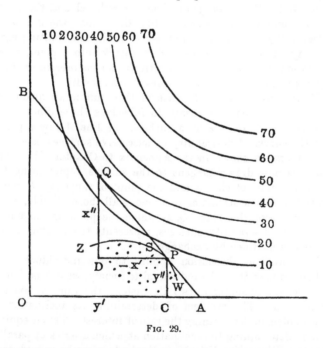

Fig. 29.

of modifying his income-stream by exchange were open to him. For, if he were shut off from exchange (*i.e.* compelled to accept P, unmodified to Q), the income-stream of maximum present value (P) would not necessarily be that of maximum desirability. In this case the maximum desirability would evidently be found at S, the point of tangency between WZ and a curve (not drawn) of desirability, and S would be chosen instead of P. The choice of P is made only if there is freedom to replace it immediately by Q of higher desirability although of the same present value.

The only difference between this determination of the point Q and that shown in the Appendix to Chapter VII, where we assumed a fixed or rigid income-stream, is that there the point P was assumed as a *fixed point*, whereas here it is considered as a point of tangency to a *fixed curve WZ*. In the previous chapter, if the rate of interest changed, the line AB revolved about the point P. Under our new and more general hypothesis, if the rate of interest changes, the line AB *rolls* upon the curve WZ. If the range of choice is reduced and the curve WZ is thereby restricted to smaller dimensions, the difference between the two cases is diminished, until, as a limiting case, we may suppose the curve WZ to shrink into a point, when the range of choice disappears entirely and the present diagram reverts to the one used in the previous Appendix.

If now we consider the case of three unknown quantities y', y'', y''', it is only necessary to introduce three dimensions, replace the curve WZ by a surface, the line AB by a plane, and the curves of desirability by successive surfaces in concentric layers, as shown in the Appendix to Chapter VII. The plane is now drawn tangent to the surface representing the effective range of choice, and the point of tangency P represents the income-stream chosen among all those eligible, while the point upon this plane Q, at which the plane is tangent to one of the desirability surfaces, represents the income-stream as finally modified by exchange.

The previous discussion applies to one individual only. When we pass from the individual to society, we can no longer consider the plane (or in two dimensions, the line) as fixed in inclination. The problem of determining its inclination is the problem of determining the rate of interest. This is equivalent to determining the inclination at which a series of parallel planes (or lines), for different individuals, must be passed, each tangent to its own surface (or curve) WZ, and such that the center of gravity of all the Q's coincides with that of all the P's. This condition will evidently make the algebraic sum of all the x''s zero, and likewise of the x'''s, etc. In other words, it will make the sums lent equal to those borrowed.

This determination may be mentally represented by considering the set of parallel planes (or lines) to be first placed in any arbitrary inclination, corresponding to an arbitrarily assumed rate of interest for each year. Each of these planes (or lines) will have a P and a Q; but unless the centers of gravity of the P's and of the Q's happen to coincide, the algebraic sum of the x''s, x''''s, etc., will not be zero, that is, the assumed rates of interest will not clear the market. We therefore now conceive the set of planes (or lines) to *roll* on their respective boundary surfaces (or curves) WZ, and to roll in unison, that is, so that they may be always mutually parallel. When such a position is found that the center of gravity of the P's coincides with that of the Q's, the market is cleared and the inclination of the planes (or lines) then found will represent the rate of interest. The rolling process here conceived simply visualizes the process given in Chapter VII, § 7, of finding tentatively the rate of interest which will clear the market.

We see, then, from our diagrams, how the different influences coöperate to determine the rate of interest, as represented by the common slope of the parallel planes (or lines). These planes (or lines) have the same slope as the two curved surfaces (or lines) to which each is tangent. There is truth, therefore, both in the subjective and objective theory of interest. That the rate of interest is equal to the subjective rates of preference is indicated by the tangency of the plane (or line) to the desirability surfaces (or curves); that it is equal to the rate of return on sacrifice is indicated by its tangency to the surface (or curve) of effective range of choice. These two equalities are not incompatible, as has too often been assumed. Interest is determined partly by objective or technical factors which supply the range of opportunity (the boundary surfaces or curves); partly by subjective factors which determine individually the choice (the desirability curves).

§ 7

We have now seen how, on the simple hypothesis that the income-stream, or the group of optional income-streams, are foreknown, the problem of the rate of interest may be represented and solved, both algebraically and geometrically. We found that two of the interest-determining conditions were based

on the principle of finding a maximum.   One of these two conditions was that the income-stream selected should have the *maximum present value;* the other was that this choice should be
modified by exchange so as to secure the *maximum desirability.*
We shall now proceed to show that these two conditions may be
united into one, namely, that both of these choices tend simply
to secure the one end of maximum present desirability.   It is
true that maximum present value and maximum present desirability are not interchangeable concepts, and we have seen
that if an individual is, for any reason, not free to borrow or
lend, his choice of income-streams will be determined in a different manner; the point of maximum desirability under these
circumstances will have nothing to do with the straight line
PQ, but will be at the point at which the curve *WPZ* of effective choice is tangent to a utility curve.   But, given the freedom
to interchange parts of the income-stream at the market rate
of interest, the individual will, under these circumstances, gain
the maximum desirability by first seeking that use of his capital
which has the maximum present value, and then modifying the
income thus obtained by the loan or sale market.   This sub-
serviency of the principle of maximum present value to the
principle of maximum desirability was made evident in Chapter
VIII.   It becomes very clear geometrically.

In Fig. 29 the individual is free to select any point on the
line *PQ,* and to place this line at any distance from the origin,
provided it passes through one of the swarm of points representing his total range of choice, and provided also that its
slope always accords with the market rate of interest.   It has
already been made clear that, wherever he places the line, the
point upon it of maximum desirability is *Q,* where it touches
a desirability curve.   It only remains to show that if the line
were drawn, not through *P,* but through a different point in
the swarm, while keeping the same slope, *Q* would be a point
of lower desirability.   This is evident, for if *PQ* is not drawn
through *P,* its only other possible position must be parallel to
that position, but not so far from the origin *O.*   But in that
case, *Q* would evidently be on a curve of lower desirability,
since the family of such curves ascends as we recede from *O.*

§ 8

We may now summarize both the geometrical and algebraic
determinations of the rate of interest: —

1. We have the condition that, for each individual, the effective range of choice among income-streams is limited to a specific set of options, owing to the technical limitations of his capital, etc.

Geometrically, this condition is represented by the surface (or curve) WZ.

Algebraically, this condition is represented by n equations of the type

$$\phi\,(y',\, y'',\, \text{etc.}) = 0,$$

each relating to an individual.

2. We have the condition that the rate of preference for each individual for each year, as estimated in the present, depends upon the future income-stream as indicated by its annual installments.

Geometrically, this condition is represented by the family of desirability surfaces (or curves). The slopes at each point correspond to the rates of preference, and the coördinates of the point correspond to the installments of the income-stream. The fact that the slopes depend upon the position of that point represents the fact that the rate of preference depends on the income-stream.

Algebraically, this condition is represented by $n(m-1)$ equations of the type

$$f = F(y' + x',\, y'' + x'',\, \text{etc.}),$$

each relating to a single individual and a pair of consecutive years.

3. We have the condition that the market rate of preference of each individual is equal to the rate of interest and to each other; or, equivalently, that his total desirability is a maximum.

Geometrically, this condition is represented by the fact that at Q the inclination of the plane (or line) is the same as that of the desirability surface (or curve) at that point, — in short, that they are there *tangent* and further that the directions of the desirability curves at all the Q's are parallel, — in short, that the planes (or lines) drawn tangent to them are parallel to each other.

Algebraically, these conditions are represented by $m-1$ continuous equations of the type

$$f_1 = f_2 = \cdots = f_n = i,$$

each relating to two successive years, making $n(m-1)$ equations in all.

4. We have the condition that out of the effective range of choice, that particular one of the income-streams is selected which possesses the maximum present value, or, equivalently, that one is selected such that, when it is compared with its nearest neighbor, the marginal rate of return on sacrifice is equal to the rate of interest.

Geometrically, this condition is represented by the fact that the plane (or straight line) AB is tangent to WZ for each individual.

Algebraically, this condition is represented by $2\,n(m-1)$ equations, consisting of $n(m-1)$ pairs, of which the following is the type

$$1+i = 1+r = \psi(y', y'', \text{ etc.}),$$

there being one such double equation for each individual for each pair of successive years.

5. We have the condition that the sum added (by borrowing and lending, or buying and selling) in any year to the income of one individual is equal to that taken from others, or, equivalently, that the algebraic sum of such modifications is zero.

Geometrically, this condition is represented by the fact that, for each individual, the center of gravity of the Q's coincides with that of the P's.

Algebraically, this condition is represented by m equations of the type

$$x_1 + x_2 + x_3 + \cdots + x_n = 0,$$

one for each year.

6. We have the condition that for each individual the positive and negative modifications of his income-stream in different years mutually offset each other in present value, or, in more common language, what is borrowed is repayable with interest.

Geometrically, this condition is represented by the fact that for each individual, P and Q lie in the same plane (or straight line) AB.

Algebraically, this condition is represented by n equations of the type

$$x' + \frac{x''}{1+i'} + \frac{x'''}{(1+i')\,(1+i'')} + \text{ etc.} = 0,$$

one for each individual.

Counting up the total number of equations thus indicated, we find : —

> For the 1st condition, n equations,
> 2d condition, $n(m-1)$ equations,
> 3d condition, $n(m-1)$ equations,
> 4th condition, $2\,n(m-1)$ equations,
> 5th condition, m equations,
> 6th condition, n equations,

making a total of $4mn + m - 2\,n$ equations, of which, for reasons given in the Appendix to Chapter VII, only $4mn + m - 2\,n - 1$ are *independent* equations.
The number of unknowns is as follows : —

> number of y's is mn,
> number of x's is mn,
> number of r's is $n(m-1)$,
> number of f's is $n(m-1)$,
> number of i's is $m-1$,

the total of which is also $4mn + m - 2n - 1$. Hence the problem of interest is determinate.

So much space has been devoted to stating these six conditions in mathematical form, because, to those conversant with the mathematical tongue, the algebraic statement will show more definitely and clearly than is otherwise possible the determinateness of the problem, owing to the equality between the number of equations and the number of unknowns; while the geometrical method enables them to form a mental picture, clearer than would otherwise be possible, of the various factors at work, and especially of the manner in which the objective or "technical" conditions, as represented by WZ, coöperate with the subjective conditions which influence the rate of interest. It was, in fact, only through the geometrical representation that the writer was first enabled to grasp the significance of the "effective range of choice" in its general bearings. If the rôle of the curve WZ is grasped, the most difficult part of the theory of interest is mastered.

APPENDIX TO CHAPTER XI

THIRD APPROXIMATION

§ 1 (to Ch. 11, § 8)

To attempt to formulate in mathematical language, in any useful manner, the complete laws determining the rate of interest under the sway of chance, would be like attempting to express the complete laws which determine the path of a projectile when affected by random gusts of wind. Such formulæ would need to be either too general or too empirical to be of much value. In science, the most useful formulæ are those which apply to the simplest cases. For instance, in the study of projectiles, the formula of most importance is that which applies to the path of a projectile in ideal vacuum. Next come the formulæ which apply to a projectile in *still* air. It is seldom that the mathematician attempts to go beyond this, and take into account the effect of wind currents; and if he does so, he still falls short of actual conditions, by assuming the wind to be constant in direction and velocity. The truth is that science always stops short of the final approximation necessary to reach reality. This is due to the nature of science itself, which is a study of what *would* happen under *assumed* conditions, and only an approximate application of what *does* happen under *actual* conditions.[1] The consequence is that, in order to reach the final goal of real conditions, we usually cut the Gordian knots which remain; and for such summary solution, especially when the solution is general instead of numerical, ordinary language is usually better than mathematical formulae. Accordingly, in treatises on projectiles we do not find any attempt to state their trajectories in general formulæ which include the effects of gusts of wind. Still less is there any attempt to construct a formula for the path of a boomerang or of a feather thrown out of a window.

To apply the analogy to the problem in hand, we have already stated the laws determining interest under the simpler

---

[1] See the writer's "Economics as a Science," in *Science*, Aug. 31, 1906.

conditions, — first, when it was assumed that the income-streams of individuals were both certain and fixed, and, secondly, when it was assumed that the income-streams were certain, but flexible. When we introduce the element of uncertainty, our formulæ cease to have the characteristics of simple clarifying shorthand which justify their use, and take on the characteristics of what Marshall calls the "lengthy translations of political economy into mathematics." While, therefore, it is not difficult to make these translations, they add little or nothing to our understanding of the problem. Inasmuch as it is our aim to employ mathematics only when they add something which cannot be conveyed without their use, we refrain from wearying the reader with cumbersome equations.

STATISTICAL DATA

§ 1

The writer has found so much difficulty in securing a long series of yearly averages for rates of interest that the results are here presented in the hope that they may be of use to others.

YEARLY AVERAGE RATES OF INTEREST[1]

	LONDON		BERLIN		PARIS		NEW YORK			CALCUTTA	TOKYO		SHANGHAI	
	Market	Bank	Market	Bank	Market	Bank	Call	60 Days	Prime 2 Name 60 Days	Bank	Market	Bank	Market	Bank
1824	.5	4.0												
1825	.9	4.0												
1826	.5	5.0												
1827	.3	4.5												
1828	3.0	4.0												
1829	3.4	4.0												
1830	2.8	4.0												
1831	3.7	4.0												
1832	3.1	4.0												
1833	2.7	4.0												
1834	3.4	4.0												
1835	3.7	4.0												
1836	4.2	4.4												
1837	4.5	5.0												
1838	3.0	4.1												
1839	5.1	5.1												
1840	5.0	5.1												
1841	4.9	5.0												
1842	3.3	4.3												
1843	2.2	4.0												

[1] The London, Berlin and Paris market rates are on first class merchants' bills. The figures for 1824-58 are from the evidence of D. B. Chapman before the Committee on the Bank Act, 1857, Sess. 2, X, pt. I, p. 463 (also reprinted in *Hunt's Merchants' Magazine*, Vol. 41 (1859), p. 95). The remaining figures are compiled from the *Economist*. For those for 1884-94, the writer is indebted to Professor F. M. Taylor of Michigan University, who had collected them from the *Economist* for a different purpose. The Bank of England rates for 1824-43 are reduced from "Burdett's Official Intelligencer" (1894), p. 1771. The remaining ones for England, Germany, and France are reduced from those given in the Report of the Royal Commission on Depression of Trade, 1886, p. 373, and the *Economist*. They represent the bank "minimum." The rates 1896-1903 are from A. Sauerbeck's tables, *Journal Royal Statistical Society*, Vol. LXVII, Part I, p. 89. The New York rates are taken, the

418

YEARLY AVERAGE RATES OF INTEREST — Continued

	LONDON		BERLIN		PARIS		NEW YORK			CALCUTTA	TOKYO		SHANGHAI	
	Market	Bank	Market	Bank	Market	Bank	Call	60 Days	Prime 2 Name 60 Days	Bank	Market	Bank	Market	Bank
1844	2.1	2.5²	. .	4.3	. .	4.0	. .	. .	. . .	. . .	. .	. .	. .	. .
1845	3.0	2.7	. .	4.4	. .	4.0	. .	. .	. . .	. . .	. .	. .	. .	. .
1846	3.8	3.3	. .	4.7	. .	4.0	. .	. .	. . .	. . .	. .	. .	. .	. .
1847	5.9	5.2	. .	4.8	. .	4.9	. .	. .	. . .	. . .	. .	. .	. .	. .
1848	3.2	3.7	. .	4.7	. .	4.0	. .	. .	. . .	. . .	. .	. .	. .	. .
1849	2.3	2.9	. .	4.0	. .	4.0	4.5	7.8	. . .	. . .	. .	. .	. .	. .
1850	2.2	2.5	. .	4.0	. .	4.0	4.8	7.2	. . .	. . .	. .	. .	. .	. .
1851	3.1	3.0	. .	4.0	. .	4.0	5.9	8.3	. . .	. . .	. .	. .	. .	. .
1852	1.9	2.2	. .	4.0	. .	3.2	5.1	7.3	. . .	. . .	. .	. .	. .	. .
1853	3.7	2.7	. .	4.2	. .	3.2	6.9	10.1	. . .	. . .	. .	. .	. .	. .
1854	4.9	2.1	. .	4.3	. .	4.3	7.7	12.5	. . .	3.9	. .	. .	. .	. .

first two columns, from a table by E. B. Elliott (afterward government actuary) in the (New York) *Banker's Magazine*, 1874. The quotations given as "60 days" apparently included single name paper. The third column to 1890 is compiled from a diagram of highest and lowest monthly rates prepared at Yale College by Mr. G. P. Robbins of the class of 1891, and has been completed from the *Financial Review*, by averaging the highest and lowest weekly rates. It has been found impossible to extend the New York table back beyond 1849, as the rates are not systematically reported. The Calcutta rates are the minimum of the Bank of Bengal and have been kindly furnished by Messrs. Place, Siddons, and Gough, brokers, of Calcutta. The market rates of Tokyo are averages of the highest and lowest rates of each year, furnished by Mr. Ichi Hara of the Bank of Japan, Tokyo. The bank rates are for the Tokyo and Yokohama Coöperative Bank and were translated by Mr. Sakata, student at Yale, from a history of Japan by Zenshiro Tsuboya. The continuation of the table after 1895 has been supplied by Mr. Hitomi, one of my students, and is based upon: Financial Report of the Department of the Treasury, Reports Tokyo Economic Magazine Publishing Co., Reports Tokyo Bankers' Association, and Reports of Department of Agriculture and Commerce. (The last three sources are in Japanese only.) The tables for Shanghai have been procured through the kindness of Prof. F. W. Williams of the department of Oriental History of Yale College, who obtained them from Mr. J. F. Seaman of Shanghai. The first column contains the rates ruling in the native market, and the second, those of the Hong Kong and Shanghai bank (under English control) on overdrawn current accounts, a species of demand loans and the ordinary form of lending in Shanghai. Mr. Seaman was told that the market rates cannot be extended back beyond 1885, as the books of the Chinese banks for previous years are burnt.

² This rate is only from September, when the operation of the Bank Act began. Previous to this the custom of the bank was to have a uniform rate for all loans.

YEARLY AVERAGE RATES OF INTEREST — *Concluded*

	LONDON		BERLIN		PARIS		NEW YORK			CALCUTTA	TOKYO		SHANGHAI	
	Market	Bank	Market	Bank	Market	Bank	Call	60 Days	Prime 2 Name 60 Days	Bank	Market	Bank	Market	Bank
1855	4.7	2.9	..	4.1	..	4.5	6.6	9.3	...	9.7	..	..	..	..
1856	5.9	6.1	..	4.9	..	5.5	7.0	9.9	...	6.5	..	..	..	..
1857	7.1	6.7	..	5.8	..	6.1	6.9	10.4	...	7.0	..	..	..	..
1858	3.1	3.2	..	4.5	..	3.7	3.8	6.7	...	6.1	..	..	..	..
1859	2.5	3.7	..	4.2	..	3.5	5.0	7.2	...	4.9	..	..	..	..
1860	4.1	4.2	..	4.0	..	3.6	6.1	8.4	7.7	4.2	Before 1868, 10 to 12 Per Cent.	..	..	..
1861	5.5	5.3	3.0	4.0	..	5.5	5.4	9.0	6.6	4.2		..	..	..
1862	2.4	2.5	3.0	4.0	..	3.8	5.6	6.8	5.4	5.1		..	..	..
1863	4.3	4.4	3.5	4.1	..	4.6	5.0	6.7	5.8	5.5		..	..	..
1864	7.4	7.4	5.1	5.3	..	6.5	7.2	9.3	8.0	8.7		..	..	..
1865	4.6	4.8	4.6	5.0	..	3.7	6.1	10.2	8.2	6.9		..	..	..
1866	6.7	6.9	6.2	6.2	..	3.7	5.9	7.8	6.3	9.1		..	..	13.
1867	2.3	2.6	2.9	4.0	..	2.7	5.9	8.7	7.2	5.1		..	..	11.
1868	1.8	2.1	2.5	4.0	..	2.5	5.8	8.8	7.3	5.8	15.	18.	..	12.
1869	3.0	3.2	3.2	4.1	..	2.5	6.0	10.8	9.1	6.0	18.	18.	..	12.
1870	3.1	3.1	4.5	4.8	..	4.0	5.1	8.1	7.2	5.7	18.	18.	..	11.
1871	2.7	2.9	3.8	4.2	..	5.7	4.5	6.0	6.1	4.7	14.	18.	..	12.
1872	3.8	4.1	4.0	4.3	4.2	5.1	5.6	9.0	8.0	5.0	14.	18.	..	10.
1873	4.5	4.8	4.5	5.0	5.0	5.2	6.3	9.8	10.3	3.9	14.	14.	..	10.
1874	3.5	3.7	3.3	4.4	4.0	4.3	3.9	6.4	6.0	6.2	12.	14.	..	10.
1875	3.0	3.2	3.7	4.7	3.2	4.0	..	..	5.5	5.7	12.	14.	..	9.
1876	2.2	2.6	3.1	4.1	2.3	3.4	..	..	5.2	6.8	12.	15.	..	9.5
1877	2.3	2.9	3.3	4.4	1.8	2.3	..	..	5.2	8.4	10.	13.	..	9.5
1878	3.5	3.8	3.4	4.3	2.0	2.2	..	..	4.8	5.3	11.	15.	..	9.
1879	1.8	2.5	2.7	3.7	2.2	2.6	..	..	5.0	6.3	11.	16.	..	9.
1880	2.2	2.8	3.1	4.2	2.5	2.8	..	..	5.2	4.6	13.	17.	..	8.5
1881	2.9	3.5	3.4	4.4	3.7	3.9	..	..	5.2	5.3	14.	17.	..	8.
1882	3.4	4.1	3.9	4.5	3.4	3.8	..	..	5.7	6.6	10.	17.	..	8.
1883	3.0	3.6	3.1	4.1	2.6	3.1	..	..	5.5	6.8	7.9	11.	..	8.
1884	2.6	3.0	2.9	4.0	2.4	3.0	..	..	5.2	6.4	12.	16.	..	8.
1885	2.0	2.9	2.9	4.1	2.5	3.0	..	..	4.1	5.4	13.	11.	4.6	7.5
1886	2.1	3.0	2.1	3.3	2.2	3.0	..	..	4.7	6.0	8.8	9.2	6.1	7.
1887	2.4	3.3	2.3	3.4	2.4	3.0	..	..	5.7	5.6	9.0	8.8	6.5	7.
1888	2.4	3.3	2.1	3.3	2.8	3.3	..	..	4.9	5.5	10.	9.7	6.0	7.
1889	2.7	3.6	2.7	3.7	2.6	3.1	..	..	4.8	7.0	10.	10.	6.2	7.
1890	3.7	4.5	3.7	4.5	2.6	3.0	..	..	6.0	5.8	11.	11.	7.2	7.
1891	2.5	3.3	3.0	3.9	2.6	3.0	..	..	5.7	3.1	9.4	9.4	3.5	7.
1892	1.5	2.5	1.8	3.2	1.8	2.7	..	..	4.3	3.5	8.3	8.4	5.0	7.
1893	2.1	3.1	3.2	4.1	2.2	2.5	..	..	7.1	4.9	7.8	7.8	6.9	7.
1894	1.0	2.1	1.7	3.1	1.8	2.5	..	..	3.4	5.4	9.3	9.4	3.8	7.
1895	.8	2.0	2.0	3.1	1.6	2.1	..	..	3.8	4.3	9.6	9.6	2.8	6.5
1896	1.4	2.5	3.0	3.7	1.8	2.0	..	..	5.8	...	11.0	9.3	..	..
1897	1.8	2.6	3.1	3.8	1.8	2.0	..	..	3.4	...	11.4	9.9	..	..
1898	2.6	3.3	3.6	4.3	2.1	2.2	..	..	3.8	...	12.3	11.4	..	..
1899	3.3	3.8	4.5	5.0	3.0	3.1	..	..	4.2	...	10.4	8.8	..	..
1900	3.7	4.0	4.4	5.3	3.2	3.3	..	..	4.4	...	12.1	10.8	..	..
1901	3.2	3.8	3.1	4.1	2.5	3.0	..	..	4.4	...	13.1	11.9	..	..
1902	3.0	3.3	2.2	3.3	2.4	3.0	..	..	4.9	...	12.1	10.4	..	..
1903	3.2	3.8	3.0	3.8	2.8	3.0	..	..	5.5	...	10.7	...	..	..
1904	2.7	3.3	3.1	4.2	2.2	3.0	..	..	4.2	...	10.8	...	..	..
1905	2.6	3.0	2.9	3.8	2.1	3.0	..	..	4.3	...	...	...	..	..
1906	4.0	4.2	4.0	5.1	2.7	3.0	..	..	5.7	...	...	...	..	..

All the rates in the foregoing table are entered as rates of "interest," though the rates for the Banks of England, Germany, and France are rates of discount. Although the two are not quite equivalent, for the purposes of the foregoing work the distinction between them is unnecessary, because, in a continuous series, the error, if any, affects all items nearly alike and thus cancels itself out in the comparisons.

Had it been necessary, some of the tables could have been extended backward. Thus the Bank of England rate could be given as far back as 1696, but it was too inflexible to be of use. The Berlin and Paris bank notes could also be extended and the Paris market rate could be given back to 1861 (except for 1870 and 1871) from data in the *Economist*.

Many of the sources from which the table has been drawn also contain other information such as the rates for other money centers than those named, the weekly or monthly rates, the variation with the seasons, etc.

§ 2

Of sources not mentioned in the above note, the chief which the writer has encountered are: —

Eleventh Census of the United States, Bulletin 71 (on real estate mortgages, 1880–89).

This is probably the most elaborate series of interest averages ever constructed.

Twelfth Census of the United States, Special Reports, wealth, debt, and taxation, pp. 143, 147, 394. Rates of interest on public debts.

"Commercial Valuation of Railway Operating Property in the United States, 1904," United States Census Bulletin 21 (1905).

Gives rates of return on railway securities to investor for 1904.

Reports of the Secretary of the Treasury.
Reports of the Comptroller of Currency.

The last two references contain statistics of rates of interest realized on some United States Government bonds.

R. A. Bayley, "National Loans of the United States" (Government Printing Office, Washington, 1882).

Gives rates of interest and price of issue of all United States loans from July 4, 1776, to June 30, 1880.

Report of the New England Mutual Life Insurance Company, Boston, 1890.

Gives rates realized by twenty representative insurance companies for 1869–88, and for Massachusetts savings banks for 1877–89, and bank dividends in Boston, New York and Philadelphia. The rates realized by the insurance companies for the twenty years, 1869–88, inclusive, were 6.0, 5.9, 6.1, 6.2, 6.5, 6.2, 6.5, 6.1, 5.6, 5.1, 5.0, 4.8, 4.8, 5.1, 5.1, 4.7, 4.7, 4.9, 4.7, 4.6, respectively. These represent (if the writer mistakes not) the average rates earned on the par value of investments of all ages, some old, some new, some terminable soon and others having many years to run. For this reason they are of little or no use for the purposes of Chapter XIV.

Lester W. Zartman, *The Investments of Life Insurance Companies*, New York (Henry Holt & Co.), 1906.

Gives earning rate of real estate, mortgage loans and bonds and stocks of the principal life insurance companies of the United States 1860–1904, and similar data for companies of England, Canada, Australia and other countries.

W. B. Hedge, "On the Rates of Interest for the Use of Money in Ancient and Modern Times. Part I." *Association Magazine*, Vol. 6 (1857), pp. 301–333.

H. W. Farnam, "Some Effects of Falling Prices," *Yale Review*, August, 1895.

F. M. Taylor, "Do we want an Elastic Currency?" *Political Science Quarterly*, March, 1896, pp. 133–157.

Gives diagram showing the relation of surplus reserves and rates of discount; also seasonal variation of rate of discount.

Carl C. Plehn, "Notes concerning the Rates of Interest in California," *Publications American Statistical Association*, Vol. VI (September 1899), p. 350.

R. M. Breckenridge, "Discount Rates in the United States," *Political Science Quarterly*, Vol. XIII (March, 1898), p. 119.

R. H. Inglis Palgrave, *Analysis of the Transactions of the Bank of England* (London, 1874).

Gives rates, 1844–72, and seasonal variation, 1844–56 and 1857–72. Shows dependence of rate on ratio of reserve to liabilities.

R. H. Inglis Palgrave, *Bank Rate and the Money Market in England, France, Germany, Holland and Belgium*, 1844-1900. New York (Dutton), 1903.

Gives bank and market rates, with special reference to variability in England, France, Germany, Holland and Belgium.

W. Stanley Jevons, *Investigations in Currency and Finance* (London, 1884).

Contains diagram for prices of consols and 3 per cent. stock from 1731, and minimum rate of interest in London from 1824 ; also monthly variation in rate of interest, p. 10. The diagram for the price of consols shows that during the middle and first half of the eighteenth century the interest realized was almost as low as in the present generation. It is interesting to note that this was a period of falling prices.

Robert Giffen, *Essays in Finance*, second series (London, 1886), p. 37.

Seasonal variations of interest in connection with bank reserves, etc.

452

Arthur Crump, *English Manual of Banking* (4th ed., London, 1879), pp. 141-144.

Gives Bank of England rates for 1694-1876.

George Clare, *Money Market Primer*, 2d ed. (London, 1905).

Diagrams for seasonal variations of interest, bank reserves, etc.

M. G. Mullhall, *Dictionary of Statistics* (London, 1892), pp. 76, 607.

Gives rates for countries of Europe by five and ten year periods since 1850.

William Farr,"On the Valuation of Railroads, Telegraphs," etc., *Journal of the Royal Statistical Society*, September, 1876, pp. 464-530.

Rates of Discount and Exchange, Banks of England, France, Prussia, Vienna, 1851-1885. Final Report Gold and Silver Commission, *Parliamentary Blue Book*, 1888, appendix, p. 207.

Commercial and Financial Statistics of British India. (Government Printing Office, Calcutta.)

Monthly Discount, Bank of Bengal, from 1861, and average quotations of government securities held in London.

Tooke, *History of Prices*, and

Tooke and Newmarch, *History of Prices from 1793 to 1856*.

J. Liegeois, *Essai sur l'histoire et la législation de l'usure* (Paris, 1863).

Saugrain (Gaston), *La baisse du taux de l'interêt — causes et consequences* (Paris, Larose, 1890).

Boucher, P. B., *Histoire de l'usure ches les Egyptiens, les Grecs, les Romains, nos au cêtres et les Chinois* (Paris, 1806, 1819).

Alph. Courtois, fils, *Histoire des Banques en France* (Paris, 1881).

Gives rate of interest at the Bank of France, 1800.

Viscomte G. D'Avenel, *Histoire économique de la proprieté, des Salaires, des Denrées et de tous les Prix en général depuis l'an 1200 jusqu'en l'an 1800* (Paris, 1894), vol. II, p. 882.

This work contains also tables of the purchasing power of money.

Dictionaire des Finances, Article "Interêt."

Gives rates at which France has borrowed.

Jahrbücher für Nationalökonomie und Statistik, February, 1896, pp. 282-83.

Gives bank and market rates for London, Paris, Berlin, Amsterdam, Brussels, Vienna and St. Petersburg, 1841-80 by decades, and 1881-95 by years.

Handwörterbuch der Staatswissenschaften, Articles "Banken" and "Zinsfuss."

Gives rates for Bank of Prussia and Germany, 1847-89 ; also for Bank of Austria, 1878-89; Switzerland, 1883-88.

Adolf Soetbeer, *Materiallen zur Währungsfrage* (Berlin, 1886), p. 78.

Covers 1851-85 for Banks of England, France and Germany and market rates of Hamburg and Vienna.

Gustav Schmoller, *Grundriss der Allgemeinen Volkswirtschaftslehre*, Leipsic (Duncker und Humblot), 1904, pp. 206–208.

> Gives résumé of course of interest rates from ancient to modern times. Also gives interest rates, London, Paris, Berlin, Amsterdam, Vienna, New York, and St. Petersburg.

Billeter, *Geschichte des Zinsfusses im Griechisch-Römischen Altertum bis auf Justinian* (Leipsic, February, 1898).

> " According to the recent researches of Billeter, the normal rate of interest on good security during the period of greatest prosperity in Athens was about 12 per cent.; while in Rome at the close of the Republic it had fallen to between 4 and 6 per cent. Starting in again during the early middle ages at a rate of 20 per cent. and 15 per cent., it gradually fell, until in the great financial centers of Holland towards the close of the eighteenth century it reached a rate of between 2 per cent. and 3 per cent." — From *Principles of Economics,* by Seligman, N.Y. (Longmans), 1905, p. 404.

E. Laspeyres, *Geschichte der volkswirthschaftlichen Ansichten der Niederländer*, Leipsic, 1863. (Preisschriften der f. Jablonowskischen Gesellschaft, Bd. XI.) [Contains Zins oder Wucher; pp. 256 ff.]

Austrian Government, *Tabellen zur Währungsfrage* (Vienna, 1892), pp. 204–206. (Second edition, 1896, and third edition, 1903, 4.)

> Covers rates since 1861 for banks of Italy, England, France, Germany, Austria, Belgium, and Holland, and market rates in Vienna since 1869.

Wilhelm von Lucam, *Die Oesterreichische Nationalbank während der Dauer des dritten Privilegiums* (Vienna, 1876).

> Gives rates for Bank of Austria, 1817–75.

Theodor Hertzka, *Währung und Handel* (Vienna, 1876).

> Gives the number of weeks each rate lasted for the Banks of England, France, Germany, and Austria during 1844–73.

G. Winter, "Zur Geschichte des Zinsfusses in Mittelalter," *Zeitschrift für Social und Wirtschaftsgeschichte* (Weimar), 1875, IV, 2; 1896, IV, 161.

W. J. Streuber, *Der Zinsus bei den Römern, eine historischantiquarische Abhandlung* (Basel, 1857).

J. Kahn, *Geschichte des Zinsfusses in Deutschland seit 1815 und die Ursachen seiner Veränderung.* (Stuttgart, J. A. Cotta, 1893.)

M. Newmann, *Geschichte des Wuchers in Deutschland bis sur Begründung der heutigen Zinsgesetze* (1654). Halle, 1865.

Sombart: *Der Moderne Kapitalismus*, I, 219.

> Gives the following table showing the rise in price of a rent of one mark (in rent purchase) in Frankfurt a. M.: in 1304, 14–15 Marks; 1314–1315, 16–17 Marks; 1323–1327, 18 Marks; 1333, 19 Marks; 1358, 24 Marks.

Rodbertus, "Ein Versuch, die Höhe des antiken Zinsfusses zu erklären." *Jahrb. f. Nat. Oek.*, Bd. XLII (Jena, 1884).

J. Conrad, *Politische Oekonomie*, Jena (Gustav Fischer), 1905, p. 175.

> Gives rates of discount 1871–1904 in London, Paris, Berlin, Vienna, and St. Petersburg.

A. N. Kiaer, *Om seddelbanker* (Kristiania, 1877).

Contains diagram of bank rates at Kristiania, Stockholm, and Kjobenhavn, 1853–76.

J. P. Norton, *Statistical Studies in the New York Money Market*, New Haven (Tuttle, Morehouse, and Taylor), 1903.

Financial and Economical Annual of Japan, Tokyo, Government Printing Office.

§ 3

The following tables of index numbers are appended in order that the reader may verify the periods of rising and falling prices which have been discussed in Chapter XIV and for the reason that many of the tables, notably those for India, Japan and China, have not been easily accessible to most readers.

INDEX NUMBERS OF PRICES IN SEVEN COUNTRIES[1]

	England	Germany	France	United States	India	Japan	China
1824 . . .	105	. . . . .	. . . . .	. . . . .	. . . . .	. . . . .	. . . .
1825 . . .	124	. . . . .	. . . . .	. . . . .	. . . . .	. . . . .	. . . .
1826 . . .	108	. . . . .	. . . . .	. . . . .	. . . . .	. . . . .	. . . .
1827 . . .	108	. . . . .	. . . . .	. . . . .	. . . . .	. . . . .	. . . .
1828 . . .	97	. . . . .	. . . . .	. . . . .	. . . . .	. . . . .	. . . .
1829 . . .	95	. . . . .	. . . . .	. . . . .	. . . . .	. . . . .	. . . .
1830 . . .	97	. . . . .	. . . . .	. . . . .	. . . . .	. . . . .	. . . .
1831 . . .	98	. . . . .	. . . . .	. . . . .	. . . . .	. . . . .	. . . .
1832 . . .	93	. . . . .	. . . . .	. . . . .	. . . . .	. . . . .	. . . .
1833 . . .	90	. . . . .	. . . . .	. . . . .	. . . . .	. . . • .	. . . .
1834 . . .	93	. . . . .	. . . . .	. . . . .	. . . . .	. . . . .	. . . .
1835 . . .	96	. . . . .	. . . . .	. . . . .	. . . . .	. . . . .	. . . .
1836 . . .	103	. . . . .	. . . . .	. . . . .	. . . . .	. . . . .	. . . .
1837 . . .	101	. . . . .	. . . . .	. . . . .	. . . . .	. . . . .	. . . .
1838 . . .	101	. . . . .	. . . . .	. . . . .	. . . . .	. . . . .	. . . .
1839 . . .	110	. . . . .	. . . . .	. . . .	. . . . .	. . . . .	. . . .
1840 . . .	104	. . . . .	. . . . .	98	. . . . .	. . . . .	. . . .
1841 . . .	102	. . . . .	. . . . .	98	. . . . .	. . . . .	. . . .
1842 . . .	90	. . . . .	. . . . .	90	. . . . .	. . . . .	. . . .
1843 . . .	85	. . . . .	. . . . .	84	. . . . .	. . . . .	. . . .
1844 . . .	83	. . . . .	. . . . .	85	. • . . .	. . . . .	. . . .
1845 . . .	89	. . . . .	. . . . .	88	. . . . .	. . . . .	. . . .
1846 . . .	89	. . . . .	. . . . .	95	. . . . .	. . . . .	. . . .
1847 . . .	94	. . . . .	. . . . .	95	. . . . .	. . . . .	. . . .
1848 . . .	82	. . . . .	. . . . .	88	. . . . .	. . . . .	. . . .
1849 . . .	77	. . . . .	. . . . .	83	. . . . .	. . . . .	. . . .
1850 . . .	77	. . . . .	. . . . .	89	. . . . .	. . . . .	. . . .
1851 . . .	79	100	. . . . .	99	. . . . .	. . . . .	. . . .
1852 . . .	78[1]	102	. . . . .	98	. . . . .	. . . . .	. . . .
1853 . . .	95	114	. . . . .	105	. . . . .	. . . . .	. . . .
1854 . . .	102	121	. . . . .	105	. . . . .	. . . . .	. . . .
1855 . . .	101	124	. . . . .	109	. . . . .	. . . . .	. . . .

INDEX NUMBERS OF PRICES IN SEVEN COUNTRIES — *Concluded*

	ENGLAND	GERMANY	FRANCE	UNITED STATES	INDIA	JAPAN	CHINA
1856 . . .	101	123	. . . . .	112	. . . . .	. . . . .	. . . .
1857 . . .	105	130	. . . . .	114	. . . . .	. . . . .	. . . .
1858 . . .	91	114	. . . . .	113	. . . . .	. . . . .	. . . .
1859 . . .	94	116	. . . . .	103	. . . . .	. . . . .	. . . .
1860 . . .	99	121	. . . . .	100	. . . . .	. . . . .	. . . .
1861 . . .	98	118	100	94	. . . . .	. . . . .	. . . .
1862 . . .	101	123	118	104	. . . . .	. . . . .	. . . .
1863 . . .	103	125	127	132	. . . . .	. . . . .	. . . .
1864 . . .	105	129	129	172	. . . . .	. . . . .	. . . .
1865 . . .	101	123	112	232	. . . . .	. . . . .	. . . .
1866 . . .	102	126	115	188	. . . . .	. . . . .	. . . .
1867 . . .	100	124	100	166	. . . . .	. . . . .	. . . .
1868 . . .	99	122	95	174	. . . . .	. . . . .	. . . .
1869 . . .	98	123	97	152	. . . . .	. . . . .	. . . .
1870 . . .	96	123	94	144	. . . . .	. . . . .	. . . .
1871 . . .	100	127	94	136	. . . . .	. . . . .	. . . .
1872 . . .	109	136	105	132	. . . . .	. . . . .	. . . .
1873 . . .	111	138	103	129	100	104	. . . .
1874 . . .	102	136	94	130	98	104	100
1875 . . .	96	130	87	129	95	105	103
1876 . . .	95	128	85	123	99	102	111
1877 . . .	94	128	82	114	121	105	101
1878 . . .	87	121	78	105	125	114	106
1879 . . .	83	117	76	95	119	145	111
1880 . . .	88	122	79	105	112	160	105
1881 . . .	85	121	76	108	99	175	110
1882 . . .	84	122	73	109	98	159	108
1883 . . .	82	122	73	107	96	130	103
1884 . . .	76	114	72	103	97	116	104
1885 . . .	72	109	70	93	95	116	105
1886 . . .	69	104	69	93	99	107	107
1887 . . .	68	102	71	94	101	109	105
1888 . . .	70	102	74	96	104	112	100
1889 . . .	72	106	80	98	107	116	105
1890 . . .	72	108	83	94	103	124	104
1891 . . .	72	109[1]	79	94	104	123	104
1892 . . .	68	106	. . . . .	89	115	124	108
1893 . . .	68	102	. . . . .	89	119	129	109
1894 . . .	63	92	. . . . .	81	. . . . .	132	. . . .
1895 . . .	62	91	. . . . .	79	. . . . .	145	. . . .
1896 . . .	61	91	. . . . .	76	. . . . .	133	. . . .
1897 . . .	62	92	. . . . .	76	. . . . .	173	. . . .
1898 . . .	64	93	. . . . .	78	. . . . .	159	. . . .
1899 . . .	68	111	. . . . .	86	. . . . .	175	. . . .
1900 . . .	75	110	. . . . .	92	. . . . .	165	. . . .
1901 . . .	70	103	. . . . .	91	. . . . .	160	. . . .
1902 . . .	69	99	. . . . .	95	. . . . .	165	. . . .
1903 . . .	69	104	. . . . .	96	. . . . .	. . . . .	. . . .
1904 . . .	70	104	. . . . .	95	. . . . .	. . . . .	. . . .
1905 . . .	72	107	. . . . .	98	. . . . .	. . . . .	. . . .
1906 . . .	77	. . . . .	. . . . .	103	. . . . .	. . . . .	. . . .

[1] For England, the figures of prices are from Jevons and Sauerbeck. Those from Sauerbeck begin in 1852. They are taken from the Aldrich Senate report on Wholesale Prices, 1893 (I, 247), and from the *Journal of the Royal Statistical Society*. Those from Jevons are from 1824 to 1852 inclusive, and are taken from his " Investigations in Currency and Finance." In order to make the tables of Jevons and Sauerbeck continuous, Jevons's number for 1852 is called 78 (*i.e.*, Sauerbeck's for that year) instead of 65, as given in the " Investigations," and all the other numbers are raised in the ratio of 78 to 65. Jevons's figures are for forty commodities ; Sauerbeck's are for forty-five.

The German numbers are from Soetbeer, Heinz, and Conrad. Those for 1851-91 inclusive, are from Soetbeer, continued by Heinz, and given in the Aldrich report (I, 294) ; those for 1891-1906 inclusive, are from Conrad, as given in his *Jahrbücher*, 1894-1906, but are all magnified in the ratio of 109 to 98 in order to make the series continuous, since Heinz's figure for 1891 is 109, and Conrad's, 98. The statistics of Soetbeer and Heinz cover 114 commodities.

The French numbers are from the Aldrich report (I, 335) founded on the figures of the *Commission permanente des valeurs*. They cover only sixteen articles.

The figures for the United States are those of Professor Falkner in the Aldrich report (I, 9, 13), the weighted averages (last method) being employed. They have been continued after 1891 by using the figures of the Bulletin of the United States Department of Labor, March, 1907, p. 250. The figures of this report have all been reduced in a fixed ratio in order to bring the initial figure for 1891 into coincidence with the figure, for that year, of the Aldrich report, 94.

Those for India, Japan, and China are from the Japanese report of the Commission for investigation of monetary systems, 1895. The writer is under great obligations to Mr. Ichi Hara, of Tokyo, for a copy of the report, and to Mr. Sakata, of Yale University, for translating the tables.

That for India is an average of three tables which cover respectively twenty-one articles of export, sixteen articles of export priced at Calcutta and Bombay, and eight grains at Bombay. That for Japan is an average of three tables, of forty-two articles at Tokyo, sixteen at Osaka, and thirty-one articles of export.

The continuation of the table after 1895 has been supplied to me by Mr. Hitomi, one of my students, and is based on Reports of the Tokyo Economic Magazine Publishing Company.

That for China is an average of three tables, of twenty inland commodities, seventeen articles of export, and fifteen food-stuffs in Shanghai.

The tables for India were based on official statistics, those for Japan on information from guilds and merchants, and those for China on the reports of the consuls of Japan and England (Mr. Jameson) in China.

In the Japanese report the prices for Japan are reduced to a silver basis. As silver was at a premium up to 1885, it has been necessary in constructing the above table to reconvert into currency by applying the premium for 1873-85, viz., 4, 4, 3, 1, 3, 10, 32, 48, 70, 57, 26, 9, 5 per cent respectively.

INDEX

429

459

Editorial Postscript
with Selected Documents

Contemporary commentary on the doctrines Fisher propounded in *The Rate of Interest* proceeded in two phases. The first dated from the publication of the work itself in 1907 and was frequently combined with reactions to *The Nature of Capital and Income* (1906). A second phase began in 1911 when Fisher – in an article published in English in an Italian journal – labelled his contribution as an "impatience theory" of interest. The book that appeared in 1907 had not used this expression.

As had been the case with *The Nature of Capital and Income*, *The Rate of Interest* attracted a fair number of critics who were disturbed by Fisher's propensity to define familiar terms in unfamiliar ways. A.W. Flux, for example, complained that Fisher's "determination to use the word 'income' as a term with a meaning other than that assigned to the word 'revenue' is responsible for a rather prolonged and . . . by no means fruitful inquiry and for unnecessary disquisitions on the failure of respected economists to appreciate certain rather obvious and fundamental truths." In addition, Flux registered his "regret at the extent to which Professor Fisher, and those who think like him, have felt it necessary to tear down what has been built before them, in order to find a place for their edifice."[a]

Fisher took strong exception to these indictments.

"It is scarcely worthwhile to insist strenuously on any particular use of terms, but it is important to point out the relative analytical value of different concepts. . . . Professor Flux in his review seems to overlook or omit the mutual relations of discount and interest which constitute the *raison d'être* for the concepts which I have called capital and income. It is chiefly because 'savings' do not enter into these discount relations on equal terms with other items of income that savings do not form a part of what I have called the income concept. I do not think that there are reasons of terminology alone sufficient to justify the inclusion of savings in income. . . .

---

[a] A.W. Flux, "Irving Fisher on Capital and Interest," *Quarterly Journal of Economics*, Vol. 23, February 1909, 307–23. Flux had been a member of the faculty of McGill University in Montreal from 1901 to 1908. Subsequently, he served as a statistical adviser to the Board of Trade in London.

Professor Flux evidently regards me somewhat of an iconoclast. As a matter of fact, I have never wished to tear down any previous economic structure so long as it was possible to build upon it. On the contrary, my aim has always been to look for agreements rather than disagreements, and I always feel satisfied when economists recognize, as Professor Flux does in one part of his article, that the presentation I have made is in many respects, if not in most, merely the older conclusion in a new dress. I would not even insist on the newness of dress, were any of the older garments sufficiently serviceable, but the truth is these older garments only partially fit. Moreover, there seemed to be no prevailing fashion. It is the history of all science that terminology and definitions will constantly change until exactly adapted to serve the concepts for which they are merely names. Even where possible, it is usually awkward to cling to older usage in light of newer analysis. The whole subject of terminology, however, occupies in my estimation a very secondary place."[a]

Fisher also used this occasion to respond in print to John R. Commons's criticism of his work on grounds that emphasis on market valuations neglected societal values. In Commons's view, Fisher's approach amounted to the substitution of "business economy" (which focussed on the study of individual interests) for "political economy" (which was concerned with society's welfare).[b] Fisher addressed this point as follows.

"The capital invested in a blackmailing newspaper, in a counterfeiting establishment, in a shop for the manufacture of burglar's tools, in a bureau for the corruption of legislatures, in an opium den, or in other enterprises injurious to society, will always be capital so long as it renders its 'services' to the owners who benefit thereby. The fact that they render disservices to others is of vital consequence, but does not directly concern the subject-matter of my books, which is to follow the causes which actually determine market valuations. The truth is that market valuation seldom, if ever, exactly registers utility to society. The building of a new railroad will increase the value of certain productive real estate and decrease that of residential districts; but we shall look in vain into the records of sales of railway shares for any indication of these effects. The study of these effects forms a subject by itself and one far too large and complicated to have been combined with a study of the topics chosen for my two books.

The proper place for a study of social pathology and therapeutics seems to me to be at the end and not at the beginning of economic analysis. We shall reach sounder conclusions in regard to the best remedies to be

---

[a] Fisher, "A Reply to Critics," *Quarterly Journal of Economics,* Vol. 23, May 1909, 538–41.

[b] See the discussion of Commons's position in the Editorial Postscript to Volume 2.

applied to social conditions if first we study those conditions exactly as they are and not as we should prefer to have them. Our analysis should be as complete and as faithful to the facts as possible."[a]

The most vigorous American challenger of formal neo-classical theorizing – Thorstein Veblen – regarded *The Rate of Interest* as no less wanting than he found *The Nature of Capital and Income* to be.[b] His review of the earlier book had characterized it as a work of "taxonomy" which was out of touch with reality. Veblen regarded *The Rate of Interest* as the type of work to be expected from a member of the "marginal utility school of economics." He credited Fisher with "development of a doctrine of interest" that was "true" to that school's "premises and traditions to a degree of nicety never excelled by any of the adepts." But that choice of analytic framework, as Veblen saw matters, imposed limitations from which "several characteristic excrescences and incongruities" followed.[c] Fisher responded at some length.

– Fisher, "Capital and Interest," *Political Science Quarterly*, Volume 14, September 1909, 504–16 (extracts).

"Having recently replied to a critic who objects that my books, while correct from the standpoint of business economy, do not pay sufficient attention to social utilities, I must now face about to meet criticism from precisely the opposite quarter. Professor Veblen's objections are that I give undue attention to utility, enjoyable income, livelihood and the 'calculus of pleasure and pain,' instead of to 'pecuniary concepts,' which, and which alone, can, in his opinion, serve as a basis for the study of modern business conditions. The first critic objects that as political economist I should not confine myself to the problems of business, but should include those of welfare; the second, that I should not specifically include the problems of welfare, but should confine myself to those of business!

The opposite character of these criticisms would suggest interesting questions as to how authors ought to be guided in distributing emphasis over the topics of which they treat. Experience has shown that progress is made most rapidly in science by the writing of monographs devoted to special parts of the wide field of human knowledge. There will always necessarily be some disagreement as to what may best be covered in any

---

[a] Fisher, *ibid.*, 536–37. For a further rejoinder to Commons's line of critique, Fisher referred his readers to his lecture entitled "Why Has the Doctrine of *Laissez-Faire* Been Abandoned?" This document is reproduced below.

[b] For Veblen's appraisal of *The Nature of Capital and Income*, see the Editorial Postscript to Volume 2.

[c] Thorstein Veblen, "Fisher's Rate of Interest," *Political Science Quarterly*, Volume 24, June 1909, 296–303.

specific monograph. It must be an advantage rather than otherwise that various minds look at the field from various angles, and that each selects for himself particular aspects for special study. While there is room for difference of opinion as to the wisdom of each choice, I hold it be a mistake – and a mistake indicative of the undeveloped state of our science – that there should exist among economists a spirit of intolerance, leading critics not merely to prefer certain points of view but to maintain that any other point of view is inadmissible.... Like some other economists, he [Veblen] is not content with following his own bent and method, but wishes to prescribe limits and to mark out paths for others; and like these other economists he makes errors chiefly in his negations, not in his affirmations. Having judged any work by his criteria and found it wanting, he seems forthwith to dismiss it *in toto*, closing his eyes to particulars. All other reviews I have yet encountered are favorable to the extent of granting the validity of my main contention, but Professor Veblen finds evidences of error everywhere. He rejects my entire presentation because I have not regarded the subject from his viewpoint and, in consequence, have put different details in the background and foreground respectively. In the last of his two articles Professor Veblen states that the study of the 'rate of interest' must be confined to the money market, and objects to the extension of the concept which is made to apply to discounting future benefits in general. Among his expressions on this point we find:

> Interest is a pecuniary concept having no validity (except by force of an ambiguity) outside of the pecuniary relations of the business community, and to construe it in other, presumably more elementary, terms is to explain it away by dissolving it into the elements out of which it is remotely derived, or rather to which it is presumed to be remotely related.

Such statements will, I believe, to most readers carry their own refutation. Without such analysis, we should revert to the superficial mercantilism with which economics began. Instead of restricting economic studies in any one direction, instead of prescribing rigid metes and bounds, why not encourage every student who has the slightest spark of the explorer's spirit to follow out any chosen chain of causation *ad libitum*, even to the extent of studying, as did Jevons, the possible effect of sunspots on economic crises?

But while Professor Veblen objects to my extending the study of interest in one direction, he at the same time objects to my failing to extend it in another. He points out that in a modern market the rate of interest is affected by the degree of development of economic institutions, and that any study of the rate of interest should include a study of the historical development of the institutions of private property and industrial organization, particularly the organization of the money market. Such a study is certainly legitimate, but forms no necessary part of the field chosen for my book, which had to do primarily with analysis and only secondarily with history.

As another example of my critic's desire to narrow many economic concepts to their money manifestation may be mentioned his attitude toward the concept of income. He maintains that, 'As a business proposition, nothing that cannot be rated in terms of money income is to be accounted income at all; which is the same as saying that no definition which goes beyond or behind the pecuniary concept can be a serviceable definition of income for modern use.' My own statement would be that no definition which does *not* go beyond or behind the pecuniary concept (or concepts) can be a serviceable definition for modern use, especially use in economic analysis. Would Professor Veblen wipe out of economic literature all study – analysis and statistics alike – of, for instance, 'real' wages as distinct from pecuniary or nominal wages? The use of the term 'real' in contradistinction to 'pecuniary' indicates the belief of economists that pecuniary income, like pecuniary concepts in general, is relatively superficial.

If Professor Veblen wishes, for the purpose of classification, to mark off a concept of money income, he is of course at liberty to do so. This, however, would seem to be inconsistent with the views expressed in his first article. Here he objects to my method because he believes it is classification merely for classification's sake. In the second article, instead of branding me as a 'taxonomist,' he confines himself to calling me a 'hedonist.' If I were compelled to accept either of these epithets, I should be inclined to argue that no one could logically merit both. Since, however, Professor Veblen has apparently overlooked the fact that I had expressly disclaimed being either an advocate of classification (Professor Veblen's 'taxonomy') or an advocate of measuring utility in terms of pleasure and pain (Professor Veblen's 'hedonistic calculus'), it may be worth while to restate here two distinctions which seem to me fundamental. One is the distinction between *classification* and *analysis*; the other, the distinction between *pleasure* and *desire*.

So far as the first distinction is concerned, I believe it will go far to show that, however else we may disagree, Professor Veblen and I substantially agree on the futility of mere classification. I even venture to think that, had Professor Veblen not mistaken me for a classifier, he would have maintained a different attitude throughout his first and perhaps also his second review. . . .

Classification is a useful process mnemonically. It serves the same purpose as the division of a book into chapters; but it has no place as a scientific process, for it yields no important conclusions. I agree heartily with Professor Veblen's opinions on this point. . . .

But if Professor Veblen's criticisms are directed against *analysis* as well as classification, I am ready to join issue. He himself draws no such distinction; yet the distinction is vital. It separates definitions which are based on classification from those which are based on analysis. These are, respectively, definitions of *things* and definitions of *relations* between things. The former relate to the concrete; the latter to the abstract. The former are useful to the user of language; the latter to the student of science. Examples of the first category (concrete or classificatory) are definitions of a house, a chair, land, money; of the second category (abstract or analytical) are definitions of an average, a circle, momentum, coëfficient of correlation, velocity of circulation of money, balance of trade. In economic analysis, as in any other branch of science, the leading rôle must be played by such concepts of relation. . . .

Many economists have gone astray in respect to the true function of analysis. The literature on 'methodology' is full of misconceptions of analysis similar to that of which Professor Veblen seems to be guilty. In particular the historical school of Roscher had no real understanding of the Baconian logic, which they professed to emulate. Otherwise they would have been no more opposed to theoretical economics than the laboratory experimenter is opposed to 'rational mechanics.' As Hume said in a passage which John Rae uses as the motto for his book on *Capital*, 'Our speculations can scarce ever be too fine, provided they be just.'

One of the best examples of Professor Veblen's confusion between classification and analysis appears when he accuses me of distinguishing 'savings' and 'income' simply in order to have two mutually exclusive classes. Professor Veblen says:

> The two ideas – 'income' and 'increase of capital' – are by no means mutually exclusive in the current usage; and ordinarily, so long as the terms are taken in their current (pecuniary) meaning, such an increase of capital would unhesitatingly be rated as income to the owner. The need of making 'income' and 'increase of capital' mutually exclusive categories is a need incident to a mechanically drawn scheme of classification, and it disappears as soon as classification for classification's sake is given up.

It would be hard to conceive of a criticism more *mal à propos*. Had I been making classification for classification's sake, I might have been tempted to include savings in income, for, as Professor Veblen indicates, there is fully as much sanction for such usage as for the opposite. But 'savings' and 'income' are not mere sub-heads under some general class of objects. They are as widely different in kind as the analytical notions of velocity and energy, and quite as much in need of careful handling if confusions are to be avoided and our economic accountings are to be self-consistent. . . .

Professor Veblen overlooks another distinction which I tried to draw in reference to the psychologic side of economic science. Here also I agree with him on the general thesis that the 'calculus of pleasure and pain' has been terribly misused by theoretical economists. Economists have burdened themselves with a crude psychology. It is unnecessary for economists to enter within the field of psychology, but it is necessary to acknowledge contact with that field. The point of contact is human *desire*. It is quite impossible for any economic theory to be completely worked out without some place in the analysis for human desires. Many economists have confused pleasure and pain with desire and aversion. If Professor Veblen has not made this confusion, he has at any rate been greatly mistaken in the views he has ascribed to me. He says: 'The day when Bentham's conception of economic life was serviceable for the purposes of contemporary science lies about one hundred years back, and Mr. Fisher's reduction of "income" to "psychic income" is late by that much.' He could scarcely have written thus had he comprehended my own views. As early as 1892 I wrote: '"Utility" is the heritage of Bentham and his theory of pleasures and pains. For us his *word* is the more acceptable, the less it is entangled with his *theory*. . . .

In short the view I have upheld is that, while we must correct wrong psychological analyses, we cannot dispense with psychologic concepts altogether. Least of all can we get along by means of 'pecuniary concepts.' Nothing has led to more errors than fixing attention on the money surface of things and neglecting the psychologic forces beneath. Money, while of the greatest service in economic practice, is and always has been the chief stumbling-block in economic theory.

The impression which Professor Veblen's two reviews have made on my mind is that he, like Leslie, is influenced by a kind of phobia against certain schools and methods. Having classified (or misclassified) me in a particular 'school,' he seems to make his attack almost indiscriminately. His criticisms are almost all generalities on methodology and concepts, and for the most part they disregard the special conclusions which differentiate my books from others on his *index expurgatorius*.

I would especially call attention to the fact that nowhere does he refer to the main point of *The Rate of Interest*, namely, the rôle played by the 'time-shape of the income stream' and the considerations which go with it, which take the place in my treatment of the 'roundabout process' of Böhm-Bawerk. Instead he inveighs against those theoretical economists who find no place for any technological element and his review would give the impression to many readers that I am one of these. My book was written largely to show that Böhm-Bawerk's handling of the technological side in his famous 'roundabout process' must be discarded and replaced by the proper use of the fact that each individual has open to him a number of optional income streams differing in size, composition, certainty and time-shape. . . .

There are doubtless many points of difference between us, but they are not in general those which Professor Veblen has mentioned. Unless unwittingly I do him injustice, his preconceptions have led him to misconceive my method and conclusions and to confuse them with methods and conclusions which we both oppose."

Professional discussion of Fisher's theory of the interest rate took a bit different turn following the publication of his article entitled "The 'Impatience Theory' of Interest: a Study of the Causes Determining the Rate of Interest" in 1911. He again rejected Böhm-Bawerk's claims concerning the impact of "round-aboutness" in production on the determination of the interest rate.[a] Some readers of this essay – as well as of Fisher's treatment of interest rates in his textbook, *Elementary Principles of Economics* (1912) – took away the impression that his emphasis on the role of "impatience" amounted to an exclusively subjective approach to the problem at hand. Henry R. Seager of Columbia University – a proponent of the Böhm-Bawerkian position and long-time critic of Fisher – maintained, for example, that Fisher denied that the productivity of capital had any influence on interest rates whatsoever.[b] Fisher protested against the charge that he had failed to attend to the productivity of capital. To the contrary, he insisted that this consideration had been assimilated into his treatment of the time-shape of income streams. Its influence on the determination of interest rates was thus recognized, but it acted indirectly rather than directly.[c]

These exchanges did not silence controversies between rival camps – i.e., the "psychological" and "technological" schools. They were still alive and well when Fisher set out to reconcile them in his *Theory of Interest* in 1930.

---

[a] This article is reproduced below.

[b] Henry R. Seager, "The Impatience Theory of Interest," *American Economic Review*, December 1912, 834–51.

[c] Fisher, "The Impatience Theory of Interest," *American Economic Review*, September 1913, 610–19.

Scientia, Bologna, 1911.

THE "IMPATIENCE THEORY" OF INTEREST

A STUDY OF THE CAUSES DETERMINING THE RATE OF INTEREST.

I. Interest and Money.

Most people imagine that the rate of interest is a technical phenomenon, concerning only money lenders or borrowers. Of explicit or contract interest this is in a measure true; but interest may be implicit as well as explicit. It is implicit in every price. If we invest in a bond, for instance, the price that we pay for the bond carries with it the *implication* of a rate of interest, — that is, the rate we expect to realize on the investment. When a man buys stocks instead of bonds, or even a house or a piece of land, the same element of implicit interest enters into the transaction. He cannot even buy a piano or an overcoat or a hat without « discounting » the value of the use which he expects to make of that particular article. The rate of interest, then, is not a narrow technical phenomenon. It touches the daily life of us all.

Concerning the verbal definition of the rate of interest, there is no dispute; but concerning its nature and its causes, which I propose to discuss, there are numerous and conflicting theories.

By definition, the rate of interest is the price of capital in terms of income, when both capital and income are measured in terms of the same unit, as, for instance, of money; or, what amounts to the same thing, the rate of interest is the excess above par which has to be paid for this year's money in terms of next year's money.

But why should there be this excess? Why should not a dollar to-day exchange on even terms for a dollar next year? And what principles determine the amount of excess? These questions are among the most perplexing with which economic science has had to deal, and for two thousand years economists have been trying to solve the riddle which they represent.

The theory of interest here briefly presented is that more fully contained in my book *The Rate of Interest*. [1] It may be called for short, the « Impatience » Theory of Interest.

First of all let us note the relation of interest to money. Among the earliest fallacies concerning the rate of interest was that it depends on the amount of money in circulation. In particular, this fallacious theory held that plentiful money makes the rate of interest low. We commonly speak of interest as the « price of money », and when the trade journals tell us that « money is easy » in Wall Street, or Lombard Street, their meaning is that interest is low, and low *because* it is easy to borrow money. Or, we are told that « the money market is tight », meaning that it is hard to borrow money. Probably the great majority of unthinking business men still believe that interest is low when money is plentiful, and high when money is scarce. We often hear the argument that the present high cost of living cannot be due to any plentifulness of money, because if money were really plentiful, it would be « cheap », meaning that the rate of interest would be low, whereas it is fairly high, and therefore, it is argued, money must be scarce.

The fallacy consists in overlooking the fact that plentiful money raises the demand for loans just as much as it raises the supply. If money becomes more abundant, prices will rise and if prices rise, any intending borrower will need to borrow more money in order to purchase the same amount of goods.

That the relative abundance of money has, under normal circumstances, no influence on the rate of interest, has been well known to those versed in this subject ever since the days of Locke; yet the opposite belief still prevails among many intelligent people. One reason for this error is found in the experience and usages of banks. If his reserves are

[1] Macmillan, New York and London, Co., publish, 1907.

low the banker raises the rate of interest to « protect » those reserves. If the reserves are abundant, he reduces the rate of interest in order to get rid of them. But he mistakes a merely *relative* scarcity or abundance of reserves (as compared with money in circulation) for an *absolute* scarcity or abundance. When he says that more money lowers the rate of interest, he ought to say « When bank reserves get an undue fraction of money, the rate of interest will be low; but when an undue fraction goes into circulation outside of banks, the rate of interest will be high ». In other words, an increase of money will operate in two different ways, according to where it happens to go first. Normally, however, and eventually an increase of money distributes itself equally among pockets, tills, and bank reserves; and, in this case the rate of interest will not be affected at all.

We conclude, then, that an inflation of the currency, as such, does not affect the rate of interest at all, *provided, however, the inflation affects the loan at the time the loan is made just as much as it affects the repayment at the time the repayment is made.* This proviso is important. For the loan and the repayment do not occur at the same time; and it may be that the degree of inflation is greater or less at the end than at the beginning of the intervening period, in which case the inflation may, through its effects on the values borrowed and repaid, affect the rate of interest *during the process of change.*

Let us consider this *transitional* effect. Suppose, for instance, that the inflation of money has proceeded at such a pace that prices have been made to rise at the rate of one per cent per annum. Then, 100 dollars lent last year is equivalent in purchasing power not to 100 dollars repayable next year, but to 101 repayable next year. If prices had not risen, the borrower would pay back in his principal of 100 the value of the same amount of goods as were represented by the 100 which he borrowed. In terms of goods he would be in the same position at the end as at the beginning, and so would the lender. But we are supposing that prices have been rising. Then the lender, when he gets back his principal of 100, does not get back as much purchasing power as he lent, and the borrower does not pay back as much purchasing power as he borrowed. Under these circumstances, the principal of a debt becomes less and less valuable. If prices are rising 1 per cent a year then the falling principal of the debt would have to be eked out each year by an indemnity of about 1 per cent in order that there should be exactly the same burden on the borrower in paying back as there would have been if prices had not risen. In practice this indemnity may be paid as 1 per cent higher interest. Likewise, if prices are rising 2 per cent per annum, 2 per cent would have to be added to the rate of interest, and so on. On the other hand, if prices are falling, the rate of interest, in order to offset the appreciation of the principal, would have to de reduced.

A study of the periods of rising and falling prices in the United States, England, Germany, France, China, Japan, and India verifies these principles. It shows that, in general, when prices are rising, the rate of interest is high, and that in general when prices are falling, the rate of interest is low.

II. Previous Theories of Interest.

We have considered the relation of the relative abundance of money to the rate of interest. We saw that the money supply has no effect on the rate of interest except during transition periods. But the real riddle of interest still remains unsolved. Why is there such a thing as a rate of interest, even when the purchasing power of money is constant, and what determines that rate?

Many theories have been proposed. One of the most persistent is the theory that « interest is due to the productivity of capital ». If a man who has never thought on the subject is asked why the rate of interest is 5 per cent, he will almost invariably answer: « Because 5 per cent is what investments pay ». Now it is true that if you have 100 dollars and invest it, and it yields you 5 per cent a year, the rate of interest is 5 per cent. A 100,000 dollars mill will produce a net income of 5000 a year. A 100,000 dollars piece of land will produce a net crop worth 5000 a year, and so on throughout the whole series of investments. When the rate of interest is 5 per cent, nothing at first sight seems more obvious than that it is 5 per cent because capital *yields* 5 per cent. Since capital is productive, it seems self-evident that an investment of 100 dollars in productive land, machinery, or any other form of capital, will yield a rate of interest proportionate to its productivity. This proposition looks attractive, but it is superficial. Why is the land worth 100,000? Simply because this is the discounted value of the expected 5000 a year. The value of capital is derived by the process of « discounting » from the value of its income, not the value of the income from that of the capital. But whenever we thus discount income, we have to *assume* a rate of interest. One hundred thousand dollars is a capitalization calculated on the basis of 5 per cent interest. If we capitalize 5000 dollars at 5 per cent, and get 100,000, we naturally find that we are getting 5 per cent on the investment, for we assumed 5 per cent in the first place. We get out exactly what we put in.

Besides the productivity theory (which itself has many variations) there are numerous other theories, such as the following: that interest represents labor saved by capital; that interest is the reward of abstinence, or of waiting; that interest is the cost of managing capital: that interest is the exploitation of laborers by capitalists. The last is the socialist's theory. To the socialist, interest appears an evil — *the* evil — and he thinks it ought to be abolished. He says: « It is all wrong that the capitalist who does not lift a finger should get any pay; he is getting something for nothing, namely interest; interest is robbery; interest is sucking the blood out of the underman, viz. the workman ».

The socialist's position involves two propositions: first, that practically all income and all capital are produced by labor; and secondly, that all income should be paid to the laborer. Now the first proposition is much more nearly correct than the second. We need not contest it in order to see the fundamental error in the theory of socialism. Let it be granted that practically every instrument of production is produced by labor; let it be granted that the capitalist is always living on the product of past labor. Yet as Böhm-Bawerk says:

« The perfectly just proposition that the laborer should receive the entire value of his product may be understood to mean either that the laborer should *now* receive the entire *present* value of his product, or should receive the entire *future* value of his product *in the future*. But Rodbertus and the socialists expound it as if it meant that the laborer should *now* receive the entire *future* value of his product ».

Finally there is Böhm-Bawerk's own theory, which, with some variations, is that of his predecessors Rae, Jevons, Sax and Launhardt, as well as some of his various successors, especially Adolphe Landry. Böhm-Bawerk calls his theory the « Agio Theory ».

Böhm-Bawerk distinguishes two problems: (1) Why does interest exist ? and (2) What determines any particular rate of interest ? In answer to the first problem, he states virtually that this world is so constituted that most of us prefer present goods to future goods of like kind and number. This preference is due, according to Böhm-Bawerk, to three circumstances: one being the « technical superiority » of present over future goods, or the fact, as Böhm-Bawerk conceives it, that the « roundabout » or « capitalistic » processes of production are more remunerative than those which yield immediate returns. This circumstance — the so-called technical superiority of present over future goods — we believe contains essential errors.

According to Böhm-Bawerk, labor invested in long processes of production will yield larger returns than labor invested in short processes, and will therefore confer a « technical advantage » upon those who have the command of that labor. This technical advantage produces, so Böhm-Bawerk believes, a preference for present over future goods which is entirely apart from and in addition to the preference due to the perspective underestimate of the future or that due to the underendowment of the present. Böhm-Bawerk regards this part of his theory as most essential, and repeatedly states that the theory must stand or fall by the truth or falsity of this part.

The fact is that the only reason any one prefers the product of a month's labor invested to-day to the product of a month's labor invested next year is that to-day's investment will mature earlier than next year's investment. If a fruit tree is planted to-day which will bear fruit in four years, the labor available to-day for planting it is preferred to the same amount of labor available next year; because, if the planting is deferred until next year, the fruit will likewise be deferred a year, maturing in five instead of four years from the present. Nor is this essential fact altered by the possibility of a number of different kinds of investments to-day. It is true that a month's labor in the present may be spent in planting slow-growing or fast-growing trees; but so may a month's labor invested next year. It is from the preference for the early over the late fruition of *any* productive process that the so-called « technical superiority of present over future goods » derives all its force and not from the superior productiveness of roundabout processes of production. The latter has no power whatever to create interest.

It is impossible in this brief article to enter into a detailed account of Böhm-Bawerk's theory and its merits and defects. For amplification of the brief statement here presented the reader is referred to my « Rate of Interest ».

III. **Human Impatience the true Basis of Interest.**

We are now ready to state briefly our own theory of interest. This is a modification of Böhm-Bawerk's agio theory. Partly to distinguish it from Böhm-Bawerk's, and partly to find a better term than « agio », it is here proposed to call the present theory the « Impatience theory ». It is odd that no one has happened heretofore to hit on this term, which seems to be the only one expressing accurately and in a single word, the real basis of interest. The term *delay* (« mora ») was used by some medioeval writers, who first sought to excuse interest taking on the ground that repayment of a loan was « delayed » and that the delay should be penalized; but the justification of interest consists not exactly in the delay in paying, but in the fact that the borrower *does not like the delay.* The term « abstinence » has had much currency; but it is not abstinence but the *inconvenience* of abstinence which is the real factor. By Professor Marshall the term « waiting » has been suggested; but it is not the waiting which is significant but the reluctance to wait. Böhm-Bawerk's term « agio » has attracted much attention; but it has no evident meaning until it is explained by a longer phrase — i. e. « a premium in the esteem of man for present over future goods ». The idea which it is sought to express by all these proposed terms — delay, abstinence, waiting, agio, as well as by other more clumsy expressions such as « labor of saving », — is simply the very familiar one expressed in daily experience by the term « impatience ». It is because a man is impatient that he thinks « delay » should be penalized; it is because he is impatient that « abstinence » from immediate indulgence or « waiting » for future indulgence, is regarded with disfavor; it is because he is impatient that he puts a premium or « agio » on present goods as compared with future.

The peculiar fitness of the term « impatience » is here emphasized because so much stress has been laid on economic catch-words and because this particular catch-word seems to have escaped notice. In my own book, « The Rate of Interest », for instance, this term was unused because unthought of, and the clumsier and less self-explanatory term « time-preference » was employed instead. The proposal to employ the term « impatience » is here made for the first time. While the use of one term or another does not in the least affect the principles involved, it does affect the popular comprehension of those principles.

Impatience is a fundamental attribute of human nature. As long as people like to have things to-day rather than to-morrow, there will be a rate of interest. *Interest is, as it were, impatience crystallized into a market rate.* The rate of interest is formed out of the various degrees or rates of impatience in the minds of different people. The rate of impatience in any individual's mind is his preference for receiving an additional dollar or dollar's worth of goods at once, over receiving it a year from to-day. In other words, it is the excess of the « marginal utility », or as I prefer to express it, « desirability » of to-day's money over that of next year's money viewed from to-day's standpoint. It can be expressed in numbers as the premium that a man is willing to pay for this year's over next year's money. If, for instance, in order to get 1 dollar at once he is willing to promise to pay 1.05 next year, then his rate of impatience is 5 per cent. The present 1 dollar is worth to him so much that, in order to get it, he is willing to pay 5 per cent more than 1 dollar in the future for it. It is because of the willingness to do this to gratify one's impatience that there is such a thing as a rate of interest. A man will prefer to have a machine to-day rather than a machine in the future; a house to-day rather than a house a year from now; a piece of land to-day rather than a piece of land when he is ten years older; he would rather have some food to-day than wait until next year for it, or a suit of clothes, or stocks, or bonds, or anything else.

But what are these present and future « goods » which are thus contrasted? At first sight it might seem that the « goods » compared are rather heterogeneous, — wealth, property, services, or any economic elements whatever. This is true but some of these cases are reducible to others. When present capital is preferred to future capital, this preference is really a preference for the *income* of the first capital as compared with the *income* of the second. As already indicated the reason we would choose a present fruit tree rather than a similar fruit tree available in ten years is that the fruit of the first will be available earlier than the fruit of the second. The reason we prefer immediate tenancy of a house to the right to occupy it in six months is that the uses of the house will begin six months earlier in one case than in the other. In short, capital available early is preferred to capital of like kind available at a more remote time, simply because the *income* of the former is available earlier than the *income* of the latter.

It will thus be seen that all rates of impatience resolve themselves into preference for early *income* over late income. Moreover, the preference for present income over future income resolves itself into the preference for present *enjoyable* income over future enjoyable income. The income from an article of capital which consists merely of an intermediate step in production is desired for the sake of the final enjoyable income to which that intermediate step paves the way. We prefer present bread baking to future bread baking because the enjoyment of the resulting bread is available earlier in the one case than in the other.

We thus see that all impatience for goods (preference for present over future goods) resolves itself, in the last analysis, into impatience for enjoyable income (a preference for early enjoyable income over late enjoyable income). The preference for present over future goods, when thus reduced to its lowest terms, i. e. a preference for enjoyable income rids the present and future values of the interest element, which, in all other attempts at explanation, is so unconsciously presupposed. For when any other goods than enjoyable income are considered, their values already imply a rate of interest.

IV. The influences on impatience.

But we have not yet wholly solved the problem of interest. It is not enough to know that the more impatient a people are, the higher will be their rate of interest, and that the more patient they are, the lower will be their rate of interest. We must also know *on what causes* the rate of impatience depends. It depends principally upon two circumstances, the character of the individual and the character of the income of which he finds himself the owner.

It is clear that the rate of impatience which corresponds to a specific income-stream will not be the same for everybody. One man may have a rate of impatience of 5 per cent and another a rate of impatience of 10 per cent, although both have the same income. The difference will be due to the personal characteristics of the individuals. These characteristics are chiefly five in number: (1) foresight, (2) self-control, (3) habit, (4) expectation of life, (5) love for posterity. We shall take these up in order.

1) First, as to foresight. Generally speaking, the greater the foresight, the less the rate of impatience, and *vice versa*. In the case of primitive races and instructed classes of society, the future is seldom considered in its true proportions. The story is told of a Southern negro that he would not mend his leaky roof when it was raining, for fear of getting more wet, nor when it was not raining, because he did not then need shelter. Among such persons the rate of impatience for present gratification is powerful because their comprehension of the future is weak. If we compare the Scotch and the Irish, we will find a contrast in this respect. The Irish, in general, lack foresight and are improvident, and the Scotch have foresight and are provident. Consequently the rate of interest is high in Ireland and low in Scotland.

These differences in degrees of foresight produce corresponding differences in the dependence of impatience on the character of income. Thus, for a given income, say 1000 dollars a year, the reckless might have a rate of impatience of 10 per cent, when the forehanded would experience a rate of only 5 per cent.

Therefore the rate of impatience, in general, will be higher in a community consisting of reckless individuals than in one consisting of the opposite type.

2) We come next to self-control. This trait, though, distinct from foresight, is usually associated with it and has very similar effects. Foresight has to do with *thinking;* self-control with *willing.* A weak will usually goes with a weak intellect, though not necessarily, and not always. The effect of a weak will is similar to the effect of inferior foresight. Like those workingmen who cannot carry their pay home Saturday night, but spend it in a grogshop on the way, many persons cannot deny themselves any present indulgence, even when they know definitely what the consequences will be in the future. Others, on the contrary, have no difficulty in controlling themselves in the face of all temptations.

3) The third characteristic of human nature which needs to be considered is habit. That to which one is accustomed exerts necessarily a powerful influence upon his valuations and therefore upon his rate of impatience. This influence may be in either direction. A rich man's son who has been brought up in habits of self-indulgence, when he finds himself with a smaller income than his father provided him during his formative years, will have a higher rate of impatience than a man who has the same income but who has climbed up instead of climbed down.

4) The expectation of life will affect a man's rate of impatience. A man who looks forward to a long life will have a relatively high appreciation of the future, which means a relatively low appreciation of the present, i. e. a low rate of impatience; whereas a man who has a short life to look forward to will want it at least to be a merry one. « Eat, drink, and be merry, for to-morrow we die », is the motto applying to this type.

5) The fifth circumstance is love for posterity. Probably the most powerful cause tending to reduce the rate of interest is love for one's children and the desire to provide for their good. When these sentiments decay, as they did decay at the time of the decline and fall of the Roman Empire,

and it becomes the fashion to exhaust wealth in self-indulgence and leave little or nothing to offspring, the rate of
impatience and the rate of interest are high. At such times
the motto « After us the deluge », indicates the feverish desire to squander in the present, at whatever cost to the future. A noted gambler, who had led a wild and selfish life,
once said, when life-insurance was first explained to him.
« I have seen many schemes for making, money, but this is
the first time I have seem a scheme where you had to die
before you could rake in the pile ». That man didn' t care for
a payment which would come in after his death. But there
are many men who do, and in fact care much more for it
than for anything else in the world. This care leads them to
insure their lives in order that they may leave the money to
their families. Their desire to provide for those who survive
them gives them a low rate of impatience. Life insurance, by
training people to provide for posterity, is acting as one of
the most powerful means of lowering the rate of impatience
and therefore the rate of interest. At present in the United
States the insurance on lives amounts to 20,000,000,000 of dollars.
This represents, for the most part, an investment of the
present generation for the next. The investment of this sum
springs out of a low rate of impatience, and tends to produce a low rate of interest.

Thus we see that men may differ in many ways which
affect the rate of impatience and rate of interest. We may
contrast two extreme types of men, irrespective of the character of their income. Men may have a high rate if they are
shortsighted, or are weak-willed, or have spendthrift habits
or look forward to a short or uncertain life, or are selfish
and without regard for posterity. They will have a low rate if
they have the opposite characteristics, — foresight, self-control,
habits of thrift, length and certainty of life, and altruism
with respect to posterity.

But not only does impatience vary as between different
individuals; it varies also for the same individual according
to circumstances. The most important circumstance affecting
an individual' s degree of impatience is the character of his
expected income in the immediate and in the remote future,

Smith' s impatience for satisfactions will depend on the
abundance of his present as compared with his future satis-

factions. If the future satisfactions that he expects and looks
forward to are very great, and his present satisfactions are
very small, he will be impatient to hurry from his present
scarcity and arrive at the expected future abundance; that
is, he will have a high rate of preference for present over
future satisfactions. This is on the same principle that prices
are high when goods are scarce. The preference for present
satisfactions is high if present satisfactions are scarce. Now the
rate of preference which Smith has for present satisfactions
over future satisfactions will depend on his whole future
stream of satisfactions, that is, what we call his final enjoyable
income. It will depend on four chief characteristics of that
income: first, as just said, it will depend on the *time-shape*
of the income, the relative abundance of his present and his
future satisfactions; second, on the *amount* of the income, i.
e. whether his satisfactions are few or many; third, on the
uncertainties of the income, i. e. to what extent his satisfactions throughout future years can be depended upon; and
fourth, on the *composition* of the income, i. e. the relative
amounts of foods, shelter, etc., of which it is composed.

For brevity we shall here consider only the time-shape of
income, i. e. the distribution of income in time. Three different types of time-shape may be distinguished: uniform income, consisting of equal yearly items, income increasing in
the future, and income decreasing in the future.

The effect of possessing an increasing income is, as we
have already indicated, to make the possessor impatient, i. e.
to make his preference for present over future income higher
than otherwise; for it means that the earlier parts of his
income are relatively scarce, and the remoter, relatively
abundant. For instance, a man who is now enjoying an income of only 1000 dollars a year, but expects in ten years to be
enjoying one of 10,000 dollars a year, will be impatient to have
ten years elapse. He has « great expectations ». He may, to satisfy his impatience, borrow money to eke out this year's income, and make repayment by sacrificing from his more
abundant income ten years later.

Reversely, a decreasing income, making, as it does, the
earlier income relatively abundant, and the remoter income
relatively scarce, tends to reduce impatience, or the preference for present as compared with future income. The man

with a descending income already has a high income without
being compelled to wait for it. With him there is little
reason for impatience; there is nothing to be impatient for;
on the contrary, the future does not look at all inviting. He
will therefore strive to save from his present abundance to
provide for coming needs.

V. The determination of the Rate of Interest.

The question now arises, will not the rates of impatience
of different individuals be very different, and if so, what relation do these different rates have to the rate of *interest?*
It might seem at first that the rates of impatience would
differ widely. In a nation of hermits, without any mutual
lending and borrowing, this would be true; the rate of impatience of individuals would diverge widely, and there would
be no common market rate of interest. It is modern society's
habit of borrowing and lending that tends to bring into
equality the rates of impatience in different minds, and it is
only because of the limitations of the loan market that absolute equality is not reached.

The chief practical limitation to lending is due to the
risk involved, and to the difficulty or impossibility of obtaining the security necessary to eliminate or reduce that risk.
Those who are most willing to borrow are oftentimes those
who are least able to give security. It will then happen that
these persons, shut off from the loan market, experience a
higher rate of impatience than the rate of interest ruling in
that market. If they can contract loans at all, it will be
only through the pawnshop or other high-rate agencies.

But for the moment let us assume a perfect market,
in which the element of risk is entirely lacking. We assume
that all individuals are initially possessed of fore-known income streams, and are free to exchange any parts of them
so that present income may be exchanged for future income.
This exchange may be effected by borrowing or lending, by
buying and selling wealth or property and by changing the
uses to which capital is put.

Under these conditions, the rates of impatience for different individuals will be perfectly equalized. Borrowing and

lending evidently affect the time-shape of the incomes of borrower and lender; and since the time-shape of their incomes affects their rate of impatience, such a modification of time-shape will react upon and modify their rate of impatience and bring the market into equilibrium.

For if, for any particular individual, the rate of impatience differs from the market rate, he will, if he can, adjust the time-shape of his income-stream so as to harmonize his rate of impatience with the interest rate. For instance, those who, for a given income-stream, have a rate of impatience above the market rate, will sell some of their surplus future income to obtain (i. e. « borrow ») an addition to their present meagre income. This will have the effect of enhancing the value of the future income and decreasing that of the present. The process will continue until the rate of impatience of this individual is equal to the rate of interest. In other words, a person whose impatience-rate exceeds the current rate of interest will borrow up to the point which will make the two rates equal. Reversely, those who, with a given income-stream, have a rate of impatience below the market rate, will sell (i. e. « lend ») some of their abundant present income to eke out the future, the effect being to increase their rate of impatience until it also harmonizes with the rate of interest.

To put the matter in figures, let us suppose the rate of interest is 5 per cent, whereas the rate of impatience of a particular individual is at first 10 per cent. Then, by hypothesis, the individual is *willing* to sacrifice 1.10 of next year's income in exchange for 1 dollar of this year's. But in the market he is *able* to obtain 1 dollar for this year by spending only 1.05 of next year. This ratio is, to him, a cheap price. He therefore borrows, say, 100 dollars for a year, agreeing to return 105 dollars; that is, he contracts a loan at 5 per cent when he is willing to pay 10 per cent. This loan, by increasing his present income and decreasing his future, tends to reduce his rate of impatience from 10 per cent to, say, 8 per cent.

Under these circumstances he will borrow another 100 dollars being now willing to pay 8 per cent, but having to pay only 5 per cent. This loan will still further reduce his rate of impatience. He will continue to borrow until his rate of

impatience has been finally brought down to 5 per cent. Then
for the last or « marginal » 100 dollars, his rate of impatience will
agree with the market rate of interest. As in the general
theory of prices, this marginal rate, 5 per cent, being once
established, applies indifferently to all his valuations of present and future income.

In like manner, if another individual, entering the loan
market from the other side, has at first a rate of impatience
of 2 per cent, he will become a lender instead of a borrower.
He is *willing* to accept 102 dollars of next year's income for
100 of this year's income, but in the market he is *able*, instead
of the 102 dollars, to get 105. As he can lend at 5 per cent when he
would gladly do so at 2 per cent, he jumps at the chance and
invests, not one 100 dollars only, but another and another. But
his present income, being reduced by the process, is now more
highly esteemed than before, and his future income, being
increased, is less highly esteemed. The result will be a higher
relative valuation of the present, which, under the influence
of successive additions to the sums lent, will rise gradually
to the level of the market rate of interest.

In such an ideal loan market, therefore, where every individual could freely borrow or lend, the rates of impatience
for all the different individuals would become equal to each
other and to the rate of interest.

The two men whom we have imagined started out with
rates of impatience different from the market rate of interest. The market rate was 5 per cent, while the first man had
a rate of impatience above this, and the second, a rate of
impatience below this. But when they finished their loan
operations or readjustments in the time-shape of their income-streams, they brought their rates of impatience each
into harmony with the rate of interest and therefore with
each other. Therefore, as long as there is a market in which
everybody can borrow or lend at will at 5 per cent, everybody will have at the margin a rate of impatience of 5 per cent.
Nobody will have a rate of impatience above 5 per cent,
because, if it is at first above it, he will borrow enough to
bring it down to the market rate; and nobody will have a
rate below it, because if it is at first below it, he will lend
enough to bring it up to the rate of interest.

Thus we see that even men of widely different natures

as to foresight, self-control, etc., will have the same *marginal* rates of impatience. This adjustment of the impatience of different individuals takes place, as we have seen, by adjusting their respective incomes, increasing their immediate income at the expense of future income or increasing their future income at the expense of immediate income. These changes in income we have supposed, for illustration, to be effected by borrowing and lending. As a matter of fact they may also take place in two other ways. One way is by buying and selling property. If a man buys property like a growing forest, which will bring him remotely future income and sells property, like household furniture, or short-time notes which brings him more immediate income it is clear that he can profoundly change the character of his present and future income. The other way is by changing the uses to which he puts his capital, e. g. changing the use of land from growing immediate crops to growing timber in the remote future. But whether he modifies this income by borrowing and lending, or by buying and selling, or by changing the uses of his capital, the essential point is that he does modify its time-shape and by so doing raises or lowers his rate of impatience so as to make it agree with the market rate of interest. For the individual the rate of interest is a relatively fixed fact, since his own rate of impatience and resulting action can affect it only infinitesimally. All he can do is to adjust his rate of impatience to it. For society as a whole, however, it is these same rates of impatience which meet in, and determine, the rate of interest. While for the individual the rate of interest determines the rate of impatience, for society the rates of impatience of the individuals determine the rate of interest. The rate of interest is simply the rate of impatience, upon which the whole community may concur in order that the market of loans may be exactly cleared. Supply and demand will work this out.

To put the matter in figures: if the rate of interest is set very high, say 20 per cent, there will be relatively few borrowers and many would-be lenders, so that the total extent to which would-be lenders are willing to reduce their income-streams for the present year for the sake of a much larger future income will be, say 100,000,000 of dollars; whereas, those who are willing to add to their present income at the high price of 20 per cent interest will borrow only, say, 1,000,000 of dollars. Under such conditions the demand for loans is far short of the supply, and the rate of interest will therefore go down. At an interest rate of 10 per cent, the present year's income offered as loans might be 50,000,000 of dollars, and the amount which would be taken at that rate only 20,000,000 of dollars. There is still an excess of supply over demand, and interest must needs fall further. At 5 per cent we may suppose the market cleared, borrowers and lenders being willing to take or give respectively 30,000,000 of dollars. In like manner it can be shown that the rate would not fall below this, as in that case it would result in an excess of demand over supply, and cause the rate to rise again.

Thus the rate of interest is the common market rate of impatience for income, as determined by the supply and demand of present and future income. Those who, having a high rate of impatience, strive to acquire more present income, at the cost of future income, tend to raise the rate of interest. These are the borrowers, the spenders, the sellers of property yielding remote income, such as bonds and stocks. On the other hand, those who — having a low rate of impatience — strive to acquire more future income at the cost of present income, tend to lower the rate of interest. These are the lenders, the savers, the investors.

VI. Verification and Conclusion.

We have sketched the main principles determining the rate of interest. Some have not been mentioned save by implication. In summary we may say the rate of interest, considered independently of fluctuations in the monetary standard, is determined by six conditions. Those which we have here considered and explained are the following three: (1) the dependence of impatience upon prospective income — its size, shape, composition, and uncertainties; (2) the tendency of rates of impatience for different individuals to become equal to each other and to the rate of interest, through the loan market; (3) the fact that supply and demand must be equal so that the modifications in the income-streams of individuals, through buying and selling, or borrowing and lending, must « clear the market. » Of the other three determining conditions the most important is that the rate of interest must be equal not only to the marginal rates of impatience but also to the « marginal rates of return on sacrifice ». This, though a fundamental and distinctive feature in my theory of interest cannot adequately be presented in this short sketch. It is fully elaborated in the « Rate of Interest ». It is there shown that this principle — that rates of return on sacrifice harmonize with the rate of interest — may also be stated in the following form: of all the optional uses to which a man may put his capital he will choose that one which at the market rate of interest maximizes the present value of his capital — the discounted value of the uses chosen.

The remaining two conditions are the very obvious ones; (1) that what is borrowed at any time by some persons, equals what is loaned at that time by other persons and (2) that what any person borrows at one time must be repaid by that person at another time with interest at the market rate.

These six determining conditions are all essential. If any one of them is omitted we shall find ourselves trying to determine the unknown quantity, the rate of interest, by means of other unknown quantities — rates of impatience, rates of return on sacrifice, amount of loans and incomes — without providing adequate means for determining these other unknown quantities also. This is the difficulty with most theories of interest, the attempt to explain *ignotum per ignotius*. There is no objection to explaining one unknown in terms of others provided only we furnish enough determining conditions for all. It is a fundamental law of algebra that in order to determine fully each one of the unknowns we must have an exactly equal number of independent equations. As is shown in « The Rate of Interest », the six sets of determining conditions above mentioned provide exactly the number of equations needful to determine all the unknown quantities involved in them including the rate of interest itself.

We have now completed our study of the causes determining the rate of interest. If they are correct, we should find that the rate of interest is low (1) if in general the people are by nature thrifty, far-sighted, self-controlled, and love their children, or (2) if they have large or descending income-streams; and that it is high (1) if the people are shiftless, short-sighted, impulsive, selfish, or (2) if they have small or ascending income-streams.

History shows that the facts accord with these conclusions. The communities and nationalities which are most noted for the qualities mentioned — foresight, self-control, and regard for posterity — are probably Holland, Scotland, England, France. Among these people interest has been low. Moreover, they have been money lenders; they have the habit of thrift or accumulation, and their instruments of wealth are in general of a durable kind.

On the other hand, among communities and peoples noted for lack of foresight and for negligence with respect to the future are China, India, Java, the negro communities in the Southern states, the peasant communities of Russia, and the North and South American Indians, both before and after they had been pushed to the wall by the white men. In all of these communities we find that interest is high, that there is a tendency to run into debt and to dissipate rather than to accumulate capital, and that their dwellings and other instruments are of a very flimsy and perishable character, built for immediate, not remote, gratification. This is true even where, as in China, the people are industrious. Industry without patience will work only for immediate gratification.

These examples illustrate the effect on the rate of interest of differences in human nature. We now turn to illustrations of differences in the time-shape of incomes. The most striking examples of increasing income-streams are found in new countries. It may be said that the United States has almost always belonged to this category. In America we see exemplified on a very large scale the truth of the theory that a rising income-stream raises, and a falling income-stream depresses, the rate of interest, or that these conformations of the income-stream work out their effects in other equivalent forms. A similar causation may be seen in particular localities in the United States, especially where changes have been rapid, as in mining communities. In California, in the two decades between 1850 and 1870, following the discovery of gold, the income-stream of that state was increasing at a prodigious rate. During this period the rates of interest were abnormally high. The current rates in the « early days » were quoted at 1 ¼ to 2 per cent a month. « The thrifty Michael Reese is said to have half repented of a generous gift to the University of California, with the exclamation : « Ah, but I lose the interest » — a very natural regret when interest was 24 per cent per annum ». After railway connection in 1869, Eastern loans began to flow in. The decade 1870-1880 was one of transition during which the phenomenon of high interest was gradually replaced by the phenomenon of borrowing from outside. The residents of California were thus able to change the time-shape of their income-streams. The rate of interest consequently dropped from 11 per cent to 6 per cent.

The same phenomena of enormous interest rates were also exemplified in Colorado and the Klondike. There were many instances in both these places during the transition period from poverty to affluence, when loans were contracted at over 50 per cent per annum, and the borrowers regarded themselves as lucky to get rates so « low. »

We have seen that the rate of interest is not a mere technical phenomenon, restricted to Wall Street and other « money markets, » but that it permeates all economic relation. It is the link which binds man to the future and by which he makes all his far-reaching decisions. It enters into the price of securities, land, and capital goods generally, as well as into rent and wages.

The rate of interest also plays a central rôle in the theory of distribution. The true problem of distribution is that of determining the amounts of capital and income possessed by different individuals in society. Individuals of the spendthrift type, if in possession of land and other durable instruments, will either sell or mortgage them in order to secure the means for obtaining enjoyable services more rapidly. The effect will be, for society as a whole, that those individuals who have an abnormally low appreciation of the future and its needs will gradually part with the more durable instruments, and that these will tend to gravitate into the hands of those who have the opposite trait. By this transfer and inequality in the distribution of capital is gradually effected, an this inequality, once achieved, tends to perpetuate itself. Hence, in some countries the rich and poor come to be widely and permanently separated, the former constituting a hereditary aristocracy and the latter a helpless and degraded peasantry.

We see, therefore, that the rate of interest is of almost universal application and importance in economic relations. It concerns not only the phenomena of borrowing and lending but of buying and selling. It enters implicitly into prices. It affects distribution. It cannot be abolished by law nor by any other means unless human impatience be abolished.

New Haven (Connecticut, U. S. A.), Yale University.

IRVING FISHER

AN ADDRESS
DELIVERED TO THE
AMERICAN ASSOCIATION
FOR THE
ADVANCEMENT
OF SCIENCE

Science, January 4, 1907

WHY HAS THE DOCTRINE OF LAISSEZ FAIRE BEEN ABANDONED?[1]

PERHAPS the most remarkable change which economic opinion has undergone

[*] See description by A. L. Carnahan in the *Mining World* of August 25, 1906, and by C. H. Taylor in *Mining and Scientific Press*, August 18, 1906.

[1] Address of the vice-president before Section I. —Social and Economic Science—at the New York meeting of the American Association for the Advancement of Science.

during the last fifty years has been the change from the extreme *laissez faire* doctrines of the classical economists to the modern doctrines of governmental regulation and social control. And yet there has been very little attempt to explain why *laissez faire* has been so generally abandoned. Its abandonment has been gradual and almost unconscious, not so much the result of any rival abstract doctrine, as the cumulative effect of experience, which in hundreds of individual cases has brought men face to face with the practical limitations of the let-alone policy. The movement is fast bringing us back to the old view by virtue of which economics was first named *political* economy.

The revival of governmental activity in economic affairs is due to causes which are partly political and partly economic. This paper has to do chiefly with the economic causes and we shall, therefore, merely note in passing the chief political aspects of the problem. One reason for the extension of governmental control of industry is the growing strength of governmental control in general and of popular confidence in it. *Laissez faire* was a natural doctrine in a time when governments were weak and inefficient. Change of power has brought change of the theory of power. Compulsory workmen's insurance we find in the strongly developed German Empire; railway rate regulation follows increased power and centralization of government. It may even be said that much of the modern government regulation of industry resulted from the attempt of governments to extend its powers in self-defense. It has been felt, for instance, that if the government did not control the railroads, the railroads would control the government. Government regulation here has taken on the aspect of a struggle for supremacy. Just as England feels the necessity of having a navy equal to the combined navies of several other European powers, so governments feel that they must overtop the corporate aggregations of wealth with which they may have to cope.

Were there space we might discuss the question how far the movement toward governmental interference can profitably be pushed. The doctrine of socialism lies at the extreme opposite pole from the doctrine of *laissez faire*, and we are moving toward socialism dangerously fast. Yet there are insuperable obstacles to the success of socialistic projects. Governmental power and efficiency are limited and, when one class of society attempts actually to rule another, there is always a tendency to corruption, inefficiency, lack of adaptability to new conditions and abuse of power. Socialism can not be put in practise without opposition, and to maintain itself socialism must hold the opposing class in subjection. Nominally this subjection would be a benevolent paternalism, but in political history it is the universal experience that the party in power, to entrench itself against attacks, soon usurps more power, employs indefensible and oppressive methods and tries to establish itself in the enjoyment of special selfish privileges.

Our present purpose, however, is to study, not the political, but the economic, side of the problem. The doctrine of *laissez faire* is that governmental interference, in economic matters at least, is unnecessary and harmful. Sometimes it is added as a corollary that not only should government let individuals alone, but also that individuals should let each other alone. 'Live and let live' and 'Each for himself' are the mottoes of this type of individualism. The advocates of extreme *laissez faire* maintain that one class is not justified in imposing its tastes upon another. They say, we must not meddle with our neighbors' affairs, even if they are wasting their lives

in what appears to us trivial, useless or positively harmful gratifications. Those who love art, science or literature have no right, we are told, to criticize those who are bored by these things, but love prize-fighting, fast horses, fast society or high living.

The reasoning by which these individualistic doctrines were supported may be briefly stated in two propositions: first, each individual is the best judge of what subserves his own interest, and the motive of self-interest leads him to secure the maximum of well-being for himself; and, secondly, since society is merely the sum of individuals, the effort of each to secure the maximum of well-being for himself has as its necessary effect to secure thereby also the maximum of well-being for society as a whole.

In the light of the experience of the last fifty years, it is not difficult to see wherein each of these two propositions is in error. First, it is not true that each man can be trusted to pursue his own best interests. Some men need enlightenment, owing to ignorance of what constitutes their best interests, and others need restraint, owing to lack of self-control in following them. The necessity for both enlightenment and restraint has always been recognized in the case of children, and an examination of actual conditions will show that they apply—often with equal force—to adults.

Liberty is certainly indispensable in a healthy society, but liberty insensibly verges upon license. While most of us would still agree that sumptuary laws are ill-advised, there is certainly good ground for maintaining that the liquor traffic should be put under some restraint, even if only by high license. It is not true that the drunkard is the best judge of what is for his own well-being and that of his family, and it is still less true that even when he thoroughly recognizes his failings he will have the self-control to act upon that knowledge. Hence the liquor problem becomes a social as well as an individual question. Again it is not true that ignorant parents are justified in imposing their ideas of education upon their children; hence the problem of child-labor, instead of concerning only the individual, as was at one time thought, has important and far-reaching relations to society as a whole. The same principles apply to the restraint of gambling, vice, the suppression of indecent literature, the compulsion upon landlords to make tenements sanitary, and many other forms of governmental regulation.

Even where governmental intervention is impracticable or inadvisable, there will still be good reason for attempting betterment of conditions through the influence of one class upon another; hence come social agitations and the efforts of one class to educate or instruct another. On this principle are based the great modern movements for human betterment as exemplified by the Society for the Study and Prevention of Tuberculosis, the Society for Sanitary and Moral Prophylaxis, the National Civic Federation, the American Institute of Social Service, the National Child Labor Committee, temperance societies, college settlements, district nurse associations and other organizations.

Strange as it may seem to those of us interested in these movements to-day, the fact is that a generation ago many of them would have been regarded by the dominant Manchester School not only as impracticable, but as unnecessary and possibly harmful. The adherents of this school seemed to treat the difference between knowledge and ignorance as a mere difference in opinion, with which the government has no more concern than with difference of religious creeds. It is certainly true that the attempts of govern-

ments to impose what is regarded by the ruling class as the 'true religion' upon the entire people have always proved ill-advised; the recognition of this has produced the modern sentiment of religious toleration. But we are carrying toleration too far when we refuse to correct errors which science demonstrates to be false. There are doubtless millions of persons to-day who jeer at the idea that indiscriminate spitting is dangerous to public health, but it would be silly to allow their ignorant prejudice to prevail. The bacteriologist knows what the ignorant do not know, and every effort should be made to pass down this knowledge to the masses as soon as possible after it is discovered. We can not let any dogma of *laissez faire* prevent us from checking suicidal ignorance.

The world consists of two classes—the educated and the ignorant—and it is essential for progress that the former should be allowed to dominate the latter. But once we admit that it is proper for the instructed classes to give tuition to the uninstructed, we begin to see an almost boundless vista for possible human betterment. Instead of regarding the present state of society as a normal and desirable one because each man naturally 'seeks his own best interests,' we permit ourselves to judge each actual case by our own ideal standard. This standard may differ widely from the average of actual usage. We must always distinguish between the ideal or *normal*, and the real or *average*.

The average represents merely conditions as they are; the normal represents conditions as they ought to be. Yet nothing is more common than confusing the two. In fact, in most anthropometric or physiologic tables, the word 'normal' is used almost synonymously with 'average.' The normal height of man, his normal weight, his normal length of life, his normal diet, strength, etc., are all identified with the average.

In this way all question of possible improvement is begged. We are stopped at the outset from asking, for instance, whether men in general are too stout, for the average weight of mankind is *assumed* as 'normal.' The absurdity of such procedure becomes apparent as soon as we consider cases in which, by common consent, the average and the normal are held to be distinct. For instance, the average adult man certainly does not have normal teeth, for they are usually half decayed; nor normal hair, for he is usually half bald; nor normal posture, for he is usually round-shouldered. Average health is below normal health, average morality below normal morality. In the absence of evidence we have no right to assume that the average and the normal are identical, even when we lack the data on which to base an opinion. It is only recently, and in consequence of the movement against tuberculosis, that experts have come to realize how widely different is the average air we breathe from air which is normal for human respiration, and that investigation has shown the average diet, in America at least, to be abnormally nitrogenous. In view of such revelations we should be open-minded enough to accept evidence—should it be offered—that the average span of life is less than half the normal span, and the average efficiency less than half the normal efficiency.

Those who habitually confuse the normal and the average are prevented from seeing the possibility of progress. They take the position, as unscientific as it is obstructive of progress, that 'whatever is is right,' presumptively at least, and brand every one who deviates from the average as an eccentric or a crank. The confusion between the normal and the average thus leads to the confusion between the eccentric

and the pioneer. An eccentric or a crank is properly a person who deviates from the *normal*, and is almost the opposite of the pioneer, who deviates from the *average*, but toward the normal.

Discrepancies between the average and the normal may apply—in fact, do apply —to the economic side as well as to other sides of life. But this the *laissez faire* doctrine denied. The world as it is was thought to be nearly, if not absolutely, the best world possible. One example of this complaisant assumption was in the use of the term 'utility' to signify the intensity of desire that men have for things. So far as I know, the only writer who has attempted systematically to distinguish between the desires of men as they are and as they should be, is Pareto, who for this purpose suggested a new term—ophelimity—to replace 'utility' as applied to man's actual desires, reserving for the term 'utility' its original sense of what is intrinsically desirable. Thus, to an opium fiend opium has a high degree of ophelimity, but no utility. Economists have not yet laid sufficient emphasis on the distinction between true utility and what Pareto calls ophelimity. A whole range of problems of social betterment is opened up through the distinction. Economists have received with derision the suggestions of reform of Ruskin. But, however impracticable his specific proposals, his point of view is certainly saner than that of most economists; for, as Ruskin has pointed out, it is absurd to regard as equivalent a million dollars of capital invested in opium culture, and a million dollars invested in schools.

But there remains to be considered a second fallacy in *laissez faire*. Not only is it false that men, when let alone, will always follow their best interests, but it is false that when they do, they will always thereby best serve society. To Adam

Smith it seemed self-evident that a man served society best who served himself best—though he would certainly have admitted that the rule had exceptions in the case of thieves, assassins and others who are obviously enemies of society. But the extent to which the classical 'economic harmonies' were pushed by some writers, while not including such persons as thieves among beneficent workers, was, nevertheless, astonishing. Herbert Spencer's advocacy of freedom of private coinage is well known, though any one familiar with 'Gresham's law' knows how chimerical such an institution would be. A still more astonishing suggestion is that which Molinari is reputed to have made at one time, namely, that even the police function of government should be left to private hands, that police corps should be simply voluntary vigilance committees, somewhat like the old-fashioned fire companies, and that rivalry between these companies would secure better service than that now obtained through government police!

If we stop to classify the social effects of individual actions, we shall find that they fall into three groups: (1) those actions which benefit the individual himself and have no effect upon others; (2) those actions which benefit the individual and at the same time benefit society; (3) those actions which benefit the individual while at the same time they injure society. It is the third group which the *laissez faire* doctrinaires have overlooked, and especially that part of the third group in which the injury to society outweighs the benefit to the individual. As Huxley said:[2]

Suppose, however, for the sake of argument, that we accept the proposition that the functions of the state may be properly summed up in the one great negative commandment—'Thou shalt not allow any man to interfere with the liberty

[2] 'Life and Letters of Thomas H. Huxley,' by Leonard Huxley, Vol. I., pp. 384-5, Appleton, New York, 1900.

of any other man '—I am unable to see that the logical consequence is any such restriction of the power of government, as its supporters imply. If my next-door neighbor chooses to have his drains in such a state as to create a poisonous atmosphere, which I breathe at the risk of typhoid and diphtheria, he restricts my just freedom to live just as much as if he went about with a pistol threatening my life; if he is to be allowed to let his children go unvaccinated, he might as well be allowed to leave strychnine lozenges about in the way of mine; and if he brings them up untaught and untrained to earn their living, he is doing his best to restrict my freedom, by increasing the burden of taxation for the support of gaols and workhouses, which I have to pay.

The higher the state of civilization, the more completely do the actions of one member of the social body influence all the rest, and the less possible is it for any one man to do a wrong thing without interfering, more or less, with the freedom of all his fellow citizens.

In the examples given by Huxley, the acts complained of are injurious not only to society, but to the individual. But even when the act of an individual is actually for his own benefit, it may not be for the benefit of society. The paradox that the intelligent actions of a million individuals, each attempting to better his condition, may result in making the aggregate condition of the million worse, is illustrated by considering the effect of individual action in the case of a burning building. When a theater is on fire, thousands of frantic individuals are struggling to get out. In the panic, it is doubtless to the best interest of any particular individual to struggle to get ahead of the others; if he does not, he is far more apt to be burned. And yet nothing is more certain than that the very intensity of such efforts in the aggregate defeat their own ends. The reason is that the effect of the effort is chiefly relative; so far as one pushes himself forward he pushes others backward.

Numerous examples exist of actions which benefit the individual but injure society, or benefit a part of society but injure society as a whole. Thus, the city of Chicago, in tapping the Great Lakes for its new sewerage system, has tended to influence the level of these lakes and thereby affect economically a large territory, including several states of the Union and also Canada. It has been estimated that the level of the lakes may be affected as much as six inches.

One reason for federal interference in irrigation is that the water supply is often controlled by citizens of one state, while the land belongs to another state or to the United States, and cooperation between the two is difficult to secure. Water, in the arid lands of the west, is a prime requisite, and without it the lands have no value. From one point, Mt. Union, in the Yellowstone Park, three rivers begin—the Missouri, the Columbia and the Colorado—flowing into the Gulf of Mexico, the Pacific and the Gulf of California, and through a large number of states and a vast extent of territory. The mutual interests of the riparian owners and those affected by irrigation could scarcely be adjusted merely through the play of individual interests.

Similarly, the act of one individual in destroying forests influences climate and water supply and thereby affects other individuals in distant parts. Where individuals in the community are allowed to seek their own interests the destruction of forests in some regions inevitably follows.

A like effect was seen a few years ago in the case of the seal dispute between the United States and Great Britain. The play of individual motive in this case tended to the actual extinction of seals, and could only be curbed by the mutual agreement of nations to prevent pelagic sealing.

Individual action can not be trusted to provide fire-proof or slow-burning construction as required in a crowded city; for the individual, although interested in protect-ing himself from his neighbors' fires, is not interested in protecting his neighbors from his own fires; hence the necessity and justification for city fire ordinances. Similarly, soft coal, in such cities as Denver, St. Louis and Pittsburg, constitutes a veritable nuisance to the entire city; and yet the individual factory owner is undoubtedly following his own best interest in not substituting hard coal or using expensive smoke-consumers. Such protective measures would redound greatly to the benefit of the community, but only slightly to his own benefit; hence the necessity and justification for smoke ordinances. Individual action would never give rise to a system of city parks, or even to any useful system of streets. And where parks exist, as in the case of Battery Park, New York, there is a constant tendency for those seeking their individual interests to encroach upon them. In Hartford and other cities certain parks have in this way gradually disappeared, much to the damage of the public.

In the cases mentioned, of a conflict between social and individual interests, legal restraints become necessary. But there are many examples in which, for one reason or another, legal restraints are impracticable. This is particularly true in cases where a number of nations are concerned. There can be no question, for instance, that the standing armies and great navies are an almost intolerable burden in Europe, and that their existence has tended to increase the cost of our own army and navy, three thousand miles away. Nevertheless, in the absence of any central international authority or mutual agreement to bring about disarmament, it must be confessed that it is to the interest of Germany or France each individually to keep up its military equipment to a level comparable to that of its neighbors. Yet the aggregate effect of international competition for military power is to cancel itself out; the advantages and disadvantages are purely relative. The nations are in a mad race each to excel the other. Their object being purely one of relative advantage, such advantage can be shifted from one to the other, but can not accrue to all. A general increase in relative advantage is a contradiction in terms, so that in the end the racers as a whole have only their labor for their pains.

An economic example of the same international character, and one which has received very scant attention, is found in the increase of the monetary metals. The production and distribution of gold and silver is the effect of individual action, each person seeking his own best interests. Yet the aggregate effect upon these individuals may be injurious. The injury referred to is not the imaginary injury of an 'unfavorable balance of trade' which was the bugbear of the mercantilists, but the exact opposite. A nation which increases its stock of money is always and necessarily a loser. This increase costs the nation either labor of mining or commodities sent out of the country, and for this cost there is no return whatever. To assume that the increase of money is itself a valuable return is to commit the fallacy of inflationism. Money is a very peculiar commodity. A general increase of other commodities is an advantage to society, but a general increase of money is not. The inflationist reasons that if a government can enrich one person by printing paper money and bestowing it upon him, it has only to do the same for everybody in order to enrich the nation. The paper-money delusion is too well understood to require comment. It is, however, not always perceived that precisely the same reasoning applies to all inflation, even the inflation which nature herself creates when she unlocks her hoards of buried treasure. The United States now has $33 of money

per capita as against $22 a few years ago, but we are no better off on that account. The smaller amount of money is as useful in exchange as the larger amount. There are, of course, transition evils in contracting or expanding the currency, but so long as the price level remains constant or certain, the absolute number of dollars of the circulating medium is a matter of indifference. It follows that any effort expended in increasing the stock of money is wasted effort, an effort without a return. This waste is a necessary concomitant of monetary individualism.

A not dissimilar case, and one which is now causing much discussion, is that of railroad rates. Those who have examined the working of competition in railroad transportation recognize the fact that this competition is of the variety called 'cut-throat' competition, and that no stable or normal rates for transportation, under which capitalists will consent to invest in railway-building, can occur through such competition. Those who advocate competition as a cure for the evils of railroad rates do not appreciate the mechanics of the problem. The effect of competition is to bring rates down to the cost of operation; it leaves no provision for interest on capital sunk in the enterprise. If the cost of operation is one cent per ton-mile, whereas two cents are required to include enough revenue to pay interest on original cost, rates under competition will inevitably sink below the two-cent level to the one-cent level. For if we assume that the two-cent rate is for a moment the ruling rate, it is clear that it would pay any individual competitor to cut under that rate in order to divert traffic away from his rivals. But as soon as he cuts below it, all the others must do likewise or lose their traffic. This competition is merely self-defense, and yet its ultimate effect is to injure, not benefit, all of the roads who engage in it. It is *cut-throat* competition. In order that rates may be maintained at the two-cent instead of the one-cent level, either competition must be absent, or it must be partial or imperfect. In the actual railroad world competition is usually present at some points and absent at others. The consequence of this mixture of competition and monopoly is that rates will be determined differently for some points than for others, and this constitutes what is called local discrimination. In a régime where monopoly is present, discrimination, not only of this local character, but discrimination as to persons and as to commodities carried, is a natural and inevitable result. It is not, of course, a desirable result; but it is no more undesirable than is the cut-throat competition which is the other horn of the dilemma. This cut-throat competition discourages the investment of capital in new railroads, and the shippers and consumers must in the end suffer. This dilemma between the evils of monopoly and of competition leads to governmental regulation, though the efficacy of this remedy is not all that could be desired. It is not our purpose to discuss the best solution of so difficult a question. We are merely concerned in pointing out that this railroad-rate problem is partly due to cut-throat competition and that cut-throat competition is one more example of the suicidal effects of blindly following individual self-interest.

Numerous other examples might be given; we shall, however, content ourselves with one. As John Rae has pointed out, there exists a species of subtle competition in private expenditure, due to social rivalry —the desire for distinction through wealth. It has frequently been remarked among ladies' social clubs which begin with simple entertainments, that each successive hostess attempts, almost unconsciously, to surpass her predecessor in the entertainment offered. Beginning with tea and cake, the club ends with elaborate and expensive collations, until it produces a heavy drain upon the resources of its members. In precisely the same way, on a larger scale, there is laid a heavy burden upon us all through the social rivalry of individuals. If we study the history of Newport or similar fashionable resorts, we find that social racing has gradually resulted in setting a pace which only the most wealthy can keep up, and that even for them expenditure represents cost rather than satisfaction. This cost often takes the form of producing fictitious values on articles merely because they are 'exclusive.' As John Rae says:[3]

A dish of nightingale's brains could scarcely be a very delicious morsel, yet Adam Smith quotes from Pliny the price paid for a single nightingale as about £66. According to Suetonius, no meal cost Vitellius less than £2,000 * * * Thus Adam Smith reckons the cost of some cushions of a particular sort used to lean on at table, at £30,000.

Nor do we need to draw our examples from ancient Rome. The 'History of Luxury' by Baudrillart will show the tendency to produce luxury out of social rivalry in all ages. It was only recently that an American in London gave a dinner party which was said to have cost $8,000. The table was placed in a large Venetian gondola set in the midst of an artificial lake, while in a smaller gondola near by a band was stationed.

Much has been said of late about the importance of living the simple life, but so far as I know there has been no analysis to show why it is not lived. This analysis would reveal that the failure to live it is due to a kind of unconscious cut-throat competition in fashionable society. When San Francisco was destroyed by earthquake and fire, much comment was made upon the fact that many did not feel their losses as

[3] 'Sociological Theory of Capital,' by John Rae, ed. by C. W. Mixter, MacMillan, 1905, p. 247.

much as might have been anticipated. One reason for this result is doubtless found in the fact that the losses were not relative. Had a single individual found himself suddenly reduced from a palace to a tent, his sense of loss and discomfiture would have been great. He could no longer return social entertainment among his former associates; he would feel 'out of it' and envy would gnaw at his breast. But after the San Francisco catastrophe there was little place for envy; all were in the same boat. There was no relative loss, there was only the absolute loss of creature comforts, and strange as it may seem to one who has not considered it, the absolute loss is the smaller of the two.

It is hard to overestimate the tax which is laid upon society through social racing. We are not conscious of this weight, because, like the weight of the atmosphere, it is always pressing upon us. The New York business man buys a silk hat as a matter of course. He does not think of its cost as a tax laid on him by society. He is satisfied because the hat fills a want, and he does not consider how that want originated. It is only when the tax varies by change of place, just as when atmospheric pressure varies by ascending a mountain, that he is at all aware of its existence. If he removes to a smaller town where social racing is less intense and the leaders in the race are unable to set so high a pace, he finds the tall hat no longer *de rigueur*. He drops off this and numerous other expenses and feels himself that much better off. A gentleman recently refused a salary of $7,000 in New York, preferring $4,000 in a smaller town, feeling that he could buy no more real satisfaction with the former than with the latter. The extra $3,000 meant simply that it would cost more to keep up with his neighbors.

The burden of social racing is laid not only on the rich but upon all classes.

A milliner in New Haven recently thought to avoid competing with existing fashionable millinery establishments by catering to the trade of shop girls. To his surprise, he found that the tyranny of fashion was quite as strong among them. He attempted to put on sale a large number of $5 and $6 hats, but found great difficulty in disposing of them, whereas the few $15 and $16 hats met with a very ready sale. The shop girls wanted these hats to 'be in the swim.' Recently in France a whole family committed suicide because they had lost the capital which they considered necessary to keep their social position.

Many ingenious arguments have been made to justify luxury and in some of them there may lie truth. The fact that luxurious expenditure can be so readily cut down in hard times provides a sort of buffer against want and famine. The relations of luxury to the growth of population deserve careful study. But whatever the indirect benefits of luxury, certain it is that it forms a tax upon society, and a heavy one. It seems also true that where luxury is greatest civilization decays.

Were there more space we might discuss remedies for this social racing; but we must content ourselves with merely describing the phenomenon. It exemplifies the manner in which the self-seeking of each may create a burden for all.

From this and the other examples which have been reviewed we see that the mechanics of individualism is not so simple as the individualists have assumed. The old individualism requires two corrections: first, the individual may often be interfered with in his own interest, because either of his ignorance or his lack of self-control; secondly, even when an individual can be trusted to follow his own best interests, it can not be assumed that he will thereby best serve the interests of

society.   A recognition of these two facts
is essential not only to clear thinking, but
as preliminary to any practical solution of
the great problems of human betterment.
We are doubtless to-day in danger of too
much socialistic experimentation; but nothing can be gained and much may be lost by
ignoring or condoning the opposite evils of
individualism.   In fact, the menace of socialism can best be met if we understand
and acknowledge the evils which it is intended to remedy.   The preliminary to
remedy is diagnosis, and an accurate diagnosis will save us from the error of both
extremes—the extreme, on the one hand,
of an overdose of socialism, and the extreme, on the other hand, of omitting all
medication whatever.

IRVING FISHER

YALE UNIVERSITY

For Product Safety Concerns and Information please contact our EU
representative GPSR@taylorandfrancis.com Taylor & Francis Verlag GmbH,
Kaufingerstraße 24, 80331 München, Germany

Printed and bound by CPI Group (UK) Ltd, Croydon, CR0 4YY
08/05/2025
01864337-0001